William Byrd, 1674—1744

William Byrd's

Histories of the Dividing Line

BETWIXT

Virginia and North Carolina

WITH INTRODUCTION AND NOTES BY
WILLIAM K. BOYD

———— • ————

AND A NEW INTRODUCTION BY
PERCY G. ADAMS
PROFESSOR OF ENGLISH
LOUISIANA STATE UNIVERSITY

———— • ————

DOVER PUBLICATIONS, INC.
New York

To
M. E. B.

Published in Canada by General Publishing Company, Ltd., 30 Lesmill Road, Don Mills, Toronto,
Ontario.
Published in the United Kingdom by Constable
and Company, Ltd., 10 Orange Street, London
WC 2.

This Dover edition, first published in 1967, is an
unabridged republication of the work first published
by the North Carolina Historical Commission in
1929. It contains a new Introduction by Percy G.
Adams.
The publisher is grateful to the library of Louisiana State University, which made available its
edition for purposes of reproduction.

Library of Congress Cataloging-in-Publication Data

Byrd, William, 1674-1744.
    William Byrd's histories of the dividing line betwixt
Virginia and North Carolina.

    "Unabridged republication of the work first published by the North Carolina Historical Commission in
1929"—Verso t.p.
    Bibliography: p.
    Includes index.
    1. Virginia—Boundaries—North Carolina.   2.
North Carolina—Boundaries—Virginia.   3. Virginia—Description and travel.   4. North Carolina—
Description and travel.   I. Boyd, William Kenneth,
1879-1938.   II. Title.
F229.B968   1987   975.5′02   87-27248

ISBN 0-486-25553-0 (pbk.)

Manufactured in the United States of America
Dover Publications, Inc.
180 Varick Street
New York, N.Y. 10014

CONTENTS

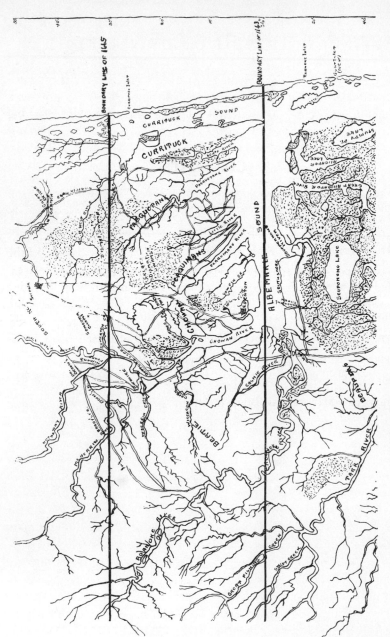

Map Showing Boundaries of the Carolina Charters

INTRODUCTION TO THE DOVER EDITION

These two "histories" written by Colonel William Byrd of Westover in the second quarter of the eighteenth century comprise a strikingly unique kind of travel book. It is not like the *Cruising Voyage* of Byrd's contemporary, Woodes Rogers, which narrates the events of a circumnavigation of the globe. Nor does it describe the exciting life of buccaneers in the southern hemisphere, as do the books of those other contemporaries Esquemeling, Ringrose, and William Dampier. Nor does it picture the sophisticated European cities which Smollett visited in the same century, nor an exotic, uncivilized nation like that seen by "Abyssinian" James Bruce, the greatest of travel writers in Africa. Instead it is the day-by-day journal that tells how in 1728 some twenty men traveled a few miles from home to survey the disputed boundary line between Virginia and North Carolina, in the process penetrating the great Dismal Swamp, visiting Indians, meeting white frontiersmen, fighting snakes, quarreling, loving. One of the histories is private and very revealing; its author was having fun when he wrote it on the spot. The other is longer, more formal, recollected in tranquility, intended for publication; its author was avoiding controversies with former companions, inserting afterthoughts and information not available on the spot, removing the barbs from the sarcasms, and excising the gossip, the sex, and the scandal. But both histories are the work of a remarkable Virginia aristocrat whose literary reputation, like that of James Boswell, has been growing with each new-found, ultimately published manuscript.

Like most other great gentlemen of colonial Virginia the author of the *Dividing Line Histories* was not entirely a self-made man. His father, William Byrd I, inherited from his uncle not only broad land holdings in the New World but a lucrative commerce with the southeastern Indians and a thriving trans-ocean trade in tobacco, slaves, and rum. At his death he left his only heir 26,000 acres and two fine houses on the James River, one called Belvidere and the other Westover. Furthermore, after joining with Nathaniel Bacon to suppress the rampaging Indians and then having discretion enough to avoid involvement in Bacon's notorious Rebellion against the governor, William Byrd I made himself a power in Virginia politics. A member of the House of Burgesses, Colonel in the militia, Auditor-General of the colony, member of the select and influential Council, he became President of that Council within a year of his death. All this drive, all this business, political, and social prestige, he passed on to William Byrd II, who was more than a worthy son to such a father.

Also like other Southern aristocrats William Byrd II had close ties with England. Born in 1674, at age seven he was sent with his two sisters to receive an English education. And it was a thorough one. With one of the best of British schoolmasters, Cristopher Glasscock in Essex, he was given a grounding in the classics and modern languages that not only remained with him throughout life but afforded him much pleasure. Then after a brief period of study with merchants in Holland, he returned to London to learn more about business with the firm of Perry and Lane, agents for the Byrd family. Finally, there were three years of training in law at the Middle Temple, including the preparation of a dozen cases tried publicly before he was admitted to the bar in 1695. In that year he came home to be elected to the House of Burgesses and to make a beginning on the career of Southern Gentleman. But his training in law and his familiarity with England brought a quick return to London as legal representative of the Virginia Assembly. In fact, from the time he was seven until he was thirty William Byrd II had only two brief visits with his family. In this period of his life he was more English than American.

There was another kind of education he acquired in London during his years with Perry and Lane, at the Temple, and as Counsellor for Virginia, an education just as necessary to the incipient Virginia gentleman. As the son of a rich colonial he was invited into the finest drawing rooms; he became an habitué of Wills and the Virginia Coffee House; and he regularly attended the theatre, counting among his friends at the Temple and afterwards three of the great dramatists of the day—William Wycherly, William Congreve, and Nicholas Rowe. Other friends, even closer, were interested in science, among them Robert Boyle, Earl of Orrery, and Sir Robert Southwell, and in 1696 the twenty-two-year-old was admitted to the Royal Society, an honor he always cherished so much that as an old man he once wrote that august body to complain that his name had been omitted from the year's membership rolls. His friends were not all primarily literary or scientific, however. Some of them, Wycherley, for example, knew the night spots, and so the young colonial learned much about taverns, gambling, women, and gallantry. When he was over sixty he could write nostalgically and teasingly to his old friend Benjamin Lynde of Salem, Massachusetts, about those days when the two "used to intrigue in the Temple." But in 1704 the period of preparation was over, for in that year William Byrd I died leaving all his land and all his business ventures to his only son, who set out immediately for America to assume the role for which he had been preparing so long.

The first duty of this most eligible of Virginia bachelors was to find a suitable wife, not only to help him assume his position in society but to help cool the ardent nature that had been even more enflamed by gay years in London. He found her in Lucy Parke, whom he married within two years after returning home. She was temperamental and sometimes more enflaming than cooling for the strong-willed William Byrd. For example, they fought over her occasional harsh punishment of a house slave, or over her desire to pluck her eyebrows, or over his attentions to another woman; but normally, as he reported in his diary, he managed to maintain his "authority." Her father, Colonel Daniel Parke, was killed in 1710 in an uprising in the Leeward Islands, where he had been sent as governor. Byrd, apparently because of pride but also because he wanted to get possession of the family lands in Virginia, assumed his father-in-law's debts, which were considerably more than he had anticipated. For most of the rest of his life he paid £500 a year on these debts and was, as a result, seldom out of financial trouble. Already a member of the House of Burgesses, in 1709 he was appointed to the twelve-member Council that constituted the upper house in the Virginia Assembly, thus following in his father's footsteps. Also like his father before him, he was appointed to the lucrative post of Receiver-General for the Crown in Virginia. Then in 1715 he went back to England, partly for business reasons, partly to represent the colony before the Board of Trade; and just as his contemporary Jonathan Swift had a few years before succeeded in getting the First Fruits for Ireland, William Byrd was successful in persuading the King to use for expenses in Virginia all the money collected there from quit-rents and duties. But within months of his arrival in London, his wife Lucy, who had joined him, was dead of the smallpox, leaving him two daughters of the four children she had given birth to in the ten years of their marriage.

For the next decade his position kept him in England most of the time. And there he made more influential friends and pursued the ladies—of all kinds—more than he had before his father's death. He was intimate with Lord Egmont, with Admiral Sir Charles Wager, with Sir Hans Sloane, President of the Royal Society. His daughter was a close friend of Teresa Blunt and apparently was entertained by Alexander Pope at Twickenham. And while he kept a mistress he fell in love with more than one fashionable lady whom he hoped to lure back to Westover. One was "Sabina," a wealthy heiress named Mary Smith, whose father, "Vigilante," preferred a baronet for a son-in-law. Another was the widow Pierson, who lived near St. James' Palace and to whom he proposed at least three times unsuccessfully. Still another was Lady Elizabeth Lee, grand-daughter of Charles II, to whom Byrd gave the name "Charmante"; but she also rejected him and some years later married Edward Young, the famous poet. Finally there was Maria Taylor of Kensington, whom he married in 1724 and who was to give him another four children, three daughters and his only surviving son, William Byrd III. In 1726 he was back in Virginia, where he was to remain until his death in 1744. During those eighteen years he was as active as he had ever been.

In the first place he adopted the favorite pastime of a hundred great Virginia families. Like William Fitzhugh of Bedford, like Robert "King" Carter of Corotoman, like his cousin, the historian Robert Beverley, William Byrd acquired land almost feverishly. But unlike another member of the Council, Colonel Philip Ludwell, he apparently acquired that land in only legitimate ways. To his father's 26,000 acres he added his father-in-law Parke's estate. He was granted vast acres for serving on the Virginia-North Carolina boundary commission, and in two purchases, he added the 26,000-

acre "Land of Eden" in North Carolina. Twice he made valiant attempts to entice Europeans, especially from Switzerland, to settle on his lands along the Roanoke River, and once he partially succeeded. At his death he was owner of nearly 180,000 acres of the best land in the South.

In the second place Byrd continued to be politically active. For years, in England and at home, he led the fight to curb the power of the royal executive in Virginia, Lieutenant-Governor Spotswood. Although Spotswood was as strong-willed as the great planters who served on the Council with him, the battle ended with more power for the Council and a kind of friendship between him and his chief adversary. Twice William Byrd led important commissions for the government, once in 1728 to settle the dispute with North Carolina, again in 1736 to survey the Northern Neck in Northwest Virginia. So busy was he with affairs of state that he kept apartments in Williamsburg in order to meet his obligations. He was, in fact, Virginia's elder statesman and in the year before he died became President of the Council, an honor that came so late only because his predecessor, Commissary James Blair, clung so tenaciously to life.

In the third place William Byrd was a cultured and busy plantation owner, a prominent member of his community, and head of a family. He helped with the planting and harvesting; he controlled many slaves and servants; he was colonel in the militia; he supervised the education of his children and often took one or more of them on overnight visits to distant parts of his estate; he was chief medical adviser for his people and even for neighboring families; his home was forever being visited by friends, whom he entertained hospitably; he played billiards, or piquet, or whist, skated on the ice pond in winter, walked constantly over his fields and grounds, and everyday did his "dance," a kind of shadow boxing exercise like that of his contemporary Joseph Addison; he expanded the beautiful garden begun by his father; he rebuilt Westover in 1735, in brick, importing English furniture and cut glass to help make his one of the most splendid of Southern mansions; he collected portraits of all his important friends, English and American, and hung them in a magnificent picture gallery; he arose every day at 5:00 or 6:00 A.M. to read Greek, Latin, Hebrew, or one of the modern languages he knew; and he put together one of the best libraries to be found anywhere in America. This amazing collection of books, which required a librarian and which was not catalogued until a generation after Byrd's death, contained 250 volumes of travel, geography, biography, and history, the best law library among many good ones in the South, most of the contemporaneous poets and dramatists, much philosophy and science, and over 500 volumes in languages other than English. That he made good use of his library is evident when we inspect his own writing, for although William Byrd II was first a gentleman, statesman, and businessman, pretending to write with his left hand only, he has come to be recognized as one of the three or four best American authors before the Revolution.

During his own lifetime, however, he was not widely noted for his writing because he published little. There was an early piece for the Royal Society that appeared in the *Philosophical Transactions*. He translated out of Petronius, but did not publish, the wonderful little story of the Wife of Ephesus. In 1710 a satire of certain members of the House of Burgesses went the rounds and was recognized as the work of William Byrd. He apparently made notes for a history of Virginia that in 1741 John Oldmixon was to acknowledge as a chief source for his own well-known history. In 1719 Byrd published a volume of light verse called *Tunbrigalia*; and in 1721, within months of Defoe's two famous books on the subject, he brought out *A Discourse on the Plague*. Throughout his life he wrote lampoons, satires, and witty character sketches, especially of women, some of which have survived to be published in the twentieth century. In his own day, however, the great age of letter writing, perhaps he was best known as a letter writer of ability, counting among his later correspondents his old friends of the literary, scientific, political, and social world of London. He received letters from Sir Hans Sloane, Robert Boyle, Mark Catesby, the botanist, even Sir Robert Walpole, whom Byrd dared to advise about the British Navy.

Today, his reputation as a writer secure and growing, Byrd is best known as a keeper of journals. Since 1939 three of his shorthand diaries have been discovered and published. They are all very personal and brief, but for months at a time he never failed to record at least a few lines every day, no matter where he was. Long before any of these journals had been discovered, Marion Harland, writing in her novel *His Great Self*, reported Byrd's habit of keeping a diary: "His minutes," she said, " were sometimes jotted down in cipher upon the pommel of his saddle, sometimes pencilled by the glare of the watch fire while his comrades slept on the bare ground around him, or scribbled in a wayside-hostelry and in the finest private mansions Virginia could boast. Every scrap was jealously guarded."[1] Although based on a Byrd family legend, this imaginary account is now seen to be substantially true. Like Samuel Sewall, his contemporary in New England, like Samuel Pepys, an older, British contemporary, Byrd felt compelled to keep a record of everything that was significant and much that was intimate. Most of all, one is reminded of that other great travel writer, William Dampier, who was a friend of important friends of Byrd, Hans Sloane, for example, and who, even as a buccaneer in Spanish America, kept a journal under the most trying conditions, protecting his notes from water by sealing them in bamboo canes.

Byrd's three shorthand diaries that have turned up cover three periods of his life after 1708 and are of inestimable importance to historians of Colonial America, who can hardly do without the hundreds of brief entries like this very typical one written at Williamsburg, June 14, 1740:

I rose about 5, read Hebrew and Greek. I prayed and had chocolate. The weather continued very hot. We had news of Colonel Spotswood's death. I breakfasted with the Commissary where we consulted what he as President was to insist upon. About 10 went to the capitol where it was agreed that the Commissary should be President during the Governor's absence, [and] the Governor and Isham Randolph should have the care of the soldiers. Colonel Grymes and I dined with the Commissary and I ate beans and bacon. After dinner we went to Lady Randolph's and about 8 walked home and prayed.

Furthermore, the entries are often entertaining and, to the uninitiated, even shocking, this one for July 30, 1710, for example:

I rose at 5 o'clock and wrote a letter to Major Burwell about his boat

---

[1]Quoted by Maude H. Woodfin in the preface to *Another Secret Diary of William Byrd of Westover, 1739–1741*, ed. Woodfin, trans. and collated, Marion Tinling (Richmond, Virginia, 1942), p. vii.

which Captain Broadwater's people had brought round and sent Tom with it. I read two chapters in Hebrew and some Greek in Thucydides. I said my prayers and ate boiled milk for breakfast. I danced my dance. I read a sermon in Dr. Tillotson and then took a little [nap]. I ate fish for dinner. In the afternoon my wife and I had a little quarrel which I reconciled with a flourish. Then she read a sermon in Dr. Tillotson to me. It is to be observed that the flourish was performed on the billiard table. I read a little Latin. In the evening we took a walk about the plantation. I neglected to say my prayers but had good health, good thoughts, and good humor, thanks be to God. This month there were many people sick of fever and pain in the heads; perhaps this might be caused by the cold weather which we had this month, which was indeed the coldest that ever was known in July in this country. Several of my people have been sick, but none died, thank God.

Although the recent discovery and publication of these three diaries have increased his reputation, as a writer of travel journals Byrd had been widely known even before the twentieth century. One of these, *A Progress to the Mines,* was the result of a trip made in 1732 to inspect some iron mines operated by Governor Spotswood. Another, *A Journey to the Land of Eden,* records his visit in 1733 to survey the 26,000-acre estate he had bought in North Carolina. Both of these journals have been published at least five times, twice in the nineteenth century, and both are livelier, wittier, and in much greater detail than the more recently discovered diaries, which were written under more comfortable conditions. Two other travel journals, now considered Byrd's most significant, are those published here—the *History* of the surveying party's experiences in running the line between Virginia and North Carolina in 1728 and the *Secret History* of that same experience.

These two versions of the same adventures and the same period of time are in general so different from each other that a reader hardly notices the few repetitions. The *History* opens with twelve pages about how the creation of certain British colonies out of Virginia gave rise to the trouble over the line between North Carolina and the parent colony and concludes with the theory that the misunderstanding had arisen because Weyanoke Creek, one of the reference points given in the King's Charter of 1665, had lost its identity and had probably become Nottoway River. The author of this background material had taken time to do some reading, looking back, for example, at the beginning of his brother-in-law's *History of Virginia.* The *Secret History* has none of this introductory material but opens with an account of how the surveying party was appointed and moves on to an exchange of letters made, on the one hand, by the three Virginia commissioners appointed for the line and, on the other, by the four commissioners from North Carolina.

Names in the two versions are also unlike. The *History* refers to each member of the surveying party by his real name. For the seven commissioners, at least, the *Secret History* uses only names invented by the author, each of which, in the tradition of the Restoration comedy of manners known so well by Byrd, revealed something about the man to whom it was given. "Firebrand," for example, was Richard Fitz-William, always ready to assert his rights vehemently or to make love to almost any white, black, or red female he saw. "Steddy" [Steady] was, of course, the name Byrd selected for himself, not altogether in jest since he felt that he was long suffering in the ordeals the party underwent and patient in settling differences among the men. The third Virginia commissioner was "Meanwell." Then there was "Dr. Humdrum," that is to say, the Reverend Peter Fontaine, whom Byrd, a good Anglican, was instrumental in having appointed chaplain for the expedition, not only because he felt that the eighteen or twenty members needed divine guidance but because the backwoodsmen along the line had long been without a minister to give them communion or baptize their children. "Plausible," "Jumble," "Shoebrush," and "Puzzle Cause" were the North Carolina commissioners, "the Flower and Cream of the Council of that Province." As soon as he began to rework his private journal for publication and to insert the real names for these eight men, most of whom were influential citizens, Byrd felt it necessary to restrain his private sarcasms and delete dozens of scandalous revelations, especially about sex life.

Sometimes the greater frankness of the private version has to do with the author of the two journals. In the *History*, for example, we are told that the Nottoway Indians had a custom of providing female bedfellows for male visitors. Then we are told,

We were unluckily so many, that they cou'd not well make us the Complement of Bed-fellows, . . . tho' a grave Matron whisper'd one of the

Commissioners very civilly in the Ear, that if her Daughter had been but one year Older, she should have been at his Devotion.

In the *Secret History* we discover that the "grave Matron" was whispering in the ear of William Byrd himself.

The private version is also frequently more dramatic. Where the *History* simply states that as a result of the great hurricane of 1726 "Both Trees and Houses were laid flat on the Ground, and several things hurl'd to an incredible distance," the *Secret History* says, "Mr. Baker's House was so unlucky as to stand in its way, which it laid flat to the Ground and blew some of his Goods above 2 Miles."

On the other hand, the version intended for publication is just as frequently more detailed. In the original journal Byrd wrote, "Then they past for several Miles together by the North Side of the Great Dismal, and after a Journey of 25 Miles, arriv'd in good Order at Major Crawford's, over against Norfolk Town." In the *History* these two and one-half lines become ten that add a description of "Candle Berries," of "Gall-Bush," and of how moss on the trees was eaten by domestic animals. Elsewhere six lines in one day's entry in the original journal name three plants used for snake bite remedies. In the more formal *History* the three plants become five and their descriptions are expanded and spread out over four entries. Although William Byrd would have seldom needed outside help for such details as these, his second, more formal, version does often demonstrate that he both read books and had taken time to reflect on how they could improve his own book. Not only does the later account make an obvious if limited use of Robert Beverley's *History*; it shows a wide acquaintance among the many travel writers in Byrd's own library. For he was able to compare American bears with those of Muscovy and Greenland or American ginseng with that of China and, more especially, with the "kama" of South Africa. He added a long description of the "paco" as a beast of burden in Chile. He even added names of some of the travel books he knew, that by Bishop Burnet of 1686 being only one.

What is important is perhaps not the fact that the two "histories" are different but that they are complementary. Where one gains in spontaneity, the other gains in detail. Where one may be impetuous in certain judgments or unfair in its attempts at sarcasm, the other may be the result of greater deliberation and a desire for more thoroughness. Taken together they reveal many sides of their author as well as many attitudes to life on the old frontier of Southern America. Certain of these facts stand out.

One is the running battle waged between Byrd and his fellow Virginian, Richard Fitz-William, whom Byrd considered not only immoderate and vulgar but traitorous because he fraternized more with the North Carolina surveyors and seemed to favor their position.

Another important element in the two journals is their information about the Indians encountered along the border, for Byrd and his companions not only employed Indian hunters to keep them supplied with game but visited several Indian villages. As a result, the journals describe the Southern Red Man's way of curing deer hides, his superstitions, his marriage customs, his endurance, and his hospitality. One of the best of the entries dealing with Indians is that which at great length records Byrd's "interview" with his companion Bearskin about religion.

One of the principal features of the "histories" is their revelation of Byrd's great interest in and knowledge of the plants and animals in his region. Although he was not the author of the book published in 1940 as *William Byrd's Natural History of Virginia*, which is largely the work of John Lawson, he could have written such a book. In fact, the Dividing Line journals, especially the more formal one, almost constitute a natural history of Byrd's colony none of which is indebted to Lawson or anyone else. For example, to test Byrd's originality and thoroughness, one can compare his longer, fuller, and more dramatic account of the elk (p. 236) with that given by Lawson[2] (p. 127), or his excellent description of the opossum (p. 248) with the equally detailed one by Lawson (p. 124), which appears almost verbatim in the book published as *William Byrd's Natural History of Virginia* (pp. 55-56).

He knew even more about plants. Here he could have learned something from his father, who started a beautiful garden at

[2]*Lawson's History of North Carolina . . .*, ed. F. L. Harriss (Third ed; Richmond, Va., 1960). [First printed in London, 1709 and 1714.]

Westover that William Byrd II enlarged and loved. He could have learned much from the Indians he knew and employed. But like John Bartram of Pennsylvania, he probably was his own best teacher as he walked his plantation, traveled the region on horseback, or read from the many scientific books in his library. That the very fine naturalist Mark Catesby would enjoy his companionship and hospitality for so many days in 1712 is evidence enough for William Byrd's interest in nature.

Sometimes, as one might expect, Byrd's natural history is not always scientific. By the time he wrote, travelers normally had outgrown the custom of padding their journals with stories out of Pliny, and Byrd seldom resorted to that practice. But he did explain gravely how alligators swallowed rocks in order to make themselves heavy enough to pull a cow under water and drown her, thereafter spewing up the rocks (p. 300). This story matches the well-known one with which John Bartram pulled the leg of the Swedish botanist Kalm telling him how bears killed a cow by making an opening in her skin and then blowing in air until the skin burst off and she died. Byrd had one or two other such tales —Indians capturing sturgeon by riding them bareback; squirrels crossing rivers on pieces of bark, using their tails as sails—but one cannot be sure that he was not smiling at these stories also.

One of Byrd's reasons for being so interested in plants is that he delighted in playing doctor to anyone who was ailing, including himself. His recently discovered diaries all demonstrate this to be one of his chief characteristics. He carefully recorded his own ills and those of his family, his servants, his neighbors, his friends in Williamsburg. He prescribed for anyone, his favorite prescriptions being sweating, blood letting, vomiting, and swimming in cold water. More than once either he or some friend such as Mark Catesby performed this last regimen, not only coming out alive but cured. His favorite medicines were "snakeroot stewed in wine" and ipecacuanha; his favorite panacea for preserving health was ginseng tea, which other American travelers found the Indians drinking as a guarantee for long life. Byrd's travel journals discover him just as busy nursing and doctoring. In the *Secret History* he tells how he handled the case of Meanwell, "Purging and vomiting" him with "Veal Broth," advising him to follow up with "a Gallon of warm Water," which finished the cure (p. 147). In one day (p. 163) he prescribed the letting of twelve ounces of blood for Puzzlecause, "the bark" for Boötes, and ipecac for his man Powell and for one of the Carolina men. One of the chief differences between the two "Histories" is that nearly all of these doctorings were omitted from the formal version.

But while he took his medicine seriously, William Byrd had a sense of humor that may have been his greatest, but to some his most provoking, asset. Certainly it makes all of his writing sparkle. The three diaries published in the last thirty years reveal him, for example, as a practical jokester who, like his contemporary Swift, delighted in putting the "bite" on someone. He could chuckle at his wife Lucy because she could not catch him cheating her at cards, or he could enjoy the irritation of his fellow members of the House of Burgesses when in his presence they read lampoons directed at them but which they did not know he wrote. Even more than these private diaries the *Secret History* has its wit. It could be mild, like the repartee he exchanged with Rachel Speight, the landlord's pretty daughter, while she was washing out his linen. When, he wrote, "I desired the Parson to make a Memorandum of his Christenings, that we might keep an Account of the good we did, she ask't me pertly, who was to keep an Account of the Evil? I told her she should be my Secretary for that, if she would go along with me" (p. 77). Or the wit in the *Secret History* could be rough, as when Byrd told how, after he had retired at camp one night, his companions stayed for drinks at a nearby plantation and lured from the kitchen a girl with a sprained wrist to drink with them. When the liquor had had its effect on the "Tallow-faced Wench," Byrd wrote, "they examined all her hidden Charms, and play'd a great many gay Pranks. While Firebrand who had the most Curiosity, was ranging over her sweet Person, he pick't off several Scabs as big as Nipples, the Consequence of eating too much Pork. The poor Damsel was disabled from making any resistance by the Lameness of her Hand; all she cou'd do, was, to sit stil, and make the Fashionable Exclamation of the Country, Flesh a live and tear it, and by what I can understand she never spake so properly in her life" (p. 59).

Such plays on words are common in Byrd's journals, for, like Swift again, he loved puns. The *Secret History* has many of them, the *History* very few. About Mr. Speight's "worthless" son, he explained, his "good Father intended him for the Mathematics, but he never cou'd rise higher in that Study than to gage a Rum Cask" (pp. 95-96). Mr. "Kinchin" was described as "a Man of Figure in these parts, and his Wife a much better Figure than he." Not only are both these puns omitted in the *History*, but there Byrd neglected the wife's handsome figure entirely while calling attention to her "tidy" housekeeping (p. 111). When he did keep a pun in the formal version, he sometimes spoiled it, as when a three-line private joke about the name of Matrimony Creek was expanded to five lines that show he did not trust his reader to get the joke (pp. 214-215). But the more formal *History* is by no means devoid of wit. For example, when Byrd was reworking his journal for publication, he was able to add two paragraphs about how a diet of bear meat not only increased the birth rate among Indians but made all his companions proud papas within nine months after returning home.

Much of Byrd's wit, it is now obvious, is concerned with sex, a fact that is true about all his journals and letters and *jeux d'esprits*. It is, of course, a fact that is true for most of the great humorists—Aristophanes, Lucian, Rabelais, Swift, Sterne, for example. And much has been said about Byrd's sex life, which has apparently been as fascinating to his readers as it was to him. He knew he had a warm "constitution," and in the Diary of 1709-1712 he took great care to record the fact every time he "rogered" his wife or gave her a "flourish." It also tells how he made her cry by throwing Mrs. Chiswell on the bed and kissing her passionately; it also made Mrs. Chiswell angry, he admitted. Written after his first wife died, Byrd's *London Journal* (1717-1721) displays a man with a constitution more than warm. While pursuing the numerous fashionable ladies each of whom he tried to marry, he could pick up wenches in the park, either for hugging or kissing or for more; on the boat back to America he could take two maids who would be more than maids to him; or he could keep at least two whores in London, one of whom he would quit because she sold her favors to other men. By the time he was sixty-five the passionate planter had lost much of his energy. Not only are the entries in his last diary (1739-1741) shorter; seldom do they announce thoughts of sex. Four times during those two years, however, the old man noted that he "played the fool" with some female other than his wife—Sarah, or Sally, or Caton.

The *Secret History* then, if not the History, can be expected to offer its readers much sex. The members of the surveying party managed to find willing women everywhere they went—white, black, and red. In one Indian village, for example, the men were out "all Night" hunting the girls while even some of the worthy Commissioners showed up the next morning with their ruffles tarnished from the bear grease which the Indian women used for cold cream. All the white women along the line were not easy conquests, however. Some barred their doors and kept loaded chamber pots handy; others were guarded all night by an anxious father. But even though Byrd recorded it all, one fact stands out about his frank exposé of the sex life of the surveyors: He never admitted that he himself was guilty of any sex act or of any offense against good manners. The only admission he made was that on a rainy morning he might lie in bed late and indulge in licentious thoughts. It is obvious that on this expedition Byrd was considering his position as cultured aristocrat and statesman: Not only did he bring along a minister and not only did he act as medical adviser to the party; he was the leader who was not going to stoop to vulgarities of any kind.

The personality of the author, the facts about men and nature, the historical significance—all these stand out in the *Dividing Line Histories* as their admirer Thomas Jefferson discovered a century and a half ago. But the two accounts have other attractive qualities, their style, for example; for Byrd was a conscious artist, a fact not so surprising in an age of clear and polished and great prose. He included literary allusions, not only to travel books but to the Bible. He made apt analogies, with London life, with domestic life, with things of nature. Like the great neo-classicists of his day, from Dryden to Dr. Johnson, he employed much parallel structure, both analogies and antitheses. Here, for example, is a sentence from his more nearly finished *History* that, in spite of its scientific error, is not only epic in its proportions and its similes but balanced in its phrases and climactic in its arrangement:

For as some Brutes have Horns and Hoofs, and others are arm'd with Claws, Teeth and Tushes for their Defense; and as Some Spit a Sort of Poison at their Adversaries, like the Paco; and others dart Quills at their Pursuers, like the Porcupine; and as some have no Weapons to help themselves but their Tongue, and others none but their Tails; so the poor Polcat's safety lies altogether in the irresistible Stench of its Water; insomuch that when it finds itself in Danger from an Enemy, it Moistens its bushy Tail plentifully with this Liquid Ammunition, and, then with great fury, Sprinkles it like a Shower of Rain full into the Eyes of its Assailant, by which it gains time to make its Escape. (p. 316)

Byrd's penchant for parallelism was that of his day, and like Dryden and Pope especially he enjoyed balancing not only phrases and clauses but smaller units—nouns or verbs. And frequently the rhetorical balance of two words was emphasized by balancing the sounds of the words too. For example, in the *Secret History* Byrd wrote that the Carolina commissioners arrived "much better provided for the Belly than the Business" (p. 45). He liked this phrase so much that he kept it intact in the formal version even though he altered all the rest of the passage. Or he could say, also in the *Secret History*, that "Firebrand chose rather to litter the Floor, than lye with the Parson" (p. 65); but this wonderful sentence, following Byrd's practice of eliminating all sarcasms directed at Richard Fitz-William, is not to be found in the final version. Another neatly balanced barb directed at Firebrand also had to be excised because it accused him of making "hot Love to honest Ruth" Speight, who was not charmed either "with his Persuasion or his Person (p. 91). Most of these parallel sounds are alliterations, but—also like Dryden and Pope—Byrd could assonate the balanced words, as when he wrote that at one point his companions became so vulgar he had to leave them, "taking as little pleasure in their low Wit, as in their low liquor" (p. 113). Partly because his words are so neatly and logically arranged, Byrd's sentences sometimes leave the impression that they are shorter than they really are.

William Byrd's Dividing Line Histories, then, are well worth reprinting in an edition easily accessible to all readers. Together they make up a volume that is important for eighteenth-century prose, for early American history, and for travel literature. They reveal the Southeastern American frontier as no other book has done. They reveal a witty, observant, intelligent, many-sided Virginia Gentleman better than anything else he wrote. They give us the unique opportunity to compare the private with the public author. And they are entertaining.

PERCY G. ADAMS

January, 1967
Baton Rouge, Louisiana

A NOTE ON THE EDITION

William Byrd's histories of the Dividing Line were almost published by the American Philosophical Society early in the nineteenth century, Thomas Jefferson being one who concerned himself very much with the two travel journals as he read them in manuscript. Judging them to be too frank in matters of sex, however, the American Philosophical Society set them aside, and it was not until 1841 that the less "shocking" *History* was first published, in a volume edited by Edmund Ruffin and containing also *A Progress to the Mines and A Journey to the Land of Eden*. These three journals came out again in 1866 in two volumes edited by Thomas H. Wynne, and again in 1901 in John Spencer Bassett's *The Works of "Colonel William Byrd of Westover, Esq.,"* and again in 1928 edited by Mark Van Doren. But it was not until 1929 that the *Secret History* was first published, edited by Professor William K. Boyd of Duke University. It is this volume that is reproduced here. The *Secret History* has been published one other time, in a handsome and scholarly but necessarily expensive book done by Harvard Press in 1966, called *The Prose Works of Colonel William Byrd of Westover* and edited by Louis B. Wright. This volume includes both *Histories*, the *Progress*, and *A Journey to the Land of Eden*. In addition, it was able to provide two manuscript pages of the *Secret History* that had not been published in any of the previous editions of Byrd's works, these being the entries for November 20, 21, 22 and coming at the very end of the journal. These pages had, however, been published in 1945 in the *William and Mary Quarterly*.

Dover has elected to reissue the Boyd edition for two chief reasons. First, it places the *History* and the *Secret History* on opposite and matching pages so that the reader can compare the two versions as he reads. Second, it retains the spelling and punctuation of the original manuscript. The entries in the *Secret History* for November 20, 21, 22, which were not in Professor Boyd's volume, have been added with the kind permission of Colonial Williamsburg, where they are to be found in the "William Byrd II Papers."

SUGGESTIONS FOR FURTHER READING

Beatty, Richmond C., *William Byrd of Westover*. New York, Houghton Mifflin Company, 1932.
  This is the only full-length biography. It is, however, much out of date, since it was written before the discovery and publication of the various "secret diaries."

Beatty, Richmond C., and William J. Mulloy, edd. and trans., *William Byrd's Natural History of Virginia; or, The Newly Discovered Eden*. Richmond, Dietz Press, 1940.
  This book, listed in nearly all bibliographies of Byrd, has been shown to be a compilation out of John Lawson, *A History of North Carolina*, and Robert Beverley, *The History and Present State of Virginia*. It first appeared in German and was used as propaganda by Samuel Jenner in Switzerland.

Byrd, William, *Another Secret Diary of William Byrd of Westover, 1739–1741*, Maude H. Woodfin, ed. Richmond, Dietz Press, 1942.

———, *The London Diary, 1717–1721*, Louis B. Wright and Marion Tinling edd. New York, Oxford University Press, 1958.

———, *The Prose Works of Colonel William Byrd of Westover*, Louis B. Wright, ed. Cambridge, Belknap Press of Harvard University, 1966.
  This volume includes both *Dividing Line Histories*, *A Progress to the Mines*, and *A Journey to the Land of Eden*. Although it modernizes the spelling and punctuation of the original manuscripts, Professor Wright's edition will be invaluable to the special student of Byrd.

———, *The Secret Diary of William Byrd of Westover, 1709–1712*, Louis B. Wright and Marion Tinling, edd. Richmond, Dietz Press, 1941.

Wright, Louis B., *The First Gentleman of Virginia*. San Marino, Huntington Library, 1940. Reprinted by the University of Virginia Press, 1964.

INTRODUCTION TO THE FIRST EDITION

I

William Byrd's *History of the Dividing Line betwixt Virginia and North Carolina* has long been regarded as a classic of the colonial period of American literature, an invaluable source for the social history of that time, and a comprehensive and dependable account of the first successful effort to establish the boundary between North Carolina and Virginia. This estimate, however, must be revised. Only the literary merits of the work can withstand criticism. Undoubtedly Byrd was a cosmopolitan "writer of quality," worthy of a place among the wits of the eighteenth century coffee houses. In all other respects, the *History of the Dividing Line* must be accepted with reservations. As a description of the frontier region along the Virginia-Carolina border its general tone is true to nature; but certain details leave on the mind of the reader misconceptions regarding conditions and policies in North Carolina. Moreover, as an account of the survey of the boundary line, it omits certain factors that were vital in shaping the results.

An important reason for such a revision of judgment is the fact that Byrd wrote another account of the survey which he called *The Secret History of the Line*, hitherto unpublished, which gives a different impression concerning the work of the boundary commission than the *History of the Dividing Line*. A comparison of the two works reveals the following divergencies.

First of all, the principal characters appear in the *Secret History* under the guise of fictitious names. Thus Byrd himself is "Steddy," his fellow-commissioners of Virginia, William Dandridge and Richard Fitz-William, are "Meanwell" and "Firebrand," and the Virginia surveyors, Alexander Irvine and William Mayo, are "Orion" and "Astrolabe"; likewise the North Carolina commissioners, Chief Justice Gale, Edward Moseley, John Lovick and William Little, are respectively "Judge Jumble," "Plausible," "Shoebrush" and "Puzzlecause," while Samuel Swann, the North Carolina surveyor, is denominated "Bo-otes." The chaplain, Rev. Peter Fountain (Fontaine) is "Dr. Humdrum." The use of these fictitious names gives to the *Secret History* a certain air of mystery and makes easy the expression of opinions regarding its leading personalities. It is not surprising, therefore, that *the Secret History* contains considerable information regarding the expedition which is not contained in the *History of the Dividing Line*.

This new information centers mainly around two personalities, Richard Fitz-William and Alexander Irvine. The former was a royal official, being Surveyor-General of Customs for the Southern Colonies, and between him and Byrd there was a strong antipathy. Fitz-William was tardy in joining the expedition, for which he made no apology, and he soon found cause to encourage dissension which had its origin in the personality and labors of Irvine, the Virginia surveyor, who was also professor of Mathematics at William and Mary. Irvine seems to have been a man with a certain literalness of mind, without a sense of humor or that spirit of comradeship so valuable when men confront the wilds of nature. Byrd certainly had little respect for his ability. In the very beginning of the survey, he aroused Byrd's distrust by relying more on the North Carolina surveyors than his Virginia colleague, William Mayo, in correcting the readings of his instruments. This placed the Virginia surveyors at odds, and Fitz-William supported Irvine; in the language of Byrd, "Firebrand took all occasion to set Orion above Astrolabe." A definite breach was not long in developing. On March 22, the surveyors emerged from the Dismal Swamp and Byrd sent forward the horse of William Mayo in order that Mayo might ride into camp. At the same time Fitz-William ordered a Virginian member of the party to send a horse for Irvine. To this there was a point-blank refusal, whereupon Fitz-William easily persuaded one of the North Carolinians to lend a horse for the purpose. The climax came some days later when Irvine resented what he believed to be insubordination by one of the Virginia party; and when Fitz-William urged Byrd to discipline the man, he refused. "After this misfortune," says Byrd, "to be formally civil was as much as we could afford to be to one another." A week later, on April 1, there was a stormy interview because Fitz-William objected to the presence among the surveyors of Joseph Mayo, a brother of William Mayo, and again complained of the rudeness shown to Irvine; but Byrd was obdurate. Fitz-William then went visiting with John Lovick, one of the North Carolina commissioners; "and," adds Byrd, "his going off was not less pleasing to us than the going off of a fever."

In all this a likely contributing factor was that Fitz-William, as a royal official of the customs, had been admitted to the Executive Council of North Carolina and was probably in sympathy with the North Carolina contention regarding the boundary. Certainly he was not in sympathy with Virginia's policy of excluding North Carolina tobacco from her ports. Alexander Irvine, also, because he was a professor in William and Mary, was a protégé of Commissary James Blair, for whom Byrd had little fondness. Fitz-William, on the other hand, seems to have been on good terms with both Irvine and Blair; according to Byrd it was through Irvine's efforts that Fitz-William was appointed one of the boundary commissioners.

When Byrd called on Governor Gooch during the suspension of the survey in the summer of 1728, he found that Fitz-William and Irvine had complained to the Governor concerning his attitude toward Irvine, and had criticised the ability of William Mayo as a surveyor. In this they were supported by the North Carolina commissioners, who had sent to Gooch letters commending Fitz-William and Irvine. Fitz-William also refused to sign Byrd's report of the survey until he learned that it was to be sent to England. He secretly supported a demand of the Carolina commissioners that the date for the resumption of the survey be September 10, instead of September 20.

Thus in the summer of 1728 there was a well-defined cleavage among the Virginia commissioners; Byrd, William Dandridge, and Surveyor Mayo composing one faction, Fitz-William and Irvine the other. According to the *Secret History*, Governor Gooch was easily persuaded to support the former. Certainly, when preparations were made to resume the survey, a decision favorable to Byrd was reached. Fitz-William objected to the employment of as many men for the expedition as Byrd desired; whereupon Byrd definitely asked to be relived of further participation in the survey and consented to continue in the work only when he was made official head of the Virginia commission with the full quota of men he had recommended. With Byrd thus exercising definite authority, there was less friction in the last than the earlier stage of the survey. Fitz-William, however, consorted with the

North Carolina members of the expedition, and when on October 5, they proposed to Byrd a suspension of the survey, Fitz-William became their advocate. Indeed, a discussion of the proposal on the part of Byrd, Fitz-William, and Dandridge almost resulted in a broil. Finally, when the North Carolina members left the expedition, Fitz-William returned to Williamsburg. The North Carolina commissioners, in recognition of his sympathy with their contentions, named on their map of the survey that tributary of the Dan now known as the Banister, Fitz-William River, while the Virginia commissioners, strange to say, left no tracing of the stream on their map, which was prepared by Surveyor Mayo.

The *Secret History* also relates a number of incidents not mentioned in the *History of the Dividing Line*. Notable are those which illustrate the attitude of the men of the expedition toward the women of the frontier. Byrd himself had an eye for feminine charms, but he also had the restraint proper in one of his station. This was not true of certain others, including some of the commissioners. Six times insult or violence to women occurred. Such conduct Byrd always took pains to prevent and always he condemned it. These incidents of violence illustrate a lack of discipline and control due, no doubt, to the cleavage between Byrd and Fitz-William. All accounts of them are omitted in the *History of the Dividing Line*.

Finally, in the *Secret History* are included a number of letters, addresses, and other documents which are missing in the text of the *History of the Dividing Line*. These consist of three letters exchanged by the North Carolina and Virginia commissioners (two drafted by the former and one by the latter), five speeches of Byrd (four delivered to the men of the expedition and one to the Virginia Council), the protest of the North Carolina commissioners against a continuance of the survey and the reply of Byrd (which are in the appendix of the *History of the Dividing Line*), and a detailed schedule indicating the distances from place to place in the territory traversed by the commissioners.

So much for the *Secret History;* in contrast is the *History of the Dividing Line,* of twice the length. It contains much information not included in the *Secret History*. This consists mainly of a sketch of English colonization in America, descriptions of the region traversed by the surveying expedition, including its fauna and flora, the customs of the Indians and the life of the pioneers, and characterizations of North Carolina and its people. Of these contrasts between the two works, none is more impressive than their respective attitudes toward North Carolina. The *Secret History* contains but one unfavorable criticism of the people of the colony, while such reflections are so numerous and so piquant in the *History of the Dividing Line* as to be one of its principal characteristics. The indolence of the North Carolinians, their lack of religion, their disrespect for government, and their poverty—these traits so freely described in the *History of the Dividing Line* are not mentioned in the *Secret History*. Likewise Edenton, a place which comes in for satirical remarks in the *History of the Dividing Line,* is barely mentioned in the *Secret History,* and apparently Byrd never visited the town. In fact, the single unfavorable reflection on North Carolina common to both documents is that the people eat so much swine's flesh as to injure their dispositions.

These contrasts of the two works raise questions of origins and literary history. Concerning the former the evidence is mainly internal. A comparison of manuscripts reveals a common penmanship, but not that of William Byrd himself; and on the first page of the *Secret History* is written the name Nancy Byrd, who was probably Byrd's daughter, Anne (1725-1757).[1]   As the *History of the Dividing Line* is twice the length of *The Secret History,* it is logical to believe that the latter was the first to be composed and that as the title indicates, it was intended only for a select few, and that the *History of the Dividing Line* was written at a later date for a wider audience. Supporting such a conclusion are letters of Byrd written in 1736 and 1737. Peter Collison, then in England, heard of Byrd's journal of the survey and wrote him asking for a copy.[2] Byrd in his reply stated that he was at work on a complete history of the expedition. Mark Catesby saw a copy of the journal and wrote Byrd a complimentary note; Byrd replied in 1737 that he had not finished the history, but according to another letter to Collison in July 1737, he expected to complete it the following winter; and as he intended to describe some of the wild animals of the frontier, he requested Collison to make

---

[1] Nancy is a vulgarized form of Anne.
[2] Byrd's journal and survey notes (transcribed from the records of the Board of Trade) are published in the *Colonial Records of North Carolina,* vol. II, pp. 750, 799.

arrangements for some plates.[3] From these facts it is probable
that Byrd finished the work mentioned early in 1738 and evidently
he intended publication. As the *History of the Dividing Line* contains much information regarding the state of civilization on the
frontier and none regarding the dissension between Byrd and Fitz-
William, it is very probable that it is the work referred to in the
correspondence with Collison and Catesby.

The preservation of the two manuscripts harmonizes with their
literary divergences. *The History of the Dividing Line* passed
into the hands of Mrs. Mary Willing Byrd, William Byrd's daughter-in-law, who gave it to her grandson, George Harrison, of Brandon. At Brandon it remained until recently and at this writing it
is in the custody of a New York trust company. It was first published in 1841;[4] a second edition appeared in 1866;[5] and a third
in 1901.[6] Meanwhile, at some time and by some process unknown,
the *Secret History of the Line* was transferred to Philadelphia and
was there deposited with the American Philosophical Society.
Although Lyman C. Draper called attention to the existence of the
Secret History in 1851,[7] it has not hitherto been published;
through the courtesy of the Philosophical Society it is now given
publicity. In this connection it is pertinent to recall that Byrd's
library was sold in Philadelphia in 1778 and that Mrs. Mary
Willing Byrd, his daughter-in-law, was a native of Philadelphia;
either by sale or by act of Mary Willing Byrd, the manuscript
probably reached that city.

II

The boundary controversy which it was the duty of Byrd and
his associates to settle, had long been a source of irritation to the

[3] Regarding this correspondence, see the Introduction to Bassett's *Writings of Colonel William Byrd*, lxxix.

[4] *The Westover Manuscripts; containing the History of the Dividing Line betwixt Virginia and North Carolina, etc.* Petersburg, 1841. Edmund Ruffin disclosed the manuscripts and was the publisher.

[5] *History of the Dividing Line and other notes, from the papers of Wm. Byrd, of Westover, in Virginia, Esquire*, 2 vols. Richmond, 1866. Thomas H. Wynne was the editor.

[6] *The Writings of "Colonel William Byrd in Virginia, Esq."* Edited by John Spencer Bassett. New York, 1901.

[7] See "The Westover Library," by Charles Campbell (*Virginia Historical Register*, vol. IV, p. 87) in which a communication from Draper regarding the Westover Manuscripts is quoted.

governments of North Carolina and Virginia. Its origin is found in the terms of the Carolina charters. That of 1663 declared the northern boundary of the colony to be 36°, but by the second charter the boundary was declared to run "from the north end of Currituck river or inlet upon a strait westerly line to Weyanoke Creek which lies within or about the degrees of 36 and thirty minutes northern latitude; and as far west, in the direct line, as far as the south seas." Thus a strip of land approximately thirty miles wide was added to Carolina. Living therein were people holding land grants from Virginia; in fact the region included all of the Albemarle section of Carolina. Until the boundary was officially established in accordance with the provisions of the second charter, a conflict of jurisdiction between North Carolina and Virginia was inevitable. That conflict began in 1680 when certain people on the border lands refused any longer to pay the Virginia quit rents, although their titles were from the Virginia land office; thereupon the Sheriff of Lower Norfolk County was ordered by the Virginia Council to collect the rents. The matter came to the attention of the Lords Proprietors and in 1681 they petitioned the Committee for Trade and Plantations that Virginia be instructed to appoint a commission to act with representatives of North Carolina in establishing the boundary as described in the charter of 1665. To this petition no reply is extant. Doubtless none was made, for at that time the question of vacating all the proprietary charters was under serious consideration by the British authorities.

In 1688 there is again evidence of conflicting jurisdiction. The people around Currituck Inlet complained to the Virginia authorities that North Carolina officials were distraining on their property for taxes. Thereupon the Virginia Council informed His Majesty's Government that North Carolina was extending its jurisdiction beyond the line 36°, the boundary named in the first charter, so manifesting ignorance regarding the boundary described in the second charter. Again there is no record of any action by the British authorities, and conflicts over jurisdiction continued. In 1697 the Lords Proprietors sent to Deputy Governor Harvey a copy of the charter of 1665, which they hoped would enable him to convince the Virginia authorities of the legality of North Carolina's jurisdiction over the area in dispute.

Two years later Harvey received from His Majesty's Government an order in council that a commission be appointed to survey and establish the Virginia boundary. Thereupon Harvey appointed Daniel Akehurst and Henderson Walker as commissioners on the part of North Carolina. They, in due time, journeyed to Williamsburg and laid before the Virginia Council their instructions. But that body proved to be recalcitrant; it refused to coöperate on the ground that Harvey was not legally Governor, because his appoinment to office had not been approved by the Crown, which approval was required under act of Parliament of 1696, and therefore any findings or decisions reached by a commission appointed by him would not be conclusive; and this view of the Virginia Council was approved by the Lords of Trade. The real motive behind the Virginia policy was perhaps a hope that the Crown might purchase Carolina and so restore the territory that had been lost. Such a policy was recommended to the Lords of Trade by Governor Nicholson in 1701.

Thus far Virginia had ignored the claims of North Carolina and sought means to avoid any survey or settlement of the dispute. But in 1705 this policy was reversed. In that year the House of Burgesses adopted resolutions that some provision should be made to establish the line between the two colonies and that a commission be appointed to coöperate with North Carolina to that end. This was agreed to by the Virginia Council, but that body also decided that a secret survey should be made before negotiations were opened with North Carolina in order to estimate how much territory might be lost and to secure the affidavits of old residents regarding the location of Weyanoke Creek, the final point named in the Carolina charter of 1665 from which the boundary was to extend westward. The North Carolina authorities doubtless heard of this action, for soon it was reported in Virginia that North Carolina surveyors were running a boundary line and taking depositions. The Virginia Council also made representations to the Lords of Trade regarding the encroachments of North Carolina land grants on grants issued by the Virginia land office. In 1709 the Lords recommended that a joint commission representing Virginia and North Carolina be appointed to survey and establish the boundary. This recommendation was favorably received; Edward Moseley and John Lawson were duly appointed by the North Carolina

authorities and Nathaniel Harrison and Philip Ludwell by the
Virginia Council. This commission undertook the task assigned
in 1710, but the results were unsatisfactory. This was due to
the obstructionary tactics of the North Carolina commissioners.
It was hard for the Virginia commissioners to arrange a meeting with them; they quibbled over the official instructions, sought
to confuse old residents of the territory in question who were
called upon to make depositions, found fault with the readings
of the instruments of the Virginia commissioners; and so prevented
any definite conclusion of the survey. Such tactics were attributed
by the Virginia Commissioners to the fact that Moseley was
secretly taking out land grants in the disputed region; but a better
explanation is found in the central contention of the surveyors,
the location of Weyanoke Creek, from which the boundary was
to extend westward. This stream had lost its original name, and
consequently there was difficulty in locating it. The Virginia commissioners claimed that it was identical with Wicocon Creek, a
tributary of the Chowan River, in the lower part of Hertford
County; the North Carolinians, that it was the Nottoway River. The
instruments of the Virginia surveyors—the only instruments used
by the Commissioners—gave a reading of 36° 40' on Wicocon
Creek and one of 37° at Nottoway River. These readings gave
support to the Virginia contention, but it is interesting to find that
Byrd in 1728 confessed that the instruments used in 1710 were
defective. However, it was not merely the additional land that
would be secured by starting the line at Nottoway River which interested the North Carolina Commissioners; there was also the
question of tobacco and commerce. As early as 1679 Virginia
had prohibited the importation of North Carolina tobacco, a condition which greatly retarded the economic development of the
northeastern part of the province, where the soil was well adapted
to tobacco culture. If the boundary ran through Nottoway River,
the North Carolina tobacco could be shipped down that and other
streams to Albemarle Sound and thence to points without the
colony. Indeed, the possibility of North Carolina tobacco being
exported without the payment of export duties was pointed out
to the Crown by the Virginia authorities in 1688 as an argument
for holding the boundary at the line 36°, and when in 1728 the
line was finally established as running by way of Nottoway River,

the North Carolina commissioners expressed one regret—a regret
that it did not run a little further northward, across Nansemond
River, which would have given the colony water transportation to
Chesapeake Bay, and thereby Virginia would not have been able
to enforce her laws against the importation of North Carolina
tobacco.

The year 1714 marked the beginning of the last phase of the
controversy. Governor Spotswood of Virginia, claiming that
North Carolina continued to grant lands in the disputed region,
and that "loose and disorderly people daily flock there," proposed
that Virginia survey a line through Nottoway River and North
Carolina one through Wicocon Creek, and that all settlers between
these lines be removed. Indeed, he went so far as to lay off a
line through Nottoway River and, when North Carolina did not
establish one through Wicocon he threatened to do so and to
remove the intervening settlers. At this juncture a new governor
appeared in North Carolina, Charles Eden. In 1715 he reached
an agreement with Spotswood, a compromise by which the boundary was to be established as follows: Beginning on the North
shore of the mouth of Currituck River or Inlet, it should run due
west; if it happened to cross Chowan River between the mouth of
the Nottoway and Wicocon Creek, that course should be continued
westward to the mountains; or if it cut the Chowan south of Wicocon it should be diverted up the Chowan to Wicocon and thence
westward; on the other hand, if it reached Blackwater River, a
stream north of the Nottoway, it should be diverted down that
stream to the middle entrance of the Nottoway and thence on to the
mountains. This proposal was referred to the Lords Proprietors
and to the Crown for their consideration. News of its approval by
the Lords Proprietors reached North Carolina in 1724 and a commission of four was promptly appointed to make the survey. But
there was delay in approval by the crown officials, for reasons unknown; not until March, 1727, did the Privy Council sanction the
compromise. Consequently, in 1728 a new commission was appointed by Governor Everard of North Carolina, consisting of
Christopher Gale, Edward Moseley, William Little, and John
Lovick. The Virginia authorities appointed William Byrd, William Dandridge, and Richard Fitz-William. To act with these
commissioners were the surveyors, Alexander Irvine and William

Mayo for the Virginians, and Samuel Swann and Edward Moseley (also a Commissioner) for those of North Carolina.[8]

The preparations of the commissioners for the survey were in keeping with the temper of the people and the governments they represented. The Virginians undertook their task in a true gala spirit, full of pride, and assuming to set standards for the expedition. "It is very proper to acquaint you in what manner we intend to come provided," they wrote to the North Carolina Commissioners, "that so you, Gentlemen, who are appointed in this same station, may if you please do the same honor to Your government. We shall have a Tent with us and a Marquis for the convenience of ourselves and our Servants. We shall be provided with as much Wine and Rum as will enable us and our men to drink every Night to the Success of the following Day, and because we understand there are many Gentiles on your frontier who never had an opportunity of being Baptised we shall have a Chaplain to make them Christians. For this Purpose we intend to rest in our Camp every Sunday that there may be leisure for so good a work. And whoever of your Province shall be desirous of novelty may report on Sundays to our Tent and hear a Sermon. Of this you may please give Public notice that the Charitable Intentions of this Government may meet with the happier Success."[9]

To this patronizing information the North Carolina Commissioners aptly replied: "we are at a Loss Gentlemen whether to thank you for the particulars you give us of your Tent Stores and the manner you design to meet us. Had you been Silent about it we had not wanted an Excuse for not meeting you in the same manner but now you force us to expose the nakedness of our Country and to tell you we can't possibly meet you in the manner our great respect to you would make us glad to do whom we are not Emulous of outdoing unless in Care and Diligence in the affair we come to meet you about. So all we can answer to that article is that we will endeavor to provide as well as Circumstances of things will permit"; and then they added, with irony barely veiled, "What we may want in necessaries we hope will be made up in

---

[8] The documents and official records relating to this boundary controversy may be found in the *Colonial Records of North Carolina* (vols. I-III) and the *Executive Journal of the Council of Colonial Virginia* (vols. I, II).
[9] *Secret History*, p. 21; *Colonial Records of North Carolina* II, p. 735.

Spiritual Comfort we expect from Your Chaplain of whom we shall give notice as you desire to all lovers of novelty and doubt not of a great many Boundary Christians."[10]

After the preliminary correspondence the Commissioners met at Currituck Inlet on March 5, 1728, which they found to be in Latitude 36 degrees, 31 minutes. Quite naturally the work began with a dispute. The official instructions of the Virginia Commissioners empowered them to carry the survey to a conclusion in case the North Carolina Commissioners should delay or refuse their coöperation. To the North Carolina Commissioners this seemed "too lordly and Positive"; there was no intimation of such power in their instructions and it seemed to give the Virginians the whip hand. The bluff reply to their criticism was that the Virginia Boundary Commission of 1710 had been required to do its work in conjunction with the North Carolina Commission, which had, by obstructive tactics, prevented any definite results, and that this should not happen again.

Then arose the question of the points from which the line should start. The Virginians claimed that it should be the Spit of Sand on the North Shore of Currituck Inlet, the North Carolinians a point of high ground 200 yards beyond; in the end the Virginians yielded, after they learned that the Spit of Sand had advanced in recent years toward the Inlet. A cedar post was then erected and from it a course due westward was taken. Across rivers and islands, over creeks and marshes, through wild lands and some settled areas, the party proceeded until on March 14 the Dismal Swamp was reached. Here was the supreme challenge of the survey. No one knew of the extent of the Dismal, none had penetrated its vast recesses. The surveyors and twelve assistants undertook its exploration, the commissioners and the remaining members of the expedition finding their way around it. By the fourteenth day thereafter, on March 28, the Dismal had been crossed and the two sections of the party were again united. Eight days later, due to fatigue from six weeks in the wilderness and because spring was well advanced, the survey was suspended until autumn. The Line had been carried as far west as the Meherrin River, a

---

[10] The phrase "to all Lovers of Novelty" is in the letter as printed in the *Colonial Records of North Carolina* II, 737, but is omitted in the version given in the *Secret History*.

distance of 73 miles, and the claims of North Carolina had been vindicated, for on April 2 the surveyors reached the Blackwater River, half a mile above the mouth of the Nottoway, and following the compromise agreement of Governors Eden and Spotswood, the Line was then run from the mouth of the Nottoway.

On September 20 the Commissioners resumed their work and soon reached the Roanoke, whose rich bottom lands so impressed Byrd that he eventually made large purchases and named the region "the Land of Eden." On October 4 the North Carolina Commissioners proposed a termination of the survey. They claimed that the important question in the boundary controversy, whether Nottoway River or Wicocon Creek corresponded to the mythical Weyanoke, had been settled, and the most difficult labor of the survey performed in the penetration of Dismal Swamp; that the region of unsettled lands had been reached, and that the line could be completed through this, when necessity demanded, by two or three surveyors instead of the large and expensive party then employed. To this the Virginia Commissioners answered that their instructions were to complete the Line; that settlers would soon push forward into the fertile lands of the Roanoke; and that expense should not be considered when the public interest was at stake. But the North Carolina Commissioners were obdurate and so turned back. The Line was then continued by the Virginia Commissioners as far as Peter's Creek, on the present borders of Stokes County, when they, too, because of the advanced season and the challenge of the Appalachians, relinquished the work. In 1749 the Line was extended by a joint commission for a distance of ninety miles to Steep Rock Creek, which is near the northwestern corner of North Carolina; and in 1779 further survey was made to a point near Bristol, Tennessee.

Thus the controversy over the boundary was settled and its location was established. But in later years there was dissatisfaction over the results. The line was marked only on trees and in time disappeared or became vague; moreover surveys of the United States Coast and Geodetic Survey showed that the eastern beginning of the line at Currituck is not 36° 30' (or as determined by the Commission of 1728, 36° 31') but 36° 33' 15", and that the western end near Bristol, Tennessee, is 36° 34' 25.5". Relocation was therefore necessary, but progress in the work was slow. In

1858 commissioners were appointed to resurvey the line from the end of the Byrd survey westward, but for reasons unknown nothing was done, and efforts to the same end in 1870 and 1871 brought no results. In 1887, however, the line was re-located from Currituck to the Nottoway River, and in 1896 from the Nottoway westward for a distance of sixty-two miles, to the eastern corner of Mecklenburg County, Virginia.

III

Concerning William Byrd, his personality and activities, extensive comment is unnecessary, but it is well to recall certain characteristics of the man and certain phases of his life.[11]

He belonged to the aristocracy of Virginia, an aristocracy not of inherited blood, but of achievement. His grandfather was a London goldsmith, John Bird, whose son William came to Virginia about 1670, signed his name Byrd, and inherited from an uncle, Thomas Stegg, 1,800 acres of land at the falls of the James and a business of merchandising and trade. This property increased until at the time of his death in 1704 he was a very wealthy man. He also acquired political distinction, rising from the office of militia captain to membership in the House of Burgesses and the Executive Council. He was also Auditor of Virginia and Receiver General of Quit Rents, offices which enabled him to increase his worldly estate. Marriage also brought him valuable contacts, for his wife, Mary Horsemanden, was a daughter of a kinsman or close friend of that Dame Frances who married three colonial governors: first, Samuel Stephens of Albemarle; second, William Berkeley of Virginia; and third, Philip Ludwell of Virginia. Ambitious for his children, he sent those who survived infancy to England for their education. Of these one daughter, Susan, married in England and remained there; the other, Ursula, returned to Virginia and married Robert Beverly, the historian. The son, William Byrd II, born in 1674 and author of the Dividing Line histories, proved himself well worthy of his opportunities. His guide and mentor in England was Sir Robert Southwell. He did not attend Oxford or Cambridge, but was under the instruction of

---

[11] For an exhaustive account of Byrd and his family, see the admirable *Introduction* to Professor Bassett's *Writings of Colonel William Byrd.*

tutors, spending some time on the Continent; he then studied law at the Middle Temple, and returned to Virginia in 1696 after twelve years' absence.

At once he assumed the position in Colonial life prepared for him by the prestige of his father. In the year of his return he became Auditor of Virginia, a position exchanged for the Receiver-Generalship of Quit Rents a little later when those offices were divorced, and in 1708 he became a member of the Executive Council, in which he continued to have a seat until his death in 1744. His record in public office indicates virility and an independent spirit. He was involved in numerous controversies with Governor Spotswood and carried his opposition to the highest authorities in England, where he resided from 1697 to 1705 and from 1715 to 1726, part of the time being agent of the colony. In Byrd Spotswood met an able opponent; in some controversies the Governor won, in others he lost; the climax was reached when he tried to have Byrd removed from the Council but failed. Yet their controversies created no personal hostility; each respected the other and when they met in 1732 they extended greetings worthy of friendship.

Byrd's aggressiveness in politics was well matched by his acquisition of property. As the years passed a veritable hunger for land possessed him. By the time of his departure for England in 1715 he had added to his patrimony 5,523 acres. The survey of the boundary quickened his speculative spirit; the sight of thousands of acres of unoccupied lands was a temptation not to be resisted. So he purchased from the North Carolina Commissioners 20,000 acres at the junction of the Dan and Irvine Rivers. To this were added 6,000 acres adjacent, patented from North Carolina in 1743. But the Land of Eden, as he called this region, was far removed from Westover, the seat of his inherited possessions, and so he dreamed of intervening plantations. Therefore between 1730 and 1738 he patented 5,211 acres in the region where the Dan and Staunton unite to form the Roanoke; then in 1742 all previous records were surpassed by patenting 105,000 acres between the junction of the Hico with the Dan and the North Carolina line. Soon thereafter he bought a small plantation of 2,429 acres on the Meherrin River, as a stopping place between Westover and his large possessions on the frontier. To these purchases must be added 9,710 acres acquired in the settlement of an estate and 1,336 from a legacy. All told he increased the Byrd possessions from 26,231 acres to 179,440. And, more than this, he had a desire for the Dismal Swamp. He believed that vast wilderness could be drained and redeemed for agriculture, especially the production of hemp. To that end he proposed the organization of a company which should secure a grant of the Dismal from the Crown, with exemption from quit rents for fifty years and from taxes for ten.[12]

In his acquisition of land and his long service in public office Byrd was typical of the ruling class of Virginia. Another trait was also characteristic of that class—his devotion to Virginia. He spent many years in England, but that did not impair his love for his native heath. After his arrival in London in 1715 he wrote that he had found the charms of the place tasteless, and soon after his second marriage, which occurred in England about 1725, he hastened to return to Virginia. To him there was in the vast open spaces, the rugged and unconquered wilderness and the natural beauty of the New World, something vastly more appealing than European civilization. And the inner shrine of Virginia was Westover, the lordly estate on the James which he inherited and improved. There he watched the turn of the seasons and marveled at the revelations of nature. He experimented in fruit-growing, studied wild herbs, and prescribed remedies for his sick friends. "A library, a garden, a grove and a purling stream are the Innocent scenes that divert our Leisure," he wrote. To this might have been added the companionship of friends, for the hospitality of Westover was known far and wide, and Byrd was the idol of a large family connection. This love of home interlocked with his political views; for as a member of the Council he was always the defender of Virginia's rights versus the prerogative of the British Government or the interests of the Empire.

Besides his acquisition of property, his devotion to the public service, and his love of Virginia, Byrd had another quality—one that links him with men of all climes and all ages—a taste for

---

[12]Byrd left in manuscript a description of the Dismal with a plan for its exploration which was published by Edmund Ruffin in the *Farmer's Register* (vol. II, pp. 521-524) and was reprinted in 1922 in Heartman's Historical Series, No. 38, by Earl G. Swem (*Description of the Dismal Swamp and a Proposal to Drain the Swamp* by William Byrd of Westover).

letters and things of the mind. He was a constant inquirer, and
was never satisfied with knowledge at hand. He therefore made
a collection of books which was the largest library in all the
colonies, numbering 4,000 volumes. He loved art, and was known
as the Black Swan by his many kinsmen. The walls of Westover
mansion were adorned with paintings, among them portraits of
Lord Orrery, Sir Wilfred Lawson, the Marquis of Halifax, Sir
Robert Southwell, Lord Egmont, William Blathwayt, and the Duke
of Argyle. With such worthies and others he had correspondence;
he was also a member of the Royal Society.[13] He wielded a gifted
pen, his letters being sprightly, humorous, and considerate. His
activity in public affairs and his business interests were such that
he attempted no formal literary work until late in life; then between 1732 and 1740 he wrote the *Progress to the Mines,
Journey to the Land of Eden,* and the histories of the Dividing
Line. Each was inspired by his love of the frontier, and all were
based on diaries or journals of his expeditions. These works reveal his view of life. All things, men and women too, are a revelation of nature and its wonders, and an understanding of nature
brings a philosophical cheer which enables the individual to carry
on and act well his part. He was critical of his fellow-men, quick
to see frailties, full of irony and sarcasm, but he also knew how
to be generous. Of social institutions he was also critical; slavery
he regarded as a liability[14] and for the Indian he had respect.
Cosmopolitan, intellectual, and devoted to the public service, he
is the best type of Virginia gentleman of the Eighteenth Century;
few, if any, were his equal in personality and wealth of ideas
until the days of the Revolution.

---

[13] He contributed to the *Transactions* of the Society one paper, "An account of a
Negro Boy that is dappled in several places of his Body with White Spots," which was
published in the issue of December, 1697.

[14] Byrd to Lord Egmont, in "Colonel William Byrd on Slavery and Indentured
Servants," (*American Historical Review,* vol. I, p. 88).

The History of the Dividing Line betwixt Virginia and North Carolina run in the year of our Lord 1728.

Before I enter upon the Journal of the Line between Virginia and North Carolina, it will be necessary to clear the way to it by shewing how the other British Colonies on the main, have one after another, been carved out of Virginia, by Grants from his Majesty's Royal Predecessors. All that part of the Northern American Continent, now under the Dominion of the King of Great Britain, and stretching quite as far as the Cape of Florida, went at first under the general name of Virginia.

The only Distinction in those early Days, was, that all the Coast to the Southward of Chesapeak Bay, was called South Virginia, and all to the Northward of it, North Virginia.

FIRST PAGE OF THE HISTORY OF THE DIVIDING LINE

HISTORY OF THE DIVIDING LINE

RUN IN THE YEAR 1728*

Before I enter upon the Journal of the Line between Virginia and
North Carolina, it will be necessary to clear the way to it, by shewing
how the other British Colonies on the Main have, one after the other,
been carved out of Virginia, by Grants from his Majesty's Royal Predecessors. All that part of the Northern American Continent now under the
Dominion of the King of Great Britain, and Stretching quite as far as
the Cape of Florida, went *at first under the General Name of Virginia.*

The only Distinction, in those early Days, was, that all the Coast to
the Southward of Chesapeake Bay was called South Virginia, and all to
the Northward of it, North Virginia.

The first Settlement of this fine Country was owing to that great Ornament of the British Nation, Sir Walter Raleigh, who obtained a Grant
thereof from Queen Elizabeth of ever-glorious Memory, by Letters Patent,
dated March the 25th, 1584.

But whether that Gentleman ever made a Voyage thither himself is
uncertain; because those who have favour'd the Public with an Account
of His Life mention nothing of it. However, thus much may be depended
on, that Sir Walter invited sundry persons of Distinction to Share in his
Charter, and join their Purses with his in the laudable project of fitting
out a Colony to Virginia.

Accordingly, 2 Ships were Sent away that very Year, under the Command of his good Friends Amidas and Barlow, to take possession of the
Country in the Name of his Roial Mistress, the Queen of England.

These worthy Commanders, for the advantage of the Trade Winds,
shaped their Course first to the Charibbe Islands, thence stretching away
by the Gulph of Florida, drop Anchor not far from Roanoak Inlet.
They ventured ashoar near that place upon an Island now called Colleton
island, where they set up the Arms of England, and Claimed the Adjacent
Country in Right of their Sovereign Lady, the Queen; and this Ceremony
being duly performed, they kindly invited the neighbouring Indians to traffick with them.

These poor people at first approacht the English with great Caution,
having heard much of the Treachery of the Spaniards, and not knowing
but these Strangers might be as treacherous as they. But, at length, discovering a kind of good nature in their looks, they ventured to draw near,
and barter their Skins and Furs, for the Bawbles and Trinkets of the
English.

---

* This is Byrd's long known version of the boundary question. The hitherto unknown and unpublished *Secret History* begins on page 13 and continues on the
odd-numbered pages to the conclusion.

These first Adventurers made a very profitable Voyage, raising at least a Thousand per cent. upon their Cargo. Amongst other Indian Commodities, they brought over Some of the bewitching Vegetable, Tobacco. And this being the first that ever came to England, Sir Walter thought he could do no less than make a present of Some of the brightest of it to His Roial Mistress, for her own Smoaking.

The Queen graciously accepted of it, but finding her Stomach sicken after two or three Whiffs, it was presently whispered by the earl of Leicester's Faction, that Sir Walter had certainly Poison'd Her. But Her Majesty soon recovering her Disorder, obliged the Countess of Nottingham and all her Maids to Smoak a whole Pipe out amongst them.

As it happen'd some Ages before to be the fashion to Santer to the Holy Land, and go upon other Quixot Adventures, so it was now grown the Humour to take a Trip to America. The Spaniards had lately discovered Rich Mines in their Part of the West Indies, which made their Maritime Neighbours eager to do so too. This Modish Frenzy being still more Inflam'd by the Charming Account given of Virginia, by the first Adventurers, made many fond of removeing to such a Paradise.

Happy was he, and still happier She, that cou'd get themselves transported, fondly expecting their Coarsest Utensils, in that happy place, would be of Massy Silver.

This made it easy for the Company to procure as many Volunteers as they wanted for their new Colony; but, like most other Undertakers who have no Assistance from the Public, they Starved the Design by too much Frugality; for, unwilling to Launch out at first into too much Expense, they Ship't off but few People at a Time, and Those but Scantily provided. The Adventurers were, besides, Idle and extravagant, and expected they might live without work in so plentiful a Country.

These Wretches were set Ashoar not far from Roanoak Inlet, but by some fatal disagreement, or Laziness, were either Starved or cut to Pieces by the Indians.

Several repeated Misadventures of this kind did, for some time, allay the Itch of Sailing to this New World; but the Distemper broke out again about the Year 1606. Then it happened that the Earl of Southampton and several other Persons, eminent for their Quality and Estates, were invited into the Company, who apply'd themselves once more to People the then almost abandon'd Colony. For this purpose they embarkt about an Hundred men, most of them Riprobates of good Familys, and related to some of the company, who were men of Quality and Fortune.

The Ships that carried them made a Shift to find a more direct way to Virginia, and ventured thro the Capes into the Bay of Chesapeak. The same Night they came to an Anchor at the Mouth of Powatan, the same as James River, where they built a Small Fort at a Place call'd Point Comfort.

This Settlement stood its ground from that time forward in spite of all the Blunders and Disagreement of the first Adventurers, and the many Calamitys that befel the Colony afterwards.

The six gentlemen who were first named of the company by the crown, and who were empowered to choose an annual President from among themselves, were always engaged in Factions and Quarrels, while the rest detested Work more than Famine. At this rate the Colony must have come to nothing, had it not been for the vigilance and Bravery of Capt. Smith, who struck a Terrour into all the Indians round about. This Gentleman took some pains to perswade the men to plant Indian corn, but they look upon all Labor as a Curse. They chose rather to depend upon the Musty Provisions that were sent from England: and when they fail'd they were forct to take more pains to Seek for Wild Fruits in the Woods, than they would have taken in tilling the Ground. Besides, this Exposd them to be knockt on the head by the Indians, and gave them Fluxes into the Bargain, which thind the Plantation very much. To Supply this mortality, they were reinforct the year following with a greater number of People, amongst which were fewer Gentlemen and more Labourers, who, however, took care not to kill themselves with Work.[1]

These found the First Adventurers in a very starving condition, but relieved their wants with the fresh Supply they brought with them. From Kiquotan they extended themselves as far as James-Town, where like true Englishmen, they built a Church that cost no more than Fifty Pounds, and a Tavern that cost Five hundred.[2]

They had now made peace with the Indians, but there was one thing wanting to make that peace lasting. The Natives coud, by no means, perswade themselves that the English were heartily their Friends, so long as they disdained to intermarry with them. And, in earnest, had the English consulted their own Security and the good of the Colony—Had they intended either to Civilize or Convert these Gentiles, they would have brought their Stomachs to embrace this prudent Alliance.

The Indians are generally tall and well-proportion'd, which may make full Amends for the Darkness of their Complexions. Add to this, that they are healthy & Strong, with Constitutions untainted by Lewdness, and not enfeebled by Luxury. Besides, Morals and all considered, I cant think the Indians were much greater Heathens than the first Adventurers, who, had they been good Christians, would have had the Charity to take this only method of converting the Natives to Christianity. For, after all that

---

[1] This paragraph appears as a note in the manuscript and the edition of the *Dividing Line* by Ruffin; Wynne and Bassett, however, incorporated it in the text, and I have followed their precedent.

[2] According to John Smith, worship at Jamestown was first conducted under an awning made by stretching an old sail between some trees. (*Advertisements for the Inexperienced*, Chapter XIV.) Soon a building was erected which was destroyed in 1608 but was restored immediately and greatly improved in 1610. On the other hand, there is no contemporary account of a tavern in early Jamestown. Indeed the absence of a tavern was one of the charges against the London Company in 1623. See Nathaniel Butler's *Unmasking*.

can be said, a sprightly Lover is the most prevailing Missionary that can be sent amongst these, or any other Infidels.

Besides, the poor Indians would have had less reason to Complain that the English took away their Land, if they had received it by way of Portion with their Daughters. Had such Affinities been contracted in the Beginning, how much Bloodshed had been prevented, and how populous would the Country have been, and, consequently, how considerable? Nor wou'd the Shade of the Skin have been any reproach at this day; for if a Moor may be washt white in 3 Generations, Surely an Indian might have been blancht in two.

The French, for their Parts, have not been so Squeamish in Canada, who upon Trial find abundance of Attraction in the Indians. Their late Grand Monarch thought it not below even the Dignity of a Frenchman to become one flesh with this People, and therefore Ordered 100 Livres for any of his Subjects, Man or Woman, that would intermarry with a Native.

By this piece of Policy we find the French Interest very much Strengthen'd amongst the Savages, and their Religion, such as it is, propagated just as far as their Love. And I heartily wish this well-concerted Scheme don't hereafter give the French an Advantage over his Majesty's good Subjects on the Northern Continent of America.

About the same time New England was pared off from Virginia by Letters Patent, bearing date April the 10th, 1608.[3] Several Gentlemen of the Town and Neighbourhood of Plymouth obtain'd this Grant, with the Ld Chief Justice Popham at their Head.

Their Bounds were Specified to Extend from 38 to 45 Degrees of Northern Latitude, with a Breadth of one Hundred Miles from the Sea Shore. The first 14 Years, this Company encounter'd many Difficulties, and lost many men, tho' far from being discouraged, they sent over Numerous Recruits of Presbyterians, every year, who for all that, had much ado to stand their Ground, with all their Fighting and Praying.

But about the year 1620, a Large Swarm of Dissenters fled thither from the Severities of their Stepmother, the Church. These Saints conceiving the same Aversion to the Copper Complexion of the Natives, with that of the first Adventurers to Virginia, would, on no Terms, contract Alliances with them, afraid perhaps, like the Jews of Old, lest they might be drawn into Idolatry by those Strange Women.

Whatever disgusted them I cant say, but this false delicacy creating in the Indians a Jealousy that the English were ill affected towards them, was the Cause that many of them were cut off, and the rest Exposed to various Distresses.

This Reinforcement was landed not far from Cape Codd, where, for their greater Security they built a Fort, and near it a Small Town, which in Honour of the Proprietors, was call'd New Plymouth. But they Still

---

[3] The Plymouth and London Companies were incorporated in the same charter, the so-called Virginia Charter of April 10, 1606.

had many discouragements to Struggle with, tho' by being well Supported from Home, they by Degrees Triumph't over them all.

Their Bretheren, after this, flockt over so fast, that in a few Years they extended the Settlement one hundred Miles along the Coast, including Rhode Island and Martha's Vineyard.

Thus the Colony throve apace, and was throng'd with large Detachments of Independents and Presbyterians, who thought themselves persecuted at home.

Tho' these People may be ridiculd for some Pharisaical Particularitys in their Worship and Behaviour, yet they were very useful Subjects, as being Frugal and Industrious, giving no Scandal or bad Example, at least by any Open and Public Vices. By which excellent Qualities they had much the Advantage of the Southern Colony, who thought their being Members of the Establish't Church sufficient to Sanctifie very loose and Profligate Morals. For this Reason New England improved much faster than Virginia, and in Seven or Eight Years New Plimouth, like Switzerland, seemed too Narrow a Territory for its Inhabitants.

For this Reason, several Gentlemen of Fortune purchas'd of the Company that Canton of New England now called Massachuset colony. And King James confirm'd the Purchase by his Royal Charter, dated March the 4th, 1628. In less than 2 years after, above 1000 of the Puritanical Sect removed thither with considerable Effects, and these were followed by such Crowds, that a Proclamation was issued in England, forbidding any more of his Majesty's Subjects to be Shipt off. But this had the usual Effect of things forbidden, and serv'd only to make the Wilful Independents flock over the faster. And about this time it was that Messrs. Hampden and Pym, and (some say) Oliver Cromwell, to show how little they valued the King's Authority, took a Trip to New England.

In the Year 1630, the famous City of Boston was built, in a Commodious Situation for Trade and Navigation, the same being on a Peninsula at the Bottom of Massachuset Bay.

This Town is now the most considerable of any on the British Continent, containing at least 8,000 houses and 40,000 Inhabitants.[4] The Trade it drives, is very great to Europe, and to every Part of the West Indies, having near 1,000 Ships and lesser Vessels belonging to it.

Altho the Extent of the Massachuset Colony reach't near one Hundred and Ten Miles in Length, and half as much in Breadth, yet many of its Inhabitants, thinking they wanted Elbow-room, quitted their Old Seats in the Year 1636, and formed 2 New Colonies: that of Connecticut and New Haven. These King Charles the 2d erected into one Government in 1664,[5] and gave them many Valuable Privileges, and among the rest,

---

[4] Byrd overestimates the population of Boston. In 1722 it was around 17,000 and somewhat less in 1741. See Winsor, *Memorial History of Boston*, II, 496, 570.
[5] The date of the Connecticut charter is April 23, 1662.

that of chusing their own Governors. The Extent of these united Colonies may be about Seventy Miles long and fifty broad.

Besides these several Settlements, there Sprang up still another, a little more Northerly, called New Hampshire. But that consisting of no more than two Counties, and not being in condition to Support the Charge of a Distinct Government, was glad to be incorporated with that of Massachuset, but upon Condition, however, of being Named in all Public Acts, for fear of being quite lost and forgot in the Coalition.

In like manner New Plymouth joyn'd itself to Massachuset, except only Rhode Island, which, tho' of small Extent, got itself erected into a Separate government by a Charter from King Charles the 2d, soon after the Restoration, and continues so to this day.

These Governments all continued in Possession of their Respective Rights and Privileges till the Year 1683,[6] when that of Massachuset was made Void in England by a Quo Warranto.

In Consequence of which the King was pleased to name Sir Edmund Andros His first Governor of that Colony. This Gentleman, it seems, ruled them with a Rod of Iron till the Revolution, when they laid unhallowed Hands upon Him, and sent him Prisoner to England.

This undutiful proceeding met with an easy forgiveness at that happy Juncture. King William and his Royal Consort were not only pleasd to overlook this Indignity offered to their Governor, but being made sensible how unfairly their Charter had been taken away, most graciously granted them a new one.

By this some new Franchises were given them, as an Equivalent for those of Coining Money and Electing a governour, which were taken away. However, the other Colonies of Connecticut and Rhode Island had the luck to remain in Possession of their Original Charters, which to this Day have never been calld in Question.

The next Country dismembered from Virginia was New Scotland,[7] claimed by the Crown of England in Virtue of the first Discovery by Sebastian Cabot. By Colour of this Title, King James the first granted it to Sir William Alexander by Patent, dated September the 10th, 1621.

But this Patentee never sending any Colony thither, and the French believeing it very Convenient for them, obtained a Surrender of it from their good Friend and Ally, king Charles the 2d, by the Treaty of Breda. And, to show their gratitude, they stirred up the Indians soon after to annoy their Neighbours of New England. Murders happend continually to his Majesty's Subjects by their Means, till Sʳ William Phipps took their Town of Port Royal, in the year 1690. But as the English are better at taking than keeping Strong Places, the French retook it soon, and re-

---

[6] Procedure against the Massachusetts charter was begun in June 1683, but judgment was not rendered until October 23, 1684. (4 Mass. Hist. Coll. II, pp. 262, 267).

[7] Nova Scotia.

maind Masters of it till 1710, when General Nicholson wrested it, once more, out of their Hands.

Afterwards the Queen of Great Britain's Right to it was recognized and confirmed by the treaty of Utrecht.

Another Limb lopt off from Virginia was New York, which the Dutch seized very unfairly, on pretence of having Purchasd it from Captain Hudson, the first Discoverer. Nor was their way of taking Possession of it a whit more justifiable than their pretended Title.

Their West India Company tamperd with some worthy English Skippers (who had contracted with a Swarm of English Dissenters to transport them to Hudson river) by no means to land them there, but to carry 'em some leagues more notherly.

This Dutch Finesse took Exactly, and gave the Company time soon after to seize the Hudson River for themselves. But Sr Samuel Argall, then governor of Virginia, understanding how the King's Subjects had been abused by these Republicans, marcht thither with a good Force, and obliged them to renounce all pretensions to that Country.[8] The worst of it was, the Knight depended on their Parole to Ship themselves to Brasile, but took no measures to make this Slippery People as good as their Word.

No sooner was the good Governor retired, but the honest Dutch began to build Forts and strengthen themselves in their ill-gotten Possessions; nor did any of the King's Liege People take the trouble to drive these Intruders thence. The Civil War in England, And the Confusions it brought forth, allowed no Leisure to such distant Considerations. Tho tis strange that the Protector, who neglected no Occasion to mortify the Dutch, did not afterwards call them to Account for this breach of Faith. However, after the Restoration, the King sent a Squadron of his Ships of War, under the Command of Sir Robert Carr,[9] and reduced that Province to his Obedience.

Some time after, His Majesty was Pleasd to grant that Country to his Royal Highness, the Duke of York, by Letters Patent, dated March the 12th, 1664. But to shew the Modesty of the Dutch to the Life, tho they had no Shaddow of Right to New York, yet they demanded Surinam, a more valuable Country, as an Equivalent for it, and our able Ministers at that time had the Generosity to give it them.

But what wounded Virginia deepest was the cutting off MARYLAND from it, by Charter from King Charles the 1st, to sir George Calvert, afterwards Ld Baltimore, bearing the date the 20th of June, 1632. The Truth of it is, it begat much Speculation in those days, how it came about that a

---

[8] Reference is to the reputed seizure in 1613, which, however, is discredited by many authorities. See Paltsits, "The Founding of New Amsterdam," *Proceedings of the American Antiquarian Society*, 1924.

[9] The leader of the expedition was Colonel Richard Nicolls; Carr was one of the other four members.

good Protestant King should bestow so bountiful a Grant upon a Zealous Roman catholic. But 'tis probable it was one fatal Instance amongst many other of his Majesty's complaisance to the Queen.

However that happened, 'tis certain this Province afterwards provd a Commodious Retreat for Persons of that Communion. The Memory of the Gun-Powder-Treason-Plot was Still fresh in every body's mind, and made England too hot for Papists to live in, without danger of being burnt with the Pope, every 5th of November; for which reason Legions of them transplanted themselves to Maryland in Order to be Safe, as well from the Insolence of the Populace as the Rigour of the Government.

Not only the Gun-Powder-Treason, but every other Plot, both pretended and real, that has been trump't up in England ever Since, has helpt to People his Lordship's Propriety.

But what has provd most Serviceable to it was the Grand Rebellion against King Charles the 1st, when every thing that bore the least tokens of Popery was sure to be demolisht, and every man that Profest it was in Jeopardy of Suffering the same kind of Martyrdom the Roman Priests do in Sweden.[10]

Soon after the Reduction of New York, the Duke was pleasd to grant out of it all that Tract of Land included between Hudson and Delaware Rivers, to the Lord Berkley and Sir George Carteret, by deed dated June the 24th, 1664. And when these Grantees came to make Partition of this Territory, His Lordp's Moiety was calld West Jersey, and that to Sir George, East Jersey.

But before the Date of this Grant, the Swedes began to gain Footing in part of that Country; tho, after they saw the Fate of New York, they were glad to Submit to the King of England, on the easy Terms of remaining in their Possessions, and rendering a Moderate Quit-rent. Their Posterity continue there to this Day, and think their Lot cast in a much fairer Land than Dalicarlia.[11]

The Proprietors of New Jersey, finding more Trouble than Profit in their new Dominions, made over their Right to several other Persons, who obtained a fresh Grant from his Royal Highness, dated March 14th, 1682.

Several of the Grantees, being Quakers and Anababtists, faild not to encourage many of their own Perswasion to remove to this Peaceful Region. Amongst them were a Swarm of Scots Quakers, who were not tolerated to exercise the Gifts of the Spirit in their own Country.

---

[10] In the seventeenth and eighteenth centuries Sweden was the most intolerant of the Protestant States. In 1593 Lutheranism definitely became the state religion, no other form of worship being allowed. In 1604 Catholics were subjected to banishment and confiscation of property. This policy was moderated in favor of those who migrated to Sweden for purposes of commerce and trade, but down to 1854 natives were forbidden to enter Catholic Churches.

[11] An ancient province of Sweden corresponding to the laen of Kopparberg or Fahlun.

Besides the hopes of being Safe from Persecution in this Retreat, the New Proprietors inveigled many over by this tempting Account of the Country: that is was a Place free from those 3 great Scourges of Mankind, Priests, Lawyers, and Physicians. Nor did they tell a Word of a Lye, for the People were yet too poor to maintain these Learned Gentlemen, who, every where, love to be paid well for what they do; and, like the Jews, cant breathe in a Climate where nothing is to be got.

The Jerseys continued under the Government of these Proprietors till the Year 1702, when they made a formal Surrender of the Dominion to the Queen, reserving however the Property of the Soil to themselves. So soon as the Bounds of New Jersey came to be distinctly laid off, it appeared that there was still a Narrow Slipe of Land, lying betwixt that Colony and Maryland. Of this, William Penn, a Man of much Worldly Wisdom, and some Eminence among the Quakers, got early Notice, and, by the Credit he had with the Duke of York, obtained a Patent for it, Dated March the 4th, 1680.[12]

It was a little Surprising to some People how a Quaker should be so much in the good Graces of a Popish Prince; tho, after all, it may be pretty well Accounted for. This Ingenious Person had not been bred a Quaker; but, in his Earlier days, had been a Man of Pleasure about the Town. He had a beautiful form and very taking Address, which made him Successful with the Ladies, and Particularly with a Mistress of the Duke of Monmouth. By this Gentlewoman he had a Daughter, who had Beauty enough to raise her to be a Dutchess, and continued to be a Toast full 30 Years.[13]

But this Amour had like to have brought our Fine Gentleman in Danger of a Duell, had he not discreetly sheltered himself under this peaceable Perswasion. Besides, his Father having been a Flag-Officer in the Navy, while the Duke of York was Lord High Admiral, might recommend the Son to his Favour. This piece of secret History I thought proper to mention, to wipe off the Suspicion of his having been Popishly inclind.

This Gentleman's first Grant confind Him within pretty Narrow Bounds, giving him only that Portion of Land which contains Buckingham, Philadelphia and Chester Counties. But to get these Bounds a little extended, He pusht His Interest still further with His Royal Highness, and obtaind a fresh Grant of the three Lower Counties, called New-Castle, Kent and Sussex, which still remain within the New York Patent, and had been luckily left out of the Grant of New Jersey.

The Six Counties being thus incorporated, the Proprietor dignifyd the whole with the Name of Pensilvania.

---

[12] 1680-81.

[13] This is a piece of gossip not found elsewhere; it calls to mind other calumnies against Penn perpetuated by Macaulay, which are refuted in Dixon's *William Penn*, pp. 338-357.

The Quakers flockt over to this Country in Shoals, being averse to go to Heaven the same way with the Bishops. Amongst them were not a few of good Substance, who went Vigorously upon every kind of Improvement; and thus much I may truly say in their Praise, that by Diligence and Frugality, For which this Harmless Sect is remarkable, and by haveing no Vices but such as are Private, they have in a few Years made Pensilvania a very fine Country.

The truth is, they have observed exact Justice with all the Natives that border upon them; they have purchasd all their Lands from the Indians; and tho they paid but a Trifle for them, it has procured them the Credit of being more righteous than their Neighbours. They have likewise had the Prudence to treat them kindly upon all Occasions, which has savd them from many Wars and Massacres wherein the other Colonies have been indiscreetly involved. The Truth of it is, a People whose Principles forbid them to draw the Carnal Sword, were in the Right to give no Provocation.

Both the French and the Spaniards had, in the Name of their Respective Monarchs, long ago taken Possession of that Part of the Northern Continent that now goes by the Name of Carolina; but finding it Produced neither Gold nor Silver, as they greedily expected, and meeting such returns from the Indians as their own Cruelty and Treachery deserved, they totally abandond it. In this deserted Condition that country lay for the Space of 90 Years, till King Charles the 2d, finding it a DERELICT, granted it away to the Earl of Clarendon and others, by His Royal Charter, dated March the 24th, 1663. The Boundary of that Grant towards Virginia was a due West Line from Luck-Island, (the same as Colleton Island), lying in 36 degrees N. Latitude, quite to the South Sea.

But afterwards Sir William Berkeley, who was one of the Grantees and at that time Governour of Virginia, finding a Territory of 31 Miles in Breadth between the Inhabited Part of Virginia and the above-mentioned Boundary of Carolina, advisd the Lord Clarendon of it. And His Lordp had Interest enough with the King to obtain a Second Patent to include it, dated June the 30th, 1665.

This last Grant describes the Bounds between Virginia and Carolina in these words: "To run from the North End of Corotuck-Inlet, due West to Weyanoke Creek, lying within or about the Degree of Thirty-Six and Thirty Minutes of Northern Latitude, and from thence West, in a direct Line, as far as the South-Sea."[14] Without question, this Boundary was well known at the time the Charter was Granted, but in a long Course of years Weynoke Creek lost its name, so that it became a Controversy where it lay. Some Ancient Persons in Virginia affirmd it was the same

---

[14] This quotation is not literal but is true to the boundary as set forth in the charter.

with Wicocon, and others again in Carolina were as Positive it was Nottoway River.

In the mean time, the People on the Frontiers Entered for Land, & took out Patents by Guess, either from the King or the Lords Proprietors. But the Crown was like to be the loser by this Incertainty, because the Terms both of taking up and seating Land were easier much in Carolina. The Yearly Taxes to the Public were likewise there less burdensom, which laid Virginia under a Plain disadvantage.

This Consideration put that Government upon entering into Measures with North Carolina, to terminate the Dispute, and settle a Certain Boundary between the two colonies. All the Difficulty was, to find out which was truly Weyanoke Creek. The Difference was too Considerable to be given up by either side, there being a Territory of 15 Miles betwixt the two Streams in controversy.

However, till that Matter could be adjusted, it was agreed on both sides, that no Lands at all Should be granted within the disputed Bounds.[15] Virginia observed this Agreement punctually, but I am sorry I cant say the Same of North-Carolina. The great Officers of that Province were loath to lose the Fees accrueing from the Grants of Land, and so private Interest got the better of Public Spirit; and I wish that were the only Place in the World where such politicks are fashionable.

All the Steps that were taken afterwards in that Affair, will best appear by the Report of the Virginia-Commissioners, recited in the Order of Council given at St. James's, March the 1st, 1710, set down in the Appendix.[16]

It must be owned, the Report of those Gentlemen was Severe upon the then commissioners of North-Carolina, and particularly upon Mr. Moseley.[17] I wont take upon me to say with how much Justice they said so many hard things, tho it had been fairer Play to have given the Parties accused a Copy of such Representations, that they might have answered what they could for themselves.

But since that was not done, I must beg leave to say thus much in behalf of Mr. Moseley, that he was not much in the Wrong to find fault with the Quadrant produced by the Surveyors of Virginia because that Instrument plact the Mouth of Notoway River in the Latitude of 37 Degrees; whereas, by an Accurate Observation made Since, it Appears to line in 36° 30′ ½′, so that there was an Error of near 30 minutes, either in the Instrument or in those who made use of it.

Besides, it is evident the Mouth of Notoway River agrees much better with the Latitude, wherein the Carolina Charter supposed Wyanoak Creek, (namely, in or about 36 Degrees and 30 minutes,) than it does with Wicocon Creek, which is about 15 Miles more Southerly.

---

[15] See *Colonial Records of North Carolina*, Vol. I, p. 853.
[16] See p. 324.
[17] Edward Moseley. See note 13 to the *Secret History*.

This being manifest, the Intention of the King's Grant will be pretty exactly answered, by a due West Line drawn from Corotuck Inlet to the Mouth of Notaway River, for which reason tis probable that was formerly calld Wyanoak-Creek, and might change its Name when the Nottoway Indians came to live upon it, which was since the Date of the last Carolina Charter.

The Lievt Governor of Virginia, at that time Colo Spotswood, searching into the Bottom of this Affair, made very Equitable Proposals to Mr. Eden, at that time Governour of North Carolina, in Order to put an End to this Controversy. These, being formed into Preliminaries, were Signd by both Governours, and transmitted to England, where they had the Honour to be ratifyed by his late Majesty and assented to by the Lords Proprietors of Carolina.[18]

Accordingly an Order was sent by the late King to Mr. Gooch, afterwards Lievt Governor of Virginia, to pursue those Preliminaries exactly. In Obedience thereunto, he was pleased to appoint Three of the Council of that colony to be Commissioners on the Part of Virginia, who, in Conjunction with others to be named by the Governor of North Carolina, were to settle the Boundary between the 2 Governments, upon the Plan of the above-mentioned Articles.

---

[18] For the agreement of Spotswood and Eden, see Appendix, p. 328, or *Colonial Records of North Carolina*, Vol. II p. 222. It was forwarded to the Lords of Trade in February, 1715, but did not receive the approval of the Crown until March, 1727. In the meantime the Lords Proprietors took favorable action in 1723.

THE SECRET HISTORY OF THE LINE

The Governor & Council of Virginia in the Year 1727 receiv'd an Express Order from his Majesty, to appoint Commissioners, who in conjunction with others to be nam'd by the Government of North Carolina, should run the Line betwixt the two Colonies. The Rule these Gentlemen were directed to go by, was a paper of Proposals formerly agreed on between the 2 Governor's, at that time Spotswood, & Eden.[1] It wou'd be a hard thing to say of so wise a man as Mr. Spotswood thought himself, that he was over reach't, but it has appear'd upon Tryal, that Mr. Eden was much better inform'd how the Land lay than he. However since the King was pleased to agree to these unequal Proposals, the Government of Virginia was too Dutifull to dispute them. They therefore appointed Steddy[2] & Merryman,[3] Commissioners, on the part

---

[1] Reference is to the compromise agreement of 1715. See page 12, note 18.
[2] William Byrd himself.
[3] Nathaniel Harrison, (1677-1727) of Wakefield, Surry County, member of the House of Burgesses, (1699-1706), and of the Council (1713-1727), County Lieutenant of Surry and Prince George in 1715 and after, and Auditor of Virginia in 1724.

Two Experienct Surveyors were at the same time directed to wait upon the Commissioners, Mr. Mayo, who made the Accurate Mapp of Barbadoes, and Mr. Irvin, the Mathematick Professor of William and Mary Colledge.[19]   And because a good Number of Men were to go upon this Expedition, a Chaplain was appointed to attend them,[20] and the rather because the People on the Frontiers of North-Carolina, who have no Minister near them, might have an Opportunity to get themselves and their Children baptizd.

---

[19] Mayo and Irvin are respectively "Astrolabe" and "Orion" in the *Secret History*. See Notes 4 and 23 to that version. No mention is made in this version of "Capricorn" (John Allen) whom Irvin replaced.

[20] Rev. Peter Fontaine, "Dr. Humdrum" of the *Secret History*. See note 9 to that version.

of Virginia to Execute that Order, and Astrolabe[4] & Capricorn[5] to be the Surveyors. But Merryman dying, Firebrand[6] & Meanwell[7] made Interest to fill his Place. Most of the Council enclin'd to favour the last, because he had offered his Services before he knew that any pay wou'd belong to the Place. But Burly[8] one of the Honble Board, perceiving his Friend Firebrand wou'd lose it, if it came to the vote, propos'd the Expedient of sending 3 Commissioners, upon so difficult and hazardous an Expedition. To this a majority agreed, being unwilling to be thought too frugal

---

[4] William Mayo, a native of Wiltshire, England, who arrived in Virginia about 1723 from the Barbadoes, whither he had migrated prior to 1712. During 1717-1721 he made a survey of the Barbadoes and also a map, preserved in the library of King's College. He was one of the justices of Goochland County and was very active as a surveyor in that county and the colony at large, laying off for Byrd the City of Richmond and aiding in establishing the boundaries of the Northern Neck. He died in 1744. Mayo's River is named for him. See Brown's *The Cabells and Their Kin*.

[5] John Allen, "Gent." See "Virginia Council Journals," Sept. 12, 1727. (*Virginia Magazine of History and Biography*, Vol. XXXII, p. 242.) He was probably that John Allen of Surry County who married Elizabeth Bassett, daughter of William Bassett of the Virginia Council, and sometime a student of William and Mary. His will was proved in 1741. See "Allen Family of Surry County" in *William and Mary College Quarterly*, Vol. VIII, p. 110.

[6] Richard Fitz-William, a royal official of whom little is known. In 1719 he was Collector of Customs for the Lower District of James River. (*Calendar of Treasury Books and Papers*, 1714-1719, p. 481.) On November 21, 1727, he was appointed "Surveyor General of all the Duties and Importations" for the Carolinas, Maryland, Virginia, Pennsylvania, the Bahama Islands and Jamaica. (Ibid., 1729-30, p. 470.) In 1733 he was replaced by George Phenny, whom he succeeded as Governor-in-Chief of the Bahama Islands. (Ibid., 1731-34, p. 93.) This position he resigned in 1738 but was not relieved by his successor, John Tinker, until 1740. Fitz-William was more in sympathy with North Carolina than his fellow-Commissioners of Virginia, having criticised to the British Government Virginia's exclusion of North Carolina tobacco from its ports and, during the survey of the boundary line, he fraternized with the North Carolina Commissioners and supported them in vital matters.

[7] William Dandridge, of King William County. He belonged to the Dandridge family of Worcestershire, England, though the name of his Viriginia home, Elsing Green, is suggestive of Norfolk, where a village and parish of that name were to be found. He migrated to Virginia early in the eighteenth century. In 1717 he was a partner of Governor Spotswood in commercial enterprises and in 1740 he took part in the naval operations against the Spanish at St. Augustine. In 1728 he was a member of the Viriginia Council. His death occurred in 1743.

[8] Rev. James Blair, Commissary of the Bishop of London in Virginia from 1685 until his death in 1743. A veritable "King Maker," for he was responsible for the recall of three governors, Andros, Nicholson and Spotswood. In 1697 Byrd represented Governor Andros before the Archbishop of Canterbury and the Bishop of London in the controversy between Andros and Blair, and lost his case.

Of these proceedings on our Part, immediate Notice was sent to Sir Richard Everard, Governor of North Carolina, who was desired to Name Commissioners for that Province, to meet those of Virginia at Corotuck-Inlet the Spring following. Accordingly he appointed Four Members of the Council of that Province to take Care of the Interests of the Lds Proprietors. Of these, Mr. Moseley[21] was to serve in a Double Capacity, both as Commissioner and Surveyor. For that reason there was but one other Surveyor from thence, Mr. Swan.[22] All the Persons being

---

[21] "Plausible" in the *Secret History*. See note 13 to that version.
[22] "Bo-otes" of the *Secret History*. See note 34 to that version.

of the Publick Money. Accordingly they were both joined with Steddy in this commission. When this was over Steddy proposed that a Chaplain might be allowed to attend the Commissioners by reason they shou'd have a Number of Men with them sufficient for a small Congregation, and were to pass thro' an ungodly Country where they shou'd find neither Church nor Minister. That besides it wou'd be an act of great Charity to give the Gentiles of that part of the world an opportunity to christen both them & their children. This being unanimously consented to, Dr. Humdrum[9] was named upon Steddy's recommendation.

Of all these proceedings Notice was dispatch'd to Sir Richard Everard[10] Governour of North Carolina desiring him to name Commissioners on the part of that Province, to meet those of Virginia the Spring following. In consequence whereof that Government named Jumble,[11] Shoebrush,[12] Plausible,[13] and Puzzle Cause,[14]

---

[9] Rev. Peter Fontaine (1691-1757), one of the six children of James Fontaine, a Huguenot refugee, all of whom as well as their parents migrated to Virginia in the second decade of the eighteenth century. Peter was educated at Dublin, Ireland, and after officiating at Wallingford, Weyanoke, Martin's Brandon, and Jamestown, became rector of Westover Parish, Charles City County, of which Byrd was a parishioner. A brother, John, was rector of St. Margaret's Parish, King William County. See Meade's *Old Churches and Families of Virginia* and Maury's *Memoirs of a Huguenot Family*.

[10] The last governor under the Proprietors (1725-31). See Haywood's "Sir Richard Everard" (*Publications of the Southern History Association*, Vol. II, No. 4, or *North Carolina Booklet* X, No. 1.)

[11] Christopher Gale, Chief Justice, a native of Yorkshire, England, and eldest son of Rev. Miles Gale, rector of Wighby. He came to North Carolina about 1700, settling at Edenton. By 1703 he was a Justice of the General Court and in 1712 was appointed Chief Justice, an office which he held until 1731, except for an intermission from 1717 to 1722 when he was in England, and a briefer one in 1724-25. In 1722 he was appointed Deputy for two Proprietors, Elizabeth Blake, widow of Joseph Blake, and James Bertie. He was Collector of the Customs at Edenton, an office he held at the time of his death in 1734, and was a vestryman of the West Parish of Pasquotank County. In the violent political controversies of his day he took an active part, antagonizing Governors Burrington and Everard. See *Colonial Records of North Carolina*, Vol. II, *passim*.

[12] John Lovick, prominent in the turbulent politics of North Carolina from 1718 to 1735, when his death is reported. He was a Deputy of the Proprietors and as such was a member of the Council from 1718 to 1731, being its secretary and also Secretary of the Province from 1722 to 1730; he was also a member of the Council under the royal administration from 1731 to 1734. In 1731 he also appears as a member of the Assembly for Chowan County. In 1729 he was a member of the Court of Chancery, and in 1732 was appointed Surveyor General. See *Colonial Records of North Carolina*, Vols. II, III, *passim*.

[13] Edward Moseley, also a member of the boundary commission of 1710, the preeminent political leader of North Carolina from his appearance in public affairs in 1705 until his death in 1749. Few men have equaled his record as a holder of public office. He was a member of the Council under four administrations, being President of that body and Acting Governor in 1725. He was also a distinguished

thus agreed upon they settled the time of Meeting to be at Corotuck, March the 5th, 1728.

[Continued on page 28]

being the Flower & Cream of the Council of that Province. The next Step necessary to be taken, was for the Commissioners on both Sides to agree upon a day of Meeting at Coratuck Inlet, in order to proceed on this Business, & the 5th of March was thought a proper time, because then Mercury & the Moon were to be in Conjunction.

It was desired by Sir Richard, that the Commissioners might meet on the Frontiers sometime in January to settle Preliminarys, and particularly that it might be previously agreed, that the present Possessors of Land in either Government, shou'd be confirm'd in their Possession, tho' it shou'd not happen to fall within the Government that granted it. This the Governor of Virginia disagreed to, not thinking it just, that either the King or the Lords Proprietors, shou'd grant away Land that did not belong to them. Nor was this proposal made on the part of Carolina purely out of good Nature, but some of the Council of that Province found their own Interest concern'd, and particularly the Surveyor or General must in Justice have return'd some of his Fees, in case the People shou'd lose the Land he survey'd for them as belonging to the Proprietors, when in truth it belong'd to the King.

---

member of the Assembly, holding the speakership in 1708, and continuously from 1715 to 1723, and again in 1731, 1733, and 1734. From 1715 to 1740 he was Treasurer of the entire colony and from 1740 to 1749 Treasurer of the Southern District; in 1743 he was also appointed Chief Baron of the Exchequer. In 1724 he was made Judge of the Admiralty Court, which office he resigned, but was reappointed in 1725. He was one of the commissioners chosen in 1709 to establish the boundary, and in 1723 he was made Surveyor General. Later he was one of the commissioners to establish the South Carolina boundary and also the boundary of the Granville District. In 1733 he prepared "a New and Correct Map of the Province of North Carolina," a copy of which is in the possession of the United States War Department. He was a defender of the rights of the Assembly against prerogative, either proprietary or royal, a friend of religious liberty, a patron of learning, a lawyer of no mean ability. His antecedents are unknown, but he was probably a kinsman of the Moseley family of Princess Anne County, Virginia. He acquired an extensive estate, bequeathing 25,000 acres of land, nearly 100 slaves, and much personal property. Originally a resident of Chowan County, he removed to New Hanover about 1730. See Shinn, "Edward Moseley" (*Publications of the Southern History Association*, Vol. I, No. 1.)

[14] William Little (1692-1733), a native of Massachusetts and a graduate of Harvard, class of 1710. While visiting in England he met Chief Justice Gale and was persuaded by him to move to North Carolina. He settled at Edenton and in 1726 married Justice Gale's daughter, Penelope. In 1725 he was appointed Attorney General and in 1726 Receiver General of Quit Rents. He was also Clerk of the General Court and in 1732 became Chief Justice, an office he held for one year. See Haywood's "Christopher Gale." (*Biographical History of North Carolina*, Vol. II, p. 28.)

The Secret History of the Line &c &c

The Governour & Council of Virginia in the Year 1727 receiv'd an Express Order from his Majesty, to appoint Commissioners, who in Conjunction with others to be nam'd by the Government of North Carolina, shou'd run the Line betwixt the two Colonies. The Rule these Gentlemen were directed to go by, was a Paper of Proposals formerly agreed on between the 2 Governors, at that time Spotswood, & Eden. It wou'd be a hard thing to say of so wise a Man as Mr Spotswood thought himself, that he was over reacht, but it has appeared upon Tryal, that Mr Eden was much better inform'd how the Land lay than he.

However since the King was pleased to agree to these unequal Proposals, the Government of Virginia was too Dutifull to dispute them. They therefore appointed Steddy & Merryman, Commissioners, on the Part of Virginia to Execute that Order, and Astrolabe & Capricorn to be the Surveyors. But Merryman dying, Firebrand & Meanwell made Interest to fill his Place. Most of the Council enclin'd to favour the last, because he had offered his Service before he knew that any pay wou'd belong to the Place. But Burly one of the Honble Board, perceiving his Friend Firebrand wou'd loose it, if it came to the Vote, propos'd the Expedient of sending 3 Commissioners, upon so difficult and ha-

FIRST PAGE OF THE SECRET HISTORY

Soon after the Commissioners for Virginia, wrote the following Letter to the worthy Commissioners of N. Carolina.[15]

Gentlemen:

We are Sorry we can't have the Pleasure of meeting you in January next as is desired by Your Governour. The Season of the Year in which that is proposed to be done, & the distance of our Habitation from your Frontier, we hope will make our Excuse reasonable. Besides his Majesty's Order marks out our Business so plainly, that we are perswaded that there can be no difficulty in the Construction of it. After this, what imaginable Dispute can arise amongst Gentlemen who meet together with minds averse to Chicane, and Inclinations to do equal Justice both to his Majesty and the Lords Proprietors, in which disposition we make no doubt the Commissioners on both Sides will find each other.

We shall have full powers to agree at our first meeting on what Preliminarys shall be thought necessary, which we hope you will likewise be, that an affair of so great Consequence may have no Delay or Disappointment.

It is very proper to acquaint You in what manner we intend to come provided, that so you, Gentlemen who are appointed in the same Station, may if you please do the same Honour to Your Government. We shall bring with us about 20 men furnish't with Provisions for 40 days. We shall have a Tent with us & a Marquis[16] for the convenience of ourselves & Servants. We shall be provided with much Wine & Rum as just enable us, and our men to drink every Night to the Success of the following Day, and because we understand there are many Gentiles on your Frontier, who never had an opportunity of being Baptized, we shall have a chaplain with us to make them Christians. For this Purpose we intend to rest in our Camp every Sunday that there may be leizure for so good a work. And whoever of your Province shall be desirous of novelty may repair on Sundays to our Camp, & hear a Sermon. Of this you may please to give publick notice that the Charitable Intentions of this Government may meet with the happier Success.

---

[15] This document is also in the *Colonial Records of North Carolina*, Vol. II, p. 735.
[16] Corruption of marquee, a tent or awning for special purposes, as banquets and dinners.

[Continued on page 28]

Thus much Gentlemen we thought it necessary to acquaint you with and to make use of this first Opportunity of Signifying with how much Satisfaction we receiv'd the News that such able Commissioners are appointed for the Government, with whom we promise our selves we shall converse with prodigious Pleasure, & Execute our Commissions to the full content of those by whom we have the Honour to be employ'd, We are

Gentlemen   Your most humble
Servants

FIREBRAND.   STEDDY
MEANWELL.

Williamsburgh
the 16th of Decem^r.
 1727

To this Letter the Commissioners of Virginia the latter End of January receiv'd the following answer.[17]

Gentlemen

We have the Honour of your Favour from Williamsburgh dated the 16th of December, in which you Signify, that the proposals already agreed on are so plain, that you are perswaded there can no difficulty arise about the Construction of them. We think so too, but if no dispute should arise in construing them, yet the Manner of our proceeding in the Execution, we thought had better be previously concerted, and the End of the Meeting we prospos'd was to remove every thing that might ly in the way to retard the Work, which we all seem equally desirous to have amicably concluded. We assure you Gentlemen we shall meet you with a hearty disposition of doing equall Justice to either Government, and as you acquaint us you shall come fully empowered to agree at our first Meeting, to settle all necessary Preliminarys,

---

[17] This letter is also in the *Colonial Records*, Vol. II, p. 737.

[Continued on page 28]

we shall endeavour to have our Instructions as large. Your Governor in his last Letter to ours, was pleas'd to mention our confering with You by Letters, about any matters previously to be adjusted. We therefore take leave to desire by this Messenger, You will let us know, after what Manner you purpose to run the Line, whether you think to go thro' the Great Swamp, which is near 30 miles thro', & thought not passable, or by taking the Latitude at the first Station to run a due West Line to the Swamp, & then to find the said Latitude on the West Side the Swamp, & continue thence a due West Line to Chowan River. Or to make the 2d Observation upon Chowan River and run an East Line to the Great Swamp. We shall also be glad to know what Instruments you intend to use to observe the Latitude, & find the Variation with, in Order to fix a due West Line. For we are told the last time the Commissioners met, their Instruments vary'd Several Minutes, which we hope will not happen again, nor any other Difficulty that may occasion any delay or disappointment, after we have been at the trouble of meeting in so remote a place, and with such a Hendrance & Equipage as you intend on your part. We are at a loss, Gentlemen, whether to thank you for the Particulars you give us of your Tent, Stores, & the Manner you design to meet us. Had you been Silent, we had not wanted an Excuse for not meeting you in the same Manner, but now you force us to expose the nakedness of our country, & tell You, we can't possibly meet you in the Manner our great respect to you, wou'd make us glad to do, whom we are not emulous of out doing, unless in Care & Diligence in the Affair we came about. So all we can answer to that Article, is, that we will endeavour to provide as well as the Circumstances of things will admit; And what we want in Necessarys, we hope will be made up in Spritual Comfort we expect from Your Chaplain, of whom we shall give notice as you desire; & doubt not of making a great many Boundary Christians. To conclude, we promise, to make ourselves as agreeable to you as possibly we can; & we beg Leave to assure you that it is a Singular Pleasure to Us, that You Gentlemen are nam'd on that Part, to see this business of so great concern & consequence to both Governments determin'd which makes it to be undertaken on our parts more cheerfully,

[Continued on page 28]

being assured your Characters are above any artifice or design. We are

Your most obedient humble Servants

PLAUSIBLE   JUMBLE

PUZZLECAUSE SHOEBRUSH

This Letter was without date they having no Almanacks in North Carolina, but it came about the beginning of January. However the Virginia Commissioners did not return an Answer to it, til they had consulted their Surveyor honest Astrolabe, as to the Mathematical Part. When that was done they reply'd in the following Terms.

Gentlemen

We shou'd have return'd an Answer sooner, had not the Cold Weather, & our remote Situation from one another prevented our Meeting. However we hope 'tis now time enough to thank you for that favour, & to assure You, that tho' we are appointed Commissioners for this Government, we encline to be very just to Yours. And as the fixing fair Boundarys between Us, will be of equal advantage to both, You shall have no reason to reproach us with making any step either to delay or disappoint so usefull a Work. If the Great Swamp you mention shou'd be absolutely impassable, we then propose to run a due West Line from Our first Station thither & then Survey around the same til we shall come on our due West course on the other Side, & so proceed til we shall be again interrupted. But if you shall think of a more proper Expedient, we shall not be fond of our own Opinion. And tho' we can't conceive that taking the Latitude will be of any use in running this Line, yet we shall be provided to do it with the greatest exactness. In performing which we shall on our part use no graduated Instrument: but our Accurate Surveyor Astrolabe tells us he will use a Method that will come nearer the Truth.[18] He likewise proposes to discover as near as possible the just variation of the Compass, by means of a true Meridian to be found by the North Star. We shall bring with us 2 or 3 very good compasses, which we hope will not differ much from Yours, tho' if there shou'd be

---

[18] The "graduated instrument" was doubtless the surveyor's pole, 16½ feet long. By sighting the north star with this, latitude could be crudely calculated. The "better method" referred to was perhaps the astrolabe.

In the Mean time, the requisite Preparations were made for so long and tiresome a Journey; and because there was much work to be done and some Danger from the Indians, in the uninhabited Part of the Country, it was necessary to provide a Competent Number of Men. Accordingly, Seventeen able Hands were listed on the Part of Virginia, who were most of them Indian Traders and expert Woodsmen.

27. These good Men were ordered to come armed with a Musquet and a Tomahack, or large Hatchet, and provided with a Sufficient Quantity of Ammunition.

They likewise brought Provisions of their own for ten days, after which time they were to be furnisht by the Government. Their March was appointed to be on the 27th of February, on which day one of the Commissioners met them at their Rendezvous, and proceeded with them as far

some little variance, 'twill be easily reconciled by two such Skilful Mathematicians as Astrolabe and Plausible.

In short Gentlemen we are so conscious of our own disposition to do right to both Colonys, & at the same time so verily perswaded of Yours, that we promise to our selves an intire harmony & good Agreement. This can hardly fail, when Justice and Reason are laid down on both Sides, as the Rule & Foundation of our Proceeding. We hope the Season will prove favourable to us, but be that as it will we intend to preserve fair Weather in our Honour, believing that even the Dismal may be very tolerable in good Company, We are without the least Artifice or design.

Gentlemen,   Your most humble Servants

S. F. M.

It was afterwards agreed by the Commissioners on both Sides, to meet on the North Shoar of Coratuck Inlet, on the 5th day of the following March in Order to run the Dividing Line. In the mean time those on the Part of Virginia divided the trouble of making the necessary preparations. It fell to Steddy's Share to provide the Men that were to attend the Surveyors. For this purpose Mr. Mumford recommended to him 15 able Woodsmen, most of which had been Indian Traders. These were order'd to meet him at Warren's Mill, arm'd with a Gun & Tomahawk, on the 27th of February, & furnisht with Provisions for ten days. Astrolabe came on the 26th in Order to attend Steddy to the Place of Rendezvous. The next day they crost the River, having first recommended all they left behind to the Divine Protection. Steddy carry'd with him 2 Servants, & a Sumpter Horse[19] for his Baggage. About 12 a Clock he met the Men at the New Church near Warren's Mill. He drew them out to the number of 15, & finding their Arms in good Order, He caus'd them to be muster'd by their Names as follows.

Peter Jones	Tho. Jones	John Ellis
James Petillo	Charles Kimball	John Evans
Tho: Short	Geo: Hamilton	Robert Hix
Tho: Wilson	Steven Evans	Tho: Jones Junr
George Tilman	Robert Allen	John Ellis Junr

[19] Pack horse.

as Colo Allen's.[23] This Gentleman is a great oeconomist, and Skilld
in all the Arts of living well at any easy expense.

---

[23] John Allen of Surry County. See *Secret History*, Notes 5 and 20.

Here after drawing out this small Troop, Steddy made them the following Speech.

Friends & Fellow Travellers.

It is a pleasure to me to see that we are like to be so well attended in this long & painfull Journey. And what may we not hope from Men who list themselves not so much for pay, as from an Ambition to serve their Country. We have a great distance to go, & much Work to perform, but I observe too much Spirit in your Countenances to flinch at either. As no care shall be wanting on my part to do every One of You Justice so I promise myself that on Yours, You will set the Carolina Men, whom we are to meet at Coratuck, a constant Pattern of Order, Industry & Obedience. Then he march'd his Men in good Order to Capricorn's Elegant Seat,[20] according to the Route before projected, but found him in dolefull Dumps for the illness of his Wife. She was really indispos'd, but not so dangerously as to hinder a Vigorous Man from going upon the Service of his Country. However he seem'd in the midst of his Concern, to discover a Secret Satisfaction, that it furnish't him with an Excuse of not going upon an Expedition, that he fancy'd wou'd be both dangerous & difficult. Upon his refusing to go for the reason abovemention'd, Steddy wrote to the Governor how much he was disappointed at the Loss of one of the Surveyors, & recommended Astrolabe's Brother[21] to Supply his Place. At the same time he dispatch't away an Express to Young Astrolabe, to let him know he had nam'd to the Governor for his Service. But not knowing how it wou'd be determin'd he cou'd promise him nothing, tho' if he wou'd come to Norfolk at his own Risque, he shou'd there be able to resolve him. This was the best Expedient he cou'd think of for the Service at that Plunge because Capricorn had in his bitterness of his Concern, taken no care to acquaint the Governor that he was prevented from going. However D[r] Arsmart who had been to Visit M[rs] Capricorn, let the

---

[20] The home of John Allen, Surry County, Virginia, probably "Bacon's Castle," built by his grandfather, Arthur Allen.

[21] Joseph Mayo, of "Powhatan Seat," on the James River, below Richmond.

28. They proceeded in good Order through Surry County, as far as the Widdow Allen's[24] who had copied Solomon's complete housewife exactly. At this Gentlewoman's House, the other two Commissioners had appointed to join them, but were detained by some Accident at Williamsburg, longer than their appointment.

29. They pursued their March thro the Isle of Wight and observed a most dreadful Havock made by a late Hurricane, which happend in

---

[24] See *Secret History*, Note 24.

Governor know that he was too tender a Husband to leave his Spouse to the Merch[22] of a Physician. Upon this Notice, which came to the Governor before Steddy's Letter, it was so managed that the learned Orion[23] was appointed to go in his room. This Gentleman is Professor of the Mathematicks in the College of William & Mary, but has so very few Scholars, that he might be well enough spared from his Post for a short time. It was urg'd by his Friends, that a Person of his Fame for profound Learning, wou'd give a grace to the Undertaking, and be able to Silence all the Mathematicks of Carolina. These were unanswerable reasons, and so he was appointed. The Rev[d] D[r] Humdrum came time enough to bless a very plentiful Supper at Capricorns. He treated his Company handsomely, and by the help of a Bowl of Rack Punch his Grief disappear'd so entirely, that if he had not sent for Arsmart, it might have been suspected his Lady's Sickness was all a Farce. However to do him Justice, the Man wou'd never be concern'd in a Plot that was like to cost him 5 Pistoles.

28. The Table was well spread again for Breakfast, but unfortunately for the poor Horses, the Key of the Corn-loft was mislaid, at least the Servant was instructed to say as much. We march't from hence in good Order to the Widdow Allen's, which was 22 Miles.[24] She entertain'd us elegantly, & seem'd to pattern Solomon's Housewife if one may Judge by the neatness of her House, & the good Order of her Family. Here Firebrand & Meanwell, had appointed to meet Steddy but fail'd; however the Tent was sent hither under the care of John Rice, of the Kingdom of Ireland, who did not arrive till 12 a Clock at Night. This disorder at first setting out, gave us but an indifferent Opinion of Firebrand's Management.

29. From hence Steddy sent a Letter to the Governor, with an account of his March to that Place, & of the Steps he had taken

---

[22] Old English for marrow, indicating "goodness" as well as substance within the bones. I have not been able to identify "Dr. Arsmart."

[23] Alexander Irvine, who held the professorship of Mathematics at William and Mary from 1729 to his death in 1732.

[24] The maiden name of this hospitable lady was Bray. She was thrice married; first to Arthur Allen, second to Arthur Smith, finally to —— Stith. In 1753 she donated £125 for a free school in the upper part of Isle of Wight County and her will revealed a bequest of £120, the interest from which was to be used for the education of "any six poor children." See *William and Mary College Quarterly*, Vol. VI, pp. 77-78.

August, 1726. The Violence of it had not reachd above a Quarter of a
Mile in Breadth, but within that Compass had levelld all before it. Both
Trees and Houses were laid flat on the Ground, and several things hurld
to an incredible distance. Tis happy such violent Gusts are confined to
so narrow a Channel, because they carry desolation wherever they go.
In the Evening they reacht Mr. Godwin's, on the South Branch of Nansemond River, where they were treated with abundance of Primitive Hospitality.

March 1. This Gentleman was so kind as to shorten their Journey,
by setting them over the river. They coasted the N E Side of the Dismal
for several miles together, and found all the Grounds bordering upon it
very full of Sloughs. The Trees that grew near it lookt very Reverend,
with the long Moss that hung dangling from their Branches. Both cattle
and Horses eat this Moss greedily in Winter when other Provender is
Scarce, tho it is apt to scowr them at first. In that moist Soil too
grew abundance of that kind of Myrtle which bears the Candle-Berries.
There was likewise, here and there, a Gall-bush, which is a beautiful Evergreen, and may be cut into any Shape. It derives its Name from its Berries turning Water black, like the Galls of an oak.

When this Shrub is transplanted into Gardens, it will not thrive
without frequent watering.

The two other commissioners came up with them just at their Journey's
end, and that evening they arrived all together at Mr. Craford's,[25] who
lives on the South Branch of Elizabeth-River, over against Norfolk.

---

[25] See *Secret History*, Note 26.

about Astrolabe's Brother. At Ten in the Morning he thank't the
clean Widdow for all her Civilitys, & march't under the Pilotage
of Mr Baker, to Col° Thomas Goddings.[25] By the way Steddy
was oblig'd to be at the Expence of a few Curses upon John Rice, /
who was so very thirsty that he call'd at every house he past by. /
The Cavalcade arrived at Col°. Goddings about 4 a Clock after a
pleasant Journey of 30 Miles. But Steddy found himself exceedingly fatigued with the March. In passing thro' the upper part
of the Isle of Wight, Mr Baker remarkt the Dismal Footsteps made
by the Hurricane which happen'd in August 1626. The violence
of it did not extend in Breadth above a Quarter of a Mile, but in
that Compass levell'd all before it. Mr Baker's House was so
unlucky as to stand in its way, which it laid flat to the Ground and
blew some of his Goods above 2 Miles. Col° Godding was very
hospitable both to Man & Beast, But the poor Man had the Misfortune to be deaf, which hinder'd him from hearing any parts
of the acknowledgments that were made to him; He prest every
Body very kindly to eat, entreating 'em not to be bashful, which
might be a great Inconvenience to Travellors. The Son & Heir of
the Family offer'd himself as a Volunteer the over Night, but
dreamt so much of Danger & Difficulties, that he declar'd off in the
Morning.

March

1. About About 9 in the Morning the Col° was so kind as to set
all his Guests over the South Branch of Nansimond River, which
shorten'd their Journey 7 or 8 Miles, & from thence his Son conducted them into the great Road. Then they past for several
Miles together by the North Side of the Great Dismal, and after a
Journey of 25 Miles, arriv'd in good Order at Maj^r Crawford's[26]
over against Norfolk Town. Just before they got hither, the Lag
Commissioners over took them, and all the Men were drawn up

---

[25] The Baker family was prominent in Isle of Wight County, Lawrence Baker,
being a vestryman of New Port Parish from 1724 to 1737 and James Baker, Clerk
of the County Court, 1732-1734. Colonel Thomas Godding was Colonel Thomas
Godwin of Nansemond County.

[26] Major William Crawford, a member of the County Court of Norfolk in 1728. See
Lower Norfolk County, Virginia, Antiquary, Vol. I, p. 80.

Here the Commissioners left the Men with all the Horses and heavy Baggage, and crosst the River with their Servants only, for fear of making a Famine in the Town.

Norfolk has most the ayr of a Town of any in Virginia. There were then near 20 Brigantines and Sloops riding at the Wharves, and oftentimes they have more. It has all the advantages of Situation requisite for Trade and Navigation. There is a Secure Harbour for a good Number of Ships of any Burthen. Their River divides itself into 3 Several Branches, which are all Navigable. The Town is so near the sea, that its Vessels may Sail in and out in a few Hours. Their Trade is Chiefly to the West-Indies, whither they export abundance of Beef, Pork, Flour and Lumber. The worst of it is, they contribute much towards debauching the Country by importing abundance of Rum, which, like Ginn in Great Britain, breaks the Constitution, Vitiates the Morals, and ruins the Industry of most of the Poor people of this Country.

This Place is the Mart for most of the Commodities produced in the Adjacent Parts of North Carolina. They have a pretty deal of Lumber from the Borderers on the Dismal, who make bold with the King's Land there abouts, without the least Ceremony. They not only maintain their Stocks upon it, but get Boards, Shingles and other Lumber out of it in great Abundance.

The Town is built on a level Spot of Ground upon Elizabeth River, the Banks whereof are neither so high as to make the landing of Goods troublesome, or so low as to be in Danger of over-flowing. The Streets are Straight, and adorned with several Good Houses, which Encrease every Day. It is not a Town of Ordinarys and Publick Houses, like most others in this Country, but the Inhabitants consist of Merchants, Ship-Carpenters and other useful Artisans, with Sailors enough to manage their Navigation. With all these Conveniences, it lies under the two great disadvantages that most of the Towns in Holland do, by having neither good Air nor good Water. The two Cardinal Vertues that make a Place thrive, Industry and Frugality, are seen here in Perfection; and so long as they can banish Luxury and Idleness, the Town will remain in a happy and flourishing Condition.

The Method of building Wharffs here is after the following Manner. They lay down long Pine Logs, that reach from the Shore to the Edge of the Channel. These are bound fast together by Cross-Pieces notcht into them, according to the Architecture of the Log-Houses in North Carolina. A wharff built thus will stand Several Years, in spight of the Worm, which bites here very much, but may be soon repaired in a Place where so many Pines grow in the Neighbourhood.

to receive them. Meanwell was so Civil as to Excuse his not meeting Steddy at Mr Allens as had been agreed; but Firebrand was too big for Apology. It was agreed to leave the Men & the heavy Baggage at Maj^r. Crawfords (having made the necessary Provision for it) & pass over to Norfolk only with the Servants & Portmantles, that the Town's Men might not be frighten'd from entertaining them. Here they divided their Quarters that as little trouble might be given, as possible, and it was Steddy's fortune, after some apprehensions of going to the Ordinary to be invited by Col° Newton.[27] To shew his regard to the Church he took the Chaplain along with him. Mrs Newton provided a clean Supper without any Luxury about 8 a Clock, and appear'd to be one of the fine Ladys of the Town, and like a true fine Lady to have a great deal of Contempt for her Husband.

2. This Morning Old Col° Boush,[28] made Steddy a visit with the tender of his Service. There was no Soul in the Town knew how the Land lay betwixt this Place & Coratuck Inlet, til at last Mr William Williams that lives upon the Borders drew a rough Sketch that gave a general Notion of it. The light given by this Draught determin'd the Commissioners to march to the Landing of Northwest River, and there embark in a Periauga in Order to meet the Commissioners of Carolina at Coratuck. It was really a pleasure to see 12 or 14 Sea Vessels, riding in the Harbour of this City, & several Wharfs built out into the River to land goods upon. The Wharfs were built with Pine Logs let into each other at the End, by which those underneath are made firm by those which lye over them. Here the Commissioners were supply'd with 2 Caggs of Wine, & 2 of Rum, 173^lb of Bread, & several other Conveniencys. Our good Landlord entertain'd Steddy, and the Chaplain at Dinner, but Firebrand refused, because he was not sent to in due form. In the Evening the Commissioners were invited to an Oyster and a Bowl by Mr Sam Smith a plain Man worth 20000 Pounds. He produc'd his 2 Nieces, whose charms were all in-

---

[27] George Newton, Lieutenant-Colonel of Militia in Norfolk County, one of the trustees of the Town of Norfolk in the transfer of land owned by the town to Norfolk Academy. In 1744 he was a member of the County Court of Norfolk. (*Lower Norfolk County, Virginia, Antiquary*, Vol. I, pp. 78-81, 117.)

[28] Samuel Boush, member of the County Court of Norfolk in 1728. Today there is a Boush Avenue in Norfolk.

The Commissioners endeavourd, in this Town, to list Three more men to serve as Guides in that dirty Part of the Country, but found that these People knew just enough of that frightful Place to avoid it.

They had been told that those Netherlands were full of Bogs, of Marshes and Swamps, not fit for Human Creatures to engage in, and this was Reason enough for them not to hazard their Persons. So they told us, flat and plain, that we might een daggle thro the mire by Our-Selves for them.

The worst of it was, we coud not learn from any body in this Town, what Rout to take to Coratuck Inlet; till at least we had the fortune to meet with a Borderer upon North Carolina, who made a rough Sketch of that Part of the Country. Thus, upon seeing how the Land lay, we determind to march directly to Prescot Landing upon N W River, and proceed from thence by Water to the Place where our Line was to begin.

4. In Pursuance of this Resolution we crosst the River this Morning to Powder-Point,[26] where we all took Horse; and the Grandees of the Town, with great Courtesy, conducted us Ten Miles on our way, as far as the long Bridge built over the S Branch of the River. The Parson of the Parish, Mr. Marston,[27] a painful Apostle from the Society, made one in this Ceremonious Cavalcade.

At the Bridge, these Gentlemen wishing us a good Deliverance, returnd, and then a Troop of Light Horse escorted us as far as Prescot-Landing, upon N W River. Care had been taken beforehand to provide 2 Periaugas

---

[26] Today a suburb of Norfolk, known as Berkeley.
[27] Rev. Richard Marsden, Lynnhaven Parish, Princess Anne County.

visible. These Damsals seem'd discontented that their Uncle Shew'd more distinction to his Housekeeper than to them. We endeavour'd to hire 2 or 3 Men, here to go a long with Us: but might for the same price have hired them to make a Trip to the Other World. They look't upon us, as Men devoted, like Codrus & the 2 Decii, to certain destruction for the Service of our Country. The Parson & I return'd to our Quarters in good time & good Order, but my Man Tom broke the Rules of Hospitality by getting extreamly drunk in a Civil house.

3d. This being Sunday we were edify'd at Church by M[r] Marston[29] with a good Sermon. People cou'd not attend their Devotion for Staring at us, just as if we had come from China or Japan. In the Mean time Firebrand and Astrolabe not having quite so much regard for the Sabbath, went to the N. W. Landing to prepare Vessels for our Transportation to Coratuck. I wrote to the Governor an account of our Progress thus far, with a Billet-doux to my Wife. The Wind blew very hard at S.W. all day: However in the Evening Steddy order'd the Men & Horses to be set over the South Branch to save time in the Morning. My Landlady gave us Tea, & sweeten'd it with the best of her Smiles. At Night we spent an hour with Col° Boush who stir'd his Old Bones very cheerfully in our Service. Poor Orion's Horse & Furniture were much disorder'd with the Journey hither. His Instrument wou'd not traverse, nor his Ball rest in the Socket. In short all his Tackle had the air of Distress. Over against the Town is Powder Point[30] where a Ship of any Burden may lye close to, and the Men of War are us'd to Careen.

4. About 8 a Clock in the Morning we crost the River to Powder Point, where we found our Men ready to take Horse. Several of the Grandees of the Town, and the Parson among the rest, did us the Honour to attend Us as far as the great Bridge over South River. Here we were met by a Troop under the command of Captain Wilson[31] who escorted us as far as his Father's Castle near the Dismal. We halted about a quarter of an Hour, and

---

[29] Rev. Richard Marsden, of Lynnhaven Parish, Princess Anne County.
[30] Today a suburb of Norfolk, known as Berkeley.
[31] Probably that Captain Willis Wilson, Jr., who was in 1744 a member of the County Court of Norfolk. See *Lower Norfolk County, Virginia, Antiquary*, Vol. I, p. 117.

to lie ready at that Place to transport us to Coratauck Inlet. Our Zeal was so great to get thither at the time appointed, that we hardly allowd our-selves leisure to eat, which in truth we had the less Stomach to, by reason the dinner was served up by the Landlord, whose Nose stood on such ticklish Terms that it was in Danger of falling into the Dish. We therefore made our Repast very short, and then embarkt with only the Surveyors and Nine chosen Men, leaving the rest at Mr. W-n's[28] to take Care of the Horses and Baggage. There we also left our Chaplain, with the Charitable Intent, that the Gentiles round about might have time and Opportunity, if they pleasd, of getting themselves and their children baptizd.

We rowd down N W River about 18 miles, as far as the Mouth of it, where it empties itself into Albemarle Sound. It was a really Delightful Sight, all the way, to see the Banks of the River adornd with Myrtle, Laurel and Bay-Trees, which preserve their Verdue the Year round, tho it must be ownd that these beautiful Plants, sacred to Venus and Appollo, grow commonly in very dirty Soil. The River is, in most Places, fifty or Sixty Yards wide, without spreading much wider at the Mouth. Tis remarkable it was never known to Ebb and flow till the year 1713, when a Violent Storm opend a new Inlet, about 5 Miles South of the old one; since which Convulsion, the Old Inlet is almost choakd up by the Shifting of the Sand, and grows both Narrower and Shoaller every day.

It was dark before we could reach the Mouth of the River, where our wayward Stars directed us to a Miserable Cottage. The Landlord was lately removed, Bag and Baggage, from Maryland, thro a Strong Antipathy he had to work and paying his Debts.[29] For want of our Tent, we were obligd to Shelter our Selves in this wretched Hovel, where we were almost devourd by Vermin of Various kinds. However, we were above complaining, being all Philosophers enough to improve such Slender Distresses into Mirth and good Humour.

5. The Day being now come, on which we had agreed to meet the Commissioners of North Carolina, we embarkd very early, which we coud the easier do, having no Temptation to stay where we were. We shapt our Course along the South End of Knot's Island, there being no Passage open on the North.

Farther Still to the Southward of us, we discoverd two Smaller Islands, that go by the names of Bell's and Churche's Isles. We also saw a small New England Sloop riding in the Sound, a little to the South of our Course. She had come in at the New-Inlet, as all other vessels have

---

[28] Probably Willis Wilson. See *Secret History*, Note 30.
[29] Andrew Dukes. See *Secret History*, p. 41.

then proceeded to N.W. Landing. Here Firebrand had provided a Dinner for us, serv'd up by the Master of the House, whose Nose seem'd to stand upon very ticklish Terms. After Dinner we chose Ten able Men & embarkt on board 2 Periaugas under the command of Capt Wilkins,[32] which carry'd us to the Mouth of N.W. River. By the way we found the Banks of the River Lined with Myrtles & Bay-Trees, which afforded a Beautiful Prospect. These beautifull Plants dedicated to Venus & Appollo grow in wet Ground, & so dos the Wild Lawrell, which in some Places is intermixt with the rest. This River is in most places about 100 Yards over, & had no Tide til the Year 1713 when a violent Tempest open'd a New Inlet about 5 miles to the Southward of the old One, which is now about clos'd up, and too Shallow for any Vessel to pass over. But the New Inlet is deep enough for Sloops. We were 4 Hours in rowing to the Mouth of the River, being about 13 Miles from the Landing. Here we took up our Lodging at one Andrew Dukes, who had lately removed, or rather run away hither from Maryland. We were forc't to ly in Bulk upon a very dirty Floor, that was quite alive with Fleas & Chinches, and made us repent that we had not brought the Tent along with Us. We had left that with the rest of the heavy Baggage at Capt Wilson's, under the Guard of 7 Men. There we had also left the Revd Dr Humdrum with the hopes that all the Gentiles in the Neighbourhood wou'd bring their Children to be Christen'd, notwithstanding some of them had never been Christen'd themselves. Firebrand had taken Care to Board his Man Tipperary with Capt Wilson, because by being the Squire of his Body he thought him too much a Gentleman to diet with the rest of the Men we left behind. This Indignity sat not easy upon their Stomachs, who were all honest house-keepers in good Circumstances.

5.   At break of Day we turn'd out properly speaking, and blest our Landlord's Eyes with half a Pistole. About 7 we embark't, & past by the South End of Knot's Island, there being no Passage on the North. To the Southward, at some Distance we saw Bells & Churches Islands. About Noon we arrived at the South Shoar of Old Coratuck Inlet, and about 2 we were join'd by Judge Jumble & Plausible, 2 of the Carolina Commissioners; the other two Shoe-

---

[32] Probably William Wilkins, Justice of Norfolk County in 1728.

done since the opening of it.   This Navigation is a little difficult, and fit
only for Vessels that draw no more than ten feet Water.

The Trade hither is engrosst by the Saints of New England, who carry
off a great deal of Tobacco, without troubling themselves with paying
that Impertinent Duty of a Penny a Pound.

It was just Noon before we arrived at Coratuck Inlet, which is now so
shallow that the Breakers fly over it with a horrible Sound, and at the
same time afford a very wild Prospect.   On the North side of the Inlet,
the High Land terminated in a Bluff Point, from which a Spit of Sand
extended itself towards the South-East, full half a Mile.   The Inlet lies
between that Spit and another on the South of it, leaving an Opening
of not quite a Mile, which at this day is not practicable for any Vessel
whatsoever.   And as shallow as it now is, it continues to fill up more and
more, both the Wind and Waves rolling in the Sands from the Eastern
Shoals.

About two a Clock in the Afternoon we were joind by two of the
Carolina Commissioners, attended by Mr. S—n, their Surveyor.   The
other two were not quite so punctual, which was the more unlucky for us,
because there could be no sport till they came.   These Gentlemen, it
seems, had the Carolina-Commission in their keeping, notwithstanding
which they coud not forbear paying too much regard to a Proverb—
fashionable in ther Country,—not to make more hast than good Speed.

However, that we who were punctual might not spend our precious
time unprofitably, we took the Several bearings of the Coast.   We also
surveyd part of the Adjacent High Land, which had scarcely any Trees
growing upon it, but Cedars.   Among the Shrubs, we were shewed here
and there a Bush of Carolina-Tea calld Japon, which is one Species of the
Phylarrea.   This is an Evergreen, the Leaves whereof have some resem-
balance to Tea, but differ very widely both in Tast and Flavour.[30]

We also found some few Plants of the Spired Leaf Silk grass, which
is likewise an Evergreen, bearing on a lofty Stemm a large Cluster of
Flowers of a Pale Yellow.   Of the Leaves of this Plant the People
thereabouts twist very strong Cordage.

A vertuoso might divert himself here very well, in picking up Shells
of various Hue and Figure, and amongst the rest, that Species of Conque
Shell which the Indian Peak is made of.   The Extremities of these Shells
are Blue and the rest white, so that Peak of both these Colours are drilld
out of one and the same Shell, Serving the Natives both for Ornament
and Money, and are esteemd by them far beyond Gold and Silver.

The Cedars were of Singular use to us in the Absence of our Tent, which

---

[30] The Yapon or Yaupon is similar to the holly tree.   From its leaves the Southern
Indians made an emetic black drink which was used ceremoniously as well as a
medicine.

brush & Puzzlecause lagg'd behind, which was the more unlucky because we cou'd enter on no Business, for want of the Carolina Commission, which these Gentlemen had in their keeping. Jumble was Brother to the late Dean of York,[33] and if his Honour had not formerly been a Pyrate himself, he seem'd intimately acquainted with many of them. Plausible had been bred in Christ's Hospital and had a Tongue as Smooth as the Commissary, and was altogether as well qualify'd to be of the Society of Jesus. These worthy Gentlemen were attended by Bo-otes, as their Surveyor, a Young Man of much Industry, but no Experience.[34] We had now nothing to do but to reconnoitre the Place. The High Land ended in a blouf Point, from which a Spit of Sand extended itself to the South East about half a Mile. The Inlet lys between this Spit & another on the South Side, leaving a shoal Passage for the Sea not above a Mile over. On the East are Shoals that ran out 2.

---

[33] Here is apparently a mistake. Thomas Gale, Dean of York, died in 1702 and his father was a Christopher Gale. The father of Chief Justice Gale was Rev. Miles Gale. (*Colonial Records of North Carolina*, Vol. II, p. 133.)

[34] This was Samuel Swann (1704-1772), son of that Major Smauel Swann who removed from Virginia to North Carolina in 1694, and grandson of William Swann of Swann's Point, opposite Jamestown, Virginia, and nephew of Edward Moseley. He was a member of the North Carolina Assembly from Perquimans County from 1725 to 1734, and also for Onslow from 1734 to 1762, and was Speaker from 1742 to 1762. See *Colonial Records of North Carolina*, Vol. IX, preface.

we had left with the rest of the Baggage for fear of overloading the Periaugas. We made a Circular Hedge of the Branches of this Tree, Wrought so close together as to fence us againt the Cold Winds. We then kindled a rouseing fire in the Center of it, and lay round it, like so many Knights Templars. But, as comfortable as this Lodging was, the Surveyors turnd out about 2 in the Morning to try the Variation by a Meridian taken from the North Star, and found it to be somewhat less than three degrees West.

The Commissioners of the Neighbouring Colony came better provided for the Belly than the Business. They brought not above two men along with them that would put their Hands to any thing but the Kettle and the Frying-Pan. These spent so much of their Industry that way, that they had as little Spirit as Inclination for Work.

6. At Noon, having a Perfect Observation, we found the Latitude of Coratuck Inlet to be 36 Degrees and 31 Minutes.

Whilst we were busied about these Necessary Matters, our Skipper row'd to an Oyster Bank just by, and loaded his Periauga with Oysters as Savoury and well-tasted as those from Colchester of Walfleet, and had the advantage of them, too, by being much larger and fatter.

About 3 in the Afternoon the two lagg Commissioners arriv'd, and after a few decent excuses for making us wait, told us they were ready to enter upon Business as soon as we pleas'd. The first Step was to produce our respective Powers, and the Commission from each Governor was distinctly read, and Copies of them interchangeably deliver'd.

It was observ'd by our Carolina Friends, that the Latter Part of the Virginia Commission had something in it a little too lordly and Positive. In answer to which we told them twas necessary to make it thus peremptory, lest the present Commissioners might go upon as fruitless an Errand as their Predecessors. The former Commissioners were ty'd down to Act in Exact Conjunction with those of Carolina, and so could not advance one Step farther, or one Jot faster, than they were pleas'd to permit them.

The Memory of that disappointment, therefore, induc'd the Government of Virginia to give fuller Powers to the present Commissioners, by Authorizing them to go on with the Work by Themselves, in Case those of Corolina should prove unreasonable, and refuse to join with them in carrying the business to Execution. And all this was done lest His Majesty's gracious Intention should be frustrated a Second time.

After both Commissions were considered, the first Question was, where the Dividing Line was to begin. This begat a Warm debate; the Virginia Commissioners contending, with a great deal of Reason, to begin at the End of the Spitt of Sand, which was undoubtedly the North Shore of Corautck Inlet. But those of Carolina insisted Strenuously, that the Point

or 3 Miles, over which the Breakers rise Mountains high with a
Terrible Noise. I often cast a longing Eye towards England, &
Sigh'd. This Night we lay for the first time in the Woods, and
being without the Tent, we made a Bower of the Branches of
Cedar, with a large Fire in Front, to guard us from the North-
Wester, which blew very smartly. At Night Young Astrolabe
came to Us, & gave great Jealousy to Orion. His Wigg was in
such Stiff Buckle, that if he had seen the Devil the Hair wou'd
not have stood on end. This Night we found the variation to be
3° West, by a due Meridian taken from the North Star.

6. We were treated at Breakfast by the Commissioners of Carolina, who coming from home by Water, were much better provided
for the Belly than the Business. At Noon we found the Latitude
to be 36° 31' according to Astrolabe, but Orion to prove his Skill
in the Mathematicks, by flat Contradiction wou'd needs have it but
36° 30'. Capt Wilkins furnish't us with excellent Oysters, as
savory & well tasted as those in England. About 3 a Cloak Messrs
Shoebrush & Puzzlecause made a Shift to come to Us, after calling at every House, where they expected any Refreshment; after
the necessary Complements, & a Thousand Excuses for making
us wait for them so long, we began to enter upon business. We
had a tough dispute where we shou'd begin: whether at the Point
of high Land, or at the End of the Spit of Sand, which we with
good reason maintain'd to be the North Shoar of Coratuck Inlet,
according to the Express Words of his Majesty's Order. They
had no argument to Support our beginning at the High-Land, but
because the former Commissioners for Virginia submitted to it.
But if what they did was to be a Rule for Us, then we ought to
allow no Variation of the Compass, because those Gentlemen
allow'd of None. This Controversy lasted til Night neither Side
receding from its Opinion. However by the lucky advice of Firebrand, I took Plausible aside & let him know the Government of
Virginia had look't upon him as the Sole Obstacle to the settling
the Bounds formerly, and if we shou'd break off now upon this
frivolous Pretence, he wou'd surely bear the Blame again. At the

of High Land ought rather to be the Place of Beginning, because that was fixt and certain, whereas the Spitt of Sand was ever Shifting, and did actually run out farther now than formerly. The Contest lasted some Hours, with great Vehemence, neither Party receding from their Opinion that Night. But next Morning, Mr. M. . . . ., to convince us he was not that Obstinate Person he had been represented, yielded to our Reasons, and found Means to bring over his Collegues.

Here we began already to reap the Benefit of those Peremptory Words in our Commission, which in truth added some Weight to our Reasons. Nevertheless, because positive proof was made by the Oaths of two Credible Witnesses, that the Spitt of Sand had advanced 200 Yards towards the Inlet since the Controversy first began, we were willing for Peace-sake to make them that allowance. Accordingly we fixed our Beginning about that Distance North of the Inlet, and there Ordered a Cedar-Post to be driven deep into the Sand for our beginning. While we continued here, we were told that on the South Shore, not far from the Inlet, dwelt a Marooner, that Modestly call'd himself a Hermit, tho' he forfeited that Name by Suffering a wanton Female to cohabit with Him.

His Habitation was a Bower, cover'd with Bark after the Indian Fashion, which in that mild Situation protected him pretty well from the Weather. Like the Ravens, he neither plow'd nor sow'd, but Subsisted chiefly upon Oysters, which his Handmaid made a Shift to gather from the Adjacent Rocks. Sometimes, too, for Change of Dyet, he sent her to drive up the Neighbour's Cows, to moisten their Mouths with a little Milk. But as for raiment, he depended mostly upon his Length of Beard, and She upon her Length of Hair, part of which she brought decently forward, and the rest dangled behind quite down to her Rump, like one of Herodotus's East Indian Pigmies.

Thus did these Wretches live in a dirty State of Nature, and were mere Adamites, Innocence only excepted.

7. This Morning the Surveyors began to run the Dividing line from the Cedar-Post we had driven into the Sand, allowing near 3 Degrees for the Variation. Without making this Just allowance, we should not have obeyd his Majesty's order in running a Due West Line. It seems the former Commissioners had not been so exact, which gave our Friends of Carolina but too just an Exception to their Proceedings.

The Line cut Dosier's Island, consisting only of a Flat Sand, with here and there an humble Shrub growing upon it. From thence it crost over a narrow Arm of the Sound into Knot's Island, and there Split a Plantation belonging to William Harding.

same time I show'd him a Representation made to the late Queen by Col° Spotswood, greatly to his disadvantage. This work't so powerfully upon his Politick that he without loss of time soften'd his Brethren in such a Manner, that they came over to our Opinion. They were the rather perswaded to this by the Peremptory Words of our Commission, by which we were directed to go on with the Business tho' the Carolina Commissioners shou'd refuse to join with us therein. However by reason of some Proof that was made to us by the Oaths Credible Persons, that the Spit of Sand was advanced about 200 Yards to the Southward since the Year 1712 when the Proposals between the Governours Eden & Spotswood were agreed upon, we thought it reasonable to allow for so much. And accordingly made our Beginning from thence. Upon the high-Land we found One kind of Silk Grass, and plenty of Japon, which passes for Tea in North Carolina, tho' nothing like it. On the Sands we saw Conque-Shells in great Number of which the Indians make both their Blue & white Peak, both colours being in different Parts of the same Shell.

7.   We drove down a Post at our Place of beginning, & then crost over to Dosior's Island, which is nothing but a flat Sand with Shrubs growing upon it. From thence we past over to the North End of Knob's Island, our Line running thro' the Plantation of Wm Harding. This Man had a wife born & bred near Temple Bar, and stil talk't of the Walks in the Temple with Pleasure. These poor People bestow'd their Wood & their Water upon us very freely. We found Shoebrush a merry good humor'd Man, and had learnt a very decent behaviour from Governour Hyde, to whom he had been Valet de Chambre, of which he still carry'd the marks by having his coat, wast-coat & Breeches of different Parishes. Puzzlecause had degenerated from a New-England Preacher for which his Godly Parents design'd him, to a very wicked, but awkward, Rake. I had almost forgot to mention a Marooner who had the Confidence to call himself an Hermit, living on the South Shoar of Coratuck near the Inlet. He has no other Habitation but a green Bower or Harbour with a Female Domestick as wild & as dirty as himself. His Diet is chiefly

The Day being far spent, we encampt in this Man's Pasture, tho' it lay very low, and the Season now inclin'd People to Aguish Distempers. He sufferd us to cut Cedar-Branches for our Enclosure, and other Wood for Firing, to correct the moist Air and drive away the Damps. Our Landlady, in the Days of her Youth, it seems, had been a Laundress in the Temple, and talkt over her Adventurers in that Station, with as much pleasure as an Old Soldier talks over his Battles and Distempers, and I believe with as many Additions to the Truth.

The Soil is good in many Places of this Island, and the Extent of it pretty large. It lyes in the form of a Wedge: the South End of it is Several Miles over, but towards the North it Sharpens into a Point. It is a Plentiful Place for Stock, by reason of the wide Marshes adjacent to it, and because of its warm Situation. But the Inhabitants pay a little dear for this Convenience, by losing as much Blood in the Summer Season by the infinite Number of Mosquetas, as all their Beef and Pork can recruit in the Winter.

The Sheep are as large as in Lincolnshire, because they are never pincht by cold or Hunger. The whole Island was hitherto reckon'd to lye in Virginia, but now our Line has given the greater Part of it to Carolina. The Principal Freeholder here is Mr. White, who keeps open House for all Travellers, that either Debt or Shipwreck happens to cast in his way.

8. By break of Day we sent away our Largest Periauga, with the Baggage, round the South end of Knot's Island, with Orders to the Men to wait for us in the Mouth of North River. Soon after, we embarkt ourselves on board the smaller Vessel, with Intent, if possible, to find a Passage round the North End of the Island.

We found this Navigation very difficult, by reason of the Continued Shoals, and often stuck fast aground; for tho' the Sound spreads many miles, yet it is in most places extremely Shallow, and requires a Skilful Pilot to Steer even a Canoe safe over it. It was almost as hard to keep our Temper as to keep the Channel, in this provoking Situation. But the most impatient amongst us strokt down their Choler and swallow'd their curses, lest, if they suffer'd them to break out, they might sound like Complaining, which was expressly forbid, as the first Step to Sedition.

At a distance we descry'd Several Islands to the Northward of us, the largest of which goes by the Name of Cedar Island. Our periauga stuck so often that we had a fair chance to be benighted in this wide Water, which must certainly have been our Fate, had we not luckily spied a Canoe that was giving a Fortune-teller a cast from Princess Anne County over to North Carolina. But, as conjurers are Sometimes mistaken, the Man mistrusted we were Officers of Justice in pursuit of a Young

Oysters, which he has just Industry enough to gather from the Neighbouring Oyster Banks, while his Concubine makes a Practice of driving up the Neighbour's Cows for the advantage of their Milk.　Orion seem'd to be grievously puzzled about Plotting off his Surveyor's Work, and chose rather to be oblig'd to the Carolina Commissioners, than to Mr Mayo, for their Instruction, which it was evident to every Body that he wanted.　The Truth of it is, he had been much more discreet to loiter on at the College, & receive his Sallary quietly (which he ows to his Relation to the pious Commissary) than to undertake a Business which discover'd he knew very little of the matter.

8.　We quitted our Camp about 7 & early dispatch't away the large Periauga with the Heavy Baggage & most of the Men round the South End of Knots Island.　About 9 we embark't ourselves on board the Resser Periauga under the Pilotage of Capt Wilkins, & steer'd our Course towards the North End of the Island.　This Navigation was so difficult by reason of the perpetual Shoals, that we were often fast aground: but Firebrand swore us off again very soon.　Our Pilot wou'd have been a miserable Man if One half of that Gentleman's Curses had taken effect.　It was remarkable to see how mild & unmov'd the poor man was under so much heavy displeasure insomuch that the most passionate Expression that escap't him was, O for ever & after! which was his form of Swearing.　We had been benighted in that wide Water, had we not met a Canoe that was carrying a Conjurer from Princess Ann to Carolina.　But as all Conjurors are sometimes mistaken, he took us at first for Pyrates, what was worse for him, he suspected afterwards that we were Officers, that were in pursuit of him & a Woman that past for his Wife.　However at last being undeceiv'd

Wench he had carry'd off along with him. We gave the Canoe Chase for more than an Hour and when we came up with her, threatend to make them all prisoners unless they would direct us into the right Channel.

By the Pilotage of these People we row'd up an Arm of the Sound, call'd the Back-Bay, till we came to the Head of it. There we were stoppt by a Miry Pocoson full half a Mile in Breadth, thro' which we were oblig'd to daggle on foot, plungeing now and then, tho' we pickt our Way, up to the Knees in Mud. At the End of this Charming walk we gain'd the Terra Firma of Princess Anne County. In that Dirty Condition we were afterwards oblig'd to foot it two Miles, as far as John Heath's Plantation, where we expected to meet the Surveyors & the men who waited upon them.

While we were performing this tedious Voyage, they had carried the Line thro' the firm Land of Knot's Island, where it was no more than half a Mile wide. After that they travers'd a large Marsh, that was exceeding Miry, and extended to an Arm of the Back-Bay. They crosst that water in a Canoe, which we had order'd round for that Purpose, and then waded over another Marsh, that reacht quite to the High Land of Princess Anne. Both these Marshes together make a breadth of five Miles, in which the Men frequently sunk up to the Middle without muttering the least complaint. On the contrary, they turn'd all these Disasters into Merriment.

It was discover'd, by this day's Work, that Knot's Island was improperly so call'd, being in Truth no more than a Peninsula. The N W Side of it is only divided from the Main by the great Marsh above-mentioned, which is seldom totally overflow'd. Instead of that, it might, by the Labour of a few Trenches, be drain'd into firm Meadow, capable of grazing as many cattle as Job, in his best Estate, was master of. In the Miry Condition it now lies, it feeds great Numbers in the Winter, tho', when the Weather grows warm, they are driven from thence by the Mighty Armies of Mosquetas, which are the Plague of the lower Part of Carolina, as much as the Flies were formerly of Egypt, and some Rabbis think those Flies were no other than Mosquetas.

All the People in the Neighbourhood flockt to John Heath's, to behold such Rarities as they fancied us to be. The Men left their belov'd Chimney Corners, the good women their Spinning Wheels, and some, of more Curiosity than Ordinary, rose out of their sick Beds, to come and stare at us. They lookt upon us as a Troop of Knight Errants, who were running this great Risque of our Lives, as they imagin'd, for the Public Weal; and some of the gravest of them question'd much whether we were not all Criminals, condemned to this dirty work for Offences against the State.

What puzzled them most was, what cou'd make our men so very Light-

in both these points, they suffer'd us to Speak with them, & directed
us in the Course we were to Steer.　By their Advice we row'd up
a Water call'd the Back-Bay, as far as a Skirt of Pocoson a quarter
of a Mile in Breadth.　Thro' this we waded up to the Knees in
Mud & got Safe on the firm Land of Princess-Ann County.　During this Voyage Shoebrush in Champing a Biscuit, forc't out one
of his Teeth, which an unlucky Flux had left loose in his Head.
And tho' one of his Feet was inflam'd with the Gout, yet he was
forc't to walk 2 Miles as well as the rest of us to John Heath's
where we took up our Quarters.　Amongst other Spectators came
2 Girls to see us, one of which was very handsome, & the other
very willing.　However we only saluted them, & if we committed
any Sin at all, it was only in our Hearts.　Cap[t] White a Grandee
of Nott's Island, & M[r] Moss a Grandee of Princess-Ann made us
a visit & helpt to empty our Liquor.[35]　The Surveyors & their attendants came to us at Night, after wading thro' a Marsh near 5
Miles in Breadth, which stretches from the West Side of Knot's
Island, to the high-Land of Princess-Ann.　In this Marsh several
of the Men had plung'd up to the Middle, however they kept up
their good Humour, & only made Sport of what others wou'd have
made a Calamity.

---

[35] Reference is doubtless to Capt. Solomon White of Princess Anne County.　There
is no record of a Moss family in that County.

hearted under such intolerable Drudgery. "Ye have little reason to be merry, My Masters," said one of them, with a very solemn Face, "I fancy the Pocoson you must Struggle with to-morrow will make you change your Note, and try what Metal you are made of. Ye are, to be sure, the first of Human Race that ever had the Boldness to attempt it, and I dare say will be the last. If, therefore, you have any Worldly Goods to dispose of, My Advice is that you make your Wills this very Night, for fear you die Intestate to-Morrow." But, alas! these frightfull Tales were so far from disheartening the men that they serv'd only to whet their Resolution.

9. The Surveyors enter'd Early upon their Business this Morning, and ran the Line thro' Mr. Eyland's Plantation, as far as the Banks of North River. They passt over it in the Periauga, and landed in Gibbs' Marsh, which was a mile in Breadth, and tolerably firm. They trudg'd thro' this Marsh without much difficulty as far as the High Land, which promis'd more Fertility than any they had seen in these Parts. But this firm Land lasted not long before they came upon the dreadful Pocoson they had been threaten'd with. Nor did they find it one Jot better than it had been painted to them. The Beavers and Otters had render'd it quite impassable for any Creature but themselves.

Our poor Fellows had much ado to drag their Legs after them in this Quagmire, but disdaining to be baulkt, they cou'd hardly be persuaded from pressing forward by the Surveyors, who found it absolutely Necessary to make a Traverse in the Deepest Place, to prevent their Sticking fast in the Mire, and becoming a Certain Prey to the Turkey-Buzzards.

This Horrible Day's Work Ended two Miles to the Northward of Mr. Merchant's Plantation, divided from N W River by a Narrow Swamp, which is causway'd over. We took up our Quarters in the open Field, not far from the House, correcting, by a Fire as large as a Roman-Funeral-Pile, the Aguish Exhalations arising from the Sunken Grounds that Surrounded us.

The Neck of Land included betwixt N River and N-West River, with the adjacent Marsh, belong'd formerly to Governor Gibbs,[31] but since his Decease to Colonel Bladen,[32] in right of his first Lady, who was Mr. Gibbs' Daughter. It would be a Valuable Tract of Land in any Country but North Carolina, where, for want of Navigation and Commerce, the best Estate affords little more than a coarse Subsistence.

---

[31] John Gibbs, of the Currituck region, who, in 1690, claimed to be Governor of North Carolina and resisted the authority of Philip Ludwell, the appointee of the Proprietors. His claim was probably due to an election by the Council after the expulsion of Seth Sothel by the Assembly. Ludwell appealed to Governor Nicholson of Virginia for intervention and Nicholson reported to the Crown that he had quieted the controversy. Ludwell and Gibbs both went to England to lay their case before the proper authorities, Ludwell winning.

[32] Martin Bladen (1680-1746), Whig politician, and member of the Board of Trade from 1717 to his death. His wife was Mary Gibbs.

9.   In the Morning we walk't with the Surveyors to the Line, which cut thro' Eyland's Plantation, & came to the Banks of North River. Hither the Girls above mention'd attended us, but an Old Woman came along with them for the Security of their Vertue. Others rose out of their Sick Beds to see such Raritys as we were. One of our Periaugas sat the Surveyors & 5 Men over North River. They landed in a miry Marsh, which led to a very deep Pocoson. Here they met with Bever Dams & Otter holes, which it was not practicable to pass in a direct Line, tho' the Men offer'd to do it with great Alacrity: But the Surveyors were contented to make a Traverse. While they were struggling with these difficultys, we Commissioners went in State in the other Periauga to N. W. River, and row'd up as high as Mr Merchants.[36]   He lives near half a mile from the River having a Causway leading thro' a filthy Swamp to his Plantation. I encampt in his Pasture with the Men, tho' the other Commissioners endulg'd themselves so far as to ly in the House. But it seems they broke the Rules of Hospitality, by several gross Freedoms they offer'd to take with our Landlord's Sister. She was indeed a pretty Girl, and therefore it was prudent to send her out of harm's Way. I was the more concern'd at this unhandsome Behaviour, because the People were extremely Civil to us, & deserv'd a better Treatment. The Surveyors came to us at Night, very much Jaded with their dirty work, and Orion Slept so Sound that he had been burn't in his Blanket, if the Centry had not been kinder to him than he deserv'd.

---

[36] There was a Willoughby Merchant, justice of Princess Anne, at this time; at the close of eighteenth century his descendants lived in Norfolk County.

10. The Sabbath happen'd very opportunely to give some ease to our jaded People, who rested religiously from every work, but that of cooking the Kettle. We observed very few corn-fields in our Walks, and those very small, which sem'd the Stranger, to us, because we could see no other Tokens of Husbandry or Improvement. But, upon further Inquiry, we were given to understand People only made Corn for themselves and not for their Stocks, which know very well how to get their own Living.

Both Cattle and Hogs ramble in the Neighbouring Marshes and Swamps, where they maintain themselves the whole Winter long, and are not fetch'd home till the Spring. Thus these Indolent Wretches, during one half of the Year, lose the Advantage of the Milk of their cattle, as well as their Dung, and many of the poor Creatures perish in the Mire, into the Bargain, by this ill Management.

Some, who pique themselves more upon Industry than their Neighbours, will, now and then, in compliment to their Cattle, cut down a Tree whose Limbs are loaden with the Moss aforemention'd. The trouble wou'd be too great to Climb the Tree in order to gather this Provender, but the Shortest way (which in this Country is always counted the best) is to fell it, just like the Lazy Indians, who do the same by such Trees as bear fruit, and so make one Harvest for all. By this bad Husbandry Milk is so Scarce, in the Winter Season, that were a Big-belly'd Woman to long for it, She would lose her Longing. And, in truth, I believe this is often the Case, and at the same time a very good reason why so many People in this Province are markt with a Custard Complexion.

The only Business here is raising of Hogs, which is manag'd with the least Trouble, and affords the Diet they are most fond of. The Truth of it is the Inhabitants of N Carolina devour so much Swine's flesh, that it fills them full of gross Humours. For want too of a constant Supply of Salt, they are commonly obliged to eat it Fresh, and that begets the highest taint of Scurvy. Thus, whenever a Severe Cold happens to Constitutions thus Vitiated, tis apt to improve into the Yaws, called there very justly the country-Distemper. This has all the Symptoms of the Pox, with this Aggravation, that no Preparation of Mercury will touch it. First it seizes the Throat, next the Palate, and lastly shews its spite to the poor Nose, of which tis apt in a small time treacherously to undermine the Foundation.

This Calamity is so common and familiar here, that it ceases to be a Scandal, and in the disputes that happen about Beauty, the Noses have in some Companies much ado to carry it. Nay, tis said that once, after three good Pork years, a Motion had like to have been made in the House of Burgesses, that a Man with a Nose shou'd be incapable of holding any Place of Profit in the Province; which Extraordinary Motion could never have been intended without Some Hopes of a Majority.

10. This being Sunday we rested the Men & Surveyors, tho' we cou'd not celebrate the Sabbath as we ought for want of our Chaplain. I had a Letter from him informing me that all was well, both Soul & Body, under his Care. Capt Wilkins went home to make his wife a Visit, and brought me a Bottle of Milk, which was better than a Bottle of Tokay. Firebrand took all Occasions to set Orion above Astrolabe, which there was no reason for, but because he had the Honour to be recommended by him. I halted as bad as old Jacob, without having wrestled with any thing like an Angel.

The Men were concern'd at it, and had observ'd so much of Firebrand's sweet Temper, that they swore they wou'd make the best of their way home if it pleas'd God to disable me from proceeding on the Business. But I walk't about as much as I cou'd, & thereby made my Hips very pliable. We found Capt Willis Wilson here, whose Errand was to buy Pork, which is the Staple Commodity of North Carolina, & which with Pitch & Tar makes up the whole of their Traffick. The Truth of it is, these People live so much upon Swine's flesh, that it don't only encline them to the Yaws, & consequently to the downfall of their Noses, but makes them likewise extremely hoggish in their Temper, & many of them seem to Grunt rather than Speak in their ordinary conversation.

Thus, considering the foul and pernicious Effects of Eating Swine's Flesh in a hot Country, it was wisely forbidden and made an Abomination to the Jews, who liv'd much in the same Latitude with Carolina.

11. We ordered the Surveyors early to their Business, who were blesst with pretty dry Grounds for three Miles together. But they paid dear for it in the next two, consisting of one continued frightfull Pocoson,[33] which no Creatures but those of the amphibious kind ever had ventur'd into before.

This filthy Quagmire did in earnest put the Men's Courage to a Tryal, and tho' I can't say it made them lose their Patience, yet they lost their Humour for Joking. They kept their Gravity like so many Spaniards, so that a Man might then have taken his Opportunity to plunge up to the Chin, without Danger of being laught at. However, this unusual composure of countenance could not fairly be call'd complaining.

Their Day's-Work ended at the Mouth of Northern's Creek, which empties itself into N W River; tho' we chose to Quarter a little higher up the River, near Mossy Point. This we did for the Convenience of an Old house to Shelter our Persons and Baggage from the rain, which threaten'd us hard. We judg'd the thing right, for there fell an heavy shower in the Night, that drove the most hardy of us into the House. Tho' indeed, our case was not much mended by retreating thither, because that Tenement having not long before been us'd as a Pork-Store, the Moisture of the Air dissolv'd the Salt that lay Scatter'd on the Floor, and made it as wet within Doors as without. However, the Swamps and Marshes we were lately accustom'd to had made such Beavers and Otters of us that Nobody caught the least cold.

We had encampt so early, that we found time in the Evening to walk near half a Mile into the Woods. There we came upon a Family of Mulattoes, that call'd themselvs free, tho' by the Shyness of the Master of the House, who took care to keep least in Sight, their Freedom seem'd a little Doubtful. It is certain many Slaves Shelter themselves in this Obscure Part of the World, nor will any of their righteous Neighbours discover them. On the Contrary, they find their Account in Settling such Fugitives on some out-of-the-way-corner of their Land, to raise Stocks for a mean and inconsiderable Share, well knowing their Condition makes it necessary for them to Submit to any Terms.

---

[33] A corruption of poquosin, Indian word of Algonquian origin, denoting low, wooded ground, often covered with water.

11. We order'd the Surveyors early to their Business with 5 of the Men to attend them. They had a tiresome day's work of it, wading thro' a deep Pocoson near 2 Miles over, in which they frequently plung'd up to the Middle. In the mean time we Commissioners row'd up the River in our Periauga much more at our ease, & drop't Anchor at Mossy-Point near a deserted Pork-Store belonging to Capt Willis Wilson. After the Men had swept out a Cart load of Dirt, we put our Baggage into it for fear of Rain. Then we sent our Periauga in quest of the Surveyors, & Firebrand believing nothing cou'd be well done without him, went in it himself attended by Puzzlecause, tho' he did no other good but favour us with his Room instead of his Company. In the mean while Shoebrush & I took a walk into the Woods, and call'd at a Cottage where a Dark Angel surpriz'd us with her Charms. Her Complexion was a deep Copper, so that her fine Shape & regular Features made her appear like a Statue en Bronze done by a masterly hand. Shoebrush was smitten at the first Glance, and examined all her neat Proportions with a critical Exactness. She struggled just enough to make her Admirer more eager, so that if I had not been there, he wou'd have been in Danger of carrying his Joke a little too far.

The Surveyors found us out in the Evening very much fatigued, & the men were more off their mettle than ever they had been in the whole Journey, tho' without the least Complaint, I took up my Lodging in the Camp, but was driven into the House about Midnight without my Breeches, like Monsr Broylio by a smart Shower of Rain. Here we all lay in Bulk the rest of the Night upon a dirty & wet Floor without taking cold.

Nor were these worthy Borderers content to Shelter Runaway Slaves, but Debtors and Criminals have often met with the like Indulgence. But if the Government of North Carolina has encourag'd this unneighbourly Policy in order to increase their People, it is no more than what Ancient Rome did before them, which was made a City of Refuge for all Debtors and Fugitives, and from that wretched Beginning grew up in time to be Mistress of a great Part of the World.[34] And, considering how Fortune delights in bringing great things out of Small, who knows but Carolina may, one time or other, come to be the Seat of some other great Empire?

12.   Every thing had been to soakt with the Rain, that we were oblig'd to lie by a good Part of the Morning and dry them. However, that time was not lost, because it gave the Surveyors an Opportunity of Platting off their Work, and taking the Course of the River. It likewise helpt to recruit the Spirits of the Men, who had been a little harass'd with Yesterday's March. Notwithstanding all this, we crosst the River before Noon, and advanc'd our Line 3 Miles. It was not possible to make more of it, by reason good Part of the way was either Marsh or Pocoson. The Line cut two or three Plantations, leaving Part of them in Virginia, and part of them in Carolina. This was a Case that happen'd frequently, to the great Inconvenience of the Owners, who were therefore oblig'd to take out two Patents and Pay for a new Survey in each Government.

In the Evening we took up our Quarters in Mr. Ballance's Pasture, a little above the Bridge built over N W River. There we discharg'd the two Periaugas, which in truth had been very Servicable in transporting us over the Many Waters in that Dirty and Difficult Part of our Business.

Our Landlord had a tolerable good House and Clean Furniture, and yet we cou'd not be tempted to lodge in it. We chose rather to lye in the open Field, for fear of growing too tender. A clear Sky, spangled with Stars, was our Canopy, which being the last thing we saw before we fell asleep gave us Magnificent Dreams. The Truth of it is, we took so much pleasure in that natural kind of Lodging, that I think at the foot of the Account Mankind are great Losers by the Luxury of Feather-Beds and warm apartments.

The curiosity of beholding so new and withal so Sweet a Method of

---

[34] Reference is to the Carolina law of 1669 which prohibited suits for the recovery of debts already contracted against those who came into the colony until five years after their arrival. (*Colonial Records of North Carolina*. Vol. I, p. 183). Virginia had adopted a similar law in 1643, which was re-affirmed in 1663 and again in 1683. In 1717 it was the subject of complaint by British merchants and in 1718 it was disallowed. The North Carolina statute was also a subject of complaint as early as 1707, when the Board of trade brought it to the attention of the Privy Council, and it was disallowed (*Colonial Records*, Vol. I, p. 717). Another North Carolina statute giving priority to local over foreign creditors in suits for the collection of debts, enacted in 1715, was disallowed in 1747; and in 1767 a third statute exempting the property of debtors from execution unless action was brought within five years from the passage of the law, was declared void. See Russell's *Review of American Colonial Legislation by the King in Council, passim.*

12. Complaint was made to Me this Morning, that the Men belonging to the Periauga, had stole our People's Meat while they Slept. This provoked me to treat them a la Dragon, that is to swear at them furiously; & by the good Grace of my Oaths, I might have past for an Officer in his Majesty's Guards. I was the more out of Humour, because it disappointed us in our early March, it being a standing Order to boil the Pot over Night, that we might not be hinder'd in the Morning. This Accident, & Necessity of drying our Bed-Cloaths kept us from decamping til near 12 a Clock. By this delay the Surveyors found time to plot off their Work, and to observe the Course of the River. Then they past it over against Northern's Creek, the Mouth of which was very near our Line. But the Commissioners made the best of their way to the Bridge, and going ashoar walkt to Mr Ballance's Plantation. I retir'd early to our Camp at some distance from the House, while my Collegues tarry'd within Doors, & refresh't themselves with a Cheerful Bowl. In the Gaiety of their Hearts, they invited a Tallow-faced Wench that had sprain'd her Wrist to drink with them, and when they had rais'd her in good Humour, they examined all her hidden Charms, and play'd a great many gay Pranks. While Firebrand who had the most Curiosity, was ranging over her sweet Person, he pick't off several Scabs as big as Nipples, the Consequence of eating too much Pork. The poor Damsel was disabled from making any resistance by the Lameness of her Hand; all she cou'd do, was, to sit stil, & make the Fashionable Exclamation of the Country, Flesh a live & tear it, & by what I can understand she never spake so properly in her Life. One of the Representatives of N. Carolina made a Midnight Visit to

encamping, brought one of the Senators of N Carolina to make us a Midnight Visit. But he was so very Clamorous in his Commendations of it, that the Centinel, not seeing his Quality, either thro' his habit or Behaviour, had like to have treated him roughly.

After excusing the Unseasonableness of his Visit, and letting us know he was a Parliament Man, he swore he was so taken with our Lodging, that he would set Fire to his House as soon as he got Home, and teach his Wife and Children to lie, like us, in the open field.

13. Early this Morning our Chaplain repair'd to us with the Men we had left at Mr. Wilson's. We had sent for them the Evening before to relieve those who had the Labour-Oar from Corotuck-Inlet. But to our great surprise, they petition'd not to be reliev'd, hoping to gain immortal Reputation by being the first of Mankind that Ventur'd thro' the great Dismal. But the rest being equally Ambitious of the same Honour, it was but fair to decide their Pretensions by Lot. After Fortune had declar'd herself, those which she had excluded offer'd Money to the Happy Persons to go in their Stead. But Hercules would have as soon sold the Glory of Cleansing the Augean Stables, which was pretty near the same Sort of Work.

No sooner was the Controversy at an end, but we sent them unfortunate Fellows back to their Quarters, whom Chance had Condemn'd to remain upon Firm Land and Sleep in a whole Skin. In the mean while the Surveyors carry'd the Line 3 Miles, which was no Contemptible day's work, considering how cruelly they were entangled with Bryars and Gall Bushes. The Leaf of this last Shrub bespeaks it to be of the Alaternus Family.

Our Work ended within a Quarter of a Mile of the Dismal abovemention'd, where the Ground began to be already full of Sunken Holes and Slashes, which had, here and there, some few Reeds growing in them.

Tis hardly credible how little the Bordering inhabitants were acquainted with this mighty Swamp, nothwithstanding they had liv'd their whole lives within Smell of it. Yet, as great Strangers as they were to it, they pretended to be very exact in their Account of its Dimensions, and were positive it could not be above 7 or 8 Miles wide, but knew no more of the Matter than Star-gazers know of the Distance of the Fixt Stars. At the Same time, they were Simple enough to amuse our Men with Idle Stories of the Lyons, Panthers and Alligators, they were like to encounter in that dreadful Place.

In short, we saw plainly there was no Intelligence of this Terra Incognita to be got, but from our own Experience. For that Reason it was resolv'd to make the requisite Dispositions to enter it next Morning. We allotted every one of the Surveyors for this painful Enterprise, with 12 Men to attend them. Fewer than that cou'd not be employ'd in clearing the way, carrying the Chain, marking the Trees, and bearing the necessary Bedding and Provisions. Nor wou'd the Commissioners themselves have Spared

our Camp, & his Curiosity was so very clamorous that it waked
Me, for which I wish't his Nose as flat as any of his Porcivorous
Countrymen.

13.   In the Morning our Chaplain came to us, & with him some
Men we had sent for, to relieve those who had waded thro' the
Mire from Coratuck.   But they beg'd they might not be reliev'd,
believing they shou'd gain immortal Honour by going thro' the
Dismal.   Only Patillo desired to be excus'd, on the Account of his
Eyes.   Old Ellis Petition'd to go in the Room of his Son, and
Kimball was depriv'd from that favour by Lot.   That griev'd him
so, that he offer'd a Crown to Hambleton to let him go in his
room, which the other wou'd not Listen to for ten times the Money.
When this great affair was settled, we dismist all the Men to their
Quarters at Capt Wilson's, except the Nine Dismalites.   Of these
we sent 5 with the Surveyors who ran the Line to the Skirts of
the Dismal, which began first with Dwarf Reeds, & moist uneven
Grounds.   We discharged our Periaugas and about Noon our good
Friend Capt Wilkins conducted us to his own House, & entertain'd
us hospitably.   We made the necessary Disposition for entering
the Dismal next Morning with 9 of our Men, & 3 of Carolina, so
many being necessary to attend the Surveyors, & for carrying the
Bedding & Provisions.   The Men were in good Spirits but poor
Orion began to repent, & wish he had Slept in a whole Skin at the
College, rather than become a prey to Turkey-buzzard.   These
reflections sunk his Courage so low, that neither Liquor nor Toast
cou'd raise it.   I hardly knew how to behave myself in a Bed,
after having lain a week in the Open Field, & seeing the Stars
twinkle over my head.

their Persons on this Occasion, but for fear of adding to the poor men's Burthen, while they were certain they cou'd add nothing to their Resolution.

We quarter'd with our Friend and Fellow Traveller, William Wilkins, who had been our faithful Pilot to Coratuck, and liv'd about a mile from the Place where the Line ended. Everything lookt so very clean, and the Furniture so neat, that we were tempted to Lodge within Doors. But the Novelty of being shut up so close quite spoil'd our rest, nor did we breathe so free by abundance, as when we lay in the open Air.

14. Before nine of the Clock this Morning, the Provisions, Bedding and other Necessaries, were made up into Packs for the Men to carry on their Shoulders into the Dismal. They were victuall'd for 8 days at full Allowance, Nobody doubting but that wou'd be abundantly Sufficient to carry them thro' that Inhospitable Place; nor Indeed was it possible for the Poor Fellows to Stagger under more. As it was, their Loads weigh'd from 60 to 70 Pounds, in just Proportion to the Strength of those who were to bear them.

Twou'd have been unconscionable to have Saddled them with Burthens heavier than that, when they were to lugg them thro' a filthy Bogg, which was hardly practicable with no Burthen at all.

Besides this Luggage at their Backs, they were oblig'd to measure the distance, mark the Trees, and clear the way for the Surveyors every Step they went. It was really a Pleasure to see with how much Cheerfulness they undertook, and with how much Spirit they went thro' all this Drudgery. For their Greater Safety, the Commissioners took care to furnish them with Peruvian-Bark, Rhubarb and Hipocoacanah,[35] in case they might happen, in that wet Journey, to be taken with fevers or Fluxes.

Altho' there was no need for Example to inflame Persons already so cheerful, yet to enter the People with better grace, the Author and two more of the Commissioners accompanied them half a Mile into the Dismal. The Skirts of it were thinly Planted with Dwarf Reeds and Gall-Bushes, but when we got into the Dismal itself, we found the Reeds grew there much taller and closer, and, to mend the matter was so interlac'd with bamo-briars, that there was no scuffling thro' them without the help of Pioneers. At the same time, we found the Ground moist and trembling under our feet like a Quagmire, insomuch that it was an easy Matter to run a Ten-Foot-Pole up to the Head in it, without exerting any un-common Strength to do it.

Two of the Men, whose Burthens were the least cumbersome, had orders to march before, with their Tomahawks, and clear the way, in order to make an Opening for the Surveyors. By their Assistance we made a Shift to push the Line half a Mile in 3 Hours, and then reacht a small piece of firm Land, about 100 Yards wide, Standing up above the rest like an

---

[35] Probably Epecacuanha, an American plant used as an emetic.

14. This Morning early the Men began to make up the Packs they were to carry on their Shoulders into the Dismal. They were victual'd for 8 Days, which was judg'd sufficient for the Service. Those Provisions with the Blankets & other Necessaries loaded the Men with a Burthen of 50 or 60^{lb} for Each. Orion helpt most of all to make these Loads so heavy, by taking his Bed, and several changes of Raiment, not forgeting a Suit for Sundays along with him. This was a little unmercifull, which with his peevish Temper made him no Favorite. We fixt them out about ten in the Morning, & then Meanwell, Puzzlecause, & I went along with them, resolving to enter them fairly into this dreadful Swamp, which no body before ever had either the Courage or Curiosity to pass. But Firebrand & Shoebrush chose rather to toast their Noses over a good Fire, & Spare their dear Persons. After a March of 2 Miles thro' very bad way, the Men sweating under their Burthens, we arriv'd at the Edge of the Dismal, where the Surveyors had left off the Night before. Here Steddy thought proper to encourage the Men by a short harangue to this effect. "Gentlemen, "we are at last arriv'd at this dreadfull place, which til now has "been thought unpassable. Tho' I make no doubt but you will "convince every Body, that there is no difficulty which may not "be conquer'd by Spirit & constancy. You have hitherto behaved "with so much Vigour, that the most I can desire of you, is to "persevere unto the End; I protest to You the only reason we don't "Share in Your Fatigue, is, the fear of adding to Your Burthens, "(which are but too heavy already,) while we are Sure we can "add nothing to your Resolution. I shall say no more, but only "pray the Almighty to prosper your Undertaking, & grant we may "meet on the other Side in perfect Health & Safety." The Men took this Speech very kindly, and answer'd it in the most cheerful manner, with 3 Huzzas. Immediately we enter'd the

Island. Here the people were glad to lay down their Loads and take a
little refreshment, while the happy man, whose lot it was to carry the Jugg
of Rum, began already, like Aesop's Bread-Carriers to find it grow a good
deal lighter.

After reposing about an Hour, the Commissioners recommended Vigour
and Constancy to their Fellow-Travellers, by whom they were answer'd
with 3 Cheerful Huzzas, in Token of Obedience. This Ceremony was no
sooner over but they took up their Burthens and attended the Motion of
the Surveyors, who, tho' they workt with all their might, could reach but
one Mile farther, the same obstacles still attending them which they
had met with in the Morning.

However small this distance may seem so such as are us'd to travel at
their Ease, yet our Poor Men, who were oblig'd to work with an unwieldy Load at their Backs, had reason to think it a long way; Especially
in a Bogg where they had no firm Footing, but every Step made a deep
Impression, which was instantly fill'd with Water. At the same time they
were labouring with their Hands to cut down the Reeds, which were Ten-
feet high, their Legs were hampered with the Bryars. Besides, the Weather
happen'd to be very warm, and the tallness of the Reeds kept off every
Friendly Breeze from coming to refresh them. And, indeed, it was a
little provoking to hear the Wind whistling among the Branches of the
White Cedars, which grew here and there amongst the Reeds, and at the
same time not have the Comfort to feel the least Breath of it.

In the mean time the 3 Commissioners return'd out of the Dismal the
same way they went in, and having join'd their Brethren, proceeded that
Night as far as Mr. Wilson's.

This worthy Person lives within sight of the Dismal, in the Skirts
whereof his Stocks range and Maintain themselves all the Winter, and yet
he knew as little of it is he did of Terra Australis Incognita. He told us a
Canterbury Tale of a North Briton, whose Curiosity Spurr'd him a long
way into this great Desart, as he call'd it, near 20 Years ago, but he having
no Compass, nor seeing the Sun for several Days Together, wander'd
about till he was almost famisht; but at last he bethought himself of a
Secret his Countrymen make use of to Pilot themselves in a Dark day.

He took a fat Louse out of his Collar, and expos'd it to the open
day on a Piece of White Paper, which he brought along with him for his
Journal. The poor Insect having no Eye-lids, turn'd himself about till he
found the Darkest Part of the Heavens, and so made the best of his way
towards the North. By this Direction he Sterr'd himself Safe out, and
gave such a frightful account of the Monsters he saw, and the Distresses he
underwent, that no mortall Since has been hardy enough to go upon the
like dangerous Discovery.

Dismal, 2 Men clearing the way before the Surveyors, to enable them to take their Sight. The Reeds which grew about 12 feet high, were so thick, & so interlaced with Bamboe-Briars, that our Pioneers were forc't to open a Passage. The Ground, if I may properly call it so, was so Spungy, that the Prints of our Feet were instantly fill'd with Water. Amongst the Reeds here & there stood a white Cedar, commonly mistaken for Juniper. Of this Sort was the Soil for about half a Mile together, after which we came to a piece of high land about 100 Yards in Breadth. We were above 2 Hours scuffling thro' the Reeds to this Place, where we refresh't the poor Men. Then we took leave, recommending both them & the Surveyors to Providence. We furnish'd Astrolabe with Bark & other Medicines, for any of the People, that might happen to be Sick, not forgetting 3 Kinds of Rattle-Snake Root made into Doses in case of Need. It was 4 a Clock before we return'd to our Quarters, where we found our Collegues under some Apprehension that we were gone with the People quite thro' the Dismal. During my Absence Firebrand was so very carefull in sending away the Baggage, that he forgot the Candles. When we had settled Accounts with our Landlord, we rode away to Capt Wilson's, who treated us with Pork upon Pork. He was a great Lover of Conversation, & rather than it shou'd drop, he wou'd repeat the same Story over & over. Firebrand chose rather to litter the Floor, than lye with the Parson, & since he cou'd not have the best Bed, he sullenly wou'd have none at all. However it broil'd upon his Stomach so much, that he swore anough in the Night, to bring the Devil into the Room had not the Chaplain been there.

15. The Surveyors pursued their work with all Diligence, but Still found the Soil of the Dismal so Spongy that the Water ouzed up into every foot-step they took. To their Sorrow, too, they found the Reeds and Bryars more firmly interwoven than they did the day before. But the greatest Grievance was from large Cypresses, which the Wind had blown down and heap'd upon one another. On the Limbs of most of them grew Sharp Snags, Pointing every way like so many Pikes, that requir'd much Pains and Caution to avoid.

These Trees being Evergreens, and Shooting their Large Tops Very high, are easily overset by every Gust of Wind, because there is no firm Earth to Steddy their Roots. Thus many of them were laid prostrate to the great Encumbrance of the way. Such Variety of Difficulties made the Business go on heavily, insomuch that, from Morning till Night, the Line could advance no further than 1 Mile and 31 Poles. Never was Rum, that cordial of Life, found more necessary than it was in this Dirty Place. It did not only recruit the People's Spirits, now almost Jaded with Fatigue, but serv'd to correct the Badness of the Water, and at the same time to resist the Malignity of the Air. Whenever the Men wanted to drink, which was very often, they had nothing more to do but to make a Hole, and the Water bubbled up in a Moment. But it was far from being either clear or well tasted, and had besides a Physical Effect, from the Tincture it receiv'd from the Roots of the Shrubbs and Trees that grew in the Neighbourhood.

While the Surveyors were thus painfully employ'd, the Commissioners discharged the long Score they had with Mr. Wilson, for the Men and Horses which had been quarter'd upon him during our Expedition to Coratuck. From thence we march'd in good Order along the East Side of the Dismal, and passt the long Bridge that lies over the South Branch of Elizabeth River. At the End of 18 Miles we reacht Timothy Ivy's Plantation, where we picht our Tent for the first Time, and were furnisht with every thing the Place afforded.

We perceiv'd the happy Effects of Industry in this Family, in which every one lookt tidy and clean, and carri'd in their countenances the chearful Marks of Plenty. We saw no Drones there, which are but too Common, alas, in that Part of the World. Tho', in truth, the Distemper of Laziness seizes the Men oftener much than the Women. These last Spin, weave and knit, all with their own Hands, while their Husbands, depending on the Bounty of the Climate, are Sloathfull in every thing but getting of Children, and in that only Instance make themselves useful Members of an Infant-Colony.

There is but little Wool in that Province, tho' Cotton grows very kindly, and, so far South, is Seldom nippt by the Frost. The Good Women mix this with their Wool for their outer Garments; tho', for want of Fulling,

15. We sent away the Baggage about 8 a Clock under the Guard of 4 Men. We paid off a long reckoning to Capt. Wilson, for our Men & Horses, but Firebrand forgot to pay for the washing of his Linen, which saved him 2 Shillings at least. He & his Flatterer Shoebrush left us to ourselves, intending to reach Capt. Meads, but losing their way, they took up at Mr Peugh's, after riding above 50 miles, & part of the way in the dark. How many Curses this Misadventure cost them I cant say, tho' at least as many as they rode Miles. I was content to tarry to see the Men fixt out & jog on fair & softly along with them, & so were Meanwell & Puzzlecause. One of our Men had a Kick on the Belly by a Horse, for which I order'd him to be instantly Blooded, & no ill consequence ensued. We left Astrolabe's Negro Sick behind us. About 11 we set off, & call'd at an Ordinary 8 Miles off, not far from the great Bridge. Then we proceeded 8 Miles farther to honest Timothy Jones who supply'd us with every thing that was necessary. He had a tal straight Daughter of a Yielding Sandy Complexion, who having the curiosity to see the Tent, Puzzlecause gallanted her thither, & might have made her free of it, had not we come reasonably to save the Damsel's Chastity. Here both our Cookery & Bedding were more cleanly than Ordinary. The Parson lay with Puzzlecause in the Tent, to keep him honest, or peradventure, to partake of his diversion if he shou'd be otherwise.

that kind of Manufacture is Open and Sleazy. Flax likewise thrives there extreamly, being perhaps as fine as any in the World, and I question not might, with a little care, and pains, be brought to rival that of Egypt; and yet the Men are here so intolerable Lazy, they seldom take the trouble to propagate it.

16. The Line was this day carry'd one Mile and half and 16 Poles. The Soil continued soft and Miry, but fuller of Trees, especially White cedars. Many of these too were thrown down and piled in Heaps, high enough for a good Muscovite Fortification. The worst of it was, the Poor Fellows began now to be troubled with Fluxes, occasion'd by bad Water and moist Lodgings: but chewing of Rhubarb kept that Malady within Bounds.

In the mean time the Commissioners decampt early in the Morning, and made a March of 25 Miles, as far as Mr. Andrew Mead's,[36] who lives upon Nansimand River. They were no sooner got under the Shelter of that Hospitable Roof, but it began to rain hard, and continued so to do great part of the Night. This gave them much Pain for their Friends in the Dismal, whose sufferings spoilt their Taste for the good Chear, wherewith they were entertain'd themselves.

However, late that Evening, these poor Men had the Fortune to come upon another Terra-firma, which was the Luckyer for them, because the Lower ground, by the rain that fell, was made a fitter Lodging for Tadpoles than men.

In our Journey we remarkt that the North Side of this great Swamp lies higher than either the East on the West, nor were the approaches to it so full of Sunken Grounds. We passt by no less than two Quaker Meeting Houses, one of which had an Awkward Ornament on the West End of it, that seem'd to Ape a Steeple. I must own I expected no such Piece of Foppery from a Sect of so much outside Simplicity.

That persuasion prevails much in the lower end of Nansimond county, for want of Ministers to Pilot the People a decenter way to Heaven.

The ill Reputation of Tobacco planted in those lower Parishes makes the Clergy unwilling to accept of them, unless it be such whose abilities are as mean as their Pay. Thus, whether the Churches be quite void or but indifferently filled, the Quakers will have an Opportunity of gaining Proselytes. Tis a wonder no Popish Missionaries are sent from Maryland to labour in this Neglected Vineyard, who we know have Zeal enough to traverse Sea and Land on the Meritorious Errand of making converts.

Nor is it less Strange that some Wolf in Sheep's cloathing arrives not from New England to lead astray a Flock that has no shepherd. People uninstructed in any Religion are ready to embrace the first that offers. Tis natural for helpless man to adore his Maker in Some Form or other,

---

[36] See note 37, *Secret History*.

16. We march't from hence about 9 always giving our Baggage
the Start of Us. We call'd at John Ive's for a Tast of good Water,
which is as rare in these parts as good Doctrine. We saw several
pretty Girls here as wild as Colts, tho' not so ragged, but drest
all in their own Industry. Even those cou'd not tempt us to alight,
but we pursued our Journey with Diligence. We past by M^r
Osheild's, & Mr Pugh's, the last of which has a very good Brick
House, & arriv'd about 4 at Capt Meads.[37] Here amongst other
Strong Liquors we had plenty of Strong Beer, with which we made
as free as our Libertines did with the Parson. The Carolina Commissioners did not only persecute him with their Wit, but with
their Kisses too, which he suffer'd with the Patience of a Martyr.
We were no sooner under the Shelter of that hospitable House,
but it began to rain & so continu'd to do great Part of the Night,
which put in some Pain for our Friends in the Dismal. The
Journey this Day was 25 Miles, yet the Baggage Horses perform'd
it without faltering.

[handwritten marginal note: almost religious sarcastic]

---

[37] Andrew Meade, of Irish parentage, who came to Virginia about 1690 and settled
on Nansemond River near Suffolk. He was a member of the House of Burgesses,
1727-1734, and of the County Court, and was Senior Captain of Militia. See Basker-
ville's *Andrew Meade of Ireland and Virginia*.

and were there any exception to this Rule, I should expect it to be among the Hottentots of the Cape of Good Hope and of North Carolina.

There fell a great deal of Rain in the Night, accompany'd with a Strong Wind. The fellow-feeling we had for the poor Dismalites, on Account of this unkind Weather, render'd the Down we laid upon uneasy. We fancy'd them half-drown'd in their Wet Lodging, with the Trees blowing down about their Ears. These Were the Gloomy Images our Fears Suggested; tho' twas so much uneasiness clear again. They happen'd to come of much better, by being luckily encampt on the dry piece of Ground afore-mention'd.

17. They were, however, forct to keep the Sabbath in Spite of their Teeth, contrary to the Dispensation our good Chaplain had given them. Indeed, their Short allowance of Provision would have justity'd their making the best of their way, without Distinction of days. Twas certainly a Work both of Necessity and Self-preservation, to save themselves from Starving. Nevertheless, the hard Rain had made everything so thoroughly wet, that it was quite impossible to do any Business. They therefore made a vertue of what they could not help, and contentedly rested in their dry situation.

Since the Surveyors had enter'd the Dismal they had laid Eyes on no living Creature: neither Bird nor Beast, Insect nor Reptile came in View. Doubtless, the Eternal Shade that broods over this mighty Bog, and hinders the sun-beams from blessing the Ground, makes it an uncomfortable Habitation for any thing that has life. Not so much as a Zealand Frog cou'd endure so Aguish a Situation.

It had one Beauty, however, that delighted the Eye, tho' at the Expense of all the other Senses: the Moisture of the Soil preserves a continual Verdure, and makes every Plant an Evergreen, but at the same time the foul Damps ascend without ceasing, corrupt the Air, and render it unfit for Respiration. Not even a Turkey-Buzzard will venture to fly over it, no more than the Italian Vultures will over the filthy Lake Avernus, or the Birds in the Holy-Land over the Salt Sea, where Sodom and Gomorrah formerly stood.[37]

---

[37] "Byrd's description of this swamp is too unfavorable. The place is not uninhabited at this day. Persons who live in the adjacent country go thither to hunt bears and deer as well as wild cats. In the swamp is Lake Drummond, a favorite angling ground for local sportsmen. The water, which from its dark color might well seem unwholesome to the observers, is discolored by the roots of juniper-trees which abound there. It is popularly called "juniper water" and is held in such high esteem as drinking water that the inhabitants of the whole region send for it for many miles. I am assured also that there are many snakes in the swamp and the only reason Byrd's surveyors did not encounter them was the early season at which the expedition was made." (Bassett's Note, p. 60 of his edition.)

17. It rain'd this Morning til 10 a Clock, which fill'd us all with the Vapours. I gave my self a thorough wash and Scrub'd off a full weeks dirt, which made me fitter to attend the Service which our Chaplain perform'd. I wrote to the Governor a particular Account of our Proceedings, & had the Complaisance to show the Letter to my Collegues. These worthy Gentlemen had hammer'd out an Epistle to the Governor containing a kind of Remonstrance against paying the Burgesses in Money, & prevail'd with our Landlord to deliver it. At Night we had a religious Bowl to the pious Memory of St. Patrick, & to shew due Regard to this Saint several of the Company made some Hybernian Bulls: But the Parson unhappily out-blunder'd all, which made his Persecutors merry at his Cost.

In these sad Circumstances, the Kindest thing we cou'd do for our Suffering Friends was to give them a place in the Litany. Our Chaplain, for his Part, did his Office, and rubb'd us up with a Seasonable Sermon. This was quite a new thing to our Brethren of North Carolina, who live in a climate where no clergyman can Breathe, any more than Spiders in Ireland.[38]

For want of men in Holy Orders, both the Members of the Council and Justices of the Peace are empower'd by the Laws of that Country to marry all those who will not take One another's Word; but for the ceremony of Christening their children, they trust that to chance.[39] If a Parson come in their way, they will crave a Cast of his office, as they call it, else they are content their Offspring should remain as Arrant Pagans as themselves. They account it among their greatest advantages that they are not Priest-ridden, not remembering that the Clergy is rarely guilty of Bestriding such as have the misfortune to be poor.

One thing may be said for the Inhabitants of that Province, that they are not troubled with any Religious Fumes, and have the least Superstition of any People living. They do not know Sunday from any other day, any more than Robison Crusoe did, which would give them a great Advantage were they given to be industrious.[40] But they keep so many Sabbaths every week, that their disregard of the Seventh Day has no manner of cruelty in it, either to Servants or Cattle.

It was with some difficulty we cou'd make our People quit the good chear they met with at this House, so it was late before we took our Departure; but to make us amends, our Landlord was so good as to conduct us Ten Miles on our Way, as far as the Cypress Swamp, which drains itself into the Dismal. Eight Miles beyond that we forded the Waters of Coropeak, which tend the same way as do many others on that side. In Six Miles more we reacht the Plantation of Mr. Thomas Spight, a Grandee of N Carolina.[41] We found the good Man upon his Crutches,

---

[38] In this and the two following paragraphs, Byrd writes with the prejudice of a member of the Established Church. So also wrote Governor Burrington. (*Colonial Records of North Carolina.* Vol. III, pp. 152-158.) The Church was established by law in 1701, but opposition by dissenters and liberal churchmen resulted in great confusion, which culminated in the Cary Rebellion. (See Weeks, S. B., *Religious Development in the Province of North Carolina,* Baltimore, 1892.) In 1715 a new church law was adopted. Prior to 1728 the Society for the Propagation of the Gospel had sent to North Carolina thirteen ministers and one schoolmaster. Three of the four North Carolina boundary commissioners were churchmen, Moseley, Gale and Little, and also Swann, the surveyor.

[39] In 1669, because of the absence of clergymen in the colony, marriage was made a civil contract. By the vestry law of 1715, magistrates were permitted to perform the marriage ceremony, "in such parishes where no minister shall be resident," and in 1741 the right was confined to the clergy of the Church of England and magistrates.

[40] Yet in 1715 the North Carolina Assembly required the observance of the Lord's Day "with the proper acts of piety," prohibiting any trade or work thereon, and declared January 30 and September 22 days of fasting and prayer, and designated May 29 as a holy day. See *Colonial Records,* Vol. XXIII, p. 3.

[41] See *Secret History,* Note 38.

[Continued on page 75]

being crippled with the Gout in both his Knees. Here we flatter'd ourselves we should by this time meet with good Tydings of the Surveyors,
but had reckon'd, alas! without our Host: on the Contrary, we were told
the Dismal was at least Thirty Miles wide at that Place. However, as
nobody could say this on his own Knowledge, we Order'd Guns to be fired
and a Drum to be beaten, but receiv'd no Answer, unless it was from that
prating Nymph Echo, who, like a loquacious Wife, will always have the
last Word, and Sometimes return three for one.

18. It was indeed no Wonder our Signal was not heard at that time,
by the People in the Dismal, because, in Truth they had not then penetrated one Third of their way. They had that Morning fallen to work
with great Vigour; and, finding the Ground better than Ordinary, drove
on the Line 2 Miles and 38 poles. This was reckon'd an Herculean day's
Work, and yet they would not have Stopp'd there, had not an impenetrable
cedar Thicket chekt their Industry. Our Landlord had seated Himself
on the Borders of this Dismal, for the Advantage of the Green Food His
Cattle find there all Winter, and for the Rooting that Supports His Hogs.
This, I own, is some convenience to his Purse, for which his whole Family
pay dear in their Persons, for they are devoured by musketas all the
Summer, and have Agues every Spring and Fall, which Corrupt all the
Juices of their Bodies, give them a cadaverous complexion, and besides
a lazy, creeping Habit, which they never get rid of.

19. We Ordered Several Men to Patrole on the Edge of the Dismal,
both towards the North and towards the South, and to fire Guns at proper
Distances. This they perform'd very punctually, but cou'd hear nothing in
return, nor gain any Sort of Intelligence. In the mean time whole Flocks
of Women and Children flew hither to Stare at us, with as much curiosity
as if we had lately Landed from Bantam or Morocco.

Some Borderers, too, had a great Mind to know where the Line wou'd
come out, being for the most part Apprehensive lest their Lands
Should be taken into Virginia. In that case they must have submitted
to some Sort of Order and Government; whereas, in N Carolina, every
One does what seems best in his own Eyes. There were some good
Women that brought their children to be Baptiz'd, but brought no Capons
along with them to make the solemnity cheerful. In the mean time it was
Strange that none came to be marry'd in such a Multitude, if it had only
been for the Novelty of having their Hands Joyn'd by one in Holy Orders.
Yet so it was, that tho' our chaplain Christen'd above an Hundred, he did
not marry so much as one Couple dureing the whole Expedition. But mar-
riage is reckon'd a Lay contract in Carolina, as I said before, and a Country
Justice can tie the fatal Knot there, as fast as an Arch-Bishop.

None of our Visiters could, however, tell us any News of the Surveyors,

18. It was not possible to get from so good a House before 11
a Clock, nor then neither for our Servants. When Firebrand ask't
his Man why he lagg'd behind, he exprest himself with great Freedom of his Master, swearing he cared for no Mortal but his dear
self, & wishing that the Devil might take him, if he ever attended
him again in any of his Travels. We made the best of our way
to Mr Tho. Speight's, who appear'd to be a Grandee of North-
Carolina.[38] There we arriv'd about 4, tho' the Distance cou'd
not be less than 25 Miles. Upon our Arrival our poor Landlord
made a Shift to crawl out upon his Crutches, having the Gout in
both his Knees. He bid us welcome, & a great Bustle was made
in the Family, about our Entertainment. We saw 2 truss[39] Damsels
stump about very Industriously, that were handsome enough upon
a March. Our Landlord gave us much Concern, by affirming with
some Assurance, that the Dismal cou'd not be less than 30 Miles
in Breadth. All our Comfort was, that his Computation depended
wholly on his own wild Conjecture. We ordered Guns to be
fired & a Drum to be beaten to try if we cou'd be answer'd out of
the Desert, but we had no answer, but from that making Slut Echo.
The Servants ty'd the Horses so carelessly that some of them did
our Landlord much Damage in his Fodder. I was the more concern'd at this, because the poor Man did all he cou'd to supply our
Wants. Firebrand & the Parson lay single while some were oblig'd
to stow 3 in a Bed. Nor cou'd lying soft & alone cure the first of
these of swearing outrageously in his Sleep.

19. We dispatch't Men to the North & South to fire Guns on the
Edge of the Dismal by way of Signal, but cou'd gain no Intelligence of our People. Men, Women, and Children flockt from the
Neighbourhood, to stare at us with as much Curiosity as if we had
been Morrocco Embassadors. Many Children were brought to

---

[38] Thomas Speight, of Perquimans County, member of the North Carolina Assembly
in 1725 and Associate Justice of the General Court, 1726-28.
[39] Stout, well-formed.

nor Indeed was it possible any of them shou'd at that time, They being still laboring in the Midst of the Dismal.

It seems they were able to carry the Line this Day no further than one mile and 61 Poles, and that whole distance was thro' a Miry cedar Bogg, where the ground trembled under their Feet most frightfully. In many places too their Passage was retarded by a great number of fallen Trees, that lay Horsing upon one Another.

Tho' many circumstances concurr'd to make this an unwholesome Situation, yet the Poor men had no time to be sick, nor can one conceive a more Calamitous Case than it would have been to be laid up in that uncomfortable Quagmire. Never were Patients more tractable, or willing to take Physick, than these honest Fellows; but it was from a Dread of laying their Bones in a Bogg that wou'd soon spew them up again. That Consideration also put them upon more caution about their Lodging.

They first cover'd the Ground with Square Pieces of Cypress bark, which now, in the Spring, they cou'd easily Slip off the Tree for that purpose. On this they Spread their Bedding; but unhappily the Weight and Warmth of their Bodies made the Water rise up betwixt the Joints of the Bark, to their great Inconvenience. Thus they lay not only moist, but also exceedingly cold, because their Fires were continually going out. For no sooner was the Trash upon the Surface burnt away, but immediately the Fire was extinguisht by the Moisture of the Soil, Insomuch that it was great part of the Centinel's Business to rekindle it again in a Fresh Place, every Quarter of an Hour. Nor cou'd they indeed do their duty better, because Cold was the only Enemy they had to Guard against in a miserable Morass, where nothing can inhabit.

20. We could get no Tidings yet of our Brave Adventurers, notwithstanding we despatcht men to the likeliest Stations to enquire after them. They were still Scuffling in the Mire, and could not Possibly forward the Line this whole day more than one Mile and 64 Chains. Every Step of this Day's Work was thro' a cedar Bog, where the Trees were somewhat Smaller and grew more into a Thicket. It was now a great Misfortune to the Men to find their Provisions grow less as their Labour grew greater; They were all forct to come to short Allowance, and consequently to work hard without filling their Bellies. Tho' this was very severe upon English Stomachs, yet the People were so far from being discomfited at it, that they still kept up their good Humor, and merrily told a young Fellow in the Company, who lookt very Plump and Wholesome, that he must expect to go first to Pot, if matters shou'd come to Extremity.

our Chaplain to be christen'd, but no Capons, so that all the good he did that way was gratis. Maj^r Alston & Capt. Baker made us a visit & din'd with us.[40] My Landlord's Daughter Rachel offer'd her Service to wash my Linnen, & regal'd me with a Mess of Hominy toss't up with Rank Butter & Glyster Sugar. This I was forc't to eat, to shew that nothing from so fair a hand cou'd be disagreeable. She was a smart Lass, & when I desired the Parson to make a Memorandum of his Christenings, that we might keep an Account of the good we did, she ask't me very pertly, who was to keep an Account of the Evil? I told her she shou'd be my Secretary for that, if she wou'd go along with me. Mr Pugh & Mr Oshield help't to fill up our House, so that my Landlady told us in her cups, that now we must lie 3 in a Bed.

20. No News yet of our Dismalities tho' we dispatch't Men to every point of the Compass to enquire after them. Our Visitors took their Leave, but others came in the Evening to supply their Places. Judge Jumble who left us at Coratuck, return'd now from Edenton, and brought 3 Cormorants along with him. One was his own Brother,[41] the 2^d was Brother to Shoebrush,[42] & the 3^d Capt. Genneau, who had sold his Commission & spent the money. These honest Gentlemen had no business, but to help drink out our Liquor, having very little at Home. Shoebrush's Brother is a Collector, & owes his Place to a Bargain he made with Firebrand. Never were understrappers so humble, as the N. Carolina Collectors are to this huge Man. They pay him the same Colirt they

---

[40] The Alstons and Bakers were families of Chowan County, North Carolina.
[41] Edmund Gale.
[42] Thomas Lovick of Chowan County, Collector of the Customs.

This was only said by way of Jest, yet it made Him thoughtful in earnest. However, for the Present he return'd them a very civil answer, letting them know that, dead or alive, he shou'd be glad to be useful to such worthy good Friends. But, after all, this Humorous Saying had one very good Effect, for that yonker, who before was a little enclin'd by his Constitution to be lazy, grew on a Sudden Extreamly Industrious, that so there might be less Occasion to carbonade him for the good of his Fellow-Travellers.

While our Friends were thus embarrast in the Dismal, the Commissioners began to ly under great uneasiness for them. They knew very well their Provisions must by this time begin to fall Short, nor cou'd they conceive any likely means of a Supply. At this time of the Year both the Cattle and Hoggs had forsaken the Skirts of the Dismal, invited by the Springing Grass on the firm Land. All our hopes were that Providence wou'd cause some Wild Game to fall in their way, or else direct them to a wholesome Vegetable for Subsistence. In Short they were haunted with so many Frights on this Occasion, that they were in truth more uneasy than the Persons whose Case they lamented.

We had several Visiters from Edenton, in the Afternoon, that came with Mr. Gale, who had prudently left us at Coratuck, to Scuffle thro' that dirty Country by our Selves. These Gentlemen, having good Noses, had smelt out, at 30 Miles Distance, the Precious Liquor, with which the Liberality of our good Friend Mr. Mead had just before Supply'd us. That generous Person had judg'd very right, that we were now got out of the Latitude of Drink proper for men in Affliction, and therefore was so good as to send his Cart loaden with all sorts of refreshments, for which the Commissioners return'd Him their Thanks, and the Chaplain His Blessing.

21. The Surveyors and their Attendants began now in good Earnest to be alarm'd with Apprehensions of Famine, nor could they forbear looking with Some Sort of Appetite upon a dog that had been the faithful Companion of their Travels.

Their Provisions were now near exhausted. They had this Morning made the last Distribution, that so each might Husband his small Pittance as he pleas'd. Now it was that the fresh Colour'd Young Man began to tremble every Joint of Him, having dreamed, the Night before, that the Indians were about to Barbacue him over live coals.

The Prospect of Famine determin'd the People, at last, with one consent, to abandon the Line for the Present, which advanced but slowly, and make the best of their way to firm Land. Accordingly they sat off very early, and, by the help of the Compass which they carried along with them, Steer'd a direct Westwardly Course. They marcht from Morning till

wou'd do, if they held their Commissions immediately from his
Will & Pleasure.   Tho' the Case is much otherwise, because their
Commissions are as good as his, being granted by the same Com-
missioners of his Majesty's Customers.   However he expects a
World of Homage from them, calling them his Officers.   Nor is
he content with homage only, but he taxes them, as indeed he
does all the other Collectors of his Province with a hundred little
Services.

At Night the Noble Captain retir'd before the rest of the company,
& was stepping without Ceremony into our Bed, but I arriv'd just
time enough to prevent it.   We cou'd not possibly be so civil to
this free Gentleman, as to make him so great a Compliment:
Much less let him take possession according to the Carolina Breeding without Invitation.   Had Ruth or Rachel my Landlord's
Daughters taken this Liberty; We shou'd perhaps have made no
Words: but in truth the Captain had no Charms that merited so
particular an Indulgence.

21.   Several Persons from several parts came to see Us amongst
which was Mr Baker & his Brother the Surveyor of Nansimond,
but cou'd tell us no Tydings from the Dismal.   We began to be
in pain for the Men who had been trotting in that Bogg so long,
& the more because we apprehended a Famine amongst them.
I had indeed given a Warrant to kill any thing that came in their
way in case of Necessity, not knowing that no living Creature cou'd
inhabit that inhospitable Place.   My Landlord thought our Stay
here as tedious as we did, because we eat up his corn and Summer
Provisions.   However the Hopes of being well paid render'd that
Evil more Supportable.   But Complaint being made that the Corn
grew low, We retrench't the poor Man's Horses to one Meal a day.
In the Evening Plausible & Puzzlecause return'd to Us from Edenton, where they had been to recover the great Fatigue of doing
nothing, & to pick up new Scandal against their Governour.

Night, and Computed their Journey to amount to about 4 Miles, which was a great way, considering the difficulties of the Ground. It was all along a Cedar-Swamp, so dirty and perplext, that if they had not travell'd for their Lives, they cou'd not have reacht so far.

On their way they espied a Turkey-Buzzard, that flew prodigiously high to get above the Noisome Exhalations that ascend from that filthy place. This they were willing to understand as a good Omen, according to the Superstitions of the Ancients, who had great Faith in the Flight of Vultures. However, after all this tedious Journey, they could yet discover no End of their Toil, which made them very pensive, especially after they had eat the last Morsel of their Provisions. But to their unspeakable comfort, when all was husht in the Evening, they heard the Cattle low, and the Dogs bark, very distinctly, which, to Men in that distress, was more delightful Music than Faustina or Farinelli cou'd have made. In the mean time the Commissioners could get no News of them from any of their Visiters, who assembled from every Point of the Compass.

But the good Landlord had Visitors of another kind while we were there, that is to say, some industrious Masters of Ships, that lay in Nansimond River. These worthy Commanders came to bespeak Tobacco from these Parts to make up their Loadings, in Contempt of the Virginia Law, which Positively forbad their taking in any made in North Carolina.[42] Nor was this Restraint at all unreasonable; because they have no Law in Carolina, either to mend the Quality or lessen the quantity of Tobacco, or so much as to prevent the turning out of Seconds, all which cases have been provided against by the Laws of Virginia. Wherefore, there can be no reason why the Inhabitants of that Province Shou'd have the same Advantage of Shipping their Tobacco in our Parts, when they will by no means submit to the same Restrictions that we do.

22. Our Patrole happen'd not to go far enough to the Northward this Morning, if they had, the People in the Dismal might have heard the Report of their Guns. For this Reason they return'd without any Tydings, which threw us into a great tho' unnecessary Perplexity. This was now the Ninth day since they enter'd into that inhospitable Swamp, and consequently we had reason to believe their Provisions were quite Spent.

We knew they workt hard, and therefore would eat heartily, so long as they had wherewithal to recruit their Spirits, not imagining the Swamp so wide as they found it. Had we been able to guess where the Line wou'd come out, we wou'd have sent men to meet them with a fresh Supply; but as we cou'd know nothing of that, and as we had neither Compass nor Surveyor to guide a Messenger on such an Errand, we were

---

[42] In 1679 Virginia prohibited the importation of North Carolina tobacco, but this was repeated in 1705 and 1726. (Hening, II 445, III 253, IV 175.) It is interesting to note that this policy was a subject of protest to the British government by Richard Fitz-William. (*Colonial Records of North Carolina*, Vol. II, pp. 684, 816.)

22.   Our disagreeable Carolina Visitors were so kind as to take their Leave, so did Mr Osheilds & Capt Toot, by which our Company & my Landlord's Trouble were considerably lessen'd.   We went out several Ways in the Morning, & cou'd get no intelligence. But in the Afternoon Bootes brought us the welcome News that the Surveyors & all the People were come safe out of the Dismal. They landed if one may so call it, near 6 Miles North of this Place about ten this Morning not far from the House of Peter Brinkley.   Here they appeas'd their Hungry Stomachs, and waited to receive our Orders.   It seems the Distance thro' the Desart where they past it was 15 Miles.   Of this they had mark't &

unwilling to expose him to no Purpose; Therefore, all we were able to do for them, in so great an Extremity, was to recommend them to a Merciful Providence.

However long we might think the time, yet we were cautious of Shewing our uneasiness, for fear of Mortifying our Landlord. He had Done his best for us, and therefore we were unwilling he should think us dissatisfy'd with our Entertainment. In the midst of our concern, we were most argeeably surpriz'd, just after Dinner, with the News that the Dismalites were all Safe. These blessed Tidings were brought to us by Mr. Swan, the Carolina-Surveyor, who came to us in a very tatter'd condition.

After very Short Salutations, we got about Him as if He had been a Hottentot, and began to Inquire into his Adventures. He gave us a Detail of their uncomfortable Voyage thro' the Dismal, and told us, particularly, they had pursued their Journey early that Morning, encouraged by the good Omen of seeing the Crows fly over their Heads; that, after an Hour's march over very Rotten Ground, they, on a Sudden, began to find themselves among tall Pines, that grew in the Water, which in Many Places was Knee-deep. This Pine Swamp, into which that of Coropeak drain'd itself, extended near a Mile in Breadth; and tho' it was exceedingly wet, yet it was much harder at Bottom than the rest of the Swamp; that about Ten in the Morning, they recovered firm Land, which they embraced with as much Pleasure as Shipwreckt Wretches do the shoar.

After these honest adventurers had congratulated each other's Deliverance, their first Inquiry was for a good House, where they might Satisfy the Importunity of their Stomachs. Their good Genius directed them to Mr. Brinkley's, who dwells a little to the Southward of the Line. This Man began immediately to be very inquisitive, but they declar'd they had no Spirits to answer Questions till after Dinner.

"But pray, Gentlemen," said he, "answer me One Question at least: what shall we get for your Dinner?" To which they replied, "No Matter what, provided it be but Enough." He kindly supply'd their Wants as soon as possible, and by the Strength of that Refreshment they made a Shift to come to us in the Evening, to tell their own Story. They all lookt very thin, and as ragged as the Gibeonite Ambassadors did in the days of Yore. Our Surveyors told us they had measur'd Ten Miles in the Dismal, and Computed the Distance they had Marcht since to amount to about five more, So they made the whole Breadth to be 15 Miles in all.

measur'd no more than ten, but had travers'd the remainder as fast as they cou'd for their Lives. They were reduced to such Straights that they began to look upon John Ellis's Dog with a longing Appetite, & John Evans who was fat & well liking, had reasons to fear that he wou'd be the next Morsel. We sent Astrolabe's Horses for him & his Brother, & Firebrand ordered Peter Jones with an air of Authority to send his Horse for Orion: but he let him understand very frankly that nobody shou'd ride his Horse but himself, so not finding his Commands obeyed by the Virginians, he try'd his Power amongst the Carolina Men, who were more at his Devotion, & sent one of their Horses for his Friend, to save his own; he also sent him a Pottle-Bottle of Strong Beer particularly, without any regard to Astrolabe, tho' the Beer Belong'd to the other Commissioners, as much as to him. We also sent Horses for the Men, that they might come to us & refresh themselves after so dreadfull a Fatigue. They had however gone thro' it all with so much Fortitude, that they discover'd as much Strength of Mind as of Body. They were now all in perfect Health, tho' their moist Lodging for so many Nights, & drinking of Standing Water tinged with the Roots of Juniper, had given them little Fevers & Slight Fluxes in their Passage, which as slight Remedys recover'd. Since I mention'd the Strong Beer, It will be but just to remember Capt Meads Generosity to Us. His Cart arriv'd here Yesterday with a very handsome present to the Commissioners of Virginia. It brought them 2 Doz. Quart Bottles of Excellent Madera Wine, 1 Doz. Pottle Bottles of Strong Beer, & half a Dozen Quarts of Jamaica Rum. To this general Present was added a particular One to Meanwell, of Naples-Biscuit from Mrs Mead. At the same time we receiv'd a very Polite Letter, which gave a good Grace to his Generosity, & doubled our Obligation. And surely never was Bounty better timed, when it enabled us to regale the poor Dismalites whose Spirits needed some Recruit. And indeed we needed comfort as well as they, for tho' we had not shared with them in the Labours of the Body yet we made it up with the Labour of the Mind, and our Fears had brought us as low, as our Fatigue had done them. I wrote a Letter of thanks

23. It was very reasonable that the Surveyors, and the men who had been Sharers in their Fatigue, should now have a little Rest. They were all, except one, in good Health and good heart, blessed be God! notwithstanding the dreadful Hardships they had gone through. It was really a Pleasure to see the Chearfulness wherewith they receiv'd the Order to prepare to re-enter the Dismal on the Monday following, in order to continue the Line from the Place where they had left off measuring, that so we might have the Exact Breadth of that Dirty Place. There were no more than two of them that cou'd be perswaded to be reliev'd on this Occasion, or Suffer the other men to Share the Credit of that bold Undertaking, Neither wou'd these have Suffer'd it had not one of them been very lame, and the Other much Indispos'd.

By the Description the Surveyors gave of the Dismal, we were convinc'd that nothing but the Exceeding dry Season we had been bless'd with cou'd have made the passing of it practicable. It is the Source of no less than five Several Rivers which discharge themselves Southward into Albemarle Sound, and of two that run northerly into Virginia. From thence tis easy to imagine that the Soil must be thoroughly Soakt with Water, or else there must be plentiful Stores of it under Ground; to supply so many Rivers; especially since there is no Lake, or any considerable Body of that Element to be seen on the Surface. The Rivers that Head in it from Virginia are the South Branch of Nansimond, and the West Branch of Elizabeth; and those from Carolina are North-west River, North River, Pasquetank, Little River, and Pequimons.

There is one remarkable part of the Dismal, lying to the south of the Line, that has few or no Trees growing on it, but contains a large Tract of tall Reeds. These being green all the Year round, and waveing with every Wind, have procur'd it the Name of the Green Sea.

We are not yet acquainted with the precise Extent of the Dismal, the whole haveing never been Survey'd; but it may be Computed at a Medium to be about 30 Miles long and 10 Miles broad, tho' where the Line crost it, twas compleatly 15 Miles wide. But it seems to grow Narrower towards the North, or at least does so in many Places. The Exhalations that continually rise from this vast Body of mire and Nastiness infect the Air for many Miles around, and render it very unwholesome for the Bordering Inhabitants. It makes them liable to Agues, Pleurisies, and many other Distempers, that kill abundance of People, and make the rest look no better than Ghosts. It wou'd require a great Sum of Money to drain it, but the Publick Treasure cou'd not be better bestow'd than to preserve the Lives of his Majesty's Liege People, and at the same time render so great a Tract of Swamp very Profitable, besides the advantage to our generous Benefactor, concluding with a Tender of the Commissioners Service & the Blessing of their Chaplain.

23.   The Surveyors described the Dismal to us in the following Manner.   That it was in many places overgrown with tall Reeds interwoven with large Briars in which the Men were frequently intangled.   And that not only in the Skirts of it, but likewise towards the Middle.   In other places it was full of Juniper Trees, commonly so call'd, tho' they seem rather to be white Cedars. Some of these are of a great Bigness: but the Soil being soft & boggy, there is little hold for the Roots, & consequently any high Wind blows many of them down.   By this means they lye in heaps, horsing upon one another, and brittling out with Sharp Snaggs, so that Passage in many places is difficult and Dangerous.   The Ground was generally very quaggy, & the Impressions of the Men's feet were immediately fill'd with Water.   So if there was any hole made it was soon full of that Element, & by that Method it was that our People supply'd themselves with drink.   Nay if they made a Fire, in less than half an Hour, when the crust of Leaves & Trash were burnt thro', it wou'd sink down into a Hole, & be extinguish't.   So replete is this Soil with Water, that it cou'd never have been passable, but in a very dry Season.   And indeed considering it is the Source of 6 or 7 Rivers, without any Visible Body of Water to supply them, there must be great Stores of it under Ground.   Some part of this Swamp has few or no Trees growing in it, but contains a large Tract of Reeds, which being perpetually green, & waving in the Wind, it is call'd the Green Sea. Gall-Bushes grow very thick in many parts of it, which are ever green Shrubs, bearing a Berry which dies a Black Colour like the Galls of the Oak, & from thence they receive their Name.

Abundance of Cypress Trees grow likewise in this Swamp, and some Pines upon the Borders towards the firm Land, but the Soil is so moist & miry, that like the Junipers a high wind mows many of them down.   It is remarkable that towards the middle of the Dismal no Beast or Bird or even Reptile can live, not only because of the softness of the Ground, but likewise because it is so overgrown with Thickets, that the Genial Beams of the Sun can

of making a Channel to transport by water-carriage goods from Albemarle Sound into Nansimond and Elizabeth Rivers, in Virginia.[43]

---

[43] Such a project was planned by Byrd himself. See Introduction, p. xxxviii.

never penetrate them. Indeed on the Skirts of it Cattle & Hogs will venture for the Sake of the Reeds, & Roots, with which they will keep themselves fat all the winter. This is a great Advantage to the Bordering Inhabitants in that particular, tho' they pay dear for it by the Agues & other distemper occasion'd by the Noxious Vapours the rise perpetually from that vast Extent of Mire & Nastiness. And a vast Extent it is, being computed at a Medium 10 Miles Broad, & 30 Miles long, tho' where the Line past it, 'twas compleatly 15 Miles broad. However this dirty Dismal is in many parts of it very pleasant to the Eye, tho' disagreeable to the other Sences, because there is an everlasting Verdure, which makes every Season look like the Spring. The way the Men took to Secure their Bedding here from moisture, was, by laying Cypress Bark under their Blankets, etc which made their Lodging hard, but much more wholesome.

It is easy to imagine the hardships the poor Men underwent in this intolerable place, who besides the Burdens on their Backs, were oblig'd to clear the way before the Surveyors, & to measure & mark after them. However they went thro' it all not only with Patience, but cheerfulness. Tho' Orion was as peevish as an old Maid all the way, & more so, because he cou'd perswade Nobody to be out of Humour but himself. The merriment of the Men, & their Innocent Jokes with one another, gave him great offence, whereas if he had had a grain of good Nature, he shou'd have rejoiced to find, that the greatest difficultys cou'd not break their Spirits, or lessen their good Humor. Robin Hix took the Liberty to make him some short replys, that discompos'd him very much, particularly one hot day when the poor Fellow had a Load fit for a Horse upon his Back, Orion had the Conscience to desire him to carry his great Coat. But he roundly refus'd it, telling him frankly he has already as great a Burden as he cou'd Stagger under. This Orion stomach't so much, that he complain'd privately of it to Firebrand as soon as he saw him, but said not one Syllable of it to me. However I was informed of it by Astrolabe, but resolved to take no Notice, unless the cause was brought before us in Form, that the Person accus'd might have the English Liberty

24. This being Sunday, we had a Numerous congregation, which flockt to our Quarters from all the adjacent Country. The News that our Surveyors were come out of the Dismal, increas'd the Number very much, because it wou'd give them an Opportunity of guessing, at least, whereabouts the Line wou'd cut, whereby they might form Some Judgment whether they belong'd to Virginia or Carolina. Those who had taken up Land within the Disputed Bounds were in great pain lest it should be found to ly in Virginia; because this being done contrary to an Expres Order of that government, the Patentees had great reason to fear they should in that case have lost their land. But their Apprehensions were now at an end, when they understood that all the Territory which had been controverted was like to be left in Carolina.

of being heard in his turn. But Firebrand Said a Gentleman
shou'd be believ'd on his bare word without Evidence, and a poor
Man condemned without Tryal, which agreed not at all with my
Notions of Justice. I understand all this at 2^n hand, but Meanwell
was let into the Secret by the Partys themselves, with the hopes of
perverting him into their Sentiments, but he was Stanch, & they
were not able to make the least Impression upon him. This was
a grievous Baulk, because if they cou'd have gain'd him over,
they flatter'd themselves they might have been as unrighteous as
they pleased by a majority. As it happens to Persons disappointed
it broil'd upon our Gentlemen's Stomacks so much, that they were
but indifferent Company; and I observ'd very plain, that Firebrand joked less a days & swore more a Nights ever after. After
these Mistfortunes, to be formally civil was as much as we cou'd
afford to be to one another. Neither of us cou'd dissemble
enough to put on a gay outside when it was cloudy within. However this inward uneasiness helpt to make the rest of our Sufferings the more intollerable. When People are join'd together in a
troublesome Commission, they shou'd endeavor to sweeten by
Complacency & good Humour all the Hazards & Hardships they
are bound to encounter, & not like marry'd People make their
condition worse by everlasting discord. Tho' in this indeed we
had the Advantage of marry'd People, that a few Weeks wou'd
part us.

24. This being Sunday the People flock't from all parts partly
out of Curiosity, & partly out of Devotion. Among the Female
part of our Congregation, there was not much Beauty, the most fell
to Maj^r. Alston's Daughter, who is said to be no niggard of it.
Our Chaplain made some Christians, but cou'd perswade nobody
to be marry'd because every Country Justice can do that Jobb for
them. Major Alston & Captain Baker dined with us. In the afternoon I equipt the Men with Provissions, & dispatch't them away
with Astrolabe & Bootes, to the Place where they were to return
into the Dismal, in order to mark & measure what they had left
unfinish't. Plausible & Shoebrush took a turn to Edenton, & invited us to go with them, but I was unwilling to go from my

In the afternoon, those who were to re-enter the Dismal were furnisht with the Necessary Provisions, and Order'd to repair the Over-Night to their Landlord, Peter Brinkley's, that they might be ready to begin their Business early on Monday Morning. Mr. Irvin was excus'd from the Fatigue, in complement to his Lungs; but Mr. Mayo and Mr. Swan were Robust enough to return upon that painful Service, and, to do them Justice, they went with great Alacrity. The Truth was, they now knew the worst of it; and cou'd guess pretty near at the time when they might hope to return to Land again.

25.* The air was chill'd this Morning with a Smart North-west Wind, which favour'd the Dismalites in their Dirty March. They return'd by the Path they had made in coming out, and with great Industry arriv'd in the Evening at the Spot where the Line had been discontinued.

After so long and laborious a Journey, they were glad to repose themselves on their couches of Cypress-bark, where their sleep was as sweet as it wou'd have been on a Bed of Finland Down.

In the mean time, we who stay'd behind had nothing to do, but to make the best observations we cou'd upon that Part of the Country. The Soil of our Landlord's Plantation, tho' none of the best, seem'd more fertile than any thereabouts, where the Ground is near as Sandy as the Desarts of Affrica, and consequently barren. The Road leading from thence to Edenton, being in distance about 27 Miles, lies upon a Ridge call'd Sandy-Ridge, which is so wretchedly Poor that it will not bring Potatoes.

The Pines in this Part of the country are of a different Species from those that grow in Virginia: their bearded Leaves are much longer and their Cones much larger. Each Cell contains a Seed of the Size and Figure of a black-ey'd Pea, which, Shedding in November, is very good Mast for Hogs, and fattens them in a Short time.

The Smallest of these Pines are full of Cones, which are 8 or 9 Inches long, and each affords commonly 60 or 70 Seeds. This Kind of Mast has the Advantage of all other, by being more constant, and less liable to be nippt by the Frost, or Eaten by the Caterpillars. The Trees also abound more with Turpentine, and consequently yield more Tarr, than either the Yellow or the White Pine; And for the same reason make more durable Timber for building. The Inhabitants hereabouts pick up Knots of Lightwood in Abundance, which they burn into tar, and then carry it to Norfolk or Nansimond for a Market. The Tar made in this method is the less Valuable, because it is said to burn the Cordage, tho' it is full as good for all other uses, as that made in Sweden and Muscovy.

Surely there is no place in the World where the Inhabitants live with

---

*Byrd's manuscript here notes a new year, 1729. This is due to the fact that in the Old Style the new year began on March 25. Following the precedent of Professor Bassett, a deviation from the text is made, the date 1728 being preserved as that, according to our calender, was the year of the survey.

Post, & expose the Men to be ill treated that I left behind. Fire-brand had a Flirt at Robin Hix, which discover'd much Nique and no Justice, because it happen'd to be for a thing of which he was wholly Innocent.

25. The Air was chill'd with a N. Wester which favour'd our Dismalites who enter'd the Desert very early. It was not so kind to Meanwell who unreasonably kick't off the Bed Clothes, & catch't An Ague. We killed the Time, by that great help to disagreeable Society, a Pack of Cards. Our Landlord had not the good Fortune to please Firebrand with our Dinner, but surely when People do their best, a reasonable Man wou'd be satisfy'd. But he en-deavour'd to mend his Entertainment by making hot Love to honest Ruth, who wou'd by no means be charm'd either with his Perswa-sion, or his Person. While the Master was employ'd in making Love to one Sister, the man made his Passion known to the other, Only he was more boisterous, & employ'd force, when he cou'd not succeed by fair means. Tho' one of the men rescu'd the poor Girl from this violent Lover; but was so much his Friend as to keep the shamefull Secret from those, whose Duty it wou'd have been to punish such Violations of Hospitality. Nor was this the only one this disorderly fellow was guilty of, for he broke open a House where our Landlord kept the Fodder for his own use, upon the belief that it was better than what he allow'd us. This was in compliment to his Master's Horses I hope, & not in blind obedience to any order he receiv'd from him.

less Labour than in N Carolina. It approaches nearer to the Description of Lubberland than any other, by the great felicity of the Climate, the easiness of raising Provisions, and the Slothfulness of the People.

Indian Corn is of so great increase, that a little Pains will Subsist a very large Family with Bread, and then they may have meat without any pains at all, by the Help of the Low Grounds, and the great Variety of Mast that grows on the High-land. The Men, for their Parts, just like the Indians, impose all the Work upon the poor Women. They make their Wives rise out of their Beds early in the Morning, at the same time that they lye and Snore, till the Sun has run one third of his course, and disperst all the unwholesome Damps. Then, after Stretching and Yawning for half an Hour, they light their Pipes, and, under the Protection of a cloud of Smoak, venture out into the open Air; tho', if it happens to be never so little cold, they quickly return Shivering into the Chimney corner. When the weather is mild, they stand leaning with both their arms upon the corn-field fence, and gravely consider whether they had best go and take a Small Heat at the Hough: but generally find reasons to put it off till another time.

Thus they loiter away their Lives, like Solomon's Sluggard, with their Arms across, and at the Winding up of the Year Scarcely have Bread to Eat.

To speak the Truth, tis a thorough Aversion to Labor that makes People file off to N Carolina, where Plenty and a Warm Sun confirm them in their Disposition to Laziness for their whole Lives.

26. Since we were like to be confin'd to this place, till the People return'd out of the Dismal, twas agreed that our Chaplain might Safely take a turn to Edenton, to preach the Gospel to the Infidels there, and Christen their Children. He was accompany'd thither by Mr. Little, One of the Carolina Commissioners, who, to shew his regard for the Church, offer'd to treat Him on the Road with a Fricassee of Rum. They fry'd half a Dozen Rashers of very fat Bacon in a Pint of Rum, both which being disht up together, serv'd the Company at once for meat and Drink.

Most of the Rum they get in this Country comes from New England, and is so bad and unwholesome, that it is not improperly call'd "Kill-Devil." It is distill'd there from forreign molosses, which, if Skilfully manag'd yields near Gallon for Gallon. Their molasses comes from the same country, and has the name of "Long Sugar" in Carolina, I suppose from the Ropiness of it, and Serves all the purposes of Sugar, both in their Eating and Drinking.

When they entertain their Friends bountifully, they fail not to set before them a Capacious Bowl of Bombo, so call'd from the Admiral of that name. This is a Compound of Rum and Water in Equal Parts, made palatable with the said long Sugar. As good Humour begins to flow, and

26. I perswaded Meanwell to take a Vomit of Ipocoacana which workt very kindly; I took all the care of him I cou'd, tho' Firebrand was so unfriendly as not to step once up Stairs to visit him. I also gave a Vomit to a poor Shoemaker that belong'd to my Landlord, by which he reap't great benefit. Puzzlecause made a Journey to Edenton, & took our Chaplain with him to preach the Gospel to the Infidels of that Town, & to baptize some of their Children. I began to entertain with my Chocolate, which every body commended, but only he that commends nothing that don't belong to himself. In the Evening I took a Solitary walk, that I might have Leizure to think on my absent Friends, which I now grew impatient to see. Orion stuck as close to his Patron Firebrand, as to the Itch does to the Fingers of many of his Country Folks.

the Bowl to Ebb, they take care to replinish it with Shear Rum, of which there always is a Reserve under the Table. But such Generous doings happen only when that Balsam of life is plenty; for they have often such Melancholy times, that neither Land-graves nor Cassicks can procure one drop for their Wives, when they ly in, or are troubled with the Colick or Vapours. Very few in this Country have the Industry to plant Orchards, which, in a Dearth of Rum, might supply them with much better Liquor.

The Truth is, there is one Inconvenience that easily discourages lazy People from making This improvement: very often, in Autumn, when the Apples begin to ripen, they are visited with Numerous Flights of para-queets, that bite all the Fruit to Pieces in a moment, for the sake of the Kernels. The Havock they make is Sometimes so great, that whole Orchards are laid waste in Spite of all the Noises that can be made, or Mawkins that can be dresst up, to fright 'em away. These Ravenous Birds visit North Carolina only during the warm Season, and so soon as the Cold begins to come on, retire back towards the Sun. They rarely Venture so far North as Virginia, except in a very hot Summer, when they visit the most Southern Parts of it. They are very Beautiful; but like some other pretty Creatures, are apt to be loud and mischievous.

27. Betwixt this and Edenton there are many thuckleberry Slashes, which afford a convenient Harbour for Wolves and Foxes. The first of these wild Beasts is not so large and fierce as they are in other countries more Northerly. He will not attack a Man in the keenest of his Hunger, but run away from him, as from an Animal more mischievous than himself.

The Foxes are much bolder, and will Sometimes not only make a Stand, but likewise assault any one that would balk them of their Prey. The Inhabitants hereabouts take the trouble to dig abundance of Wolf-Pits, so deep and perpendicular, that when a Wolf is once tempted into them, he can no more Scramble out again, than a Husband who had taken the Leap can Scramble out of Matrimony.

Most of the Houses in this Part of the Country are Log-houses, covered with Pine or Cypress Shingles, 3 feet long, and one broad. They are hung upon Laths with Peggs, and their doors too turn upon Wooden Hinges, and have wooden Locks to Secure them, so that the Building is finisht without Nails or other Iron-Work. They also set up their Pales without any Nails at all, and indeed more Securely than those that are nail'd. There are 3 Rails mortised into the Posts, the lowest of which serves as a Sill with a Groove in the Middle, big enough to receive the End of the Pales: the middle Part of the Pale rests against the Inside of the Next Rail, and the Top of it is brought forward to the outside of the uppermost. Such Wreathing of the Pales in and out makes them stand firm, and much harder to unfix than when nail'd in the Ordinary way.

27. Tho' it threaten'd Rain both Yesterday & today, yet Heaven was so kind to our Friends in the Dismal as to keep it from falling. I perswaded Meanwell to take the Bark, which He did with good Effect, tho' he continued very faint & low-Spirited. He took Fire-brand's Neglect in great Dudgeon, and amidst all his good Nature cou'd not forbear a great deal of Resentment; but I won his Heart entirely by the tender Care I took of him in his illness. I also gain'd the Men's Affection by dressing their wounds, & giving them little Remedys for their complaints. Nor was I less in my Land-lords Books, for acting the Doctor in his Family. Tho' I observ'd some Distempers in it, that were past my Skill to cure. For his Wife & Heir Apparent were so enclin'd to a cheerfull Cup, that our Liquor was very unsafe in their keeping. I had a long time observed that they made themselves happy every day, before the Sun had run one third of his course, which no doubt gave some uneasiness to the Old Gentleman: but Custome that reconciles most Evils, made him bear it with Christian Patience.

As to the Young Gentleman, he seem'd to be as worthless as any homebred Squire I had ever met with, & much the worse for hav-ing a good Opinion of himself. His good Father intended him for the Mathematicks, but he never cou'd rise higher in that Study

Within 3 or 4 Miles of Edenton, the Soil appears to be a little more fertile, tho' it is much cut with Slashes, which seem all to have a tendency towards the Dismal.

This Town is Situate on the North side of Albemarle Sound, which is there about 5 miles over. A Dirty Slash runs all along the Back of it, which in the Summer is a foul annoyance, and furnishes abundance of that Carolina plague, musquetas. They may be 40 or 50 Houses, most of them Small, and built without Expense. A Citizen here is counted Extravagant, if he has Ambition enough to aspire to a Brick-chimney. Justice herself is but indifferently Lodged, the Court-House having much the Air of a Common Tobacco-House. I believe this is the only Metropolis in the Christian or Mahometan World, where there is neither Church, Chappel, Mosque, Synagogue, or any other Place of Publick Worship of any Sect or Religion whatsoever.[44]

What little Devotion there may happen to be is much more private than their vices. The People seem easy without a Minister, as long as they are exempted from paying Him. Sometimes the Society for propagating the Gospel has had the Charity to send over Missionaries to this Country; but unfortunately the Priest has been too Lewd for the people, or, which oftener happens, they too lewd for the Priest. For these Reasons these Reverend Gentlemen have always left their Flocks as arrant Heathen as they found them. Thus much however may be said for the Inhabitants of Edenton, that not a Soul has the least taint of Hypocrisy, or Superstition, acting very Frankly and above-board in all their Excesses.

Provisions here are extremely cheap, and extremely good, so that People may live plentifully at triffleing expense. Nothing is dear but Law, Physick, and Strong Drink, which are all bad in their Kind, and the last they get with so much Difficulty, that they are never guilty of the Sin of Suffering it to Sour upon their Hands. Their Vanity generally lies not so much in having a handsome Dining-Room, as a Handsome House of Office: in this Kind of Structure they are really extravagant.

They are rarely guilty of Flattering or making any Court to their governors, but treat them with all the Excesses of Freedom and Familiarity. They are of Opinion their rulers wou'd be apt to grow insolent, if they grew Rich, and for that reason take care to keep them poorer, and more dependent, if possible, than the Saints in New England used to do their

---

[44] Within a mile of the courthouse at Edenton was a chapel of the Church of England, built by the vestrymen of St. Pauls about 1703. See "The First Church Built in North Carolina" (*North Carolina Hist. and Geneal. Register*, Vol. I, No. 2.)

than to gage a Rum Cask. His Sisters are very sensible Industrious Damsels, who tho' they see Gentlemen but Seldom, have the Grace to resist their Importunitys, & tho' they are innocently free, will indulge them in no dangerous Libertys. However their cautious Father having some Notion of Female Frailty, from what he observed in their Mother, never suffers them to lie out of his own Chamber.

Governors. They have very little coin, so they are forced to carry on their Home-Traffick with Paper-Money. This is the only Cash that will tarry in the Country, and for that reason the Discount goes on increasing between that and real Money, and will do so to the End of the Chapter.[45]

28. Our Time passt heavily in our Quarters, where we were quite cloy'd with the Carolina Felicity of having nothing to do. It was really more insupportable than the greatest Fatigue, and made us even envy the Drudgery of our Friends in the Dismal. Besides, tho' the Men we had with us were kept in Exact Discipline, and behav'd without Reproach, yet our Landlord began to be tired of them, fearing they would breed a Famine in his Family.

Indeed, so many keen Stomachs made great Havock amongst the Beef and Bacon, which he had laid in for his Summer Provision, nor cou'd he easily purchase More at that time of the Year, with the Money we paid him, because the People having no certain Market seldom provide any more of these Commodities than will barely supply their own Occasions. Besides the Weather was now grown too warm to lay in a fresh Stock so late in the Spring. These Considerations abated somewhat of that chearfulness with which he bidd us Welcome in the Beginning, and made him think the time quite as long as we did till the Surveyors return'd.

While we were thus all hands uneasy, we were comforted with the News that this Afternoon the Line was finisht through the Dismal. The Messenger told us it had been the hard work of three days to measure the Length of only 5 Miles, and mark the Trees as they past along, and by the most exact Survey they found the Breadth of the Dismal in this Place to be completely 15 Miles.

How wide it may be in other Parts, we can give no Account, but believe it grows narrower towards the North; possibly towards Albemarle Sound it may be something broader, where so many Rivers issue out of it. All we know for certain is, that from the Place where the Line enter'd the Dismal, to where it came out, we found the Road round that Portion of it which belongs to Virginia to be about 65 Miles. How great the Distance may be from Each of those Points, round that Part falls within the Bounds of Carolina, we had no certain Information: tho' tis conjectur'd it cannot be so little as 30 Miles. At which rate the whole Circuit must be about an Hundred. What a Mass of Mud and Dirt is treasur'd up within this filthy circumference, and what a Quantity of Water must perpetually drain into it from the riseing ground that Surrounds it on every Side?

Without taking the Exact level of the Dismal, we may be sure that it declines towards the Places where the Several Rivers take their Rise, in order to carrying off the constant Supplies of Water. Were it not

---

[45] For the colonial money of North Carolina, see Bullock's *Essays on the Monetary History of the United States*, Part II (New York, 1900).

28.   I had a little stifness in my Throat, I fancy by lying alone
for Meanwell being grown restless, in his Indisposition chose to
be by Himself.   The Time past heavily, which we endeavour'd
to make lighter by Cards & Books.   The having nothing to do here
was mose insupportable than the greatest Fatigue, which made me
envy the Drudging of those in the Dismal.   In the Evening we
walk't several ways just as we drew in the day, but made a Shift
to keep within the Bounds of Decency in our behaviour.   However
I observ'd Firebrand had something that broil'd upon his Stomach,
which tho' he seem'd to stiffle in the Day, yet in the Night it burst
out in his Sleep in a Volley of Oaths & Imprecations.   This being my Birth day, I adored the Goodness of Heaven, for having
indulged me with so much Health & very uncommon happiness, in
the Course of 54 Years in which my Sins have been many, & my
Sufferings few, my Opportunitys great, but my Improvements
small.   Firebrand & Meanwell had very high Words, after I went
to Bed, concerning Astrolabe, in which Conversation Meanwell
show'd most Spirit, & Firebrand most Arrogance & Ill Nature.

for such Discharges, the whole Swamp would long Since have been converted into a Lake. On the other Side this Declension must be very gentle, else it would be laid perfectly dry by so many continual drains; Whereas, on the contrary, the Ground seems every where to be thoroughly drencht even in the dryest Season of the Year.

The Surveyors concluded this day's Work with running 25 chains up into the Firm Land, where they waited further Orders from the Commissioners.

29. This day the Surveyors proceeded with the Line no more than 1 Mile and 15 Chains, being Interrupted by a Mill Swamp, thro' which they made no difficulty of wading, in order to make their work more exact.

Thus, like Norway-Mice, these worthy Gentlemen went right forward, without Suffering themselves to be turned out of the way by any Obstacle whatever.

We are told by some Travellers, that those Mice march in mighty Armies, destroying all the fruits of the Earth as they go along. But Something Peculiar to those obstinate little Animals is, that nothing stops them in their career, and if a House happened to stand in their way, disdaining to go an Inch about, they crawl up one side of it, and down the other: or if they meet with any River, or other Body of Water, they are so determin'd, that they swim directly over it, without varying one Point from their course for the Sake of any Safety or Convenience.

The Surveyors were also hinder'd some Time by Setting up Posts in the great Road, to shew the Bounds between the two Colonies.

Our Chaplain return'd to us in the Evening from Edenton, in Company with the Carolina Commissioners. He had preacht there in the Court-House, for want of a consecrated Place, and made no less than 19 of Father Hennepin's Christians.

By the permission of the Carolina Commissioners, Mr. Swan was allow'd to go home, as soon as the Survey of the Dismal was finisht; He met with this Indulgence for a Reason that might very well have excust his coming at all; Namely, that he was lately marry'd.[46]

What remain'd of the Drudgery for this Season was left to Mr. Moseley, who had hitherto acted only in the capacity of a Commissioner. They offer'd to employ Mr. Joseph Mayo as their Surveyor in Mr. Swan's stead, but He thought it not proper to accept of it, because he had hitherto Acted as a Volunteer in behalf of Virginia, and did not care to change Sides, tho' it might have been to his Advantage.

30. The line was advanc'd this day 6 Miles and 35 chains, the Woods, being pretty clear, and interrupted with no Swamp, or other wet Ground.

---

[46] His bride was Mildred Lyon, daughter of John Lyon of the Cape Fear region of North Carolina.

29. I wrote a Letter to the Governor which I had the Complaisance to show to my Collegues to prevent Jealousies & Fears. We receiv'd Intelligence that our Surveyors & people finisht their business in the Dismal last Night, & found it no more than 5 Miles from the Place where they left off. Above a Mile before they came out, they waded up to the Knees in a Pine Swamp. We let them rest this day at Peter Brinkleys, & sent orders to them to proceed the next Morning. Bootes left them & came to us with intent to desert us quite, & leave the rest of the Drudgery to Plausible, who had indulged his Old Bones hitherto. Our Parson return'd to us with the Carolina Commissioners from Edenton, where he had preach't in their Court house, there being no Place of Divine Worship in that Metropolis. He had also Christen'd 19 of their Children, & pillag'd them of some of their Cash, if Paper Money may be allow'd that appellation.

30. This Morning all the ill-humour that Firebrand had so long kept broiling upon his Stomach broke out. First he insisted that

The Land hereabout had all the Marks of Poverty, being for the most Part Sandy and full of Pines. This kind of Ground, tho' unfit for Ordinary Tillage, will however bring Cotton and Potatoes in Plenty, and Consequently Food and Raiment to such as are easily contented, and, like the Wild Irish, find more Pleasure in Laziness than Luxury.

It also makes a Shift to produce Indian-corn, rather by the Felicity of the climate than by the Fertility of the Soil. They who are more Industrious than their Neighbours may make what Quantity of tar they please, tho' indeed they are not always sure of a Market for it.

The Method of burning Tar in Sweden and Muscovy Succeeds not well in this Warmer Part of the World. It seems they kill the Pine-Trees, by barking them quite round at a certain Height, which in those cold countreys brings down the Turpentine into the Stump in a Year's time. But experience has taught us that in warm Climates the Turpentine will no so easily descend, but is either fixt in the upper parts of the Tree, or fryed out by the intense Heat of the Sun.

Care was taken to Erect a Post in Every Road that our Line ran thro', with Virginia carv'd on the North-Side of it, and Carolina on the South, that the Bounds might every where appear. In the Evening the Surveyors took up their Quarters at the House of one Mr. Parker, who, by the Advantage of a better Spot of Land than Ordinary, and a more industrious Wife, lives comfortably, and has a very neat plantation.

31. It rain'd a little this Morning, but this, happening again upon a Sunday, did not interrupt our Business. However the Surveyors made no Scruple of protracting and platting off their work upon that good day, because it was rather an Amusement than a Drudgery.

Here the Men feasted on the fat of the Land, and believing the dirtiest part of their work was over, had a more than Ordinary Gaiety of Heart. We christen'd two of our Landlord's children, which might have remained Infidels all their lives, had not we carry'd Christianity home to his own Door.

The Truth of it is, our Neighbours of North Carolina are not so zealous as to go much out of their way to procure this benefit for their children: Otherwise, being so near Virginia, they might, without exceeding much Trouble, make a Journey to the next Clergyman, upon so good an Errand.

And indeed should the Neighbouring Ministers, once in two or three years, vouchsafe to take a turn among these Gentiles, to baptize them and their children, twould look a little Apostolical, and they might hope to be requited for it hereafter, if that be not thought too long to tarry for their Reward.

[April

quite dis-
les. They
hat there
vince of

a deep
several
w our

more
nta-
ers
tly
a:
e,

nger with the Surveyors to be a
t Voluntiers were always employ'd
y useful in assisting Orion, and had
aving his defects so well Supply'd.
Rudeness of Robin Hix to Orion, &
isht for it. To this I answer'd that if
a to make against Robin Hix, it had been
y before all the Commissioners, that the
have an Opportunity to make his Defence,
r his complaints in private to one Gentleman,
e suspecting the Justice of the rest. That Word
him home, & make him raise his voice, & roll
eat Fury, & I was weak enough to be as loud &
. However it was necessary to shew that I was
ay'd either with his big looks or his big Words, and
n he found this, he cool'd as suddenly as he fired.
himed in with my Sentiments in both these Points,
carry'd them by a fair Majority. However to shew my
nor, & love of Peace I desired Young Astrolabe to concern
no more with the Surveying part, because it gave uneasi-
ut only to assist his Brother in protracting, & plotting of
ork. After this Storm was over Firebrand went with Shoe-
sh to Mr Oshields for some Days, and his going off was not
ss pleasing to us than the going off of a Fever.

31.   This was Sunday, but the People's Zeal was not warm enough
to bring them thro' the Rain to Church, especially now their
Curiosity was satisfy'd. However we had a Sermon & some of
the nearest Neighbours came to hear it. Astrolabe sent word that
he had carry'd the Line 7 miles yesterday but was forced to wade
up to the Middle thro' a Mill Swamp. Robins sent his mate hither
to treat with my Landlord about shipping his Tobacco; they role
it in the Night to Nansimond River, in Defiance of the Law against
bringing of Tobacco out of Carolina into Virginia: but t'were unreasonable to expect that they shou'd obey the Laws of their
Neighbours, who pay no regard to their own. Only the Masters
of Ships that load in Virginia shou'd be under some Oath, or

April 1.   The Surveyors getting now upon better Ground,
engag'd from Underwoods, pusht on the Line almost 12 M
left Sommerton Chappel near two Miles to the Northward, so
was now no Place of Publick Worship left in the whole Pro
North Carolina.

The high Land of North Carolina was barren, and cover'd with
Sand; and the Low Grounds were wet and boggy, insomuch that
of our Horses were mir'd, and gave us frequent Opportunitys to she
Horsemanship.

The Line cut William Spight's Plantation in two, leaving little
than his dwelling House and Orchard in Virginia. Sundry other Pla
tions were Split in the same unlucky Manner, which made the Own
accountable to both Governments. Wherever we passed we constan
found the Borderers laid it to Heart if their Land was taken into Virgin
They chose much rather to belong to Carolina, where they pay no Tribut
either to God or to Caesar.

Another reason was, that the Government there is so Loose, and the
Laws so feebly executed, that, like those in the Neighbourhood of Sydon
formerly, every one does just what seems good in his own Eyes. If the
Governor's hands have been weak in that Province, under the Authority
of the Lord Proprietors, much weaker then were the hands of the Magis-
trate, who, tho' he might have had Virtue enough to endeavour to punish
Offendors, which very rarely happen'd, yet that vertue had been quite
Impotent, for want of Ability to put it in execution.

Besides, their might have been some Danger, perhaps, in venturing
to be so rigorous, for fear of undergoing the Fate of an honest Justice
in Corotuck Precinct. This bold Magistrate, it seems, taking upon him to
order a fellow to the Stocks, for being disorderly in his Drink, was, for
his intemperate Zeal, carry'd thither himself, and narrowly escap'd being
whippt by the Rabble into the Bargain.

This easy day's work carried the Line to the Banks of Somerton-Creek,
that runs out of Chowan River, a little below the Mouth of Nottoway.

2.   In less than a Mile from Somerton creek the Line was carry'd to
Black-water, which is the Name of the upper Part of Chowan, running some
Miles above the Mouth of Nottoway. It must be observ'd that Chowan,
after taking a compass round the most beautiful part of North Carolina,
empties itself into Albemarle Sound, a few Miles above Edenton. The
Tide flows 7 or 8 miles higher than where the River changes its Name, and
is Navigable thus high for any small vessel. Our Line intersected it

regulation about it. Sunday seem'd a day of rest indeed, in the absence of our Turbulent Companion who makes every day uneasy to those who have the pain of his conversation.

April

1. We prepar'd for a March very early, & then I discharg'd a long Score with my Landlord, & a Short one with his Daughter Rachel for some Smiles that were to be paid for in Kisses. We took leave in form of the whole Family, & in 8 Miles reach't Richard Parkers,[43] where we found Young Astrolabe & some of our Men. Here we refresh't ourselves with what a Neat Landlady cou'd provide, & Christen'd 2 of her Children, but did not discharge our reckoning that way. Then we proceeded by Somerton Chappel (which was left 2 Miles in Virginia) as far as the Plantation of William Speight, that was cut in Two by the Line, taking his Tobacco House into Carolina. Here we took up our Quarters & fared the better for a Side of fat Mutton sent us by Captain Baker. Our Lodging was exceedingly Airy, the Wind having a free circulation quite thro' our Bed-Chamber, yet we were so hardy as to take no Cold tho' the Frost was Sharp enough to endanger the Fruit. Meanwell entertain'd the Carolina Commissioners with several Romantick Passages of his Life, with Relation to his Amours, which is a Subject he is as fond of, as a Hero to talk of Battles he never fought.

2. This Morning early Capᵗ Baker came to make us a Visit, & explain'd to us the Reason of the present of Mutton which he sent us Yesterday. It seems the Plantation where he lives is taken into Virginia which without good Friends might

---

[43] Son of that Richard Parker who came to Virginia about 1650 and patented lands in the Nansemond River. (*Virginia Mag. of Hist. and Biog.*, XIX, p. 191.)

exactly half a Mile to the northward of the mouth of Nottoway. However, in Obedience to his Majesty's Command, we directed the Surveyors to come down the River as far as the Mouth of Nottoway, in order to continue our true West Line from thence.

Thus we found the Mouth of Nottoway to lye no more than half a Minute farther to the Northward than Mr. Lawson[47] had formerly done. That Gentleman's Observation, it seems, placed it in 36° 30′, and our Working made it out to be 36° 30½′—a very inconsiderable Variance.

The Surveyors crost the River over against the Middle of the Mouth of Nottoway, where it was about 80 yards wide. From thence they ran the Line about half a Mile through a dirty Pocoson, as far as an Indian Field. Here we took up our Lodging in a moist Situation, having the Pocoson above mention'd on one Side of us, and a Swamp on the other.

In this Camp 3 of the Meherin Indians made us a Visit. They told us that the Small Remains of their Nation had deserted their Ancient Town, situated near the Mouth of Meherin River, for fear of the Cataubas, who had kill'd 14 of their People the Year before; and the few that Survived that Calamity, had taken refuge amongst the English, on the East side of Chowan. Tho', if the complaint of these Indians were true, they are hardly used by our Carolina Friends. But they are the less to be pitied, because they have ever been reputed the most false and treacherous to the English of all the Indians in the Neighbourhood.

Not far from the Place where we lay, I observ'd a large Oak which had been blown up by the Roots, the Body of which was Shiver'd into perfect Strings, and was, in truth, the most Violent Effects of Lightning I ever saw.

But the most curious Instance of that dreadful meteor happen'd at York, where a man was kill'd near a Pine Tree in which the Lightening made a Hole before it Struck the Man, and left an exact Figure of the Tree upon his Breast, with all its Branches, to the wonder of all that beheld it, in which I shall be more particular hereafter.

We made another tryal of the Variation in this place, and found it some Minutes less than we had done at Coratuck-Inlet, but so small a Difference might easily happen thro' some defect in one or other of the Observations, and, therefore, we alter'd not our compass for the Matter.

3. By the advantage of clear woods, the Line was extended 12 miles and three Quarters, as far as the Banks of Meherin. Tho' the Mouth of this River lye 15 miles below the Mouth of Nottoway, yet it winds so much to the Northward, that we came upon it, after running this Small

---

[47] John Lawson, first historian of North Carolina, and Surveyor General of the Province, a member of the boundary commission of 1710.

prejudice him in his Surveyor's Place of Nansimond County. But we promised to employ our Interest in his Favour. We made the best of our way to Chowan River, crossing the Line several times. About a Mile before we came to that River, we crost Somerton Creek. We found our Surveyors at a little Cottage on the Banks of Chowan over against the Mouth of Nottoway River. They told us that our Line cut Black-Water River, about half a Mile to the Northward of that Place but in Obedience to his Majesty's Order in that Case, we directed them to continue the Line from the Middle of the Mouth of Nottoway River. According the Surveyors post Cowan there, & carry'd the Line over a miry Swamp more than half a mile thro', as far as an Indian Old-Field.

In the meantime our Horses & Baggage were ferry'd over the River, a little lower, to the same Field, where we pitch't our Tent, promising ourselves a comfortable Repose: but our Evil Genius came at Night & interrupted all our Joys. Firebrand arriv'd with his most humble Servant Shoebrush, tho' to make them less unwelcome, they brought a present from Mr Oshields, of 12 Bottles of Wine, & as many of Strong Beer. But to say the Truth we had rather have drunk Water the whole Journey to have been fairly quit of such disagreeable Company.

Our Surveyor found by an Observation made this Night, that the Variation was no more than 2°.30″ Westerly, according to which we determined to proceed in the rest of our Work towards the Mountains. Three of the Meherin Indians came hither to see us from the Place where they now live about 7 Miles down the River, they being lately removed from the Mouth of Meherin. They were frighten'd away from thence by the late Massacre committed upon 14 of their Nation by the Catawbas. They are now reduced to a small Number and are the less to be pity'd because they have always been suspected to be very dishonest & treacherous to the English.

3. We sent away the Surveyors about 9 a Clock & follow'd them at ten. By the way Firebrand & Shoebrush having spy'd a House that promised good Chear filed off to it, & took it in Dudgeon that we wou'd not follow their Vagarys. We thought it our Duty to attend the Business in hand, & follow the Surveyors. These we overtook about Noon, after passing several Miry Branches, where

Distance. During the first 7 Miles, we observed the Soil to be poor and Sandy; but as we approacht Meherin it grew better, tho' there it was cut to pieces by Sundry Miry Branches, which discharge themselves into that River, Several of our Horses plunged up to the Saddle-Skirts, and were not disengaged without Difficulty.

The latter Part of our Day's work was pretty laborious, because of the unevenness of the way, and becauss the low Ground of the River was full of Cypress-Snags, as Sharp and Dangerous to our Horses as so many chevaux-de-frize. We found the whole distance from the Mouth of Nottaway to Meherin River, where our Line intersected it, thirteen Miles and a Quarter.

It was hardly possible to find a level large enough on the Banks of the River whereupon to pitch our Tent. But tho' the Situation was, on that Account, not very convenient for us, yet it was for our poor Horses, by reason of the Plenty of Small Reeds on which they fed voraciously.

These Reeds are green here all the Year round, and will keep cattle in tolerable good Plight during the Winter. But whenever the Hogs come where they are, they destroy them in a Short time, by ploughing up their Roots, of which, unluckily, they are very fond.

The River was in this place about as wide as the River Jordan, that is, 40 Yards, and wou'd be Navigable very high for flat Bottom-Boats and Canoes, if it were not so choakt up with large Trees, brought down by every Fresh. Tho' the Banks were full 20 feet high from the Surface of the Water, yet we saw certain Marks of their having been Overflow'd.

These Narrow Rivers that run high up into the Country are Subject to frequent Inundations, when the Waters are roll'd down with such Violence as to carry all before them. The Logs that are then floated are very fatal to the bridges built over these rivers, Which can hardly be contriv'd Strong enough to stand against so much Weight and Violence join'd together.

The Isle of Wight County begins about 3 Miles to the East of Meherin River, being divided from that of Nansimond only by a Line of Markt trees.

4. The River was here hardly fordable, tho' the Season had been very dry. The Banks too were so Steep that our Horses were forced to climb like Mules to get up them. Nevertheless we had the Luck to recover the Opposite Shore without Damage.

We halted for half an hour at Charles Anderson's, who lives on the Western Banks of the River, in order to christen one of his children. In the mean time, the Surveyors extended the Line 2 Miles and 39 chains, in which small Distance Meherin River was so serpentine, that they crost it 3 times.

I had like to have Stuck fast. However this only gave me an Opportunity to shew my Horsemanship, as the fair spoken Plausible told me. After passing several Dirty Places & uneven Grounds, we arriv'd about Sun Set on the Banks of Meherin, which we found 13¼ Miles from the mouth of Notoway River. The County of Isle of Wight begins about 3 miles to the East of this River, parted from Nansimond by a dividing Line only. We pitch't our Tent, & flatter'd ourselves we shou'd be secure from the disturber of our Peace one Night more, but we were mistaken for the Stragglers came to us after it was dark with some Danger to their Necks, because the Low Grounds near the River were full of Cypress Snaggs as dangerous as so many Cheveaua de Frise. But this deliverance from Danger was not enough to make Firebrand good Humour'd, because we had not been so kind as to rejoice at it.

4. Here we call'd a Council of War, whether we shou'd proceed any farther this season, and we carry'd it by a Majority of votes to run the Line only about 2 Miles beyond this place. Firebrand voted for going on a little longer, tho' he was glad it was carry'd against him. However he thought it gave him an Air of Industry to vote against leaving off so soon, but the Snakes began to be in great Vigour which was an unanswerable Argument for it.

The River was hardly fordable & the Banks very Steep, which made it difficult for our Baggage Horses to pass over it. But

Then we went on to Mr. Kinchin's,[48] a Man of Figure and Authority in N Carolina, who lives about a Mile to the Southward of the Place where the Surveyors left off. By the Benefit of a little pains, and good Management, this worthy Magistrate lives in much Affluence.

Amongst other Instances of his Industry, he had planted a good Orchard, which is not common in that Indolent climate; nor is it at all Strange, that such improvident People, who take no thought for the Morrow, shou'd save themselves the Trouble to make Improvements that will not pay them for several Years to come. Tho' if they cou'd trust futurity for any thing, they certainly wou'd for Cyder, which they are so fond of, that they generally drink it before it is done working, lest the Fermentation might unluckily turn it Sowr.

It is an Observation, which rarely fails of being true, both in Virginia and Carolina, that those who take care to plant good Orchards are, in their General characters, Industrious People. This held good in our LANDLORD, who had many Houses built on this Plantation, and every One kept in decent Repair. His Wife, too, was tidy, his Furniture clean, his Pewter bright, and nothing seem'd to be wanting to make his Home comfortable.

Mr. Kinchin made us the Compliment of his House, but because we were willing to be as little troublesome as possible, we order'd the Tent to be pitch'd in his Orchard, where the Blossoms of the Apple Trees contributed not a little to the sweetness of our Lodging.

Because the Spring was not pretty forward, and the Rattle-Snakes began to crawl out of their Winter-Quarters, and might grow dangerous, both to the Men and their Horses, it was determin'd to proceed no farther with the Line till the Fall. Besides, the Uncommon Fatigue the People had undergone for near 6 Weeks together, and the Inclination they all had to visit their Respective Familys, made a Recess highly reasonable.

The Surveyors were employ'd great part of the Day, in forming a Correct and Elegant Map of the Line, from Corotuck-Inlet to the Place where they left off. On casting up the account in the most accurate manner, they found the whole distance we had run to amount to 73 Miles and 13 chains. Of the Map they made two fair copies, which agreeing exactly, were subscrib'd by the Commissioners of both colonies, and one of them was delivered to those on the Part of Virginia, and the other to those on the Part of North Carolina.

---

[48] See *Secret History*, Note 44.

thank God we got all well on the other Side without any Damage.
We went to a House just by the River-Side, belonging to a Man,
who learnedly call'd himself Carolus Anderson, where we christen'd his child. Then we proceeded to Mr Kinchin's a Man of
Figure in these parts, & his Wife a much better Figure than he.[44]
They both did their utmost to entertain us & our People in the best
Manner. We pitch't our Tent in the Orchard, where the Blos-
soms of the Apple Trees mended the Air very much. There Mean-
well & I lay; but Firebrand & his Flatterers stuck close to the
House. The Surveyors crost this River 3 times with the Line in
the Distance of 2½ Miles, & left off about half a Mile to the
Northward of this Place.

5. Our Surveyors made an Elegant Plat of our Line, from Coratuck Inlet to the Place where they left off, containing the Distance
of 73 Miles & 13 Polls. Of this exact Copys were made, & being
carefully examin'd were both Sign'd by the Commissioners of
each Colony. This Plat was chiefly made by Astrolabe, but one
of the Copys was taken by Plausible; but Orion was content with
a Copy which the Parson took for him. However he deliver'd me
the minutes which he had kept of our Proceedings by Order of
the Commissioners. The poor Chaplain was the common Butt at
which all our Company aim'd their profane Wit, & gave him the
Title of Dear Pipp, because instead of a Prick't Line, he had been
so maidenly as to call it a Pipp't Line. I left the Company in

---

[44] Doubtless William Kinchen of Bertie County, North Carolina.

6. Thus we finish'd our Spring Campaign, and having taken leave of our Carolina-Friends, and agreed to meet them again the Tenth of September following, at the same Mr. Kinchin's, in order to continue the Line, we crost Meherin River near a Quarter of a Mile from the House. About ten Miles from that we halted at Mr. Kindred's Plantation, where we Christen'd two Children.

It happen'd that some of Isle of Wight militia Were exercising in the Adjoining Pasture, and there were Females enough attending that Martial Appearance to form a more invincible corps.

Ten miles farther we passed Nottoway River at Bolton's Ferry, and took up our Lodgings about three Miles from thence, at the House of Richard Parker, an honest Planter, whose Labours were rewarded with Plenty, which, in this country is the Constant Portion of the Industrious.

7. The Next day being Sunday, we order'd Notice to be sent to all the Neighbourhood that there wou'd be a Sermon at this Place, and an Opportunity of Christening their Children. But the Likelihood of Rain got the better of their Devotion, and what perhaps, Might Still be a Stronger motive of their Curiosity. In the Morning we despacht a runner to the Nottoway Town,[49] to let the Indians know we intend them a Visit that Evening, and our honest Landlord was so kind as to be our Pilot thither, being about 4 Miles from his House.

Accordingly in the Afternoon we marcht in good Order to the Town, where the Female Scouts, station'd on an Eminence for that purpose, had no sooner spy'd us, but they gave Notitce of our Approach to their Fellow-Citizens by continual Whoops and Cries, which cou'd not possibly have been more dismal at the Sight of their most implacable Enemys.

This Signal Assembled all their Great Men, who receiv'd us in a

---

[49] The Nottoway Indians belonged to the Iroquois family and were closely kin to the Tuscaroras. As late as 1825 a group of forty-seven were living in a village in Southampton County, Virginia.

good time, taking as little pleasure in their low Wit, as in their low liquor which was Rum Punch. Here we discharg'd 6 of the Men, that were near their own Habitations.

6.   We paid our Scores, settled our Accounts, & took leave of our Carolina Friends. Firebrand went about 6 Miles with us as far as one Corkers, where we had the grief to part with that sweet temper'd Gentleman, & the Burr that stuck with him Orion. In about ten Miles we reach't a Musterfield near Mr Kindred's House, where Capt Gerald was exercising his Company. There were Girls enough come to see this Martial Appearance to form another Company, & Beauty's enough among them to make Officers of. Here we call'd & Christen'd 2 Children, and offered to marry as many of the Wenches as had got Sweethearts, but they were not ripe for Execution. Then we proceeded ten Miles farther to Bolton's Ferry, where we past Nottoway River at Mr Symonds's Quarter. From hence we intended to proceed to Nottaway Town to satisfy the Curiosity of some of our Company, but loseing our Way we wander'd to Richard Parkers Plantation, where we had formerly met with very kind Entertainment. Our Eyes were entertain'd as well as our Stomachs by the Charms of pretty Sally the Eldest Daughter of the Family.

7.   This being Sunday we had a Sermon to which very few of the Neighbours resorted, because they wanted timely Notice. However some good Christians came & amongst them Molly Izzard the smartest Damsel in these Parts. Meanwell made this Girle very Vain by saying sweet things to her, but Sally was more engaging, whose wholesome Flesh & Blood, neither had nor needed any Ornament. Nevertheless in the Afternoon we cou'd find in our Hearts to change these fair Beauty's for the Copper Colour'd Ones of Nottaway Towne. Thither we went having given Notice by a Runner that we were coming, that the Indians might be at home to entertain us. Our Landlord shew'd us the way, and the Scouts had no sooner spy'd us, but they gave Notice of our Approach, to the whole Town, by perpetual Whoops & Crys, which to a Stranger sound very dismal. This call'd their great Men to the Fort, where we alighted, & were conducted to the best Cabins.

Body, and conducted us into the Fort. This Fort was a Square Piece of
Ground, inclos'd with Substantial Puncheons, or Strong Palisades, about
ten feet high, and leaning a little outwards, to make a Scalade more
difficult.

Each side of the Square might be about 100 Yards long, with Loop-
holes at proper Distances, through which they may fire upon the Enemy.

Within this Inclosure we found Bark Cabanes Sufficient to lodge all their
people, in Case they should be obliged to retire thither. These Cabanes
are no other but Close Arbours made of Saplings, arched at the top,
and cover'd so well with Bark as to be proof against all Weather. The
fire is made in the Middle, according to the Hibernian Fashion, the Smoak
whereof finds no other Vent but at the Door, and so keeps the whole
family Warm, at the Expense both of their Eyes and Complexion.

The Indians have no standing Furniture in their Cabanes but Hurdles
to repose their Persons upon, which they cover with Mats or Deer-skins.
We were conducted to the best Appartments in the Fort, which just before
had been made ready for our Reception, and adorn'd with new Mats, that
were sweet and clean.

The Young Men had Painted themselves in a Hideous Manner, not so
much for Ornament as Terror. In that frightful Equipage they entertain'd
us with Sundry War-Dances, wherein they endeavour'd to look as formidable as possible. The Instrument they danct to was an Indian-drum,
that is, a large Gourd with a Skin bract tort over the Mouth of it. The
Dancers all Sang to this Musick, keeping exact Time with their feet, while
their Heads and Arms were screw'd into a thousand Menacing Postures.

Upon this occasion the Ladies had array'd themselves in all their finery.
They were Wrapt in their Red and Blue Match-Coats, thrown so Negli-
gently about them, that their Mehogony Skins appear'd in Several Parts,
like the Lacedaemonian Damsels of Old. Their Hair was breeded with
white and Blue Peak, and hung gracefully in a large Roll upon their
Shoulders.

This peak Consists of Small Cylinders cut out of a Conque-Shell, drill'd
through and Strung like Beads. It serves them both for Money and
Jewels, the Blue being of much greater Value than the White, for the
same reason that Ethiopian Mistresses in France are dearer than French,
because they are more Scarce. The Women wear Necklaces and Bracelets
of these precious Materials, when they have a mind to appear lovely.
Tho' their complexions be a little Sad-Colour'd, yet their Shapes are
very Strait and well porportion'd. Their Faces are Seldom handsome,
yet they have an Air of Innocence and Bashfulness, that with a little less
dirt wou'd not fail to make them desirable. Such Charms might have had
their full Effect upon Men who had been so long deprived of female
conversation, but that the whole Winter's Soil was so crusted on the Skins
of those dark Angels, that it requir'd a very strong Appetite to approach
them. The Bear's oyl, with which they anoint their Persons all over,

All the Furniture of those Appartments was Hurdles cover'd with clean Mats. The Young Men had painted themselves in a Hideous Manner, not for Beauty, but Terrour, & in that Equipage entertain'd us with some of their War Dances. The Ladies had put on all their Ornaments to charm us, but the whole Winter's Dirt was so crusted on their Skins, that it requir'd a strong appetite to accost them. Whatever we were, Our Men were not quite so nice, but were hunting after them all Night. But tho' Meanwell might perhaps want Inclinations to these sad-colour'd Ladys, yet curiousity made him try the difference between them & other Women, to the disobligation of his Ruffles, which betray'd what he had been doing. Instead of being entertain'd by these Indians, we entertain'd them with Bacon & Rum, which they accepted of very kindly, the Ladys as well as the Men. They offer'd us no Bedfellows, according to the good Indian fashion, which we had reason to take unkindly. Only the Queen of Weynoke told Steddy that her Daughter had been at his Service if She had not been too Young. Some Indian Men were lurking all Night about our Cabin, with the felonious intent to pilfer what they cou'd lay their hands upon, & their Dogs slunk into us in the Night, & eat up what remain'd of our Provisions.

makes their skins Soft, and at the Same time protects them from every Species of Vermin that use to be troublesome to other uncleanly People.

We were unluckily so many, that they cou'd not well make us the Complement of Bed-fellows, according to the Indian Rules of Hospitality, tho' a grave Matron whisper'd one of the Commissioners very civily in the Ear, that if her Daughter had been but one year Older, she should have been at his Devotion.

It is by no means a loss of Reputation among the Indians, for Damsels that are Single to have Intrigues with the Men; on the contrary, they count it an Argument of Superior Merit to be liked by a great Number of Gallants. However, like the Ladys that Game they are a little Mercenary in their Amours, and seldom bestow their Favours out of Stark Love and Kindness. But after these Women have once appropriated their Charms by Marriage, they are from thencefourth faithful to their Vows, and will hardly ever be tempted by an Agreeable Gallant, or be provokt by a Brutal or even by a fumbling Husband to go astray.

The little Work that is done among the Indians is done by the poor Women, while the men are quite idle, or at most employ'd only in the Gentlemanly Diversions of Hunting and Fishing.

In this, as well as in their Wars, they now use nothing but Fire-Arms, which they purchase of the English for Skins. Bows and Arrows are grown into disuse, except only amongst their Boys. Nor is it ill Policy, but on the contrary very prudent, thus to furnish the Indians with Fire-Arms, because it makes them depend entirely upon the English, not only for their Trade, but even for their subsistence. Besides, they were really able to do more mischief, while they made use of Arrows, of which they wou'd let Silently fly Several in a Minute with Wonderful Dexterity, whereas now they hardly ever discharge their Firelocks more than once, which they insidiously do from behind a Tree, and then retire as nimbly as the Dutch Horse us'd to do now and then formerly in Flanders.

We put the Indians to no expense, but only of a little Corn for our Horses, for which in Gratitude we cheer'd their hearts with what Rum we had left, which they love better than they do their Wives and Children.

Tho' these Indians dwell among the English, and see in what Plenty a little Industry enables them to live, yet they chuse to continue in their Stupid Idleness, and to Suffer all the Inconveniences of Dirt, Cold, and Want, rather than to disturb their hands With care, or defile their Hands with labour.

The whole Number of People belonging to the Nottoway Town, if you include Women and Children, amount to about 200. These are the only Indians of any consequence now remaining within the Limits of Virginia. The rest are either removed, or dwindled to a very inconsiderable Number, either by destroying one another, or else by the Small-Pox and other Diseases. Tho' nothing has been so fatal to them as their ungovernable

[Continued on page 123]

Passion for Rum, with which, I am sorry to say it, they have been but too liberally supply'd by the English that live near them.

And here I must lament the bad Success Mr. Boyle's Charity[50] has hitherto had towards converting any of these poor Heathens to Christianity. Many children of our Neighbouring Indians have been brought up in the College of William and Mary. They have been taught to read and write, and have been carefully Instructed in the Principles of the Christian Religion, till they came to be men. Yet after they return'd home, instead of civilizeing and converting the rest, they have immediately Relapt into Infidelity and Barbarism themselves.

And some of them too have made the worst use of the Knowledge they acquir'd among the English, by employing it against their Benefactors. Besides, as they unhappily forget all the good they learn, and remember the Ill, they are apt to be more vicious and disorderly than the rest of their Countrymen.

I ought not to quit this Subject without doing Justice to the great Prudence of Colo Spotswood in this Affair. That Gentleman was lieut Governor of Virginia when Carolina was engaged in a Bloody War with the Indians. At that critical Time it was thought expedient to keep a Watchful Eye upon our Tributary Savages, who we knew had nothing to keep them to their Duty but their Fears.

Then it was that he demanded of each Nation a Competent Number of their great Men's Children to be sent to the College, where they serv'd as so many Hostages for the good Behaviour of the Rest, and at the same time were themselves principled in the Christian Religion. He also Plac'd a School-Master among the Saponi Indians, at the salary of Fifty Pounds P Annum, to instruct their Children. The Person that undertook that Charitable work was Mr. Charles Griffin,[51] a Man of good Family, who by the Innocence of his Life, and the Sweetest of his Temper, was perfectly well qualify'd for that pious undertaking. Besides, he had so much the

----

[50] Robert Boyle, English chemist, who in his will provided that £4,000 from his estate should be employed for "pious and charitable uses." Through the efforts of Dr. James Blair, Boyle's nephew and executor was persuaded to make an investment in the Manor of Brafferton, the income from which, excepting £45 per annum to Harvard and a similar amount to the Society for the Propagation of the Gospel in Foreign Parts, should go to William and Mary for the education of Indians; hence Brafferton Hall at that institution. During the Revolution the income was diverted to the education of Negroes in the West Indies. (See Tyler's *Colonial Williamsburg, passim.*)

[51] Charles Griffin appears in North Carolina as an immigrant from the West Indies in the early eighteenth century. About 1705 he opened a school in Pasquotank Precinct and was acknowledged as lay leader of the Church of England. In 1808 he moved to Chowan Precinct where he is reported to have fallen into immorality and Quakerism. In 1716 he appears in Virginia as head of the Indian school subsidized by Spotswood and in 1720 he became teacher in the Indian school of William and Mary. In 1712 another Indian school was reported at Sarum, on the border of North Carolina and Virginia, to which Indians were admitted. It was conducted by a Mr. Mashburn.

[Continued on page 123]

Secret of mixing Pleasure with instruction, that he had not a Scholar, who did not love him affectionately.

Such Talents must needs have been blest with a Proportionable Success, had he not been unluckily remov'd to the College, by which he left the good work he had begun unfinisht. In short, all the Pains he had undertaken among the Infidels had no other Effect but to make them something cleanlier than other Indians are.

The Care Colo Spotswood took to tincture the Indian Children with Christianity produc'd the following Epigram, which was not publisht during his Administration, for fear it might then have lookt like flattery.

> Long has the Furious Priest assay'd in Vain,
> With Sword and Faggot, Infidels to gain,
> But now the Milder Soldier wisely tryes
> By Gentler Methods to unveil their Eyes.
> Wonders apart, he knew 'twere vain t' engage
> The fix'd Preventions of Misguided Age.
> With fairer Hopes he forms the Indian Youth
> To early Manners, Probity and Truth.
> The Lyon's whelp thus on the Lybian Shore ⎫
> Is tam'd and Gentled by the Artful Moor, ⎬
> Not the Grim Sire, inured to Blood before. ⎭

I am sorry I can't give a Better Account of the State of the Poor Indians with respect to Christianity, altho' a great deal of Pains has been and still continues to be taken with them. For my Part, I must be of Opinion, as I hinted before, that there is but one way of Converting these poor Infidels, and reclaiming them from Barbarity, and that is, Charitably to intermarry with them, according to the Modern Policy of the most Christian King in Canada and Louisiana.

Had the English done this at the first Settlement of the Colony, the Infidelity of the Indians had been worn out at this Day, with their Dark Complexions, and the Country had swarm'd with People more than it does with Insects.

It was certainly an unreasonable Nicety, that prevented their entering into so good-Natur'd an Alliance. All Nations of men have the same Natural Dignity, and we all know that very bright Talents may be lodg'd under a very dark Skin. The principal Difference between one People and another proceeds only from the Different Opportunities of Improvement.

The Indians by no means want understanding, and are in their Figure tall and well-proportion'd. Even their Copper-colour'd Complexion wou'd admit of Blanching, if not in the first, at the farthest in the Second Generation.

I may safely venture to say, the Indian Women would have made altogether as Honest Wives for the first Planters, as the Damsels they us'd

[Continued on page 123]

to purchase from aboard the Ships. It is Strange, therefore, that any good Christian Shou'd have refused a wholesome, Straight Bed-fellow, when he might have had so fair a Portion with her, as the Merit of saving her Soul.

8. We rested on our clean Mats very comfortably, tho' alone, and the next Morning went to the Toilet of some of the Indian Ladys, where, what with the Charms of their Persons and the Smoak of their Apartments, we were almost blinded. They offer'd to give us Silk-Grass Baskets of their own making, which we Modestly refused, knowing that an Indian present, like that of a Nun, is a Liberality put out to Interest, and a Bribe plac'd to the greatest Advantage.

Our Chaplain observ'd with concern, that the Ruffles of Some of our Fellow Travellers were a little discolour'd with pochoon,[52] wherewith the good Man had been told those Ladies us'd to improve their invisible charms.

About 10 a Clock we marched out of Town in good order, & the War Captains saluted us with a Volley of Small-Arms. From thence we proceeded over Black-water Bridge to colo' Henry Harrisons, where we congratulated each other upon our Return into Christendom.

Thus ended our Progress for this Season, which we may justly say was attended with all the Success that could be expected. Besides the Punctual Performance of what was Committed to us, we had the Pleasure to bring back every one of our Company in perfect Health. And this we must acknowledge to be a Singular Blessing, considering the Difficulties and Dangers to which they had been expos'd.

We had reason to fear the many Waters and Sunken Grounds, thro' which We were oblig'd to wade, might have thrown the men into Sundry Acute distempers; especially the Dismal, where the Soil was so full of Water, and the Air so full of Damps, that nothing but a Dutchman cou'd live in them.

Indeed the Foundation of all our Success was the Exceeding dry Season. It rain'd during the whole Journey but rarely, and then, as when Herod built his Temple, only in the Night or upon the Sabbath, when it was no hindrance at all to our progress.

---

[52] The puccoon, or bloodroot, which yields dark red or yellow juices, called Indian paint.

8. When we were drest, Meanwell & I visited most of the
Princesses at their own Appartments, but the Smoke was so great
there, the Fire being made in the middle of the Cabbins, that we
were not able to see their Charms.   Prince James' Princess sent
my Wife a fine Basket of her own making, with the Expectation
of receiving from her some present of ten times its Value.   An
Indian Present like those made to Princes, is only a Liberality put
out to Interest, & a bribe placed to the greatest Advantage.   I cou'd
discern by some of our Gentlemen's Linnen, discolour'd by the
Soil of the Indian Ladys, that they had been convincing themselves
in the point of their having no furr.   About Ten we march't out
of the Town, some of the Indians giving us a Volley of small
Arms at our departure.   We drank our Chocolate at one Jones's
about 4 Miles from the Town, & then proceeded over Black-Water
Bridge to Col° Henry Harrisons,[45] where we were very handsomely
entertain'd, & congratulated one another upon our Return into
Christendome.

9. We scrubb'd off our Indian dirt, & refresht our selves with
clean Linnen.   After a plentifull Breakfast, we took our Leave,
& set our Faces towards Westover.   By the way we met Boller
Cocke & his Lady, who told me my Family was well, Heaven be
prais'd; When we came to the New Church near Warren's Mill,
Steddy drew up his Men, & harangued them in the following Manner.   "Friends & Fellow Travellers, It is a great Satisfaction to
"me, that after so many difficultys & Fatigues, you are return'd
"in safety to the place where I first Join'd you.   I am much
"oblidg'd to you for the great readiness & Vigour you have shew'd
"in the business we went about, & I must do you all, the Justice to
"declare, that you have not only done your Duty but also done it
"with Cheerfullness & Affection.   Such a Behaviour, you may be
"sure will engage us, to procure for you the best Satisfaction we

[45] Henry Harrison (1691-1732), of Surry County, son of Benjamin Harrison of
"Berkley," James River, member of the House of Burgesses in 1715 and later years,
and of the Council in 1730.

[Continued on page 138]

"can from the Government. And besides that you may depend "upon our being ready at all times to do you any manner of Kind-"ness, You are now blessed be God, near your own dwellings, "I doubt not, willing to be discharg'd. I heartily wish you may "every one find your Friends & Your Familys in perfect Health, "& that your Affairs may have suffer'd as little as possible by your "Absence." The Men took this Speech very kindly, & were thankful on their part for the affectionate care we had taken of them during the whole Journey. Upon the whole matter it was as much as we cou'd do to part with dry Eyes. However they filed off to Prince George Court, where they entertain'd their Acquaintance with the History of their Travels, and Meanwell with the 2 Astrolabes past over the River with me to Westover, where I had the Pleasure of meeting all my Family in perfect Health, nor had they been otherwise since I left them. This great Blessing ought to inspire us all with the deepest Sentiments of Gratitude, as well as convince us of the Powerfull Effect of Sincere & hearty Prayers to the Almighty in all our undertakings.

Thus ended our Progress for this Season, & it shou'd be remember'd that before we parted with the Commissioners of N. Carolina we agreed to meet again at Kinchins on the 10th of September, to continue the Line from thence towards the Mountains, upon this Condition nevertheless, that if the Commissioners on either Side shou'd find it convenient to alter the Day, they shou'd give timely Notice to the other. I had been so long absent from home, that I was glad to rest my self for a few Days, & therefore went not down to Williamsburgh 'till the 17th of April. And then I waited upon the Governor to give an Account of my Commission, but found my Reception a little cooler than I thought my Behaviour in the Service had deserv'd. I must own I was surpriz'd at it, 'til I came to understand, that several Storys had been whisper'd by Firebrand & Orion to my Disadvantage.

Those Gentlemen had been so indiscreet as to set about several ridiculous Falshoods, which cou'd be prov'd so, by every Man that was with us. Particularly that I had treated Orion not only without Ceremony, but without Justice, denying him any Assistance from the Men, & supporting them in their rudeness to him. And because they thought it necessary to give some Instance of my unkindness to that worthy Gentleman, they boldly affirm'd,

[Continued on page 138]

that I wou'd not send one of the Men from Capt James Wilson's to Norfolk Town for his Horse, which he had left there to be cured of a Sore back. The Father of Lies cou'd not have told one more point Blank against the Truth than this was, because the Author of it knew in his own Conscience, that I had order'd one of the Men to go upon this Errand for him, tho' it was more than 50 Miles backward & forward, & tho' his own Servant might as well have gone, because he had at that time nothing to hinder him, being left behind at Wilsons, where the Men were, & not attending upon his Master. And this I cou'd prove by Meanwell who wrote the Order I sign'd for this purpose. & by Dr Humdrum who receiv'd it, & thereupon had sent one of the Men to Norfolk for him. Nor were these Gentlemen content with doing this wrong to Me, but they were still more & more unjust to Astrolabe, by telling the Governor, that he was ignorant in the Business of Surveying, that he had done nothing in running of the Line, but Orion had done all; which was as Opposite to Truth, as Light is to darkness, or Modesty to Impudence. For in Fact Astrolabe had done all, & Orion had done nothing, but what expos'd not only his awkwardness in the Practice, but his Ignorance in the Theory: nor was this a bare untruth only with regard to Astrolabe, but there was Malice in it, for they had so totally preposest the Commissary with his being Ignorant in the Art of Surveying, that, contrary to his promise formerally given, he determined not to make him Surveyor of GoochLand, nor had he yielded to it at last, without the interposition of the Governor. So liable is Humane Nature to prepossession, that even the Clergy is not exempt from it.

They likewise circulated a great many other ridiculous Stories in the Gaiety of their Hearts, which carry'd a keener Edge against themselves than Steddy, & therefore merited rather my Contempt, than Resentment. However it was very easy when Meanwell & I came to Town, not only to disprove all their Slander, but also to set every thing in a true light with Regard to themselves. We made it as clear as the Noon Day, that all the Evidence they had given was as much upon the Irish, as their Wit & their Modesty. The Governour was soon convinced, & exprest himself very freely to those Gentlemen & particularly to Orion, who had with great confidence impos'd upon him. He was also so fully perswaded of Astrolabes Abilities, that he perfectly constrain'd the Commissary

[Continued on page 138]

to appoint him Surveyor of Goochland, to the Mortification of his
Adversarys.

As soon as I cou'd compleat my Journal, I sent it to Firebrand
for his Hand if he found it right; but after many Days he return'd
it me unsign'd, tho' he cou'd make no Objection. I gave myself
no further Trouble about him, but desir'd M[r] Banister[46] to give
it to the Governour subscrib'd by Meanwell & Me. Upon his asking Firebrand why he would not grace the Journal with his Hand,
his Invention cou'd find no other Reason, but, because it was too
Poetical. However he thought proper to Sign this Poetical Journal
at last, when he found it was to be sent to England without it.

Sometime in June Plausible made me a Visit, & let me know
in the Name of his Brother Commissioners of N. Carolina, that it
was their common Request, that our Meeting to continue the Line,
might be put off to the 20th of September, & desir'd me to communicate their Sentiments to the other Commissioners for Virginia. I beg'd he wou'd make this request in Writing by way of
Letter, lest it might be call'd in question by some unbelievers.
Such a Letter he wrote, & a few days after I show'd it to Firebrand & let him know Meanwell & I had agreed to their Desire,
& intended to write them an Answer accordingly. But he believing
this Alteration of the Day to have been made in Compliment to
me (because he knew I had always been of this Opinion) immediately sent away a Letter, or rather an Order to the Commissioners for Carolina, directing them to stick to their first
day of meeting, being the Tenth of September, & to disown their
Order to Plausible to get it put off. A precept from so great a
Man, three of these worthy Commissioners had not the Spirit to
disobey, but meanly swallow'd their own Words, & under their
Hands deny'd they had ever desired Plausible to make any such
Motion. The Renegade Letter of these Sycophants was afterwards produced by Firebrand to the Governour & Council of Virginia. In the meantime I sent them an Epistle sign'd by Meanwell
& myself, that we, in compliance with their Desire deliver'd by
Plausible had agreed to put off our meeting to the 20th of Sep-

---

46 John Banister, collector of the Customs for the Upper James District, son of Rev.
John Banister, naturalist and entomologist, who arrived in Virginia about 1678. The
Banister plantation was near Petersburg.

[Continued on page 138]

tember. This servile Temper in these 3 Carolina Commissioners, show'd of what base Metal they were made, & had discover'd itself in another pitifull Instance not long before.

Firebrand despairing of a good Word from his Virginia Collegues, with great Industry procured a Testimonial from his Carolina Flatterers, as well for himself as his Favorite Orion. And because the Complement might appear too gross if addrest to himself it was contriv'd that the Gentlemen abovemention'd shou'd join in a Letter to the Commissary[47] (with whom by the way they had never before corresponded) wherein without Rhyme or Reason, they took care to celebrate Firebrand's Civility, and Orion's Mathematicks.

This Certificate was soon produced by the good Commissary to our Governour, who cou'd not but see thro' the Shallow Contrivance. It appear'd ridiculous to him, but most abject & monstrous to us, who knew them to be as ill Judges of the Mathematicks, as a deaf Man cou'd be of Musick. So that to be sure it was a great Addition to the character of our Professor, to have the honour of their Testimonials, And tho' we shou'd allow Men of their Education to be Criticks in Civility, yet at first these very men complain'd of Firebrand's haughty Carriage, tho' now they have the meanness to write to the Commissary in Commendation of his civility. These are such Instances of a poor Spirit as none cou'd equal but themselves in other Passages of their behaviour. And tho' the Subject be very low, yet I must beg leave to mention another Case, in which not only these, but all the Council of N. Carolina discover'd a Submission below all Example. They suffer'd this Firebrand to come in at the head of their Council, when at his first Admission he ought to have been at the Tail. I can't tell whether it was more pretending in him to ask this precedence or more pitifull in them to submit to it. He will say perhaps that it befitted not a Gentleman of his Noble Family & high Station, to set below a Company of Pyrates, Vagabonds, & Footmen: but surely if that be their Character, he ought as little to sit among them at all. But what have they to say in their Excuses for Prostituting the Rank in which the Lords Proprietors had placed them, since the Person to whom they made this Complement has no other Title to the Arms

---

[47] James Blair, Commissary of the Church of England in Virginia.

[Continued on page 138]

he bears, and the name he goes by, but the Courtesy of Ireland. And then for his Office, he is at most but a Publican & holds not his Commission from his Majority, but from the Commissioners of the Customs. So they had no other Reason to give this Man place, but because their own worthlessness flow in their Faces. Sometime in July I receiv'd a Letter from Firebrand in which he accus'd me of having taken too much upon me in in our last Expedition, by pretending to a Sole Command of the Men. That then the Number of our Men was too great, & brought an unnecessary charge upon the Publick, that 9 or 10 wou'd be sufficient to take out with us next time, of which he wou'd name 3. This was the Sum & Substance of his Letter, tho' there were Turns in it & some Raillery which he intended to be very ingenious, & for which he belabour'd his poor Brains very much. I did not think this Epistle worth an Answer, but fancy'd it wou'd be time enough to dispute the Points mention'd therein, at our next Council. It happen'd in August upon the News of some disturbance among the Indians, that the Governor call'd a small Council compos'd only of the Councellors in the Neighbourhood, judging it unnecessary to give us the Trouble of a Journey, who liv'd at a greater Distance. At this Council assisted only Firebrand, the Commissary & 3 other Gentlemen. Neither Meanwell nor I were there, nor had any Summons or the least Notice of it. This Firebrand thought a proper Occasion to propose his Questions concerning the Reduction of the Number of our Men, & the day when we were to meet the Carolina Commissioners. He was seconded by his Friend the Commissary, who surpriz'd the rest of the council into their Opinion, there being nobody to oppose them, nor any so just as to put off the Question, til the 2 Commissioners that were absent might be heard in a matter that concern'd them. However these unfair & short sighted Politicks were so far from prospering, that they turn'd to the Confusion of him that contriv'd them. For having quickly gain'd Intelligence of this proceeding, I complain'd of the Injustice of it in a Letter I wrote to the Governor, and he was so much convinc'd by my Reasons, that he wrote one word, he wou'd call a general Council the Week following, to overhawle that Matter again. Indeed he had been so prudent at the little Council as to direct the Clerk not to enter what had been there determin'd, upon the Council Books, that it might not stand as an

[Continued on page 138]

Order but only as Matter of Advice to us Commissioners. Upon
Receipt of this Letter I dispatcht an Express to Meanwell, ac-
quainting him with this whole Matter, & intreating him to call
upon me in his way to the next Council. When he came we consulted what was fittest for us to do after such Treatment, & upon
weighing every Circumstance we resolv'd at last that since it was
not possible for us to agree with Firebrand, We wou'd absolutely
refuse to go with him upon the next Expedition, lest his Majesty's
Service might suffer by our perpetual Discord. Full of this Resolution we went down to Williamsburgh, & begg'd the Governor,
that he wou'd be pleas'd to dispence with our serving any more
with Firebrand in running the Line; because he was a Person of
such uneasy Temper, that there were no hopes of preserving any
Harmony amongst us. The Governor desired we wou'd not abandon a Service in which we had acquitted ourselves so well, but
finish what we had began, tho' he own'd we were join'd by a Gentleman too selfish & too arrogant to be happy with him. I reply'd
that since he did me the Honour to desire me to make another
Journey with him, I wou'd do it, but hoped I might have 20 Men
& have the Sole command of them to prevent all Disputes upon
that Chapter. He thought what I ask't was so reasonable, that
if I wou'd propose it to the Council, I might easily carry it.

According to the Governor's Advice, Meanwell & I, yielded to
put it to the Council, & when it was met, & our Business enter'd
upon, I deliver'd my self in the following Terms. "I humbly
"conceive that the Business of running the Line towards the Moun-
"tains will require at least 20 Men, if we intend to follow it with
"Vigour. The Chain-carriers, the Markers, & the Men who carrys
"the Instrument after the Surveyor must be constantly reliev'd.
"These must be 5 in Number always upon Duty, & where the
"Woods are thick, which will frequently be the Case, there shou'd
"be 2 more Men to clear the way & upon the Prospect to the Sur-
"veyors. While this Number is thus employ'd, their Arms must
"be carry'd, & their Horses led after them by as great a Number.
"This will employ at least 10 Men constantly, And if we must
"have no more, who must then take care of the Baggage & Provi-
"sions which will need several Horses, & in such Pathless Woods,
"each Horse must be led by a carefull Man, or the Packs will soon
"be torn off their Backs. Then besides all these, some Men shou'd

[Continued on page 138]

"be at Leizure to hunt & keep us in Meat, for which our whole
"dependance must be upon the Woods. Nor ought we in an Affair
"of so much Consequence, be ty'd down to so small a Number of
"Men, as will be exactly requisite for the dayly business, some
"may be sick, or Lame, or otherwise disabled. In such an Exi-
"gence must we return Home, for want of Spare Hands to supply
"such Misfortune? Ought we not to go provided against such
"common Disasters as these? At this rate we shou'd lose more
"in the length of time, than we shou'd save by the shortness of
"our Number, which wou'd make our Frugality, as it often hap-
"pens, an extravagant Expence to Us. Nor wou'd it be prudent
"or safe to go so far above the Inhabitants, without a competent
"Number of Men for our Defence. We shall cross the Path, which
"the Northern Indians Pass to make War upon the Catawba's,
"& shall go thro' the very Woods that are frequented by those
"Straggling Savages, who commit so many Murders upon our
"Frontiers. We ought therefore to go provided with a Force suf-
"ficient to secure us from falling into their hands. It may possibly
"be objected, that the Carolina Men will encrease our Number,
"which is certain, but they will very little encrease our Force.
"They will bring more Eaters than Fighters, at least they did so
"the last time, and if they shou'd be better provided with Arms
"now, their Commissioners have so little Command over the Men,
"that I expect no good from them if we shou'd be so unfortunate
"as to be attack't. From all which I must conclude, that our
"safety, our Business, & the Accidents that attend it, will require
"at least 20 Men. And in order to make this Number more use-
"full, there ought to be no confusion in the Command. We are
"taught both by reason & Experience, that when any Men in Arms
"are sent on an Expedition, they ought to be under the Command
"of one Person only. For shou'd they be commanded by several
"claiming equal Power, the Orders given by so many might happen
"to be contradictory, as probably they wou'd happen to be in our
"Case. The consequence of which must follow, that the Men
"wou'd not know whom to obey. This must introduce an endless
"distraction, & end in defeating the Business, you are sending us
"about. It were ridiculous to say the Command ought to rest in
"the Majority, because then we must call a Council every time any
"Orders are to be issued. It wou'd be still more absurd to pro-

The tenth of September being thought a little too soon for the Commissioners to meet, in order to proceed on the Line, on account of Snakes, 'twas agreed to put it off to the twentieth of the same Month, of which due Notice was sent to the Carolina-Commissioners.

"pose, that such Persons claiming equal Power, shou'd command
"by Turns, because then one Commander may undo this day, what
"his Collegue had directed the day before, & so the men will be
"perplext with a Succession of Jaring Orders. Besides the pre-
"ference, & distinction which these poor Fellows might have Rea-
"son to shew to One of these Kings of Branford, may be punish't
"by the other, when it comes to his turn to be in power. This be-
"ing the Case, what Men of Spirit or Common Sence wou'd list
"themselves under such uncertain Command, where they cou'd not
"know whom to please, or whom to obey? For all which Reason
"Sʳ I must conclude, that the Command of the Men ought to rest
"in One Person, & if in One, then without Controversy in him
"who has the Honour to be first in Commission.

The Council as well as the Governor was convinc't by these
Arguments, & unanimously voted 20 Men were few enough to go
out with us, & thought it reasonable that the Command of them
shou'd be given to me, as being the first in Commission. Firebrand oppos'd each of these Points with all his Eloquence, but to
little purpose no Body standing by him, not so much as his new
Ally the Commissary. He seem'd at first to befriend him with
a Distinction, which he made between the day of Battle, & a Day
of Business: but having no Second, he ran with the Stream. However in pure Compassion to poor Firebrand, for fear he shou'd
want somebody to run of his Errands for him, it was agreed he
shou'd have 3 Men to fetch & carry for him.

I had the same success in getting the day of Meeting which the
Carolina Commissioners desired might be put off till the 20ᵗʰ
of September, notwithstanding Firebrand produced Letters from
Messʳˢ Jumble & Shoebrush that they had not desired their Collegue Plausible to procure our Rendezvous to be deferr'd. I con-
fronted these Letters with that Epistle I had from Plausible which
flatly contradicted them. Thus it was evident there was a Shamefull untruth on one Side or the other, but if we consider the Characters of the Men, & the Influence of Firebrand over those two,
whose Brothers were Collectors, One may guess where it lies,
especially since this was not the first time their Pens had been
drawn in his Service. However these Letters did no Service. But
the Governor declared he wou'd write to Sʳ Richard Everard, that

[Continued on page 144]

we shou'd meet the Commissioners of his Government on the 20th
of September with 20 Men.   How much the Pride of Firebrand
was mortify'd by so intire a Defeat in every one of his points,
may be easily guest by the loud Complaint he made afterwards,
how unhumanely the Council had treated him, and by the Pains
he took with the Governor to get the Order of Council soften'd
with relation to the Command.   But remembering how unjustly he
had reproach't me with having taken too much upon me in our
former Trip I insisted upon the Order of Council in the fullest
Extent.   Upon seeing me so Sturdy he declar'd to the Governor,
he cou'd not go on such dishonourable Terms, & swore to others
he wou'd not, but Interest got the better of his Oath & Honour
too, and he did vouchsafe to go at last, notwithstanding all the
Disgraces which he thought had been put upon him.   From hence
we may fairly conclude, that Pride is not the Strongest of his
Passions, tho' strong enough to make him both ridiculous & de-
testable.

After these necessary Matters were settled, I ordered 1000 lb
of Brown Biscuit, & 200 lb of white to be provided, & 6 Baggage
Horses to carry it, at the rate of 3 Baggs containing 200 lb.
each Horse.   As for meat I intended to carry none, but to depend
intirely upon Providence for it.   But because the Game was not
like to be plentifull till we got above the Inhabitants, I directed
all the men to find themselves with 10 day's Provision.   I augu-
mented my Number of Men to 17, which together with 3 which
Firebrand undertook to get made up the Complement of 20.   For
these I provided Ammunition after the Rate of 2lb of Powder a
Man, with Shot in proportion.   On the 16th of September Meanwell & Astrolabe came to my House in Order to set out with me
the day following towards the Place of Rendezvous.

September

17.   About 10 in the Morning I having recommended my Wife
& Family to the Protection of the Almighty past the River with
Messrs Meanwell & Astrolabe at Mr Ravenscroft's Landing.[48]   He

---

[48] Reference is to the Maycox plantation, across the James from Westover, which
was purchased in 1723 by Thomas Ravenscroft. In the late eighteenth century it
passed into the ownership of David Meade who made it one of the famous show
places of Virginia. See Tyler, *Cradle of the Republic*, p. 212.

[Continued on page 144]

was so complaisant as to accompany us as far as the New Church,[49] where 8 of our Men were attending for us, Namely, Peter Jones, George Hamilton, James Patillo, Thomas Short, John Ellis Jun[r], Richard Smith, George Tilman & Abraham Jones. The rest were to meet us at Kinchin's, which lay more convenient to their Habitations. Only I had order'd 3 of them who were absent to convoy the Bread Horses thither, the nearest Road they cou'd go, namely Thomas Jones, Thomas Jones Jun[r], & Edward Powel, to the last of which the Bread Horses belong'd.

We proceeded with the 8 Men abovemention'd to Col[o] Harvy Harrisons,[50] where our Chaplain D[r] Humdrum was arriv'd before us. We were handsomely entertain'd & after Dinner furnish't ourselves with several small Conveniences out of the Store. There we took a turn to the Cold Bath, where the Col[o] refreshes himself every Morning. This is about 5 Feet Square, & as many deep, thro which a pure Stream continually passes, & is cover'd with a little House just big enough for the Bath & a Fireing Room. Our Landlord who us'd formerly to be troubled both with the Gripes & the Gout, fancys he receives benefit by plunging every day in cold Water. This good House was enough to spoil us for Woodsmen, where we drank Rack-Punch[51] while we sat up, & trod on Carpets when we went to Bed.

18.   Having thankt the Col[o] for our good Cheer, we took leave about ten, not at all dismay'd at the liklihood of Rain. We travelled after the Rate of 4 Miles an Hour passing over Blackwater Bridge, & ten Miles beyond that over another call'd Assamousack Bridge. Then we filed off to Richard Parker's Plantation, where we had been kindly us'd in our return home. We found the distance 24 Miles going a little astray for want of a Guide, & there fell a Sort of Scots Mist all the way. We arriv'd about 5 a Clock & found things in much disorder, the good Woman being lately dead, & those that surviv'd sick. Pretty Sally

---

[49] Reference is probably to a chapel built in 1723, the contractor being a Mr. Thomas Jefferson. See Meade, *Old Churches, Ministers and Families*, Vol. I, p. 440.
[50] Henry Harrison. See above, note 44.
[51] A beverage containing rum distilled from molasses.

19.   We, on the part of Virginia, that we might be sure to be punctual, arriv'd at Mr. Kinchin's, the place appointed, on the 19th, after a Journey of three days, in which nothing Remarkable happen'd.

We found three of the Carolina-Commissioners had taken Possession of the House, having come thither by water from Edenton.   By the Great Quantity of Provisions these Gentlemen brought, and the few men they had to eat them, we were afraid they intended to carry the Line to the South sea.

They had 500 ℔s of bcaon and dry'd Beef, and 500 ℔s of Bisket, and not above three or four men.   The misfortune was, they forgot to provide Horses to carry their good things, or else trusted to the Incertainty of hireing them here, which, considering the Place, was leaving too much to that Jilt, Hazard.

On our part we had taken better Care, being completely furnisht with everything necessary for transporting our Baggage and Provisions.   Indeed we brought no other Provisions out with us but 1000 ℔s of Bread and had Faith enough to depend on Providence for our Meat, being desirous to husband the publick Money as much as possible.

We had no less than 20 men, besides the Chaplain, the Surveyors and all the Servants, to be Subsisted upon this Bread.   However, that it might hold out the better, our men had been Order'd to provide themselves at Home with Provision for Ten days, in which time we judg'd we should get beyond the Inhabitants, where Forest-Game of all sorts was like to be plenty at that time of the Year.

had lost some of her Bloom by an Ague, but none of her good humour. They entertain'd us, as well as they cou'd, & what was wanting in good cheer was made up in good humour.

19. About 10 this Morning we wish't Health to Sally & her Family, & forded over Notoway River at Bolton's Ferry, the water being very low. We call'd upon Samuel Kindred again who regaled us with a Beef Steak, & our Men with Syder. Here we had like to have listed a Mulatoo Wench for Cook to the Expedition, who formerly lived with Col° Ludwell. After halting here about an Hour, we pursued our Journey, & in the way Richard Smith Shew'd me the Star-Root,[52] which infallibly cures the Bite of the Rattlesnake. Nine Miles from thence we forded over Meherin River near Mr Kinchin's, believing we shou'd be at the place of meeting before the rest of the Commissioners. But we were mistaken, for the first Sight my Eyes were blest with, was that of Orion, & finding the Shadow there I knew the Substance cou'd not be far off.

Three Commissioners on the Part of N. Carolina came that Night, tho' Jumble & Puzzlecause were order'd by their Governor to stay behind, lest their Genl. Court might be delay'd. But they came notwithstanding, in the Strength of their Interest with the Council, but seem'd afraid of being pursued, & arrested. They put on very gracious Countenances at our first greeting: but yet look't a little conscious of having acted a very low part in the Epistles they had written. For my part I was not Courtier enough to disguise the Sentiments I had of them & their Slavish proceeding, & therefore cou'd not smile upon those I despis'd. Nor cou'd I behave much better to Firebrand & his Eccho Orion, nevertheless I constrain'd myself to keep up a stiff Civility. The last of these Gentlemen remembering the just Provocation he had given me, thought it necessary to bring a Letter from the Governor, recommending him to my favour & Protection. This therefore had the air of confessing his former Errors, which made me after some gentle Reproofs, assure him, he shou'd have no Reason to complain of my Treatment. Tho' I carry'd fair weather to Firebrand,

---

[52] The stargrass or colicroot, a shrub bearing white or yellow flowers. Its roots were used medicinally.

20. This being the day appointed for our Rendezvous, great part of it was Spent in the careful fixing our Baggage and Assembling our Men, who were order'd to meet us here. We took care to examine their Arms, and made proof of the Powder provided for the Expedition.

Our Provision-Horses had been hinder'd by the rain from coming up exactly at the Day; but this Delay was the less Disappointment, by reason of the ten days' Subsistence the men had been directed to provide for themselves.

Mr. Moseley did not join us till the afternoon, nor Mr. Swan till Several Days after.

Mr. Kinchin had unadvisedly sold the Men a little Brandy of his own making, which produced much disorder, causing some to be too cholerick, and others too loving; Insomuch that a Damsel, who assisted in the Kitchen, had certainly Suffer'd what the Nuns call Martyrdom, had she not capitulated a little too soon.

This outrage would have call'd for some severe Discipline, had she not bashfully withdrawn herself early in the Morning, & so carry'd off the Evidence.

yet Meanwell cou'd not, but all Ceremony, Notice, & Conversation seem'd to be cancell'd betwixt them. I caus'd the Tent to be pitch'd in the Orchard, Where I & my Company took up Our Quarters, leaving the House to Firebrand & his Faction.

20. This Morning Meanwell was taken a Purging & vomiting for which I dosed him with Veal Broth, & afterwards advis'd him to a Gallon of warm Water, which finish't his Cure. We herded very little with our Brother Commissioners & Meanwell frankly gave Jumble to understand, that we resented the impertinent Letters he & some of his Collegues had writ to Virginia. He made a very lame Apology for it, because the Case wou'd not bear a good One. He & his Brethren were lamentably puzzled how to carry their Baggage & Provisions. They had brought them up by Water near this Place & had depended on fortune to get Horses there to carry them forward. I believe too they rely'd a little upon us to assist them, but I was positive not to carry One Pound Weight. We had Luggage enough for our own Horses, & as our Provisions lighten'd, the shortness of their Provenders wou'd require them to be lighten'd too. I was not so complaisant to these worthy Gentlemen as Firebrand for he brought a Tent for them out of the Magazine at Williamsburgh, to requite the dirty work they had been always ready to do for him. At last they hired something like a Cart to carry their Lumber as far as it cou'd go towards Roanoke River.

In the Evening 6 more of our Men join'd us, namely, Robert Hix, John Evans, Stephen Evans, Charles Kimball, Thomas Wilson, & William Pool, but the 3 Men that conducted the Bread-Horses, came not up as yet, which gave me some Uneasiness tho' I concluded they had been stop't by the Rain. Just after Sunset Capt Hix & Capt Drury Stith[53] arriv'd & made us the complement to attend us as far as Roanoke. The last of these Gentlemen bearing some Resemblance to Sr Richard Everard put Messrs Jumble & Puzzlecause into a Panick lest the Knight was come to put a Stop to their Journey. My Landlord had unluckily sold our Men some Brandy, which produced much disorder, making some too Cholerick, and others too loving. (So that a Damsel who came

---

[53] Colonel Drury Stith, Sheriff of Charles City County in 1719-20 and 1724-25. He removed to Brunswick County and was its first County Clerk.

21. We despatcht away the Surveyors without Loss of Time, who, with all their diligence, could carry the Line no farther than 3 Miles and 176 Poles, by reason the Low-Ground was one entire Thicket. In that distance they crost Meherin River the 4th time. In the mean while the Virginia-Commissioners thought proper to conduct their Baggage a farther way about, for the Convenience of a clearer Road.

The Carolina-Gentlemen did at length, more by Fortune than forecast, hire a clumsy Vehicle, something like a cart, to transport their Effects as far as Roanoak. This wretched Machine, at first Setting out, met with a very rude choque, that broke a Case-Bottle of Cherry Brandy in so unlucky a Manner that not one precious Drop was saved. This Melancholy Beginning forboded an unprosperous Journey, and too quick a Return, to the Persons most immediately concern'd.

In our way we crosst Fountain's Creek, which runs into Meherin River, so call'd from the disaster of an unfortunate Indian Trader who had formerly been drowned in it, and, like Icarus, left his Name to that fatal stream. We took up our Quarters on the Plantation of John Hill, where we pitcht our Tent, with design to tarry till such time as the Surveyors cou'd work their way to us.

22. This being Sunday, we had an Opportunity of resting from our Labours. The expectation of such a Novelty as a Sermon in these Parts brought together a Numerous Congregation. When the Sermon was over our Chaplain did his part towards making Eleven of them Christians.

Several of our men had Intermitting feavers, but were soon restor'd to their Health again by proper Remedies. Our chief Medicine was Dogwood Bark,[53] which we used, instead of that of Peru, with good Success. Indeed, it was given in larger Quanty, but then, to make the Patients amends, they swallowed much fewer Doses.

---

[53] The Cornus florida, used widely in the antebellum South in treatment of fevers and as a tonic. See Porcher, F. A., *Resources of Southern Fields and Forests.* (1863), pp. 59-61.

to assist in the Kitchen wou'd certainly have been ravish't, if her timely consent had not prevented the Violence. Nor did my Land-lady think herself safe in the hands of such furious Lovers, and therefore fortify'd her Bed chamber & defended it with a Chamber-Pot charg'd to the Brim with Female Ammunition. I never cou'd learn who the Ravisher was; because the Girl had walk't off in the Morning early, but Firebrand & his Servant were the most suspected, having been engag'd in those kind of Assaults once before. In the Morning Meanwell join'd us.

21. We sent away the Surveyors about 9 who could carry the Line no more than 3½ Miles because the Low Grounds were cover'd with Thickets. As soon as we had paid a very exorbitant Bill, and the Carolina Men had loaded their Vehickle & dispos'd of their Lumber, we mounted, & conducted our Baggage about 10 Miles. We took up our Quarters at the Plantation of John Hill, where we pitch't our Tent with design to rest there 'til Monday. This Man's House was so poorly furnish't, that Firebrand & his Carolina Train cou'd not find in their Hearts to lodge in it, so we had the Pleasure of their Company in the Camp. They per-fumed the Tent with their Rum Punch, & hunted the poor Parson with their unseemly Jokes, which turn'd my Stomach as much as their Fragrant Liquor. I was grave & speechless the whole Evening, & retired early, by all which, I gave them to understand, I was not fond of the Conversation of those whose Wit, like the Commons at the University & Inns of Court is eternally the same.

22. This being Sunday we had a large Congregation, & tho' there were many Females, we saw but one Beauty bright enough to disturb our devotions. Our Parson made 11 Christians. Mr Hill made heavy complaint that our Horses did much Damage to his Corn-Field. Upon which I order'd those that were most Vicious that way to be ty'd up to their good Behaviour. Among these Hum-drum's & Astrolabes were the greatest Trespassers. After Church I gave John Ellis a Vomit for his Ague with good Success, & was forc'd myself to soften my Bowels with Veal Broth for a Loose-ness. I also recommended Warm-Water to Capt Stith for the Cholick, which gave him immediate Ease.

In the afternoon our Provision-Horses arrived Safe in the Camp. They had met with very heavy Rains, but, thank God, not a Single Bisket receiv'd the least Damage thereby.

We were furnisht by the Neighbours with very lean Cheese and very fat Mutton, upon which occasion twill not be improper to draw one conclusion, from the Evidence of North Carolina, that Sheep would thrive much better in the Woods than in Pasture Land, provided a careful Shepherd were employed to keep them from Straying, and, by the help of Dogs, to protect them also from the wolves.

23. The Surveyors came to us at Night, tho' they had not brought the Line so far as our Camp, for which reason we thought it needless to go forward till they came up with us. They cou'd run no more than 4 Miles and 5 Poles, because the Ground was every where grown up with thick Bushes.

The Soil here appear'd to be very good, tho' much broken betwixt Fountain creek and Roanoak River. The Line crost Meherin the 5th and last time, nor were our People sorry to part with a Stream the Meanders of which had given them so much Trouble.

Our Hunters brought us four wild Turkeys, which at that Season began to be fat and very delicious, especially the Hens.

These Birds seem to be of the Bustard kind, and fly heavily. Some of them are exceedingly large, and weigh upwards of 40 Pounds; Nay, some bold Historians venture to say, upwards of 50. They run very fast, stretching forth their Wings all the time, like the Ostrich, by way of Sails to quicken their Speed.

They roost commonly upon very high Trees, Standing near some River or Creek, and are so stupify'd at the Sight of Fire, that if you make a Blaze in the Night near the Place where they roost, you may fire upon them Several times successively, before they will dare to fly away.

Their Spurs are so Sharp and Strong that the Indians used formerly to point their Arrows with them, tho' now they point them with a Sharp white Stone. In the Spring the Turkey-Cocks begin to gobble, which is the Language wherein they make Love.

It rain'd very hard in the Night, with a violent Storm of Thunder and Lightening, which oblig'd us to trench in our Tent all round, to carry off the Water that fell upon it.

24. So soon as the men could dry their Blankets, we sent out the Surveyors, who now meeting with more favourable Grounds, advanc'd the line 7 Miles and 82 Poles. However, the Commissioners did not think proper to decamp that day, believing they might easily overtake the Surveyors the next. In the mean time they sent out some of their most expert Gunners, who brought in four more wild Turkeys.

In the Afternoon our 3 Men arriv'd with the Bread-Horses, having been kept so long behind by the Rain, but thank God it had receiv'd no Damage. I took a walk with Plausible, & told him of the Letter his Collegues had writ, to falsify what he had told me concerning their Request, to put off the time of our Meeting. He justify'd his own Veracity, but shew'd too much Cold Blood in not been (sic) piqued at so flagrant an Injury. Firebrand & his Followers had smelt out a House about half a Mile off, to which they sent for the Silver Bowl, & spent the Evening by themselves both to their own Statisfaction & ours. We hoped to be rid of them for all night, but they found the way to the Camp just after we were gone to Bed, & Firebrand hindered us from going to sleep so soon, by his Snoring & swearing.

23. We continu'd in our Camp, & sent the Surveyors back to the Place where they left off. They cou'd run the Line no more than 4 Miles by reason that it was overgrown with Bushes. I sent several of the Men out a Hunting & they brought us 4 Wild Turkeys. Old Capt Hix kill'd 2 of them, who turn'd his Hand to everything notwithstanding his great Age, disdaining to be thought the worse for Threescore & ten. Beauty never appear'd better in Old Age, with a Ruddy complexion, & Hair as white as Snow. It rain'd a little in the Evening, but did not hinder our Rum-Commissioners from Stepping over to John Hill's to swill their Punch, leaving the Tent clear to Us. After Midnight, it rain'd very hard with a Storm of Thunder & Lightening, which oblidged us to trench in our Tent to cast off the Water. The Line crost Meherin 5 times in all.

24. So Soon as the Men cou'd dry their Blankets, we sent away the Surveyor who made a Shift to carry the Line 7 Miles. But we thought it proper not to decamp believing we might easily overtake the Surveyors before to Morrow Night. Our Shooters kill'd 4 more Wild Turkeys. Meanwell & Capt Stith pretended to go a hunting, but their Game was 2 fresh colour'd Wenches, which were not hard to hunt down. The Neighbours supply'd us with pretty good Cheese & very fat Mutton. I order'd a View of John Hill's Damage in his Corn field, & paid him for 6 Barrels on

This part of the Country being very proper for raising Cattle and Hogs, we observ'd the Inhabitants lived in great plenty without killing themselves with Labour.

I found near our Camp some Plants of that kind of Rattle-Snake Root, called Star-grass.[54] The Leaves shoot out circularly, and grow Horizontally and near the Ground. The Root is in Shape not unlike the Rattle of that Serpent, and is a Strong Antidote against the bite of it. It is very bitter, and where it meets with any Poison, works by Violent Sweats, but where it meets with none, has no Sensible Operation but that of putting the Spirits into a great Hurry, and so of promoting Perspiration.

The Rattle-snake has an utter Antipathy to this Plant, insomuch that if you Smear your hands with the Juice of it, you may handle the Viper Safely. Thus much I can say of my own Experience, that once in July, when these Snakes are in their greatest Vigour, I besmear'd a Dog's Nose with the Powder of this Root, and made him trample on a large Snake Several times, which, however, was so far from biting him, that it perfectly Sicken'd at the Dog's Approach, and turn'd its Head from him with the Utmost Aversion.

Our Chaplain, to shew his Zeal, made an excursion of 6 Miles to christen 2 children, but without the least regard to the good Chear at these Solemnities.

25. The Surveyors taking the Advantage of clear Woods, pusht on the Line 7 Miles and 40 Poles. In the mean time the Commissioners marcht with the Baggage about 12 miles, and took up their Quarters near the Banks of the Beaver Pond, (which is one Branch of Fountain's creek,) just by the place where the Surveyors were to finish their day's work.

In our march one of the men kill'd a Small Rattle-Snake, which had no more than two Rattles. Those Vipers remain in Vigour generally till towards the End of September, or Sometimes later, if the Weather continue a little warm. On this consideration we had provided three Several Sorts of Rattle-Snake-Root, made up into proper Doses, and ready for immediate use, in case any one of the Men or their Horses had been bitten.

We crosst Fountain's Creek once more in our Journey this day, and found the Grounds very Rich, notwithstanding they were broken and Stony.

Near the place where we encampt the county of Brunswick is divided from *the* Isle of Wight. These Counties run quite on the back of Surry and Prince George, and are laid out in very irregular Figures.

As a Proof the Land mended hereabouts, we found the Plantations began to grow thicker by much than we had found them lower down.

26. We hurry'd away the Surveyors without Loss of time, who ex-

---

[54] Byrd here confuses two herbs. Rattlesnake Root is the Prenanthes Serpentaria, tribe of Chichoriaeceae; Stargrass belongs to the tribe Hypoxidae.

that Account. Firebrand instructed one of the 3 Men which he listed on the Publick Service to call him Master, thereby endeavouring to pass him on the Carolina Commissioners for his Servant, that he might seem to have as many Servants as Steddy, but care was taken to undeceive them in this matter & expose his Vanity. The Carolina Men liv'd at Rack & Manager[54] without any Sort of Occonomy, thereby shewing they intended not to go very far with us, tho' we took time to set them a better example. Our Chaplain had leave to go home with Robert Hix, who lived no more than 6 Miles from this place to christen his Child & the Old Captain went along with them. We had the comfort to have the Tent to ourselves, the Knights of the Rum-Cask retiring in the Evening to the House, & wasting the Liquor & double refined Sugar as fast as they cou'd.

25.   Our Surveyors proceeded to run little more than 7 Miles. Firebrand & his Gang got out this Morning before us, on pretence of providing our Dinner; but they outrid the Man that carry'd the Mutton, & he not knowing the way was lost, so that instead of having our Dinner sooner, we run a hazard of having none at all. We came up to them about 4 a Clock & thank't them for the prudent care they had taken. This was a Sample of these Gentlemen's Management, whenever they undertook anything. We encampt near Beaver Pond Creek, & on our Way thither Peter Jones kill'd a small Rattlesnake. The Surveyors made an End very near where we lay. Orion was exceedingly awkward at his Business, that Astrolabe was obliged to do double Duty. There being no house at hand to befriend us, we were forced to do pennance at the Tent with the Topers.

26.   This Morning we dispatch't the Surveyors early, & they ran about 10½ Miles. By the way the Men that were with him kill'd 2 large Rattlesnakes. Will Pool trod upon one of them without receiving any hurt, & 2 of the Chain Carriers had march't over the other, but he was so civil as to bite neither of them, however one of these Vipers struck at Wilson's horse, and misst him. So many Escapes were very providential, tho' the Danger proves, that my Argument for putting off our Business was not without

_____
[54] Without economy or restraint.

tended the Line 10 Miles and 160 Poles, the Grounds proving dry and free from Under-woods. By the way the chain-carriers kill'd two more Rattle-Snakes, which I own was a little ungrateful, because two or three of the Men had Strided over them without receiving any Hurt; tho' one of these Vipers had made bold to Strike at one of the Baggage Horses, as he went along, but by good Luck his Teeth only grazed on the hoof, without doing him any Damage. However, these Accidents were, I think, so many Arguments that we had very good Reason to defer our coming out till the 20th of September.

We observ'd Abundance of St. Andrew's Cross[55] in all the Woods we passed thro', which is the common Remedy used by the Indian traders to cure their horses when they are bitten by Rattle-Snakes.

It grows on a Strait Stem, about 18 Inches high, and bears a Yellow Flower on the Top, that has an Eye of Black in the Middle, with Several Pairs of Narrow Leaves Shooting out at right Angles from the Stalk over against one another.

This Antidote grows Providentially all over the Woods, and upon all Sorts of Soil, that it may be every where at hand in Case a Disaster should Happen, and may be had all the hot Months while the Snakes are dangerous.

About four a'clock in the Afternoon we took up our Quarters upon Caban Branch, which also discharges itself into Fountain Creek. On our way we observed Several Meadows cloth'd with very rank-Grass, and Branches full of tall Reeds, in which Cattle keep themselves fat good part of the Winter. But Hogs are as injurious to both as Goats are said to be to Vines, and for that Reason it was not lawful to Sacrifice them to Bacchus. We halted by the way to Christen two Children at a Spring, where their Mothers waylaid us for that good Purpose.

27. It was ten of the clock before the Surveyors got to work, because some of the Horses had straggled to a great Distance from the Camp. Nevertheless, meting with Practicable Woods, they advanct the Line 9 Miles and 104 Poles. We crosst over Pea-Creek about four Miles from our Quarters, and three Miles farther, Lizzard-Creek, both which empty their Waters into Roanoak River.

Between these two Creeks a poor Man waited for us with five Children to be baptiz'd, and we haited till the Ceremony was ended. The Land seem'd to be very good, by the largeness of the Trees, tho' very Stony. We proceeded as far as Pidgeon-Roost-Creek, which also runs into Roanoak, and there Quarter'd.

We had not the pleasure of the Company of any of the Carolina-Commissioners in this day's March, except Mr. Moseley's, the rest tarrying behind to wait the coming up of their Baggage-Cart, which they had now

---

[55] See note 56, *Secret History.*

Foundation. We march't upon the Line after the Surveyors, & about 4 a Clock encampt upon Cabin Branch, which is one of the Branches of Fountain's Creek. Before we sat off this Morning, we christen'd 2 Children. One of them was brought by a Modest Lass, who being asked how she liked Captain Stiff reply'd not at all, nor Capt Limber neither, meaning Orion. We saw Abundance of Ipocoaceanna in the Woods, & the Fern Rattlesnake Root,[55] which is said to be the strongest Antidote against the Bite of that Viper. And we saw St Andrew's-Cross[56] almost every Step we went, which serves for the same Purpose. This Plant grows on all kinds of Soil, every where at hand during the Summer months, when the Snakes have Vigour enough to do Mischief. Old Capt. Hix entertain'd us with One of his Trading Songs, which he quaver'd out most Melodiously & put us all into a good humour.

27. We sent away the Surveyors before 10 a Clock & follow'd with the Baggage at 11. But Firebrand thought proper to remain with 3 of the Carolina Commissioners til their Cart came up, & took it ill that we tarry'd not with them likewise. But I cou'd not complement away our Time at that Rate. Here they made broad Hints to carry some of their Luggage for them, I wou'd put not such hardships upon our Men, who had all enough to carry of their Own, so we left them there, to make the best shift they cou'd, & follow'd the Line with all Diligence. We past Pea-hill-Creek, & sometime after Lizzard Creek, which empties itself

---

[55] An herb of the chicory family. Its milky juice was taken internally and its leaves when steeped, were applied externally in the treatment of snake wounds.
[56] A small plant of the St. Johns-wort family, so called because its petals open into shape like the St. Andrews cross.

not seen nor heard (though the Wheels made a Dismal Noise) for several days past.

Indeed it was a very difficult Undertaking to conduct a Cart thro' such pathless and perplext Woods, and no wonder if its Motion was a little Planetary. We would have payd them the Complement of waiting for them, cou'd we have done it at any other Expense but that of the Publick.

In the Stony Grounds we rode over we found great Quantity of the true Ipocoacanna,[56] which in this part of the World is call'd Indian-Physick. This has Several Stalks growing up from the Same Root about a Foot high, bearing a Leaf resembling that of a Straw-Berry. It is not so strong as that from Brazil, but has the same happy Effects, If taken in Somewhat a larger Dose. It is an Excellent Vomit, and generally cures intermitting Fevers and Bloody Fluxes at once or twice taking. There is abundance of it in the upper part of the Country, where it delights most in a Stony Soil intermixt with black Mold.

28. Our Surveyors got early to work, yet cou'd forward the Line but 6 miles and 121 Poles, because of the uneven Grounds in the Neighbourhood of Roanoak, which they crosst in this Day's work.

In that Place the River is 49 Poles wide, and rolls down a crystal Stream of very Sweet water, Insomuch that when there comes to be a great Monarch in this Part of the World, he will cause all the Water for his own Table to be brought from Roanoak, as the great Kings of Persia did theirs from the Nile and Choaspis, because the Waters of those Rivers were light, and not apt to corrupt.[57]

The great Falls of Roanoak lie about 20 Miles lower, to which a Sloop of Moderate Burthen may come up. There are, besides these, many Smaller Falls above, tho' none that entirely intercept the Passage of the River, as the great Ones do, by a Chain of Rocks for 8 Miles together.

The River forks about 36 Miles higher, and both Branches are pretty equal in Breadth where they divide, tho' the Southern, now call'd the Dan, runs up the farthest. That to the North runs away near Northwest, and is call'd the Staunton, and heads not far from the Source of Appamatuck River, while the Dan stretches away pretty near West & runs clear thro' the great Mountains.

We did not follow the Surveyors till towards Noon, being detain'd in our camp to Christen Several more Children. We were conducted a nearer way, by a famous Woodsman, call'd Epaphroditus Bainton. This Forester Spends all his time in ranging the Woods, and is said to make

---

[56] The herb Gillenia, which corresponds to the Epecacuanha of Brazil, from which the drug epecac is derived. It was also used as a tonic and as a remedy for milk sickness.

[57] "The same humor prevails at this day in the Kings of Denmark who order all the East India Ships of that nation to call at the Cape of Good Hope and take in a But of Water from a Spring on the Table Hill, and bring it to Coppenhagen for their Majesty's own Drinking." (Byrd's Note).

into Roanoke River. Here we halted 'til our Chaplain baptized
5 Children. Then we proceeded to Pigeon-Roost Creek, where we
took up our Quarters, having carry'd the Line above 9 Miles.

28. We hurry'd away the Surveyors, who cou'd run no more
than 6 Miles because of the Uneven Grounds near Roanoke-River.
We did not follow with the Baggage til 10, being staid to christen
6 Children, & to discourse a very civil Old Fellow, who brought us
2 fat Shoats for a present. The Name of our Benefactor was
Epaphroditus Bainton, who is Young enough at 60 Years of Age,
to keep a Concubine, & to Walk 25 miles in a day. He has for-
sworn ever getting on a Horse back, being once in Danger of
breaking his Neck by a fall. He spends most of his time in hunting & ranging the Woods, killing generally more than 100 Deer
in a Year. He pretends to Skill in the Virtues of many Plants,
but I cou'd learn nothing of that kind from him. This Man was
our Guide to Maj[r] Mumford's Plantation,[57] under the Care of
Miles Riley, where we were regaled with Milk, Butter, & many
other Refreshments. The Maj[r]. had order'd some Wine to be
lodged here for us, & a fat Steer to be at our Service; but the last
we refus'd with a great many thanks. From hence we continu'd
our Journey to the Canoe-Landing upon Roanoke River, where
Young Mumford & M[r] Walker met us. Here we ferry'd over
our Baggage & our Persons, ordering the men with the Horses to
the Ford near a mile higher, which leads to the Trading Path.
Here my Old Friend Cap[t] Hix took his Leave committing us to

---

[57] Robert Mumford (Munford), Justice and Colonel of Militia in Prince George
County, vestryman of Bruton Parish, and member of the House of Burgesses in
1720-22.

great Havock among the Deer, and other Inhabitants of the Forest, not much wilder than Himself.

We proceeded to the Canoe-Landing on Roanoak, where we passt the River with the Baggage. But the Horses were directed to a Ford about a Mile higher, call'd by the Indians Moni-seep,[57] which signifies, in their Jargon, Shallow Water. This is the Ford where the Indian-Traders used to cross with their Horses, in their way to the Catauba Nation.

There are many Rocks in the River thereabouts, on which grows a kind of Water Grass, which the wild Geese are fond of, and resort to it in great Numbers.

We landed on the South Side of Roanoak at a Plantation of Colo. Mumford's,[59] where, by that Gentlemen's Special Directions, we met with Sundry Refreshments. Here we picht our Tent, for the benefit of the Prospect, upon an Eminence that overlookt a broad Piece of Low Ground, very rich, tho' liable to be overflow'd.

By the way, one of our Men kill'd another Rattle-Snake, with 11 Rattles, having a large Gray Squirrel in his Maw, the head of which was already digested, while the Body remain'd Stil entire.

The way these Snakes catch their Prey is thus: They Ogle the poor little animal, till by force of the Charm he falls down Stupify'd and Senseless on the Ground. In that condition the Snake approaches, and moistens first one Ear and then the Other with his Spawl, and after that the other Parts of the Head, to make all Slippery. When that is done, he draws this Member into his Mouth, and after it, by Slow Degrees, all the rest of the Body.

29. This being Sunday, we had Divine Service and a Sermon, at which Several of the Borderers assisted, and we concluded the Duties of the Day in the Christening five Children. Our Devotion being perform'd in the Open Field, like that of Mr. Whitfield's Flocks, and unfortunate Shower of Rain had almost disperst our Congregation. About four in the Afternoon the Carolina-Commissioners made a Shift to come up with us, whom we had left at Pidgeon-Roost Creek the Fryday before, waiting for their Provisions. When their Cart came up they prudently discharg'd it, and rather chose to hire two Men to carry some part of their Baggage. The Rest they had been Obliged to leave behind, in the Crotch of an Old Tree, for want of proper Conveniences to transport it any farther.

We found in the low Ground Several Plants of the Fern Root,[60] which is said to be much the Strongest Antidote yet discover'd against the Poison

---

[58] This ford is one mile west of the point at which the Roanoke River crosses the North Carolina-Virginia boundary. It was the crossing of the Indian Trading Path, which ran from Bermuda Hundred, Virginia, to the lands of the Catawba Indians in upper South Carolina.

[59] See Note 57, *Secret History*.

[60] The Prenanthes Serpentaria, or Snake Root.

our kind Star. We were set ashoar at another Plantation belonging to Major Mumford, under the Management of a Man they call'd Natt. Here was another fat Steer ordered for Us, which we thankfully accepted of for the Sake of the Men. We pitch't the Tent near the House, which supply'd all out Wants. Poor Miles Riley received a kick from one of the Horses, for which I order'd him to be instantly blooded, & hindered all bad consequences. I interceeded with Plausible in behalf of the Virginians whose Land was left by the Line in Carolina, & he promis'd to befriend them. George Hamilton kill'd a Snake with 11 Rattles having a Squirrell in his Belly, which he had charm'd & only the head of it was digested. Also the Chain-carriers kill'd another small one the same day.

29. Being Sunday we had a Sermon, but 'twas interrupted with a Shower of Rain which dispers't our Congregation. A littl before Noon the Carolina Baggage came up, & the Servants blest us with the News that their Masters wou'd come in the Evening. They also inform'd us they lay last Night at John Youngs, & had hired him & his Brother to assist them upon the Line. That for want of Horses to carry their Luggage, they had left some of it behind. Our Chaplain Baptised 5 Children, & I gave Thomas Wilson a Vomit that work't powerfully, & carry'd off his Feaver. I wrote to the Governor a full & true account of all our proceedings, & sent the Letter by M^r. Mumford, who took his Leave this Evening. About 4 in the Afternoon Firebrand & his Carolina Guards came to us, as likewise did some of the Sapponi Indians.[58] I had sent Charles Kimball to Christanna to perswade 2 of their most able Huntsmen to go the Journey, to help supply us with meat. I had observ'd that our Men were unfortunate Gunners, which made me more desirous to have some that had better luck. Out of 5 which came I chose Bearskin & another, who accepted the Terms I proposed to them. From this time forward the Carolina Men & their Leader, honour'd us with their Company only at Dinner, but Mornings & Evenings they had a distinct Fire to our great Comfort, at which they toasted their Noses. Indeed the whole time of our being together, our dear Collegue acted more

---

[58] See Note 62, *History of the Dividing Line.*

of the Rattle-Snake. The Leaves of it resemble those of Fern, from whence it obtain'd its Name. Several Stalks shoot from the same Root, about 6 Inches long, that ly mostly on the Ground. It grows in a very Rich Soil, under the Protection of Some tall Tree, that Shades it from the Meridian Beams of the Sun. The Root has a faint Spicy tast, and is preferr'd by the Southern Indians to all other Counter-poisons in this Country.

But there is another sort preferr'd by the Northern Indians, that they call Seneca Rattle-Snake-Root, to which wonderful Vertues are ascrib'd in the Cure of Pleurisys, Feavers, Rhumatisms, and Dropsys; besides it being a powerful Antidote against the Venom of the Rattle-Snake.[61]

In the Evening the Messenger we had sent to Christanna return'd with five Saponi Indians.[62] We cou'd not entirely rely on the Dexterity of our own Men, which induced us to send for some of the Indians. We agreed with two of the most expert of them, upon reasonable Terms, to hunt for us the remaining Part of our Expedition. But one of them falling Sick soon after, we were content to take only the other, whose Hunting Name was Bear-skin.

This Indian, either by his Skill or good Luck, Supply'd us plentifully all the way with Meat, Seldom discharging his piece in vain.

By his Assistance, therefore, we were able to keep our men to their Business, without Suffering them to Straggle about the Woods, on pretence of furnishing us with Necessary Food.

30. It had rain'd all night, and made every thing so wet, that our Surveyors cou'd not get to their Work before Noon. They cou'd therefore measure no more than four Miles and 220 Poles, which, according to the best information we cou'd get, was near as high as the uppermost Inhabitant at that time.

We crost the Indian Trading path above-mention'd about a Mile from our Camp, and a Mile beyond that forded Haw-Tree-Creek. The Woods we passed thro' had all the Tokens of Sterility, except a small Poison'd Field, on which grew no Tree bigger than a Slender Sapling. The larger Trees had been destroyed, either by Fire or Caterpillars, which is often the Case in the upland Woods, and the places where such Desolation happens are call'd Poison'd Fields.

[61] See Tennent, John, *An Epistle to Dr. Richard Mead concerning the Epidemical Diseases of Virginia, particularly plurisy and Perepneumony; wherein is shown the surprising efficacy of the Seneca Rattle-Snake Root.* (Edinburgh, 1838.)

[62] The *Dividing Line* is one of the principal sources for the history of the Saponi. In 1701 Lawson found them on the Yadkin. Soon after they moved to the region of the Roanoke River, establishing Saponi Town about 15 miles west of Windsor, Bertie County, North Carolina; later they were located by Governor Spotswood at Fort Christanna. About 1740 they and the Tutelo, a kindred tribe, moved northward, stopping first at Shamokin, Pennsylvania, and then joined the Cayugas of New York. About 1779 the Tutelo went to Canada. See Mooney, "The Siouan Tribes of the Eeast" (*Bulletin of the American Bureau of Ethnology*, 1894.) For description of these Indians by Byrd, see page 308.

like a Commissioner for Carolina, than Virginia, & not only
herded with them perpetually, but in every Instance join'd his
Politicks with theirs in their consultations.   No wonder then they
acted so wisely in their Conduct, & managed their Affairs with
such admirable Prudence.   It rain'd the whole Night long & held
not up til break of day.

30.   The Tent & Baggage was so wet, that we cou'd not get them
dry til 12 a Clock, at which Hour we sent the Surveyors out &
they carry'd the Line about 4½ Miles, which we computed, was
as high as any Inhabitants.   But we mov'd not til 2 with the
Baggage.   We past over Haw-Tree Creek, 2 Miles from our Camp,
marching over poison'd Fields.   By the way a very lean Boar
crost us, & several claim'd the Credit of killing it, but all agreed
twas Stone dead before Firebrand fired, yet he took the Glory of
this Exploit to himself, so much Vanity he had, that it broke out
upon such paltry Occasions.   Before we sat off this Morning,
Orion came to me with a Countenance very pale & disordered, desiring that Astrolabe might have Orders never to concern himself,
when it was his turn to survey, because when he needed to be reliev'd, he chose rather to be beholden to Bootes, than to him.   I
cou'd by no means agree to this Request, telling him that none was
so proper to assist one Virginia Surveyor, as the other.   I let him
know too, that such a Motion savour'd more of Pique & Peevish-

We took up our Quarters upon a Branch of Great Creek, where there was tolerable good Grass for the poor Horses. These poor Animals having now got beyond the Latitude of Corn, were obliged to Shift as well as they cou'd for themselves.

On our way the men rous'd a Bear, which being the first we had seen since we came out, the poor Beast had many pursuers. Several Persons contended for the Credit of killing him: tho' he was so poor he was not worth the Powder. This was some Disappointment to our Woodsmen, who commonly prefer the Flesh of Bears to every kind of Venison. There is Something indeed peculiar to this Animal, namely, that its fat is very firm, and may be eaten plentifully without rising in the Stomach. The Paw (which, when stript of the hair, looks like a Human Foot,) is accounted a dilicious Morsel by all who are not Shockt at the ungracious Resemblance it bears to a Human Foot.

Oct. 1.   There was a white Frost this morning on the Ground, occasion'd by a North-West Wind, which stood our Friend in dispersing all Aguish Damps, and making the Air wholesome at the Same time that it made it cold. Encourag'd therefore by the Weather, Our Surveyors got to work early, and by the Benefit of Clear Woods, and Level Ground, drove the Line 12 Miles and 12 Poles.

At a Small Distance from our Camp we crost Great Creek, and about 7 Miles farther Nut-bush Creek, so call'd from the many Hazle-Trees growing upon it. By good Luck Many Branches of these Creeks were full of Reeds, to the great comfort of our Horses. Near five Miles from thence we encamp on a Branch that runs into Nut-Bush Creek, where those Reeds flourisht more than Ordinary. The Land we marcht over was for the most part broken and Stony, and in some places cover'd over with Thickets almost impenetrable.

At Night the Surveyors, taking Advantage of a very clear Sky, made a third Tryal of the Variation, and found it Still something less than 3 Degrees, so that it did not diminish by advancing towards the West, or by approaching the Mountains, nor yet by encreasing our distance from the Sea; but remain'd much the Same we had found it at Corotuck-Inlet.

One of our Indians kill'd a large Fawn, which was very welcome, tho', like Hudibras's Horse, it had hardly Flesh enough to cover its Bones.

In the low Grounds the Carolina Gentlemen shew'd us another Plant, which they said was used in their country to cure the Bite of the Rattle-Snake. It put forth Several Leaves in figure like a Heart, and was clouded so like the common Assarabacca,[63] that I convinced it to be of that Family.

2.   So soon as the Horses cou'd be found, we hurry'd away the Surveyors, who advanct the Line 9 Miles and 254 Poles. About 3 Miles from

---

[63] An aromatic herb popularly known as Wild Ginger.

ness than Reason. However I desir'd him to ask the Opinion of
the other Commissioners, if he was not satisfy'd with mine: but he
found it proper to ask no more Questions. Puzzlecause had a sore
Throat, which incommoded him very much indeed, for he cou'd
not swallow so much as Rum-Punch without Pain. But I advis'd
him to part with 12 Ounces of Blood, which Open'd the Passage
to his Stomach. I recommended the Bark to Bootes for an Ague,
& gave one of the Carolina Men a dose of Ipocoaccanna, for the
same Distemper as I did to Powell one of our own Men.

October

1.　We sent out the Surveyors early & by the benefit of clear
Woods &, even Ground they carry'd the Line 12 Miles & 12 Poles.
One of our Baggage Horses being missing we decampt not til
Noon, which gave Firebrand & his Crew an Opportunity to get
the Start of Us about an hour. However we came up with the
Surveyors before them. We forded over Great Greek not far
from the Place where we encampt, & past Nutbush Creek about
7 Miles from thence. And 5 Miles further we quarter'd near a
Branch, which we call'd Nutbush Branch, believing it ran into
the Creek of that Name. One of the Indians kill'd a Fawn, which
with the Addition of a little Beef made very Savory Soupe. The
Surveyors by the help of a clear Night took the Variation & found
it something more than 2°: 30', so that it did not diminish by
approaching the Mountains, or by advanceing towards the West,
or encreasing our Distance from the Sea, but continued much the
same we found it at Coratuck.

2.　The Surveyors got out about 9 a clock, & advanc't the Line
about 9 Miles. We follow'd with the Baggage at 11, & past at
3 Miles distance from our Camp, Mossamory Creek, an Indian
Name signifying Paint Creek, from red Earth found upon the
Banks of it, which in a fresh tinges the Water of that Colour.

the Camp they crosst a large Creek, which the Indians call'd Massamoni, Signifying, in their Language, Paint-Creek, because of the great Quantity of Red ochre[64] found in its banks. This in every Fresh tinges the Water just as the same Mineral did formerly, and to this day continues to tinge, the famous River Adonis, in Phoenicia, by which there hangs a celebrated Fable.[65]

Three Miles beyond that we past another Water with difficulty, call'd Yaypatsco, or Bever Creek. Those industrious Animals had damm'd up the water so high, that we had much ado to get over. Tis hardly credible how much work of this kind they will do in the Space of one Night. They bite young Saplings into proper Lengths with their Fore-teeth, which are exceeding Strong and Sharp, and afterwards drag them to the Place where they intend to Stop the Water.

Then they know how to join Timber and Earth together with so much Skill, that their Work is able to resist the most violent Flood that can happen. In this they are qualify'd to instruct their Betters, it being certain their damms will stand firm when the Strongest that are made by men will be carry'd down the Stream.

We observed very broad low Grounds upon this Creek, with a growth of large Trees, and all the other Signs of Fertility, but seem'd subject to be every where overflow'd in a fresh.

The certain way to catch these Sagacious Animals is thus: Squeeze all the Juice out of the large Pride of the Beaver, and 6 drops out of the small Pride. Powder the inward Bark of Sassafras, and mix it with this Juice, then bait therewith a Steel Trap, and they will eagerly come to it, and be taken.

About three Miles and a half farther we came to the Banks of another creek, call'd, in the Saponi Language, Ohimpa-moni, Signifying Jumping Creek, from the frequent Jumping of Fish during the Spring Season.

Here we encampt, and by the time the Horses were hobbled, our Hunters brought us no less than a Brace and a half of Deer, which made great Plenty, and consequently great content in our Quarters.

Some of our People had Shot a great Wild Cat, which was that fatal moment making a comfortable Meal upon a Fox-Squirrel, and an Ambitious Sportsman of our Company claim'd the merit of killing this monster after it was dead.

The Wild-cat is as big again as any Household-Cat, and much the fiercest Inhabitant of the Woods. Whenever 'tis disabled, it will tear its own Flesh for madness. Altho' a Panther will run away from a Man, a Wild-cat will only make a Surly Retreat, now and then facing about, if he be too

---

[64] A red colored mineral containing oxid of iron.

[65] The legend that Adonis, son of Cunyrus, founder and king of Cyprus, was slain by a boar and his blood colored the water of a river which was therefore named for him.

Three Miles farther we got over Yapatoco, or Bever Creek with some difficulty, the Bevers having rais'd the Water a great way up. We proceeded 3¼ Miles beyond this, & encampt on the West Side of Ohimpamony Creek, an Indian Name which signifys Fishing Creek.   By the way Firebrand had another Occasion to show his Prowess, in killing a poor little Wild Cat, which had been crippled by 2 or 3 before.   Poor Puss was unhappily making a Meal on a Fox Squirrel when all these misfortunes befell her.   Meanwell had like to have quarrell'd with Firebrand & his Carolina Squadron, for not halting for me on the West Side of Yapatsco, having been almost mired in crossing that Creek while they had the fortune to get over it at a better place.   The Indians kill'd 2 Deer & John Evans a third, which made great plenty & consequently great content in Israel.

closely pursued; and will even pursue in his turn, if he observe the least
Sign of Fear or even of caution in those that pretend to follow Him.

The Flesh of this Beast, as well as of the Panther, is as white as veal, and
altogether as sweet and delicious.

3. We got to work early this Morning, and carry'd the line 8 Miles
and 160 Poles. We forded Several Runs of Excellent Water, and afterwards traverst a large levil of high land full of lofty Walnut, Poplar, and
White Oak Trees, which are certain Proofs of a fruitful Soil. This levil
was near two Miles in length, and of an unknown breadth, quite out of
Danger of being overflow'd, which is a misfortune most of the Low
Grounds are liable to in those Parts. As we marcht along we saw many
Buffalo-Tracks, and abundance of their Dung very Fresh, but could not
have the pleasure of seeing them. They either Smelt us out, having that
sense very Quick, or else were alarm'd at the Noise that so many People
must necessarily make in marching along. At the Sight of a Man they
will Snort and Grunt, cock up their ridiculous Short Tails, and tear up
the Ground with a Sort of Timorous Fury.

These wild Cattle hardly ever range alone, but herd together like those
that are tame. They are Seldom seen so far North as 40° of latitude, de-
lighting much in canes and Reeds, which grow generally more Southerly.

We quarter'd on the Banks of a Creek that the Inhabitants call Tewahominy, or Tuskarooda creek, because one of that Nation had been kill'd
thereabouts, and his Body thrown into the Creek.

Our People had the Fortune to kill a Brace of does, one of which we
presented to the Carolina-Gentlemen, who were glad to partake of the
Bounty of Providence, at the same time that they sneer'd at us for depending upon it.

4. We hurry'd away the Surveyors about 9 this Morning, who extended the Line 7 Miles and 160 Poles, notwithstanding the Ground was
exceedingly uneaven. At the Distance of five Miles we forded a stream
to which we gave the Name of Blewing creek, because of the great Number of those Fowls that then frequented it.[66]

About 2½ Miles beyond that, we came upon Sugar-Tree-Creek, so call'd
from the many Trees of that kind that grow upon it. By tapping this
Tree, in the first Warm weather in February, one may get from 20 to 40
Gallons of Liquor, very sweet to the tast and agreeable to the Stomach.
This may be boil'd into moloses first, and afterwards into very good
Sugar, allowing about 10 Gallons of the Liquor to make a Pound. There's
no doubt, too, that a very fine Spirit may be distill'd from the molasses,
at least as good as Rum. The Sugar Tree delights only in Rich Ground,

---

[66] Reference is to the Bluewing, a small creek-water duck, much esteemed as a
delicacy.

3.   We hurry'd away the Surveyors by 9, who ran something more than 8½ Miles.   We follow'd them at 11, & crost several Branches of Excellent Water.   We went thro' a large level of very rich high-Land, near 2 Miles in Length & of an unknown Breadth.   Our Indian kill'd one Deer, & William Pool another, & this last we graciously gave to the Carolina Men, who deserv'd it not, because they had declared they did not care to rely on Providence.   We encampt upon Tewahominy or Tuscoruda Creek.   We saw many Buffalo Tracks, & abundance of their Dung, but the Noise we made drove them all from our Sight.   The Carolina Commissioners with their Leader, lagg'd behind to stop the Cravings of their Appetites, nor were we ever happy with their Conversation, but only at Dinner, when they play'd their Parts more for spite than Hunger.

4.   The Surveyors got to work a little after 9, & extended the Line near 8 Miles, notwithstanding the Ground was very uneven.   We decampt after them about 11, & at 5 Miles Distance crost Blewing Creek,[58] & 3 Miles beyond that, we forded Sugar-Tree Creek, & pitch't our Tent on the West Side of it.   This Creek receiv'd its Name from many Sugar Trees, which grow in the Low-Grounds of it.   By tapping the Sugar Tree in the Spring, a great Quantity of Sugar flows out of it, which may be boil'd up into good Sugar. It grows very tall, & the Wood of it is very soft & Spungy.   Here we also found abundance of Spice Trees, whose Leaves are fragrant, & the Berry they bear is black when dry, & hot like Pepper. Both these Trees grow only in a very rich Soil.   The Low Ground upon this Creek is very wide, sometimes on One Side, sometimes

---

[58] See Note 66, *History of the Dividing Line.*

where it grows very tall, and by the Softness and Spunginess of the Wood shou'd be a quick Grower.

Near this Creek we discovered likewise Several Spice-Trees, the Leaves of which are fragrant, and the Berries they bear are black when dry, and of a hot tast, not much unlike Pepper.

The low Grounds upon the creek are very wide, sometimes on one Side, Sometimes on the Other; tho' most commonly upon the Opposite Shore the high-land advances close to the Bank, only on the North-Side of the Line it spreads itself into a great Breadth of rich low Ground on both sides the Creek for four Miles together, as far as this Stream runs into Hico-River, whereof I shall presently make mention.

One of our Men Spy'd three Buffaloes, but his Piece being loaded only with Goose-shot, he was able to make no effectual Impression on their thick hides; however, this Disappointment was made up by a Brace of Bucks, and as many Wild Turkeys, kill'd by the rest of the company.

Thus Providence was very Bountiful to our Endeavours, never disappointing those that Faithfully rely upon it, and pray heartily for their Daily Bread.

5. This day we met with such uneven Grounds, and thick Underwoods, that with all our Industry we were able to advance the Line but 4 Miles and 312 Poles. In this small Distance it intersected a large stream four times, which our Indian at first mistook for the South Branch of Roanoke River; but, discovering his Error soon after, he assur'd us 'twas a River called Hicootomony,[67] or Turkey-Buzzard River, from the great Number of those unsavoury Birds that roost on the tall Trees growing near its banks.

Early in the Afternoon, to our very great surprize, the Commissioners of Carolina acquainted us with their Resolution to return Home. This Declaration of theirs seem'd the more abrupt, because they had not been so kind as to prepare us, by the least Hint, of their Intention to desert us.

We therefore let them understand they Appear'd to us to abandon the Business they came about with too much Precipitation, this being but the 15th day since we came out the last time. But, altho' we were to be so unhappy as to lose the Assistance of their great Abilities, yet we, who were concern'd for Virginia, determin'd by the Grace of God, not to do our Work by Halves, but, all deserted as we were like to be, shou'd think it our duty to push the Line quite to the Mountains; and if their Government should refuse to be bound by so much of the Line as was run without their Commissioners, yet at least it would bind Virginia, and Stand as a Direction how far his Majesty's Lands extend to the Southward.

In short, these Gentlemen were positive, and the most we could agree upon was to Subscribe plats of our work as far as we had Acted together;

---

[67] The Hico.

on the other, but on the Opposite Side the high land advances close to the Creek. It ought to be remember'd, that the Commissioners of Carolina, made a complement of about 2000 Acres of Land lying on this Creek to Astrolabe, without paying any Fees. Robert Hix saw 3 Buffalos, but his gun being loaden only with Shot cou'd do no Execution. Bootes shot one Deer, & the Indians kill'd 3 more, & one of the Carolina men 4 Wild Turkeys. Thus Providence was very plentifull to us, & did not disappoint us who rely'd upon it.

5.   This day our Surveyors met with such uneven Ground & so many Thickets, that with all their Diligenece they cou'd not run the Line so far as 5 Miles. In this small Distance it crost over Hico-ott-mony Creek no less than 5 times. Our Indian Ned Bearskin informed us at first, that this Creek was the South Branch of Roanoke River, but I thought it impossible, both by reason of its Narrowness & the small Quantity of Water that came down it. However it past so with us at present til future Experience cou'd inform us better.

About 4 a Clock this afternoon Jumble advanc't from the rest of his Company to tell me, that his Collegues for Carolina wanted to speak with me. I desired if they had any thing to communicate, that they wou'd please to come forward. It was some time before I heard any more of these worthy Gentlemen, but at last Shoebrush as the Mouth of the rest, came to acquaint me that their Government had ordered them to run the Line but 30 or 40 Miles above Roanoke, that they had now carry'd it near 50, & intended to go no further. I let them know, it was a little unkind they had not been so gracious as to acquaint us with their Intentions before. That it had been Neighbourly to have inform'd us with their Intentions before we sat out, how far they intended to go that we might also have receiv'd the Commands of our Government in that Matter. But since they had fail'd in that Civility we wou'd go on without them, since we were provided with Bread for 6 Weeks longer. That it was a great Misfortune to lose their Company; but that it wou'd be a much greater to lose the Effect of our Expedition, by doing the Business by halves. That tho' we went by our selves, our Surveyors wou'd continue under the same Oath to do impartial Right both to his Majesty, & the Lords Proprietors; & tho' their Government might chuse perhaps, whether it wou'd be bound by our Line, yet it wou'd **at**

tho' at the same time we insisted these Plats should be got ready by
Monday Noon at farthest, when we on the Part of Virginia intended, if we
were alive, to move forward without farther loss of Time, the Season being
then too far advanct to admit of any unnecessary or complaisant delays.

least be a direction to Virginia how far his Majesty's Land extended to the Southward.

Then they desired that the Surveyors might make a fair Plot of the distance we had run together, And that of this there might be two Copys sign'd by the Commissioners of both Governments. I let them know I agreed to that, provided it might be done before Monday Noon, when, by the Grace of God, we wou'd proceed without Loss of time, because the Season was far advanc't, & wou'd not permit us to waste one Moment in Ceremony to Gentlemen who had shew'd none to us. Here the Conversation ended 'til after Supper, when the Subject was handled with more Spirit by Firebrand. On my repeating what I had said before upon this Subject, he desir'd a Sight of Our Commission. I gave him to understand, that since the Commissioners were the same that acted before, all which had heard the Commission read, & since those for Carolina had a Copy of it, I had not thought it necessary to cram my Portmanteau with it a Second time. And was therefore sorry I cou'd not oblige him with a Sight of it. He immediately said he wou'd take a Minute of this, and after being some time in scrabbling of it, he read to this Effect. That being ask't by him (by him) for a sight of my Commission, I had deny'd it upon pretence that I had it not with me. That I had also refus'd the Commissioners of Carolina, to tarry on Monday, til the necessary Plats cou'd be prepar'd & exchanged, but resolv'd to move forward as soon as the Tent shou'd be dry, by which Means the Surveyors wou'd be oblig'd to work on the Sunday. To this, I answer'd that this was a very smart Minute, but that I objected to the word pretence, because it was neither decent, nor true, that I deny'd him a Sight of our Commission upon any pretence, but for the honest Reason that I had it not there to shew; most of the Company thinking my objection just, he did vouchasafe to soften that Expression, by saying I refus'd to shew him the Commission, alledging I had not brought it.

Soon after when I said that our Governor expected that we shou'd carry the Line to the Mountains, he made answer, that the Governor had exprest himself otherwise to him, & told him that 30 or 40 Miles wou'd be sufficient to go beyond Roanoke River. Honest Meanwell hearing this, & I suppose not giving entire Credit to it, immediately lugg'd out his Pencil, saying in a Comical Tone,

6. We lay still this day, being Sunday, on the Bank of Hico River, and had only Prayers, our Chaplain not having Spirits enough to preach.

that since he was for Minutes, I-Gad he wou'd take a Minute of
that. The other took Fire at this, & without any preface or Ceremony seized a Limb of our Table, big enough to knock down an
Ox, and lifted it up at Meanwell, while he was scratching out his
Minutes. I happening to see him brandish this dangerous Weapon, darted towards him in a moment, to stop his hand, by which
the Blow was prevented, but while I hinder'd one mischief, I
had like to have done another, for the Swiftness of my Motion
overset the Table, & Shoebrush fell under it, to the great hazard
of his gouty Limbs. So soon as Meanwell came to know the
favour that Firebrand intended him, he saluted him with the Title
he had a good right to, namely, of Son of a W—e, telling him
if they had been alone, he durst as well be damn'd as lift that
Club at him. To this the other reply'd with much Vigour, that
he might remember, if he pleas's, that he had now lifted a Club at
him.

I must not forget that when Firebrand first began this Violence,
I desir'd him to forbear, or I shou'd be obliged to take him in
Arrest. But he telling me in a great Fury that I had no Authority,
I call'd to the Men, & let him know, if he wou'd not be easy, I
wou'd soon convince him of my Authority. The Men instantly
gather'd about the Tent ready to execute my Orders, but we made
a Shift to keep the Peace without coming to Extremitys. One of
the People, hearing Firebrand very loud, desired his Servant to
go to his Assistance. By no means, said he, that's none of my
Business, but if the Gentleman will run himself into a Broil, he
may get out of it as well as he can.

This Quarrel ended at last as all Publick Quarrels do, without
Bloodshed as Firebrand has Experienced several times, believing
that on such Occasions a Man may shew a great deal of Courage
with very little Danger. However knowing Meanwell was made
of truer Metal, I was resolv'd to watch him narrowly, to prevent
further Mischief. As soon as this Fray was compos'd the Carolina Commissioners retir'd very soon with their Champion, to
flatter him, I suppose, upon the great Spirit he had shew'd in their
Cause against those who were join'd with him in Commission.

6. This being Sunday we had Prayers, but no Sermon, because
our Chaplain was indispos'd. The Gentlemen of Carolina were

The Gentlemen of Carolina assisted not at our Publick Devotions, because they were taken up all the Morning in making a formidable Protest against our Proceeding on the Line without them.

When the Divine Service was over, the Surveyors sat about making the Plats of so much of the Line as we had run this last Campaign. Our pious Friends of Carolina assisted in this work with some Seeming Scruple, pretending it was a Violation of the Sabbath, which we were the more Surpriz'd at, because it happen'd to be the first Qualm of Conscience they had ever been troubled with dureing the whole journey. They had made no Bones of Staying from prayers to hammer out an unnecessary Protest, tho' Divine Service was no Sooner over, but an unusual Fit of Godliness made them fancy that finishing the Plats, which was now matter of necessity, was a prophanation of the Day. However, the Expediency of losing no time, for us who thought it our duty to finish what we had undertaken, made such a Labour pardonnable.

In the Afternoon, Mr. Fitz William, one of the Commissioners for Virginia, acquainted his Collegues it was his Opinion, that by his Majesty's Order they could not proceed farther on the Line, but in Conjunction with the Commissioners of Carolina; for which reason he intended to retire, the Next Morning, with those Gentlemen.

This lookt a little odd in our Brother Commissioner; tho' in Justice to Him, as well as to our Carolina Friends, they stuck by us as long as our good Liquor lasted, and were so kind to us as to drink our good Journey to the Mountains in the last Bottle we had left.

all the Morning breaking their Brains to form a Protest against our Proceeding on the Line any further without them. Firebrand stuck close to them, & assisted in this elegant Speech, tho' he took some pains to perswade us he did not. They were so intent upon it, that we had not their good Company at Prayers. The Surveyors however found time for their Devotions, which help't to excuse their working upon their Plats, when the Service was over. Besides this being a work of necessity was the more pardonable. We dined together for the last time, not discovering much concern that we were soon to part. As soon as dinner was over the Protesters return'd to their Drudgery to lick their Cubb into shape. While I was reading in the Tent in the Afternoon, Firebrand approach't with a gracious smile upon his Face, & desir'd to know if I had any Commands to Williamsburgh, for that he intended to return with the Carolina Commissioners. That it was his Opinion we had no Power to proceed without them, but he hoped this difference of Sentiment might not widen the Breach that was between us, that he was very sorry anything had happen'd to set us at Variance, & wish't we might part Friends. I was a little surpriz'd at this Condescention but humour'd his Inclinations to peace, believing it the only way to prevent future Mischief. And as a proof that I was in earnest, I not only accepted of these peaceable Overtures myself, but was so much his Friend as to persuade Meanwell to be reconcil'd to him. And at last I join'd their Hands, & made them kiss One another.

Had not this Pacification happen'd thus luckily, it would have been impossible for Meanwell to put up the Indignity of holding up a Clubb at him, because in a Court of honour, the Shaking of a Cudgel at a Gentleman, is adjudged the same affront as striking him with it. Firebrand was very sensible of this, & had great Reason to believe that in due time he must have been call'd to an Account for it by a Man of Meanwells Spirit. I am sorry if I do him wrong, but I believe this Prudent Consideration was the true Cause of the pacifick advances he made to us, as also of his returning back with his dear Friends of Carolina. Tho' there might have still been another Reason for his going home before the Gen¹ Court. He was it seems left out of the Instructions in the List of Councellors, & as that matter was likely to come upon the Carpet at that time, he thought he might have a better

7. The Duplicates of the plats cou'd not be drawn fair this day before Noon, when they were countersign'd by the Commissioners of Each Government. Then those of Carolina deliver'd their Protest, which was by this time lickt into form, and sign'd by them all. And we have been so just to them as to set it down at full length in the Appendix, that their Reasons for leaving us may appear in their full Strength.[68]

After having thus adjusted all our Affairs with the Carolina Commissioners, and kindly supply'd them with Bread to carry them back, which they hardly deserv'd at our hands, we took leave both of them and our colleague, Mr. Fitzwilliam.

This Gentleman had stil a Stronger Reason for hurrying him back to Williamsburg, which was, that neither the General Court might lose an able Judge, nor himself a double Salary, not despairing in the least but he shou'd have the whole pay of Commissioner into the Bargain, tho' he did not half the Work. This, to be sure, was relying more on the Interest of his Friends than on the Justice of his cause; in which, however, he had the misfortune to miscarry, when it came to be fairly considered.

It was two a clock in the Afternoon before these arduous Affairs could be despatcht, and then, all forsaken as we were, we held on our course towards the West. But it was our misfortune to meet with so many Thickets in this Afternoon's Work, that we cou'd advance no further than 2 Miles and 260 Poles.

In this small Distance we crosst the Hico the fifth time, and Quarter'd near Buffalo-Creek, so nam'd from the frequent Tokens we discover'd of that American Behemoth.

---

[68] See p. 332.

chance to get the matter determin'd in his favour when 2 of his
Adversarys were absent. Add to this the Lucre of his Attendance
during the Gen¹ Court, which wou'd be so much clear Gain if he
cou'd get so much Interest as to be paid as bountifully for being
out 4 Weeks, as we for being 10, out upon the Publick Service.
This I know he was so unconscionable as to expect, but without
the least Shadow of Reason or Justice. Our Reconciliation with
Firebrand, naturally made us Friends with his Allys of Carolina,
who invited us to their Camp to help finish their Wine. This we
did as they say, tho' I suspect they reserv'd enough to keep up
their Spirits in their Return: while we that were to go forward did
from hence forth depend altogether upon pure Element.

7. This Morning I wrote some dispatches home, which Firebrand
was gracious as to offer to forward by an Express, so soon as he
got to Williamsburgh. I also wrote another to the Governor
signifying how friendly we parted with our Brother-Commissioner.
This last I shew'd to my Collegues to prevent all Suspicion, which
was kindly taken. The Plats were Countersign'd about Noon, and
that which belong'd to Virginia, we desired Firebrand to carry
with him to the Governor. Then the Commissioners for Carolina
deliver'd their Protest sign'd by them all, tho' I did not think
Plausible wou'd have join'd in so ill concerted a Piece. I put it
up without reading, to shew the Opinion I had of it, & let the
Gentlemen know, we wou'd Endeavour to return an Answer to it
in due time. But that so fine a piece may be preserved I will
give both that & the Answer to it a place in my Journal. The
Protest is in the following Words.⁵⁹ WE THE UNDERWRIT-
TEN COMMISSIONERS for the Government of North Carolina
in Conjunction with the Commissioners on the part of Virginia,
having run the Line for the Division of the 2 Colonys from Coratuck Inlet to the Southern Branch of Roanoke River, being in the
whole about 170 Miles, & near 50 Miles without the Inhabitants,
being of Opinion we had run the Line as far as wou'd be requisite
for a long time, judg'd the carrying of it farther wou'd be a needless charge & trouble; & the Grand Debate which had so long sub-

---

⁵⁹ See Appendix to the *History of the Dividing Line*, p. 332.

Here the Bushes were so intolerably thick, that we were oblig'd to cover the Bred Baggs with our Deer Skins, otherwise the Joke of one of the Indians must have happen'd to us in good Earnest, that in a few days We must cut up our House to make Bags for the Bread, and so be forct to expose our Backs in compliment to our Bellys.

We computed we had then Bisquet enough left to last us, with good Management, Seven Weeks longer; And this being our chief Dependence, it imported us to be very careful both in the Carriage and the Distribution of it.

We had no other Drink but what Adam drank in Paradise, tho' to our comfortwe found the Water excellent, by the Help of which we perceiv'd our Appetites to mend, our Slumbers to Sweeten, the Stream of Life to run cool and peaceably in our Veins, and if ever we dreamt of Women, they were kind.

Our men kill'd a very fat Buck and Several Turkeys. These two kinds of Meat boil'd together, with the addition of a little Rice or French Barley, made excellent Soupe, and, what happens rarely in Other good things, it never cloy'd, no more than an Engaging Wife wou'd do, by being a Constant Dish.

Our Indian was very Superstitious in this Matter, and told us, with a face full of concern, that if we continued to boil Venison and Turkey together, we Shou'd for the future kill nothing, because the Spirit that presided over the Woods would drive all the Game out of our Sight. But we had the Happiness to find this an Idle Superstition, and tho' his Argument could not convince us, yet our repeated Experience at last, with much ado, convinc'd Him.

We observ'd abundance of Colt's foot[69] and Maiden-hair[70] in many Places, and nowhere a larger Quantity than here. They are both Excellent Pectoral Plants, and seem to have greater Vertues much in this part of the World than in more Northern climates; and I believe it may pass for a Rule in Botanicks, that where any Vegetable is planted by the hand of Nature, it has more Vertue than in Places whereto it is transplanted by the Curiosity of Man.

---

[69] The Tusilago Farfara, whose leaves were formerly used as a medicine, especially for coughs and colds.
[70] A fern of the genus Adiantum.

sisited between the Two Governments about Weyanoak River or Creek being Settled at our former meeting in the Spring, when we were ready on our Parts to have gone with the Line to the Outmost Inhabitants, which if it had been done the Line at any time after might have been continu'd at an easy Expence by a Surveyor on each Side, & if at any time hereafter there shou'd be occasion to carry the Line on farther, than we have now run it, which we think will not be in an Age or Two, it may be done in the same easy manner, without that great Expence that now attends it; and on a Conference of all the Commissioners, we having communicated our Sentiments thereon, declared our Opinion that we had gone as far as the Service requir'd, & thought proper to proceed no farther, to which it was answer'd by the Commissioners for Virginia, that they shou'd not regard what we did, but if we desisted, they wou'd proceed without us. But we conceiving by his Majesty's Order in Council, they were directed to Act in Conjunction with the Commissioners appointed for Carolina, & having accordingly run the Line jointly so far, & exchanged Planns, thought they cou'd not, carry on the Bounds Singly, but that their proceedings without us wou'd be irregular & invalid & that it wou'd be no Boundary, & thought it proper to enter our Dissent thereto; Wherefore for the Reasons aforesaid, in the Name of his Excellency the Palatine, & the rest of the true & absolute Lords Proprietors of Carolina, we dissent & disallow of any farther Proceedings with the Bounds without our Concurrence, & pursuant to our Instructions do give this our dissent in writing.

| | PLAUSIBLE. | JUMBLE. |
| | PUZZLECAUSE. | SHOEBRUSH. |

October
7th 1728

To this Protest the Commissioners for Virginia made the following Answer.[60]

WHERAS on the 7th day of October a Paper was deliver'd to us by the Commissioners of N. Carolina in the Style of a PRO-

---

[60] This document is also in the *Colonial Records of North Carolina*, (Vol. II, p. 787) being included in Byrd's journal of the expedition which was sent to London. It is also in the Appendix to the *History of the Dividing Line*, p. 333.

[Continued on page 188]

TEST, against our carrying any farther without them the Dividing Line between the 2 Governments, we the Underwritten Commissioners on the part of Virginia having maturely consider'd the Reasons offer'd in the said Protest, why those Gentlemen retired so soon from that Service, beg Leave to return the following Answer.

They are pleas'd to alledge in the first place by way of Reason, that having run the Line near 50 Miles without the Inhabitants it was sufficient for a long time, & in their Opinion for an Age or two. To this we answer, that they by breaking off so soon did very imperfectly obey his Majesty's Order, assented to by the Lords Proprietors. The plain meaning of that Order was, to ascertain the Bounds betwixt the 2 Governments, as far towards the Mountains as we cou'd, that neither the King's Grants may hereafter encroach upon the Lords Proprietors, nor theirs on the Right of his Majesty. And tho' the distance towards the Mountain be not precisely determin'd by the said Order, yet surely the West Line shou'd be carry'd as near to them as may be, that both the Land of the King, & of the Lords may be taken up the faster, & that his Majesty's Subjects may as soon as possible extend themselves to that Natural Barrier. This they will do in a very few Years, when they know distinctly in which Government they may enter for the Land, as they have already done in the more Northern Parts of Virginia, So that 'tis Strange the Carolina Commissioners shou'd affirm, that the distance of 50 Miles beyond the Inhabitants, shou'd be sufficient to carry the Line for an Age or two, especially considering that a few days before the Signing of this Protest, Astrolabe had taken up near 2000 Acres of Land, granted by themselves within 5 Miles of the Place where they left us. Besides if we reflect on the goodness of the Soil in those Parts, & the fondness of all Degrees of People to take up Land, we may venture to foretell, without the Spirit of Dwinahun that there will be many settlements much higher than these Gentlemen went in less than ten Years, & perhaps in half that time. The Commissioners of N. Carolina protested against proceeding on the Line for another Reason, because it wou'd be a needless charge & trouble alledging that the rest may be done by One Surveyor on a Side, in an easy Manner when it shall be thought necessary. To this we answer, that Frugality of the Publick Money is a great Vertue, but when the Publick Service must suffer by it, it degenerates into a

[Continued on page 188]

Vice, & this will ever be the Case, when Gentlemen execute the Orders of their Superiors by halves. But had the Carolina Commissioners been sincerely frugal for their Government, why did they carry out Provisions sufficient to support themselves & their Men for 8 Weeks, when they intended to tarry out no longer than half that time. This they must confess to be true, since they had provided 500^{lb} of Bread, & the same Weight of Beef & Bacon, which was sufficient allowance for their Complement of Men for 2 Months, if it had been carefully managed. Now after so great an Expence in their Preparations, it had been but a small addition to their charge, if they had endur'd the Fatigue a Month longer. It wou'd have been at most no more than what they must be at, whenever they finish their work, even tho' they think proper to entrust it to the Management of a Surveyor, who must have a necessary Strength to attend him both for his Attendance & Defence. These are all the Reasons these Gentlemen think fit to mention in their PROTEST, tho' in Truth they had a much Stronger Argument for their retiring so abruptly, which because they forgot, it will be but neighbourly to help them out, and remind them of it. The Provision they brought along with them, for want of Providing Horses to carry it, was partly left behind upon a high Tree, to be taken down as they return'd, and what they did carry, was so carlessly handled, that after 18 days, which was the whole time we had the honour of their Company, they had by their own confession no more left than 2^{lb} of Bread for each Man to carry them home. However tho' in Truth this was an invincible Reason why they left the Business unfinish't, it was none at all to us, who had at that time Biscuit Sufficient for 6 Weeks longer. Therefore lest their want of Management shou'd put a Stop to his Majesty's Service, we conceiv'd it our Duty to proceed without them, & have extended the Dividing Line so far West, as to leave the Mountains on each Hand to the Eastward of us. This we have done with the same Fidelity & Exactness, as if those Gentlemen had continu'd with us. Our Surveyors acted under the same Oath which they had taken in the Beginning, & were Persons whose Integrity will not be call'd in Question. However tho' the Government of N. Carolina shou'd not hold itself bound by the Line, we made in the absence of its Commissioners, yet it will continue to be a direction to the Government of Virginia,

[Continued on page 188]

how far the King's Lands reach towards Carolina, & how far his Majesty may grant them away without Injustice to the Lords Proprietors. To this we may also add that having the Authority of our Commission to Act without the Commissioners of N. Carolina in case of their Disagreement or Refusal, we thought it necessary on their deserting, to finish the Dividing Line without them, lest his Majesty's Service might Suffer by any neglect or Mismanagement on their Part. Given under our Hands the 7th of December 1728.

MEANWELL.   STEDDY.

Tho' the foregoing Answer was not immediately return'd to the Protest, as appears by the Date, yet it can't be placed better in this Journal, than next to it, that the Arguments on each Side may be the better compared & understood. Thus after we had compleated our Business with our dear Friends of Carolina, & supply'd 'em with some small matters that cou'd be spared, they took their Leave, & Firebrand with them, full of Professions of Friendship & good Will. Just like some Men & their Wives, who after living together all their time in perpetual Discord & uneasiness, will yet be very good Friends at the Point of Death, when they are sure they shall part forever.

A General Joy discover'd itself thro' all our Camp, when these Gentlemen turn'd their Backs upon us, only Orion had a cloud of Melancholly upon his Face, for the loss of those with whom he had spent all his leizure Hours. Before these Gentlemen went he had perswaded Puzzlecause to give him a Certificate concerning the Quarrel betwixt Firebrand & Meanwell, not because he was ignorant how it was, because he was sitting by the fire within hearing all the time of the Fray, but because he shou'd not be able to tell the Truth of the Story, for fear of disobliging his Patron, & to disguise & falsify the Truth, besides making himself a Lyar, wou'd give just Offence to Meanwell. In this Dilemma he thought it safest to perswade Puzzlecause to be the Lyar, by giving him a Certificate, which soften'd some things & left out others, & so by his (New England) way of cooking the Story, made it tell less shocking on the Side of Firebrand. This was esteem'd wonderfull

[Continued on page 188]

Politick in Orion, but he was as blameable, to circulate an untruth, in another's Name, & under another hand, as if it had been altogether his own Act & Deed, & was in Truth as much resented by Meanwell, when he came to hear it.

Because Firebrand desired that one of the Men, might return back with him, I listed one of the Carolina Men to go on with us in his room, who was indeed the best Man they had. One of our Horses being missing, we quitted not our Camp 'til 2 a Clock. This & the thick Woods were the reason we carry'd the Line not quite 3 Miles. We crost Hico-atto-moni-Creek once more in this day's work, & encampt near another Creek that runs into it call'd Buffalo Creek, so call'd from the great Signs we saw of that Shy Animal. Now we drank nothing but the Liquor Adam drank in Paradise, & found it mended our Appetite not only to our Victuals, of which we had Plenty, but also (to Women of which we had none. It also) promoted digestion, else it had been impossible to eat so voraciously, as most of us did, without Inconvenience.

Tom Short kill'd a Deer, & several of the Company kill'd Turkeys. These 2 kinds of Flesh together, with the help of a little Rice, or French Barley made the best Soupe in the World. And what happens very rarely in other good things, it never cloys by being a constant Dish. The Bushes being very thick began to tear our Bread Bags so intollerably, that we were obliged to halt several times a day to have them mended. And the Carolina Men pleas'd themselves with the Joke of one of the Indians, who said we shou'd soon be forced to cut up our House (meaning the Tent) to keep our Baggs in Repair. And what he said in Jest wou'd have happen'd true in Earnest, If I had not order'd the Skins of the Deer which we kill'd, to be made use of in covering the Bags. This prov'd a good expedient by which they were guarded, & consequently our Bread preserv'd. I cou'd not forbear making an Observation upon our Men, which I believe holds true in others, that those of them who were the foremost to Stuff their Guts, were ever the most backward to work, & were more impatient to eat their Supper than to earn it. This was the Character of all the Carolina Men, without Exception.

8. Notwithstanding we hurry'd away the Surveyors very early, yet the Underwoods embarrass'd them so much that they cou'd with Difficulty advance the Line 4 Miles and 20 Poles.

Our Cloaths Suffer'd extreamely by the Bushes, and it was really as much as both our hands could do to preserve our Eyes in our Heads. Our poor Horses, too, could hardly drag their Loads thro' the Saplings, which stood so close together that it was necessary for them to draw and carry at the same time.

We quarter'd near a Spring of very fine Water, Soft as oyl and as cold as Ice, to make us amends for the want of Wine. And our Indian knockt down a very fat Doe, just time enough to hinder us from going Supperless to Bed.

The heavy Baggage cou'd not come up with us, because of the Excessive badness of the Ways. This gave us no Small uneasiness, but it went worse with the poor men that guarded it. They had nothing in the World with them but dry Bread, nor durst they eat any of that, for fear of inflaming their Thirst, in a Place where they could find no Water to quench it.

This was, however, the better to be endured, because it was the first Fast any one had kept dureing the whole Journey, and then, Thanks to the gracious Guardian of the Woods! there was no more than a Single Meal lost to a few of the Company.

We were entertain'd this Night with the Yell of a whole Family of Wolves, in which we cou'd distinguish the Treble, Tenor and Bass, very clearly. These Beasts of Prey kept pretty much upon our Track, being tempted by the Garbage of the Creatures we kill'd every day; for which we were Serenaded with their Shrill Pipes almost every Night. This Beast is not so untamable as the Panther, but the Indians know how to gentle their Whelps, and use them about their cabans instead of Dogs.

9. The Thickets were hereabouts so impenetrable, that we were obliged, at first setting off this Morning, to order four Pioneers to clear the way before the Surveyors. But after about 2 Miles of these rough-woods, we had the Pleasure to meet with Open Grounds and not very uneven, by the help of which we were enabled to push the Line about 6 Miles.

The Baggage that lay Short of our camp last Night came up about Noon, and the Men made heavy Complaints, that they had been half Starv'd, like Tantalus, in the midst of plenty, for the Reason above mention'd.

The Soil we past over this Day was generally very good, being cloath'd with large Trees, of Poplar, Hiccory, and Oak. But another certain Token of its Fertility was, that wild Angelica[71] grew plentifully upon it.

---

[71] The Archangelica Atropurpurea, an herb with a strong aromatic flavor.

8.   We hurry'd the Surveyors out about 9, & follow'd ourselves
with the Baggage about 11, Yet the Woods were so thick we cou'd
advance little better than 4 Miles.   I spirited up our Men, by
telling them that the Carolina Men were so arrogant as to fancy
we cou'd make no Earnings of it without them.   Having yet not
Skins enough to cover all our Bread Bags, those which had none
suffer'd much by the Bushes, as in Truth did our Cloaths & our
Baggage, nor indeed were our Eyes safe in our Heads.   Those
difficulty's hinder'd Tom Jones from coming up with some of the
loaded Horses to the Camp where we lay.   He was forced to
stop short about a Mile of us, where there was not a drop of
Water, But he had the Rum with him which was some Comfort.
I was very uneasy at their absence, resolving for the future to put
all the Baggage before us.   We were so lucky as to encamp near
a fine Spring, & our Indian kill'd a fat Doe, with which Providence
supply'd us just time enough to hinder us from going supperless
to Bed.   We call'd our Camp by the Name of Tear-Coat-Camp,
by reason of the rough thickets that Surrounded it.   I observ'd
some of the Men were so free as to take what share of the Deer
they pleas'd and to secure it for themselves, while others were at
work, but I gave such Orders as put a Stop to those Irregularitys
I divided the People into Messes, among which the Meat was fairly
to be distributed.

9.   The Surveyors went to work about 9, but because the Bushes
were so intollerably thick, I order'd some hands to clear the way
before them.   This made their Business go on the Slower, however
they carry'd the Line about 6 Miles, by reason the Thicket reach't
no farther than a Mile, & the rest of the Way was over clear Woods
& even Grounds.   We tarry'd with the Rear-Guard till 12 for our
absent Men, who came to the Camp as hungry as Hawks, for having no Water to drink, they durst not eat for fear of Thirst, which
was more uneasy than Hunger.   When we had supply'd our Wants
we followed the Tracks of the Surveyors, passing over 2 Runs of
Excellent Water, one at 3, & the other at 4 Miles Distance from
our last Camp.   The Land was for the most part very good, with

The Root of this Plant being very warm and Aromatick, is covered by Woodsmen extremely as a dry Dram, that is, when Rum, that cordial for all Distresses, is wanting.

Several Deer came into our View as we marcht along, but none into the Pot, which made it necessary for us to sup on the Fragments we had been so provident as to carry along with us. This being but a temperate Repast, made some of our hungry Fellows call the Place we lodg'd at that Night, Bread and Water Camp.

A great Flock of Cranes flew over our Quarters, that were exceeding Clamorous in their Flight. They seem to steer their Course towards the South (being Birds of Passage) in Quest of Warmer Weather. They only took this Country in their way, being as rarely met with, in this part of the World, as a Highwayman or a Begger.

These Birds travel generally in Flocks, and when they roost they place Sentinels upon some of the highest Trees, which constantly stand upon one leg to keep themselves waking.[72]

Our Indian kill'd nothing all day but a Mountain Patridge, which a little resembled the common Partridge in the Plumage, but was near as large as a Dunghill Hen. These are very frequent towards the Mountains, tho' we had the fortune to meet with very few. They are apt to be Shy, and consequently the Noise of so great a Number of People might easily Scare them away from our Sight.

We found what we conceiv'd to be Good Limestone in several Places, and a great Quantity of Blue Slate.

10. The day began very fortunately by killing a Fat Doe, and Two Brace of wild Turkeys; so the Plenty of the Morning made amends for the Short Commons over Night. One of the new men we brought out with us the last time was unfortunately heard to wish himself at Home, and for that Shew of Impatience was publickly reprimanded at the Head of the men, who were all drawn up to witness his Disgrace.

He was askt how he came so soon to be tired of the Company of so many brave Fellows, and whether it was the Danger of Fatigue of the Journey that dishearten'd Him? This publick Reproof from thenceforward put an effectual Stop to all complaints, and not a man amongst us after that pretended so much as to wish himself in Paradise.

---

[72] "Nor are these Birds the only Animals that point scouts to keep the main Body from being surprised for the Baboons, whenever they go on any mischievous Expedition, such as robbing Orchards they place Sentinels to look out towards every Point of the Compass and give notice of any danger. Then ranking themselves in one File that reaches where they harbour to the Orchard they intend to rob, some of them toss the Fruits from the Trees to those that stand nearest, these throw them to the next, and so from one to another, til the fruit is all secured in a few minutes out of Harm's way. In the meantime, if any of the Scouts should be careless at their Posts & suffer any Surprise they are torn to pieces without Mercy. In case of danger these centinels set up a fearful cry upon which the rest take the alarm and Scour away to the mountains as fast as they can." (Byrd's Note.)

Plenty of Wild Angelica growing upon it. Several Deer came into
our Sight but none into our Quarters, which made short Commons
& consequently some discontent. For this reason some of the Men
call'd this Bread & Water Camp, but we call'd it Crane-Camp, because many of those Fowls flew over our Heads being very clamorous in their Flight. Our Indian kill'd a Mountain Partridge resembling the smaller Partridge in the Plumage, but as large as a
Hen. These are common towards the Mountains tho' we saw very
few of them, our Noise scareing them away.

10. We began this day very luckily by killing a Brace of Turkeys
& One Deer, so that the Plenty of our Breakfast this Morning,
made amends for the Shortness of our Supper last Night. This
restor'd good Humour to the Men, who had a mortal Aversion to
fasting. As I lay in my Tent, I overheard one of them, call'd
James Whitlock, wish that he were at home. From this I reprov'd
him publickly, asking him whether it was the Danger, or the
Fatigue of the Journey that dishearten'd him, wondring how he
cou'd be tired so soon of the Company of so many Brave Fellows.
So reasonable a Reprimand put an effectual Stop to all Complaints, and no Body after that day was ever heard so much as
to wish himself in Heaven. A small distance from our Camp we
crost a Creek which we call'd Cocquade Creek, because we there
began to wear the Beards of Wild Turkey-Cocks in our Hats by
way of Cocquade. A little more than a Mile from thence we came
to the true Southern Branch of Roanoke River, which was about
150 Yards over with a swift Stream of Water as clear as Chrystal.
It was fordable near our Line, but we were oblig'd to ride above
100 Yards up the River to the End of a Small Island, & then near
as far back again on the other Side of the Island before we cou'd
mount the Bank. The West Side of this fine River was fringed with
tall Canes, a full furlong in Depth, thro' which our Men clear'd
a Path Broad enough for our Baggage to pass, which took up a
long time. The Bottom of the River was pav'd with Gravel, which
was every where Spangled with small Fleaks of Mother of Pearl,
that almost dazzled our Eyes. The Sand on the Shoar sparkled
with the same. So that this seem'd the most beautiful River that
I ever saw. The Difficulty of passing it & cutting thro' the Canes
hinder'd us so much, that we cou'd carry the Line little more than

A Small Distance from our Camp we crosst a pleasant Stream of Water call'd Cocquade Creek, and something more than a Mile from thence our Line intersected the South Branch of Roanoak River the first time, which we call'd the Dan. It was about 200 Yards wide we forded it, and when we came over to the West Side, we found the Banks lin'd with a Forest of Tall canes, that grew more than a furlong in depth. So that it cost us abundance of time and Labour to cut a Passage thro' them wide enough for our Baggage.

In the mean time we had leizure to take a full view of this charming River. The Stream, which was perfectly clear, ran down about two Knots, or two Miles, an Hour, when the water was at the lowest. The Bottom was cover'd with a coarse Gravel, Spangled very thick with a Shining Substance, that almost dazzled the eye, and the Sand upon either Shore Sparkled with the same Splendid Particles.

At first Sight, the Sun-Beams giving a Yellow cast to these Spangles made us fancy them to be Gold-Dust, and consequenty that all our Fortunes were made. Such Hopes as these were the less extravagant, because several Rivers lying much about the Same Latitude with this have formerly abounded with Fragments of that tempting Metal. Witness the Tagus in Portugal, the Heber in Thrace, and the Pactolus in Lesser Asia; Not to mention the Rivers on the Gold Coast in Africa, which ly in a more Southern Climate.

But we soon found our Selves mistaken, and our Gold Dust dwindled into small Flakes of ising-glass. However, tho' this did not make the River so rich as we cou'd wish, yet it made it exceedingly Beautiful.

We marcht about two Miles and a half beyond this River, as far as Cane Creek, so call'd from a Prodigious Quantity of tall canes that fring'd the Banks of it.

On the West side of this Creek we markt out our Quarters, and were glad to find our Horses fond of the canes, tho' they Scowred them smartly at first, and discolor'd their Dung. This beautiful Vegetable grows commonly from 12 to 16 feet High, and some of them as thick as a Man's wrist.

Tho' these appear'd large to us, yet they are no more than Spires of Grass, if compar'd to those which some curious Travellers tell us grow in the East Indies, one Joint of which will make a Brace of Canoes, if saw'd in two in the Middle. Ours continue green thro' all the Seasons during the Space of Six Years, and the Seventh shed their Seed, wither away and Die. The Spring following they begin to Shoot again, and reach their former Stature the Second or third Year after.

They grow so thick, and their Roots lace together so firmly, that they are the best Guard that can be of the River-Bank, which wou'd otherwise be washt away by the frequent Inundations that happen in this part of the World.

3 Miles. We crost a Creek 2½ Miles beyond the River, call'd Cane Creek, from very tall Canes, which lin'd its Banks. On the West Side of it we took up our Quarters. The Horses were very fond of those Canes but at first they purg'd them exceedingly, & seem'd to be no very heartening Food. Our Indian kill'd a Deer, & the other Men some Turkeys, but the Indian begg'd very hard that our Cook might not boil Venison & Turkey together, because it wou'd certainly spoil his luck in Hunting, & we shou'd repent it with fasting & Prayer. We call'd this South Branch of Roanoke the Dan, as I had call'd the North Branch the Stanton before.

They would also serve excellently well to plant on the Borders of Fish-Ponds and Canals, to secure their sides from falling in; tho' I fear they would not grow kindly in a cold Country, being seldom seen here so Northerly as 38 Degrees of Latitude.

11. At the Distance of 4 Miles and 60 Poles from the Place where we encampt, we came upon the River Dan a Second time; tho' It was not so wide in this Place as where we crosst it first, being not above a 150 yards over.

The West Shore continued to be cover'd with the Canes above mention'd, but not to so great a Breadth as before, and 'tis Remarkable that these canes are much more frequent on the West Side of the River than on the East, where they grow generally very scattering.

It was Still a beautiful Stream, rolling down its limpid and murmuring waters among the Rocks, which lay scatter'd here and there, to make up the variety of the Prospect.

It was about two Miles from this River to the End of our Day's Work, which led us mostly over Broken Grounds and troublesome Underwoods. Hereabout, from one of the Highest hills, we made the first Discovery of the Mountains, on the Northwest of our course. They seem'd to lye off at a vast Distance, and lookt like Ranges of Blue clouds rising one above another.

We encampt about two Miles beyond the River, where we made good chear upon a very fat Buck, that luckily fell in our way. The Indian likewise Shot a Wild Turkey, but confest he wou'd not bring it us, lest we shou'd continue to provoke the Guardian of the Forrest, by cooking the Beasts of the Field and the Birds of the Air together in one vessel.

This Instance of Indian Superstition, I confess, is countenanced in some measure by the Levitical Law, which forbad the mixing of things of a Different Nature together in the Same field, or in the Same Garment, and why not then in the same Kettle?

But, after all, if the Jumbleing of two Sorts of Flesh together be a Sin, how intolerable an Offence must it be to make a Spanish Ole, that is, a Hotchpotch of every kind of thing that is eatable? And the good People of England wou'd have a great deal to answer for, for beating up so many different Ingredients into a Pudding.

12. We were so cruelly intangled with Bushes and Grape-Vines all day, that we could advance the Line no farther than 5 Miles and 28 Poles.

The Vines grow very thick in these Woods, twineing lovingly round the Trees almost every where, especially to the Saplings. This makes it evident how Natural both the Soil and Climate of this Country are to Vines, tho' I believe most to our own Vines.

11. We hurry'd away the Surveyors at 9, & follow'd with the Baggage about 11. In about 4½ Miles we crost the Dan the 2ᵈ time, & found it something Narrower than before, being about 110 Yards over. The West Banks of it, were also thick set with Canes, but not for so great a Breadth as where we past it first. But it was here a most charming River, having the Bottom spangled as before, with a limpid Stream gently flowing, & murmuring among the Rocks, which were thinly scatter'd here & there to make up the variety of the Prospect. The Line was carry'd something more than 2 Miles beyond the River, in which Distance the Thickets were very troublesome. However we made a Shift to run 6½ Miles in the whole, but encampt after Sun-set. I had foretold on the Credit of a Dream which I had last Sunday-Night, that we shou'd see the Mountains, this day, & it proved true, for Astrolabe discover'd them very plain to the N W of our Course, tho' at a great Distance. The Rich Land held about a Mile broad on the West Side the River. Tom Jones kill'd a Buck, & the Indian a Turkey, but he wou'd not bring it us, for fear we shou'd boil it with our Venison against his ridiculous Superstition. I had a moderate cold which only spoil'd my Voice, but not my Stomach. Our Chaplain having got rid of his little lurking Feavers, began to eat like a Cormorant.

12. The Surveyors were dispatch't by 9, but the thick Woods made the Horses so hard to be found, that we did not follow with the Baggage til after Twelve. The Line was extended something more than 5 Miles, all the way thro' a Thicket. We judg'd by the great Number of Chestnut Trees that we approach't the Mountains,

The Grapes we commonly met with were black, tho' there be two or three kinds of White Grapes that grow wild. The Black are very Sweet, but Small, because the Strength of the Vine spends itself in Wood; tho' without Question a proper Culture would make the same Grapes both larger and Sweeter. But, with all these Disadvantages, I have Drunk tolerably good Wine prest from them, tho' made without Skill. There is then good Reason to believe it might Admit of great Improvement, if rightly managed.

Our Indian kill'd a Bear, of two years old, that was feasting on these Grapes. He was very fat, as they generally are in that season of the year. In the fall, the Flesh of this Animal has a high Relish, different from that of other Creatures, tho' inclining nearest to that of Pork, or rather of Wild Boar.

A true Woodsman prefers this Sort of meat to that of the fattest Venison, not only for the *Hautgout* but also because the Fat of it is well tasted, and never rises in the stomach. Another proof of the goodness of this meat is, that it is less apt to corrupt than any other we are acquainted with. As agreeable as such rich Diet was to the men, yet we who were not accustom'd to it, tasted it at first with some sort of Squeamishness, that Animal being of the Dog-kind; tho' a little Use soon reconcil'd us to this American Venison. And that its being of the Dog kind might give us the less disgust, we had the Example of that Ancient and polite People, the Chinese, who reckon Dog's Flesh too good for any under the Quality of a mandarin.

This Beast is in truth a very clean Feeder, living, while the Season lasts, upon Acorns, Chestnuts and Chinkapins, Wild-Hony and Wild-Grapes. They are naturally not carniverous, unless Hunger constrains them to it, after the Mast is all gone, and the Products of the Woods quite exhausted.

They are not provident enough to lay up any Hoard, like the Squirrels, nor can they, after all, live very long upon licking their Paws, as Sr John Mandevil and some Travellers tell us, but are forct in the Winter Months to quit the Mountains, and visit the Inhabitants.

Their Errand is then to Surprise a poor Hog at a Pinch to keep them from Starving. And to shew that they are not Flesh-Eaters by Trade, they devour their Prey very awkwardly.

They don't kill it right out, and feast upon its Blood and Entrails, like other ravenous Beasts, but having, after a fair pursuit, seiz'd it with their Paws, they begin first upon the Rump, and so devour one collop after another, till they come to the Vitals, the poor Animal crying all the while, for several Minutes together. However, in so doing, Bruin acts a little imprudently, because the dismal outcry of the Hog alarms the Neighbourhood, and 'tis odds but he pays the forfeit with his Life, before he can Secure his Retreat.

But Bears soon grow weary of this unnatural Diet, and about January, when there is nothing to be got in the Woods, they retire into some cave or

which several of our Men discover'd very plainly. The Bears are
great Lovers of Chesnuts, and are so discreet as not to Venture
their unwieldy Bodys upon the smaller Branches of the Trees,
which will not bear their Weight. But after walking upon the
Limbs as far as is safe, they bite off the Limbs which falling down,
they finish their Meal upon the Ground. In the same cautious
Manner they secure the Acorns that grow on the outer Branches
of the Oak. They eat Grapes very greedily which grow plentifully in these Woods, very large Vines wedding almost every Tree
in the Rich Soil. This shews how Natural the Situation of this
Country is to Vines. Our Men kill'd a Bear of 2 Years Old which
was very fat. The Flesh of it hath a good relish, very savory,
& inclining nearest to that of Pork. The Fat of this Creature is
the least apt to rise in the Stomach of any other. The Men for
the most part chose it rather than Venison, the greatest inconvenience was that they eat more Bread with it. We who were not accustom'd to eat this rich Dyet tasted it at first with some squeamishness, but soon came to like it. Particularly our Chaplain lov'd
it so passionately, that he wou'd growl like a Wild-Cat over a
Squirrel. Towards the Evening the Clouds gather'd thick &
threaten'd rain, & made us draw a Trench round the Tent, &
take the necessary Precaution to secure the Bread, but no Rain
fell. We remember'd our Wives & Mistresses in a Bumper of excellent Cherry Brandy. This we cou'd afford to drink no oftener
than to put on a clean Shirt, which was once a Week.

hollow Tree, where they Sleep away two or three Months very comfortably. But then they quit their Holes in March, when the Fish begin to run up the Rivers, on which they are forct to keep Lent, till some Fruit or Berry comes in Season.

But Bears are fondest of chestnuts, which grow plentifully towards the Mountains, upon very large Trees, where the Soil happens to be rich. We were curious to know how it happen'd that many of the outward Branches of those Trees came to be brok off in that Solitary Place, and were inform'd that the Bears are so discreet as not to trust their unwieldy Bodies on the Smaller Limbs of the Tree, that would not bear their weight; but after venturing as far as is safe, which they can judge to an Inch, they bite off the End of the Branch, which falling down, they are content to finish their Repast upon the Ground. In the same Cautious Manner they secure the Acorns that grow on the weaker Limbs of the Oak. And it must be allow'd that, in these Instances, a Bear carries Instinct a great way, and Acts more reasonably than many of his Betters, who indiscreetly Venture upon frail Projects that wont bear them.

13. This being Sunday, we rested from our Fatigue, and had leisure to reflect on the signal Mercies of Providence.

The great Plenty of Meat herewith Bearskin furnisht us in these lonely Woods made us once more Shorten the men's allowance of Bread, from 5 to 4 Pounds of bisket a week. This was the more necessary, because we knew not yet how long our Business might require us to be out.

In the Afternoon our Hunters went forth, and return'd triumphantly with three brace of wild Turkeys. They told us they cou'd see the Mountains distinctly from every Eminence, tho' the Atmosphere was so thick with Smoak that they appear'd at a greater Distance than they really were.

In the Evening we examin'd our Friend Bearskin, concerning the Religion of his Country and he explain'd it to us, without any of that Reserve to which his Nation is Subject.

He told us he believ'd there was one Supreme God, who had Several Subaltern Deities under Him. And that this Master-God made the World a long time ago. That he told the Sun, the Moon, and Stars, their Business in the Beginning, which they, with good looking after, have faithfully perform'd ever Since.

That the same Power that made all things at first has taken care to keep them in the same Method and Motion ever since.

He believ'd God had form'd many Worlds before he form'd this, that those Worlds either grew old and ruinous, or were destroyed for the Dishonesty of the Inhabitants.

That God is very just and very good—ever well pleas'd with those men who possess those God-like Qualities. That he takes good People into his safe Protection, makes them very rich, fills their Bellies plentifully,

13. This being Sunday we rested from our Fatigue, & had a
Sermon. Our Weather was very louring with the Wind hard at
N W with great liklihood of Rain. Every Sunday I constantly
order'd Peter Jones to weigh out the weekly allowance of Bread
to each Man, which hitherto was 5 Pounds. This with Plenty of
Meat was sufficient for any reasonable Man, & those who were unreasonable, I wou'd by no means indulge with Superfluitys. The
rising ground when we encampt was so surrounded with Thickets,
that we cou'd not walk out with any Comfort; however after Dinner, several of the Men ventur'd to try their Fortune; & brought
in no less than 6 Wild Turkeys. They told us they saw the Mountains very distinctly from the Neighbouring Hills.

In the Evening I examin'd our Indian Ned Bearskin concerning his Religion, & he very frankly gave me the following Account of it. That he believ'd there was a Supream Being, that
made the World & every thing in it. That the same Power that
made it still preserves & governs it. That it protects and prospers
good People in this World, & punishes the bad with Sickness & Poverty. That after Death all Mankind are conducted into one great
Road, in which both the good & bad travel in Company to a certain
Distance when this great Road branches into 2 Paths the One extremely Levil, & the other Mountainous. Here the good are parted
from the bad, by a flash of Lightening, the first fileing to the Right,

preserves them from sickness, and from being surpriz'd or Overcome by
their Enemies.

But all such as tell Lies, and Cheat those they have Dealings with, he
never fails to punish with Sickness, Poverty and Hunger, and, after all
that, Suffers them to be knockt on the Head and scalpt by those that
fight against them.

He believ'd that after Death both good and bad People are conducted
by a strong Guard into a great Road, in which departed Souls travel
together for some time, till at a certain Distance this Road forks into two
Paths, the one extremely Levil, and the other Stony and Mountainous.

Here the good are parted from the Bad by a flash of Lightening, the
first being hurry'd away to the Right, the other to the Left. The Right
hand Road leads to a charming warm Country, where the Spring is everlasting, and every Month is May; and as the year is always in its Youth,
so are the People, and particularly the Women are bright as Stars, and
never Scold.

That in this happy Climate there are Deer, Turkeys, Elks,and Buffaloes
innumerable, perpetually fat and gentle, while the Trees are loaded with
delicious Fruit quite throughout the four Seasons.

That the Soil brings forth Corn Spontaneously, without the Curse of
Labour, and so very wholesome, that None who have the happiness to eat
of it are ever Sick, grow old, or dy.

Near the Entrance into this Blessed Land Sits a Venerable Old Man
on a Mat richly woven, who examins Strictly all that are brought before
Him, and if they have behav'd well, the Guards are order'd to open the
Crystal Gate, and let them enter into the Land of Delights.

The left Hand Path is very rugged and uneaven, leading to a dark
and barren Country, where it is always Winter. The Ground is the whole
year round cover'd with Snow, and nothing is to be seen upon the Trees
but Icicles.

All the People are hungry, yet have not a Morsel of any thing to eat,
except a bitter kind of Potato, that gives them the Dry-Gripes, and fills
their whole Body with loathsome Ulcers, that Stink, and are unsupport-
ably painfull.

Here all the Women are old and ugly, having Claws like a Panther,
with which they fly upon the Men that Slight their Passion. For it seems
these haggard old Furies are intolerably fond, and expect a vast deal of
Cherishing. They talk much and exceedingly Shrill, giving exquisite
Pain to the Drum of the Ear, which in that Place of the Torment is so
tender, that every Sharp Note wounds it to the Quick.

At the End of this Path sits a dreadful old Woman on a monstrous
Toad-Stool, whose head is cover'd with Rattle-Snakes instead of Tresses,
with glaring white Eyes, that strike a Terror unspeakable into all that
behold her.

the other to the Left. The Right hand Road leads to a fine warm
country, where the Spring is perpetual, & every Month is May,
And as the Year is always in its Youth, so are the People, and the
Women beautifull as Stars, & never scold. That in this happy
Climate there are Deer innumerable perpetually fat, & the Trees
all bear delicious Fruit in every Season. That the Earth brings
forth Corn spontaneously without Labour, which is so very wholesome, that none that eat of it are ever Sick, grow Old or Die. At
the Entrance into this blessed Land sits a venerable Old Man who
examines every One before he is admitted, & if he has behav'd
well the Guards are order'd to open the Chrystal Gates & let him
into this Terrestrial Paradise. The left hand Path is very rough
& uneven, leading to a barren Country, where 'tis always Winter,
the Ground was cover'd with Snow, & nothing on the Trees but
Iciles. All the People are old, have no teeth, & yet are very
hungry. Only those who labour very hard make the Ground Produce a Sort of Potato pleasant to the Tast, but gives them the dry
Gripes, & fills them full of Sores, which stinks and are very painfull. The Women are old & ugly arm'd with sharp Claws like a
Panther, & with those they gore the Men that slight their passion.
For it seems these haggard old Furies are intollerably fond. They
talk very much, & very shrill, giving most exquisite pain to the
Drum of the Ear, which in that horrid Climate grows so tender,
that any sharp Note hurts it. On the Borders sits a hideous Old
Woman whose Head is cover'd with Rattle-Snakes instead of
Tresses, with glaring white Eyes, sunk very deep in her Head. Her
Tongue is 20 Cubits long arm'd with sharp Thorns as strong as
Iron. This Tongue besides the dreadfull Sound it makes in
pronouncing Sentence, serves the purpose of an Elephant's Trunk,
with which the Old Gentlewoman takes up those she has convicted
of Wickedness & throws them over a vast high wall hewn out of one
Solid Rock, that Surrounds this Region of Misery, to prevent
Escapes. They are receiv'd on the inside by another Hideous Old
Woman who consigns them over to Punishments proper for their
Crimes. When they have been Chastiz'd here a certain Number of
Years according to their degrees of Guilt, they are thrown over
the Wall again, & drawn once more back into this World of Trial,
where if they mend their Manners they are conducted into the
abovemention'd fine Country after their Death. This was the Sub-

This Hag pronounces Sentence of Woe upon all the miserable Wretches that hold up their hands at her Tribunal. After this they are deliver'd over to huge Turkey-Buzzards, like harpys, that fly away with them to the Place above mentioned.

Here, after they have been tormented a certain Number of years, according to their several Degrees of Guilt, they are again driven back into this World, to try if they will mend their Manners, and merit a place the next time in the Regions of Bliss.

This was the Substances of Bearskin's Religion, and was as much to the purpose as cou'd be expected from a meer State of Nature, without one Glimpse of Revelation or Philosophy.

It contain'd, however, the three Great Articles of Natural Religion: The Belief of a God; The Moral Distinction betwixt Good and Evil; and the Expectation of Rewards and Punishments in Another World.

Indeed, the Indian Notion of a Future Happiness is a little Gross and Sensual, like Mahomet's Paradise. But how can it be otherwise, in a People that are contented with Nature as they find Her, and have no other Lights but what they receive from purblind Tradition?

14. There having been great Signs of Rain yesterday Evening, we had taken our Precautions in Securing the Bread, and trenching in our Tent.

The men had also Stretcht their Blankets upon Poles, Penthouse fashion, against the Weather, so that nobody was taken unprepar'd.

It began to fall heavily about three a'clock in the Morning, and held not up till near Noon. Everything was so thoroughly Soakt, that we laid aside all thoughts of decamping that Day.

This gave leizure to the most expert of our Gunners to go and try their Fortunes, and they succeeded so well, that they return'd about Noon with three fat Deer, and 4 wild Turkeys. Thus Providence took care of us, and however short the Men might be in their Bread, 'tis certain they had Meat at full Allowance.

The Cookery went on Merrily all Night long, to keep the Damps from entering our Pores; and in truth the Impressions of the Air are much more powerful upon empty Stomachs.

In such a Glut of Provisions, a true Woodsman, when he has nothing else to do, like our honest countrymen the Indians, keeps eating on, to avoid the imputation of Idleness; Though, in a Scarcity, the Indian will fast with a much better Grace than they. They can Subsist Several days upon a little Rockahominy, which is parcht Indian Corn reduc'd to powder. This they moisten in the hollow of their Hands with a little water, and 'tis hardly credible how small a Quantity of it will Support them. Tis true they grow a little lank upon it, but to make themselves feel full, they gird up their Loins very tight with a Belt, taking up a Hole every day. With this Slender Subsistence they are able to travel very long Journeys;

stance of Bearskin's Religion, which he told us with a Freedom uncommon to the Indians.

14.　It began to rain about 3 a Clock this Morning but so gently
that we had leisure to secure the Bread from damage.　It continued raining all Night & til near Noon, when it held up, the
Clouds look't very heavy, & frighten'd us from all thoughts of decamping.　Meanwell & I lay abed all the Morning, believing
that the most agreeable situation in Wet Weather.　The Wind
blowing hard at NE made the air very raw & uncomfortable.
However several of the Men went hunting in the afternoon, & kill'd
a Deer & 4 Turkeys, so that the Frying Pan was not cool til next
Morning.　The Chaplain disdaining to be usefull in one Capacity only, condescended to darn my Stockins, he acquired that with
his other University Learning at the College of Dublin.　At 6 it
began to rain again, & held not up til 9, when the Clouds seem'd to
break away & give us a Sight of the Stars.　(I dreamt the 3 Graces
appear'd to me in all their naked Charms, I singled out Charity
from the rest, with whom I had an Intrigue.)

but then, to make themselves Amends, when they do meet with better Chear, they eat without ceasing, till they have raven'd themselves into another Famine.

This was the first time we had ever been detain'd a whole day in our camp by the Rain, and therefore had Reason to bear it with the more patience.

As I sat in the Tent I overheard a learn'd conversation between one of our men and the Indian. He ask't the Englishman what it was that made that rumbling noise when it thunder'd?

The man told him merrily, that the God of the English was firing his great Guns upon the God of the Indians, which made all the roaring in the clouds, and that the Lightening was only the Flash of those Guns.

The Indian carrying on the Humour reply'd very gravely, He believed that might be the case indeed, and that the Rain which follow'd upon the Thunder must be occasion'd by the Indian God's being so scar'd he could not hold his Water.

The few good Husbands amongst us took some thought of their Backs as well as their Bellies, and made use of this Opportunity to put their Habiliments in repair, which had Suffer'd wofully by the Bushes.

The Horses got some rest by reason of the bad weather, but very little Food, the chief of their Forage being a little wild Rosemary, which resembles the Garden Rosemary pretty much in Figure, but not at all in taste or smell. This Plant grows in small Tufts here and there on the Barren Land in these upper Parts, and the Horses liked it well, but this misfortune was, they cou'd not get enough of it to fill their Bellies.

15. After the Clouds brake away in the Morning, the People dryed their Blankets with all diligence. Nevertheless, it was Noon before we were in condition to move forward, and then were so puzzled with passing the river twice in a Small Distance, that we could advance the Line in all no farther than One Single Mile and 300 Poles.

The first time we past the Dan this day was 240 Poles from the Place where we lay, and the Second time was one Mile and Seven Poles beyond that. This was now the fourth time we forded that fine River, which still tended westerly, with many Short and returning Reaches.

The Surveyors had much Difficulty in getting over the River, finding it deeper than formerly. The Breadth of it here did not exceed fifty Yards. The Banks were about 20 feet high from the Water, and beautifully beset with canes.

Our Baggage Horses crost not the River here at all, but, fetching a compass, went round the Bent of it. On our Way we forded Sable-Creek, so call'd from the Dark Colour of the Water, which happen'd, I suppose, by its being Shaded on both Sides with canes.

15. The Weather promiseing to be fair, we hurry'd away the Surveyors as early as we cou'd, but did not follow with the Baggage til One a Clock, because the thick Woods made it difficult to find the Horses. Interpos'd very seasonably to decide a Wager betwixt two of the Warmest of our Men which might otherwise have inflamed them into a Quarrel. In about a Mile's march we past over a large Creek whose Banks were fring'd with Canes. We call'd it Sable Creek from the Colour of its Water. Our Surveyors crost the Dan twice this Day. The first time was 240 Poles from our Camp, & Second in one Mile & 7 Poles farther, & from thence proceeded with the Line only 59 Poles, in all no more than one Mile & 300 Poles. The difficulty they had in passing the River twice, made their days work so small. The Baggage did not cross the River at all but went round the Bent of it, & in the Evening we encamp on a charming piece of Ground that commanded the

In the Evening we quarter'd in a Charming Situation near the angle
of the River, from whence our Eyes were carried down both Reaches,
which kept a Straight Course for a great way together.

This Prospect was so beautiful, that we were perpetually climbing
up to a Neighbouring eminence, that we might enjoy it in more Perfection.

Now the Weather grew cool, the Wild Geese began to direct their Flight
this way from Hudson's Bay, and the Lakes that lay North-west of us.

They are very lean at their first coming, but fatten soon upon a Sort of
Grass that grows on the Shores and Rocks of this River.

The Indians call this Fowl Cohunks, from the hoarse Note it has,
and begin the year from the Coming of the Cohunks, which happens
in the Beginning of October.

These Wild Geese are guarded from cold by a Down, that is exquisitely
soft and fine, which makes them much more valuable for their Feathers
than for their Flesh, which is dark and coarse.

The Men chast a Bear into the River that got safe over, notwithstanding
the continual fire from the Shore upon Him. He Seem'd to Swim but
heavily, considering it was for his Life.

Where the Water is Shallow, 'tis no Uncommon thing to see a Bear
sitting, in the Summer time, on a heap of Gravel in the Middle of the
River, not only to cool himself, but likewise for the Advantage of Fishing,
particularly for a small Shellfish, that is brought down with the Stream.

In the upper part of James River I have observed this Several times,
and wonder'd very much, at first, how so many heaps of small Stones came
to be piled up in the Water, till at last we spy'd a Bear Sitting upon one of
them looking with great attention on the Stream, and rakeing up Something with his Paw, which I take to be the Shell-fish above mention'd.

16. It was Ten a'clock this Morning before the Horses cou'd be found,
having hidden themselves among the canes, whereof there was great
plenty just at hand. Not far from our camp we went over a Brook,
whose Banks were edg'd on both Sides with these canes. But three Miles
further we forded a larger Stream, which we call'd Low Land Creek, by
reason of the great Breadth of Low Grounds inclos'd between that and the
River.

The high Land we travell'd over was very good, and the low Grounds
promis'd the greatest Fertility of any I had ever seen.

At the End of 4 Miles and 311 Poles from where we lay, the Line intersected the Dan the fifth time. We had day enough to carry it farther,
but the Surveyors cou'd find no Safe ford over the River.

This obliged us to ride two Miles up the River in quest of a Ford, and
by the way we traverst Several Small Indian Fields, where we conjectur'd

Prospect of the Reaches of the River, which were about 50 Yards over & the Banks adorn'd with Canes. We pitch't the Tent at the Bottom of a Mount, which we call'd Mount Pleasant, for the Beauty of the Prospect from thence. This Night Astrolabe's Servant had his Purse cut off, in which he lost his own Money, & some that my Man had put into his keeping. We cou'd suspect no Body but Holmes of the Kingdom of Ireland, who had watched it seems that Night for several of the Men, without which he cou'd not have had an Opportunity. He had also the Insolence to strike Meanwells Servant, for which he had like to have been toss't in a Blanket. Astrolabe's Horse fell with him in the River which had no other Consequence but to refresh him, & make the rest of the Company merry. Here the Low-Ground was very narrow, but very dry, & very delightfull.

16. The Surveyors got to work about 9, & we follow'd with the Baggage at 11. They carry'd the Line about 4½ Miles, & were stop't by the River over which they cou'd not find a Ford. We past a small Creek near our Camp, which had Canes on each side on which our Horses had feasted. The Constant Current in the River may be computed to run about 2 Knots, & we discover'd no Fall, over which a Canoe might not pass. Our Journey this day was thro' very Open Woods. At 3 Miles distance we crost another Creek, which we call'd Lowland Creek from a great Breadth of Low Land made by this Creek & the River, which ran about ¼ of a Mile to the Northward of us. We were obliged to go 2 Miles higher than where our Line intersected the River, because we

the SAWRO'S[73] had been used to plant Corn, the Town where they had liv'd lying Seven or Eight Miles more Southerly, upon the Eastern Side of the River.

These Indian Fields produc'd a Sweet kind of Grass, Almost knee-high, which was excellent Forage for the Horses.

It must b observ'd, by the way, that Indian Towns, like Religious Houses, are remarkable for a fruitful Situation; for being by Nature not very Industrious, they choose such a Situation as will Subsist them with the least Labour.

The Trees grew Surprisingly large in this low-Ground, and amongst the rest we observ'd a tall kind of hiccory, peculiar to the Upper Parts of the Country. It is cover'd with a very rough Bark, and produces a Nut with a thick Shell that is easily broken. The Kernel is not so rank as that of the Common Hiccory, but altogether as oily.

And now I am upon the Subject of these Nuts, it may not be improper to remark, that a very great benefit might be made of Nut-Oyl in this Colony. The Walnuts, the Hickory-Nuts, and Nig-nuts,[74] contains a vast deal of Oyl, that might be press'd out in great abundance with proper Machines.

The Trees grow very kindly, and may be easily propagated. They bear plenty of Nuts every year, that are now of no other use in the World but to feed Hogs. 'Tis certain there is a large Consumption of this Oyl in Several of our Manufactures, and in some parts of France, as well as in other Countries, it is eaten instead of Oyl-Olive, being tolerably Sweet and wholesome.

The Indian kill'd a fat Buck, and the men brought in four Bears and a Brace of wild Turkeys, so that this was truly a Land of Plenty, both for man and Beast.

17. We detacht a Party this morning early in Search of a Ford, who after all cou'd find None that was safe; tho' dangerous as it was, we determin'd to make use of it, to avoid all further delay. Accordingly we rode over a Narrow Ledge of Rocks, Some of which lay below the Surface of the Water, and some above it.

Those that lay under the Water were as Slippery as Ice; and the Current glided over them so swiftly, that tho' it was only Water, it made us perfectly drunk. Yet we were all so fortunate as to get safe over to the West Shore, with no other Damage than the Sopping some of our Bread by the flounceing of the Horses.

---

[73] The Cheraws, who originally lived in the mountain region of Western North Carolina where they were known as the Suale. Some time prior to 1700 they moved to the valley of the Dan and established two villages. About 1710 they migrated to South Carolina, where they ultimately united with the Catawbas.

[74] The fruit of the brown hickory.

cou'd not find a Ford. In our way we went thro' several large Indian Fields where we fancy'd the Sauro Indians[61] had formerly planted Corn. We encampt near one of these Indian Corn Fields, where was excellent Food for our Horses. Our Indian kill'd a Deer & the Men knock't down no less than 4 Bears & 2 Turkeys, so that this was truly a Land of Plenty both for Man & Beast. Dr Humdrum of this Camp first discover'd his Passion for the delicious Flesh of Bear.

17. The Surveyors mov'd early, & went back at least 2 Miles on the South Side of the River before they cou'd get over. Nor was it without difficulty, & some Danger, that they & we crost this Ford, being full of Rocks & Holes, & the currant so swift that it made them giddy. However Heaven be prais'd we all got safe on the other Side, Only One Baggage Horse stumbled, & sopt a little of the Bread. The puzzle in crossing the River, & the thick Woods hinder'd our Surveyors from carrying the Line farther than 2 Miles & 250 Poles, to the Banks of Caskade Creek, so call'd from several Water Falls that are in it. We encampt the sooner because

---

[61] See Note 73, *History of the Dividing Line.*

14

The tedious time Spent in finding out this Ford, and in getting all the Horses over it, prevented our carrying the Line more than 2 Miles and 250 Poles.

This was the last time we crost the Dan with out Line, which now began to run away more Southerly, with a very flush and plentfiul Stream, the Description whereof must be left to future Discoveries, tho' we are well assured by the Indians that it runs thro' the Mountains.

We conducted the Baggage a round about way for the Benefit of evener Grounds, and this carry'd us over a broad Levil of exceeding rich Land, full of large Trees, with Vines marry'd to them, if I may be allow'd to speak so Poetically.

We untreed a young Cub in our March, that made a brave Stand against one of the best of our Dogs. This and a Fawn were all the Game that came in our way.

In this day's Journey, as in many others before, we saw beautiful Marble of Several Colours, and particularly that of the Purple kind with white Streaks, and in some places we came across large pieces of pure Alabaster.

We markt out our Quarters on the Banks of a purling Stream, which we call'd Casquade Creek, by reason of the Multitude of Water-Falls that are in it. But, different from all other Falls that ever I met with, the Rocks over which the water roll'd were Soft and would Split easily into broad Flakes, very proper for Pavement; and some Fragments of it seem'd soft enough for Hones, and the Grain fine enough.

Near our Camp we found a prickly Shrub, riseing about a foot from the Ground, something like that which bears the Barberry, tho' much Smaller. The Leaves had a fresh, agreeable Smell, and I am perswaded the Ladies would be apt to fancy a Tea made of them, provided they were told how far it came, and at the Same time were obliged to buy it very dear.

About a Mile to the South-West of our Camp rose a regular Mount, that commanded a full Prospect of the Mountains, and an Extensive View of the Flat Country. But being, with respect to the high Mountains, no more than a Pimple, we call'd it by that Name.

Presently after Sunset we discovered a great Light towards the West, too bright for a fire, and more resembling the Aurora Borealis. This, all our Woodsmen told us, was a Common Appearance in the High Lands, and generally foreboded bad Weather. Their Explanation happen'd to be exactly true, for in the Night we had a Violent Gale of Wind, accompany'd with Smart Hail, that rattled frightfully amongst the Trees, tho' it was not large enough to do us any Harm.

(18). We crost Casquade Creek over a Ledge of Smooth Rocks, and then Scuffled thro' a mighty Thicket, at least three Miles long. The whole

it threaten'd Rain the Wind strong at N E. In our way to this Place we went over abundance of good Land, made so by the River, & this Creek. Our Dogs catch't a Young Cubb, & the Indian kill'd a young Buck. Near the Creek we found a very good kind of Stone that flaked into thin Pieces fit for Pavement. About a Mile S W from our Camp was a high Mount that commanded a full Prospect of the Mountains, & a very extensive view of all the flat country. But being with Respect to the Mountains no more than a Pimple, we call'd it by that Name.

18. The Weather clearing up with a brisk N Wester, we dispatch't the Surveyors about 9, who carry'd the Line about 6 Miles

was one continued Tract of rich high Land, the woods whereof had been
burnt not long before. It was then overgrown with Saplings of Oak,
Hiccory and Locust, interlac'd with Grape Vines. In this fine Land,
however, we met with no Water, till at the End of three Miles we luckily
came upon a Chrystal Stream, which, like some Lovers of Conversation,
discover'd every thing committed to its faithless Bosom.

Then we came upon a piece of Rich Low Ground, covered with large
Trees, of the extent of half a Mile, which made us fancy ourselves not far
from the River; tho' after that we ascended gently to higher Land, with
no other Trees growing upon it except Butter-wood, which is one Species of
White Maple.

This being a dead Levil, without the least Declivity to carry off the
Water, was moist in many Places, and produc'd abundance of Grass. All
our Woodsmen call these flat Grounds High-Land-Ponds, and in their
Trading Journeys are glad to halt at such Places for Several days together,
to recruit their Jaded Horses, especially in the Winter Months, when there
is little or no Grass to be found in other Places.

This High-Land-Pond extended above two Miles, our Palfrey's Snatch-
ing greedily at the Tufts of Grass, as they went along. After we got over
this Level, we descended some Stony Hills for about half a Mile, and
then came upon a large Branch of the River, which we christen'd the
Irvin, in honour of our learned Professor. This River we forded with
much Difficulty and some Danger, by reason of the Hollow-Spaces betwixt
the Rocks, into which our Horses plunged almost every Step.

The Irvin runs into the Dan about four Miles to the Southward of the
Line, and seem'd to roll down its Waters from the N. N. W. in a very full
and Limpid stream, and the Murmur it made, in tumbling over the Rocks,
caus'd the Situation to appear very Romantick, and had almost made some
of the Company Poetical, tho' they drank nothing but Water.

We encampt on a pleasant Hill, overlooking the River, which seem'd
to be deep every where except just where we forded. In the mean time,
neither the Chain of Rocks, nor any other that we could observe in this
Stream, was so uninterrupted, but that there were Several Breaks where a
Canoe, or even a Moderate Flat-bottom'd Boat, might Shear clear. Nor
have we reason to believe there are any other Falls (except the great ones,
thirty Miles below Moniseep-Ford) that reach quite across, so as to interrupt the Navigation for Small Craft. And I have been inform'd that,
even at those Great Falls, the Blowing up a few Rocks wou'd open a
Passage at least for canoes, which certainly wou'd be an unspeakable
Convenience to the Inhabitants of all that beautiful Part of the Country.

The Indian kill'd a very fat Doe, and came across a Bear, which had
been put to Death and was half devour'd by a Panther. The last of these
Brutes reigns absolute Monarch of the Woods, and in the keenness of his
hunger will venture to attack a Bear; tho' then 'tis ever by surprize, as
all Beasts of the cat kind use to come upon their Prey.

& 30 Poles to a Branch of the Dan, which we call'd the Irvine. We did not follow with the Baggage til 12. We crost Cascade Creek over a Ledge of Rocks, & march't thro' a large Plane of good Land but very thick Woods, for at least 4 Miles together. We met with no Water in all that Distance. A little before Sunset we crost the Irvine at a deep Ford, where the Rocks were so slippery the Horses cou'd hardly keep their Feet. But by the great Care of Tom Jones we all got safe over, without any Damage to our Bread. We encamp't on a Pleasant Hill in Sight of the River, the Sand of which is full of Shining particles. Bearskin kill'd a fat Doe, & came across a Bear, which had been kill'd, & half devour'd by a Panther. The last of these Brutes reigns King of the Woods, & often kills the poor Bears, I believe more by surprize than fair Fight. They often take them Napping. Bears being very Sleepy Animals, & tho' they be very Strong, yet is their Strength heavy, & the Panthers are much Nimbler. The Doctor grutch't the Panther this Dainty Morsel, being so fond of Bear, that he wou'd rise before day to eat a Griskin of it.

Their Play is to take the poor Bears napping, they being very drowsy Animals, and tho' they be exceedingly Strong, yet their Strength is heavy, while the Panthers are too Nimble and cunning to trust themselves within their Hugg.

As formidable as this Beast is to his Fellow Brutes, he never has the confidence to venture upon a Man, but retires from him with great respect, if there be a way open for his Escape. However, it must be confesst, his Voice is a little contemptible for a Monarch of the Forrest, being not a great deal lowder nor more awful than the Mewing of a Household Cat.[75]

In South Carolina they call this Beast a Tyger, tho' improperly, and so they do in some parts of the Spanish West Indies. Some of their Authors, a little more properly, complement it with the Name of Leopard. But none of these are the Growth of America, that we know of.

The Whole Distance the Surveyors advanc'd the Line this day amounted to 6 Miles and 30 Poles, which was no small Journey, considering the Grounds we had traverst were exceedingly rough and uneven, and in many Places intolerably entangled with Bushes. All the Hills we ascended were encumber'd with Stones, many of which seem'd to contain a Metallick Substance, and the Vallies we crost were interrupted with Miry Branches. From the Top of every Hill we cou'd discern distinctly, at a great Distance to the Northward, three or four Ledges of Mountains, rising one above another; and on the highest of all rose a Single Mountain, very much resembling a Woman's Breast.

19. About four Miles beyond the River Irvin, we forded Matrimony Creek, call'd so by an unfortunate marry'd man, because it was exceedingly noisy and impetuous. However, tho' the Stream was Clamorous, yet, like those Women who make themselves plainest heard, it was likewise perfectly clear and unsully'd.

Still half a Mile further we saw a Small Mountain, about five Miles to the North-west of us, which we call'd the Wart, because it appeared no bigger than a Wart, in Comparison of the great Mountains which hid their haughty Heads in the Clouds.

We were not able to extend the Line farther than 5 Miles and 135 Poles, notwithstanding we began our March Early in the Morning, and did not encamp till it was almost dark.

We made it the later by endeavouring to Quarter in some convenient Situation, either for Grass or Canes. But Night Surprising us, we were

---

[75] "Some authors who have given an Account of the Southern Continent of America wou'd make the World believe there are lyons when in all likelihood they were mistaken, imagining these Panthers to be Lyons. What makes this probable is, that the Northern and Southern parts of America join'd by the Isthmus of Darian if there were Lyons in either they would find their way into the other, the Latitudes of each being equally proper for that generous animal." (Byrd's Note.)

19. About 9 the Surveyors took their Departure, and advanct
with the Line 5 Miles & 135 Poles, Nor was this a small Days work
considering the way was more uneven & full of Thickets than ever.
We did not follow them til 12, because some of the Bread-Horses
were missing. Astrolabe wou'd have feign sent out 2 of the Men
to find out where the Dan & the Irvine fork't, but I wou'd not consent to it, for fear they shou'd fall into some disaster, We being
now near the Path which the Northern Indians take when they
march against those of the South. Something more than 4 Miles
from our Camp we crost Matrimony Creek, which receiv'd its
Name from being very Noisy, the water murmuring Everlastingly
amongst the Rocks. Half a Mile beyond this Creek we discover'd
5 Miles to the N W of the Line, a small Mountain which we call'd
the Wart. We would willingly have marcht to a good place for
our Horses which began to grow very weak, but Night coming on,
we were oblig'd to encamp on very uneven Ground, so overgrown
with Bushes & Saplins, that we cou'd with difficulty see 10 Yards

oblig'd to Lodge at last upon High and uneven Ground, which was so overgrown with Shrubs and Saplings, that we cou'd hardly see ten yards around us.

The most melancholy part of the Story was, that our Horses had Short Commons. The poor Creatures were now grown so weak that they Stagger'd when we mounted them. Nor wou'd our own Fare have been at all more plentiful, had we not been so provident as to carry a Load of Meat along with us. Indeed, the Woods were too thick to shew us any sort of Game but one Wild Turkey, which help'd to enrich our Soup.

To make us amends, we found abundance of very Sweet Grapes, which, with the help of Bread, might have furnish'd out a good Italian Repast, in the Absence of more Savoury Food.

The men's Mouths water'd at the Sight of a Prodigious Flight of Wild Pigeons, which flew high over our Heads to the Southward.

The Flocks of these Birds of Passage are so amazingly great, Sometimes, that they darken the Sky; nor is it uncommon for them to light in such Numbers on the Larger Limbs of Mulberry-Trees and Oaks as to break them down.

In their Travels they make vast Havock among the Acorns and Berries of all Sorts, that they waste whole Forrests in a short time, and leave a Famine behind them for most other Creatures; and under Some Trees where they light, it is no Strange thing to find the ground cover'd three Inches thick with their Dung. These Wild Pigeons commonly breed in the uninhabitated parts of Canada, and as the Cold approaches assemble their Armies and bend their Course Southerly, Shifting their Quarters, like many of the Winged kind, according to the Season. But the most remarkable thing in their Flight, as we are told, is that they never have been observ'd to return to the Northern Countries the same way they came from thence, but take quite another Rout, I suppose for their better Subsistence.

In these long Flights they are very lean, and their Flesh is far from being white or tender, tho' good enough upon a March, when Hunger is the sauce, and makes it go down better than Truffles and Morels wou'd do.

20. It was now Sunday, which we had like to have spent in Fasting as well as Prayer; for our Men, taking no Care for the Morrow, like good Christians, but bad Travellers, had improvidently Devour'd all their Meat for Supper.

They were order'd in the Morning to drive up their Horses, lest they shou'd stray too far from the Camp and be lost, in case they were let alone all day. At their Return they had the very great Comfort to behold a monstrous fat Bear, which the Indian had kill'd very Seasonably for their Breakfast.

before us. Here our Horses met with short Commons, & so shou'd
we too, if we had not brought a Horse Load of Meat along with
Us. All that our Hunters cou'd kill was only one Turkey, which
helpt however to Season the Broth.

20. This being Sunday, I wash't off all my weeks Dirt, & refresht
myself with clean Linnen. We had Prayers & a Sermon. We
began here to fall from 5 to 4 Pounds of Bread a Man for the following Week, computeing we had enough at that rate to last a
Month longer. Our Indian had the Luck to kill a monstrous fat
Bear, which came very seasonably, for our Men having Nothing
else to do, had eat up all their Meat, & began to look very pensive.

We thought it still necessary to make another Reduction of our Bread, from four to three Pounds a Week to every man, computing that we had still enough in that Proportion to last us Three weeks longer.

The Atmosphere was so smoaky all round us, that the Mountains were again growing invisible. This happen'd not from the Hazyness of the Sky, but from the fireing of the Woods by the Indians, for we were now near the Route the Northern Savages take when they go out to War against the Cataubas and other Southern Nations.

On their way the Fires they make in their camps are left burning, which, catching the dry Leaves they ly near, soon put the adjacent Woods into a flame.

Some of our men in Search of their Horses discovered one of those Indian camps, where not long before they had been Furring and dressing their Skins.

And now I mention the Northern Indians, it may not be improper to take Notice of their implacable Hatred to those of the South. Their Wars are everlasting, without any Peace, Enmity being the only Inheritance among them that descends from Father to Son, and either Party will march a thousand Miles to take their Revenge upon such Hereditary Enemies.

These long Expeditions are Commonly carry'd on in the following Manner; Some Indian, remarkable for his Prowess, that has rais'd himself to the Reputation of a War-Captain, declares his Intention of paying a Visit to some southern Nation; Hereupon as many of the Young Fellows as have either a Strong Thirst of Blood or Glory, list themselves under his command.

With these Volunteers he goes from One Confederate Town to another, listing all the Rabble he can, til he has gather'd together a competent Number for Mischief.

Their Arms are a Gun and Tomahawk, and all the Provisions they carry from Home is a Pouch of Rockahominy. Thus provided and accoutr'd, they march towards their Enemy's Country, not in a Body, or by a certain Path, but Straggling in Small Numbers, for the greater convenience of Hunting and passing along undiscover'd.

So soon as they approach the Grounds on which the Enemy is used to hunt, they never kindle any Fire themselves, for fear of being found out by the smoak, nor will they Shoot at any kind of Game, tho' they shou'd be half Famisht, lest they might alarm their Foes, and put them upon their Guard.

Sometimes indeed, while they are still at some distance, they roast either Venison or Bear, till it is very dry, and then having Strung it on their Belts, wear it round their Middle, eating very Sparingly of it, because they know not when they shall meet with a fresh Supply. But coming nearer, they begin to look all round the Hemisphere, to watch if any smoke ascends, and listen continually for the Report of Guns, in order to make some happy Discovery for their own advantage.

But our starv'd Horses had no such good Fortune, meeting with no other Food, but a little Wild Rosamary that grows on the high Ground. This they love very well if they had had enough of it, but it grew only in thin Tufts here & there. Tom Short brought me a Hat full of very good wild-Grapes which were plentifull all over these Woods. Our Men, when the Service was over, thought it no Breach of the Sabbath to wash their Linnen, & put themselves in Repair, being a Matter of indispensible necessity. Meanwell was very handy at his needle, having learn't the Use of that little Implement at Sea, & flourish his Thread with as good a Grace as any Merchant Taylor.

It is amazing to see their Sagacity in discerning the Track of a Human Foot, even amongst dry leaves, which to our Shorter Sight is quite undiscoverable.

If by one or more of those Signs they be able to find out the Camp of any Southern Indians, they Squat down in some Thicket, and keep themselves hush and Snug till it is dark; Then creeping up Softly, they approach near enough to observe all the Motions of the Enemy. And about two a Clock in the Morning, when they conceive them to be in a Profound Sleep, for they never keep Watch and Ward, pour in a Volley upon them, each Singling out his Man. The Moment they have discharg'd their Pieces, they rush in with their Tomahawks, and make sure work of all that are disabled.

Sometimes, when they find the Enemy Asleep around their little Fire, they first Pelt them with little Stones to wake them, and when they get up, fire in upon them, being in that posture a better Mark than when prostrate on the Ground.

Those that are kill'd of the Enemy, or disabled, they Scalp, that is, they cut the Skin all around the Head just below the hair, and then clapping their Feet to the poor Mortal's Shoulders, pull the Scalp off clean, and carry it home in Triumph, being as proud of those Trophies, as the Jews used to be of the Foreskins of the Philistines.

This way of Scalping was practised by the Ancient Scythians, who us'd these hairy Scalps as Towels at Home, and Trappings for their Horses when they went abroad.

They also made Cups of their Enemies' Skulls, in which they drank Prosperity to their country, and Confusion to all their Foes.

The Prisoners they happen to take alive in these expeditions generally pass their time very Scurvily. They put them to all the Tortures that ingenious Malice and cruelty can invent. And (what shews the baseness of the Indian Temper in Perfection) they never fail to treat those with the greatest Inhumanity that have distinguish'd themselves most by their Bravery; and, if he be a War-Captain, they do him to Honour to roast him alive, and distribute a Collop to all that had a Share in stealing the Victory.[76]

They are very cunning in finding out new ways to torment their unhappy Captives, tho', like those of Hell, their usual Method is by Fire. Sometimes they Barbecue them over live-Coals, taking them off every now and then, to prolong their Misery; at other times they will Stick Sharp Pieces of Lightwood all over their Body's, and setting them afire, let them

---

[76] Tho' who can reproach the poor Indians for this when Homer makes his celebrated hero, Achilles, drag the Body of Hector at the Tail of his chariot for having fought gallantly for the defense of his Country. Nor was Alexander the Great with all his Fam'd Generosity, less inhuman to the brave Tyrians 2,000 of whom he ordered to be crucified in cold Blood, for no other fault but for having defended their City most courageously against Him, dureing a Seige of Seven Months. And what was still more brutal, he drag'd alive at the Tail of his Chariot thro' all the Streets for defending the Town with so much Vigour." (Byrd's Note.)

[Continued on page 223]

burn down into the Flesh to the very Bone. And when they take a Stout
Fellow, that they believe able to endure a great deal, they will tear all the
Flesh off his Bones with red hot Pincers.

While these and such like Barbarities are practising, the Victors are
so far from being touch'd with Tenderness and Compassion, that they
dance and Sing round these wretched Mortals, shewing all the Marks of
Pleasure and Jollity. And if such cruelties happen to be executed in their
Towns, they employ their Children in tormenting the Prisoners, in order
to extinguish in them betimes all Sentiments of Humanity.

In the mean time, while these poor Wretches are under the Anguish
of all this inhuman Treatment, they disdain so much as to groan, Sigh,
or shew the least Sign of Dismay or concern, so much as in their Looks;
on the Contrary, they make it a Point of Honour all the time to Soften
their Features, and look as pleas'd as if they were in the Actual Enjoyment
of Some Delight; and if they never sang before in their Lives, they will be
sure to be Melodious on this sad and Dismal Occasion.

So prodigious a Degree of Passive Valour in the Indians is the more to
be wonder'd at, because in all Articles of Danger they are apt to behave
like Cowards. And what is still more Surprizeing, the very Women
discover, on such Occasions, as great Fortitude and Contempt, both of
Pain and Death, as the Gallantest of their Men can do.

21. The Apprehension we had of losing the Horses in these Copse
Woods were too well founded, nor were the Precautions we us'd Yesterday
of driveing them up Sufficient to prevent their Straying away afterwards,
notwithstanding they were securely hobbled.

We therefore Order'd the men out early this Morning to look diligently
for them, but it was late before any cou'd be found. It seems they had
straggled in quest of Forrage, and, besides all that, the Bushes grew thick
enough to conceal them from being Seen at the Smallest Distance. One
of the People was so bewilder'd in search of his Horse, that he lost
Himself, being no great Forester.

However, because we were willing to save time, we left two of our most
expert Woodsmen behind to beat all the Adjacent Woods in Quest of Him.

In the mean while the Surveyors proceeded vigorously on their Business,
but were so perplext with Thickets at their first setting off, that their
Progress was much retarded.

They were no sooner over that Difficulty, but they were oblig'd to encounter another. The rest of the day's-Work lay over very Sharp Hills,
where the dry leaves were so Slippery that there was hardly any hold for
their Feet. Such Rubbs as these prevented them from Measuring more
than 4 Miles and 270 Poles.

Upon the Sides of these Hills the Soil was rich, tho' full of Stones, and
the Trees reasonably large.

21. Our Surveyors got to work about 9, & carry'd the Line 4 Miles & 270 Poles, great Part of that Distance being very hilly, & grown up with Thickets, But we cou'd not follow them til after 2. Both Hamilton & his Horse were missing, & tho' I sent out several Men in quest of them, they were able to find neither. At last fearing we shou'd not overtake the Surveyors, I left Tom Jones & another Man to beat all the adjacent Woods for them. We past tho' intollerable Thickets to the great Danger of our Eyes, & damage of our Cloaths, Insomuch that I had enough to do to keep my Patience & sweet Temper. With all our Diligence, we cou'd fight our way thro' the Bushes no farther than 2½ Miles before Sunset, so that we cou'd not reach the Surveyors. This was a sensible Grief to us, because they had no Bedding with them, & probably no Victuals. And even in the last Article we were not mistaken, for tho' our Indians kill'd a Bear, he had left it on the Line for us to pick up. Thus our Dear Friends run a risque of being doubly starv'd, both with Cold & Hunger. I knew this wou'd ill agree with Orion's delicate Constitution, but Astrolabe I was in less pain for, because he had more Patience & cou'd subsist longer upon licking

The Smoak continued still to Veil the Mountains from our Sight, which made us long for Rain, or a brisk Gale of Wind, to disperse it. Nor was the loss of this wild Prospect all our concern, but we were apprehensive lest the Woods shou'd be burnt in the Course of our Line before us, or happen to take fire behind us, either of which wou'd effectually have Starv'd the Horses, and made us all Foot Soldiers. But we were so happy, thank God! as to escape this Misfortune in every Part of our Progress.

We were exceedingly uneasy about our lost man, knowing he had taken no Provision of any kind, nor was it much Advantage towards his Support, that he had taken his Gun along with him, because he had rarely been guilty of putting any thing to Death.

He had unluckily wander'd from the Camp Several Miles, and after Steering Sundry unsuccessful Courses, in order to return, either to us or to the Line, was at length so tired he could go no Farther. In this Distress he sat himself down under a Tree, to recruit his jaded Spirits, and at the same time indulge a few Melancholy Reflections.

Famine was the first Phantom that appear'd to him, and was the more frightfull, because he fancy'd himself not quite Bear enough to Subsist long upon licking his Paws.

In the mean time the two Persons we had sent after him hunted diligently great part of the day without coming upon his Track. They fir'd their Pieces towards every Point of the Compass, but cou'd perceive no fireing in return. However, advancing a little farther, at last they made a lucky Shot, that our Straggler had the good Fortune to hear, and he returning the Salute, they soon found each other with no Small Satisfaction. But tho' they lighted of the man, they cou'd by no means light of his Horse, and therefore he was oblig'd to be a Foot Soldier all the rest of the Journey.

Our Indian shot a Bear so prodigiously fat, that there was no way to kill Him but by fireing in at his Ear.

The fore part of the Skull of that Animal being guarded by a double Bone, is hardly penetrable, and when it is very fat, a Bullet aim'd at his Body is apt to lose its force, before it reaches the Vitals. This Animal is of the Dog kind, and our Indians, as well as Woodsmen, are as fond of its Flesh as the Chinese can be of that of the Common Hound.

22. Early in the Morning we sent back two men to make further Search for the horse that was Stray'd away. We were unwilling the Poor man shou'd Sustain such a Damage as wou'd eat out a large Part of his Pay, or that the Publick shou'd be at the Expense of reëmbursing Him for it.

These foresters hunted all over the Neighbouring Woods, and took as much pains as if the Horse had been their own Property, but all their Diligence was to no purpose.

his Paws. We had the Comfort to encamp where our Horses fared well, And we drank Health to our Absent Friends in pure Element. Just as it was dark Tom Jones brought poor Hamilton to us without his Horse. He had contriv'd to loose himself being no great Woodsman, but pretended that he was only bogued. He looked very melancholly for the Loss of his Horse, til I promis't to employ my Interest to procure him satisfaction. For want of Venison Broth for Supper, we contented our selves with some Greasy Soup (de Jam bon,) which tho' it slip't down well enough sat not very easy on our Stomachs. So soon as we encampt I dispatch't John Evans to look for the Surveyors, but he return'd without Success, being a little too sparing of his Trouble. We saw a small Mountain to the N. W. which we call'd Wart.

22. This Morning early I sent John Evans with Hamilton back to our last Camp to make a farther Search for the Stray Horse, with orders to spend a whole day about it. At the same time I dispatch't Richd Smith to the Surveyors with some Provisions to stop their Mouths as well as their Stomachs. It was 11 a Clock before we cou'd get up all the Horses, when we follow'd our Sur-

The Surveyors, in the mean time, being fearful of leaving these men too far behind, advanc'd the Line no farther than One Mile and 230 Poles.

As we rode along we found no less than three Bears and a fat Doe, that our Indian, who went out before us, had thrown in our Course and we were very glad to pick them up.

About a Mile from the Camp we crost Miry Creek, So call'd because Several of the Horses were mired in its Branches. About 230 Poles beyond that, the Line intersected another River, that seem'd to be a Branch of the Irvin, to which we gave the Name of the Mayo, in complement to the other of our Surveyors. It was about 50 Yards wide where we forded it, being just below a Ledge of Rocks, which reacht across the River, and made a natural casquade.

Our Horses cou'd hardly keep their feet over these Slippery Rocks, which gave Some of their Riders no small Palpitation.

This River forks about a Quarter of a Mile below the Ford, and has Some Scattering Canes growing near the Mouth of it.

We picht our Tent on the Western Banks of the Mayo, for the Pleasure of being lull'd to Sleep by the Casquade. Here our Hunters had leisure to go out and try their Fortunes, and return'd loaden with Spoil. They brought in no less than Six Bears, exceedingly fat, so that the frying pan had no rest all Night. We had now the Opportunity of trying the speed of these lumpish Animals by a fair Course it had with the Nimblest of our Surveyors.

A Cubb of a year Old will run very fast, because, being upon his growth, he is never encumber'd with too much fat; but the Old ones are more Sluggish and unwieldy, especially when Mast is Plenty. Then their Nimblest Gait is only a heavy Gallop, and their Motion is still Slower down hill, where they are oblig'd to Sidle very awkwardly, to keep their Lights from riseing up into their Throat.

These Beasts always endeavour to avoid a man, except when they are wounded, or happen to be engaged in the Protection of their Cubbs.

By the force of these Instincts and that of Self-Preservation, they will now and then throw off all Reverence for their Maker's Image. For that Reason, excess of hunger will provoke them to the same Desperate Attack, for the support of their Being.

A Memorable Instance of that last Case is said to have happen'd not long ago in New England, where a Bear assaulted a Man just by his own Door, and rearing himself upon his Haunches, offer'd to take him lovingly into his Hug. But the Man's Wife observing the Danger her Husband was in, had the courage to run behind the Bear, and thrust her two Thumbs into his Eyes. This made Bruin quit the Man, and turn short upon the Woman to take his Revenge, but She had the Presence of mind to spring back with more than Female Agility, and so both their Lives were preserv'd.

veyors, & in a Mile & a half reach't the Camp where they had lain. The Woods were extremely thick in the beginning of this day's March, but afterwards grew pretty Open. As we road along, we found no less than 3 Bears & a half a Deer left upon the Line, with which we loaded our light Horses.

We came up with the Surveyors on the Banks of the Western Branch of the Irvin, which we call'd the Mayo. Here they had halted for us, not knowing the Reason why we staid behind so long. And this was the cause they proceeded no farther with the Line than One Mile & 230 Poles. About a Mile before we reach't this River, we crost a small Creek, which we call'd Miry Creek because several of the Branches of it were Miry. We past the Mayo just below a Ledge of Rocks, where Meanwell's Horse slipt, & fell upon one of his Legs, & wou'd have broke it, if his Half-Jacks had not guarded it. As it was his Ancle was bruis'd very much, & he halted several Days upon it.

After the Tent was pitch't, Astrolabe, Humdrum, & I clamber'd up a high Hill to see what we cou'd discover from thence. On the Brow of the Hill we spy'd a Young Cubb on the top of a high Tree at Supper upon some Acorns. We were so indiscreet as to take no Gun with us, & therefore were oblig'd to hallow to the Men to bring One. When it came Astrolabe undertook to fetch the Bear down, but mist him. However the poor Beast hearing the Shot Rattle about his Ears, came down the Tree of his own Accord, & trusted to his Heals. It was a pleasant Race between Bruin & our grave Surveyor, who I must confess runs much better than he shoots; Yet the Cubb out ran him even down Hill where Bears are said to Sidle, lest their Guts shou'd come out of their mouths. But our Men had better luck, & kill'd no less than 6 of these unwieldly Animals. We sent our Horses back to Miry Creek, for the benefit of the Canes & Winter Grass which they eat very greedily. There was a Waterfall in the River just by our Camp, the Noise of which gave us Poetical Dreams, & made us say our Prayers in Metre when we awaked.

23.   At the Distance of 62 Poles from where we lay, we crost the South
Branch of what we took for the Irvin, nor was it without Difficulty we got
over, tho' it happen'd to be without Damage.

Great part of the way after that was Mountainous, so that we were no
sooner got down one Hill, but we were oblig'd to climb up another.
Only for the last Mile of our Stage, we encounter'd a Locust Thicket that
was level but interlac'd terribly with Bryars and Grape Vines.

We forded a large creek, no less than five times, the Banks of which
were so steep that we were forc'd to cut them down with a Hough.

We gave it the Name of Crooked creek, because of its frequent Meanders.   The Sides of it were planted with Shrub-Canes, extremely inviting
to the Horses, which were now quite jaded with clambering up so many
Precipices, and tugging thro' so many dismal Thickets, notwithstanding
which we pusht the Line this day Four Miles and 69 Poles.   The men were
so unthrifty this Morning as to bring but a Small Portion of their
Abundance along with them.   This was the more unlucky, because we
cou'd discover no Sort of Game the whole livelong Day.   Woodsmen are
certainly good Christians in one respect, at least, that they always leave
the Morrow to care for itself; tho' for that very reason they ought to
pray more fervently for their Dayly Bread than most of them remember
to do.

The Mountains were still conceal'd from our Eyes by a cloud of Smoak.
As we went along we were alarmed at the Sight of a great Fire, which
shewed itself to the Northward.   This made our small Corps march in
closer Order than we us'd to do, lest perchance we might be waylaid by
Indians.   It made us look out Sharp to see if we cou'd discover any Track
or other Token of these insidious Forresters, but found none.   In the
mean time we came often upon the Track of Bears, which can't without
some Skill be distinguisht from that of Human Creatures, made with
Naked Feet.   And Indeed a Young Woodsman wou'd be puzzled to find out
the Difference, which consists principally in a Bear's Paws being something Smaller than a Man's foot and in its leaving sometimes the Mark
of its Claws in the Impression made upon the Ground.

The Soil where the Locust Thicket grew, was exceedingly rich, as it
constantly is, where that kind of Tree is Naturally and largely produc'd.

But the Desolation made there lately, either by Fire or Caterpillars,
had been so general, that we could not see a Tree of any Bigness standing
within our Prospect.   And the Reason why a Fire makes such a Havock
in these lonely Parts is this.

The Woods are not there burnt every year, as they generally are amongst
the Inhabitants.   But the dead Leaves and Trash of many years are heapt
up together, which being at length kindled by the Indians that happen
to pass that way, furnish fewel for a conflagration that carries all before it.

23. Our Surveyors mov'd forward & proceeded with the Line 4 Miles & 69 Poles. At the distance of 62 Poles from our Camp, we past over another Branch of the Irvin with difficulty about half a Mile from where it fork't. It was extremely Mountainous great Part of the Way, & the last Mile we encounter'd a dreadfull Thicket enterlaced with Briars & Grape-Vines. We crost a large Creek no less than 5 Times with our Line, which for that Reason we call'd Crooked Creek, The Banks of it were steep in many Places & border'd with Canes. With great luck for our Horses we encampt where these Canes were plentifull. This Refreshment was very seasonable after so tiresome a Journey, in which these poor Beasts had clamber'd up so many Precepices. About Sunset Evans & Hamilton came up with us, but had been so unlucky as not to find the Horse. Our Men eat up a Horseload of Bear, which was very unthrifty Management, considering we cou'd meet with no Game all this Day. But woodsmen are good Christians in one Respect, by never taking Care for the Morrow, but letting the Morrow care for itself, for which Reason no Sort of People ought to pray so fervently for their daily Bread as they.

There is a beautiful Range of Hills, as levil as a Terrass-Walk, that overlooks the Valley through which Crooked Creek conveys its Spiral Stream.

This Terrass runs pretty near East and West, about two Miles South of the Line, and is almost Parallel with it.

The Horses had been too much harass'd to permit us to ride at all out of our way, for the pleasure of any Prospect, or the gratification of any Curiosity. This confin'd us to the Narrow Sphere of our Business, and is at the same time a just Excuse for not animating our Story with greater Variety.

24. The Surveyors went out the sooner this Morning, by reason the men lost very little time in cooking their Breakfast. They had made but a Spare Meal over Night, leaving nothing but the Hide of a Bear for the Morrow. Some of the keenest of them got up at Midnight to Cook that nice Morsel after the Indian Manner.

They first Singed the Hair clean off, that none of it might Stick in their Throats; then they boil'd the Pelt into Soup, which had a Stratum of Grease Swimming on it full half an Inch Thick. However, they commenced this Dish extremely; tho' I believe the Praises they gave it were more owing to their good Stomach than to their good Tast.

The Line was extended 6 Miles and 300 Poles, and in that Distance crosst Crooked Creek at least eight times more.

We were forct to scuffle through a Thicket about two Miles in breadth, planted with Locusts and hiccory Sapplings, as close as they cou'd stand together. Amongst these there was hardly a Tree of Tolerable Growth within View. It was a dead Plane of Several Miles Extent, and very fertile Soil. Beyond that the Woods were open for about three Miles, but Mountainous. All the rest of our Day's Journey was pester'd with Bushes and Grape Vines, in the thickest of which we were obliged to take up our Quarters, near one of the Branches of Crooked creek.

This Night it was the Men's good fortune to fare very sumptuously. The Indian had kill'd two large Bears, the fatest of which he had taken napping. One of the People too Shot a Raccoon, which is also of the Dogkind, and as big as a small Fox, tho' its Legs are Shorter, and when fat has much a higher relish than either Mutton or Kid. 'Tis naturally not Carniverous, but very fond of Indian corn and Parsimons.

The fat of this Animal is reckon'd very good to assuage Swellings and Inflammations. Some old Maids are at the Trouble of breeding them up tame, for the pleasure of seeing them play over as many Humorous Tricks as a Munkey. It climbs up small Trees, like a Bear, by embracing the Bodies of them.

Till this Night we had accustom'd ourselves to go to Bed in our Night-Gowns, believing we should thereby be better secur'd from the cold: but

24. The Men feasted so plentifully last Night, that some of them paid for it by fasting this Morning. One who had been less provident than the rest broke his fast very odly. He sing'd all the Hair off of a Bearskin, & boil'd the Pelt into Broth. To this he invited his particular Friends, who eat very heartily & commended the Cookery, by supping it clean up. Our Surveyors hurry'd away a little after 8, & extended the Line 6 Miles & 300 Poles. We did not follow them till about 11, & crost a Thicket 2 full Miles in Breadth, without any great Trees near it. The Soil seem'd very rich & Levil, having many Locust & Hicory Saplins. The Reason why there are no high Trees, is probably, because the Woods in these remote parts are burnt but seldom. During those long intervals the Leaves & other Trash, are heapt so thick upon the Ground, that when they come to be set on Fire, they consume all before them, leaving nothing either standing or lying upon the Ground. Afterwards our way was Mountainous & the Woods open for about 2½ Miles. Then Level & Overgrown with Bushes all the remaining distance. The Line crost Crooked Creek 10 times in this day's Work, & we encampt upon a Branch of it where our Horses fared but indifferently. The Men came off better for the Indian kill'd 2 Bears on which they feasted till the Grease ran out of their Mouths. Till this Night I had always lain in my Night Gown, but upon Tryal, I found it much warmer to strip to my shirt, & lie in naked Bed with my gown over me. The Woodsmen put all off, if they have no more than one Blanket, to lye in, & agree that 'tis much more comfortable than to lye with their Cloaths on, tho' the Weather be never so cold.

upon tryal found we lay much warmer by Stripping to our Shirts, and Spreading our Gowns over us.

A True Woodsman, if he have no more than a Single Blanket, constantly pulls all off, and, lying on one part of it, draws the other over him, believing it much more refreshing to ly so, than in his cloaths; and if he find himself not warm enough, Shifts his Lodging to Leeward of the Fire, in which Situation the smoak will drive over him, and effectually correct the cold Dews that wou'd otherwise descend upon his Person, perhaps to his great damage.

25. The Air clearing up this Morning, we were again agreeably surprized with a full Prospect of the Mountains. They discover'd themselves both to the North and South of us, on either side, not distant above ten Miles, according to our best Computation.

We cou'd now see those to the North rise in four distinct Ledges, one above another, but those to the South form'd only a Single Ledge, and that broken and interrupted in many Places; or rather they were only single Mountains detacht from each other.

One of the Southern Mountains was so vastly high, it seem'd to hide its head in the Clouds, and the West End of it terminated in a horrible Precipice, that we call'd the Despairing Lover's Leap. The Next to it, towards the East, was lower, except at one End, where it heav'd itself up in the form of a vast Stack of Chimnys.[76]

The Course of the Northern Mountains seem'd to tend West-South-West, and those to the Southward very near West. We cou'd descry other Mountains ahead of us, exactly in the Course of the Line, tho' at a much greater distance. In this Point of View, the Ledges on the right and Left both seem'd to close, and form a Natural Amphi-Theater.

Thus, 'twas our Fortune to be wedg'd in betwixt these two Ranges of Mountains, insomuch that if our Line had run ten Miles on either Side, it had butted before this day either upon one or the other, both of them now Stretching away plainly to the Eastward of us.

It had rain'd a little in the Night, which disperst the smoak and open'd this Romantick Scene to us all at once, tho' it was again hid from our Eyes as we mov'd forwards by the rough Woods we had the Misfortune to be engag'd with. The Bushes were so thick for near four Miles together, that they tore the Deer-Skins to Pieces that guarded the Bread-Bags. Tho', as rough as the Woods were, the Soil was extremely good in all the way, being washt down from the Neighbouring Hills into the Plane Country. Notwithstanding all these Difficulties, the Surveyors drove on the line 4 Miles and 205 Poles.

In the mean time we were so unlucky as to meet with no Sort of

---

[77] This was probably Pilot Mountain in Surry County, North Carolina.

25. The Surveyors got to work soon after 8, & run the Line 4 Miles & 205 Poles. We did not follow them til near 2, by reason Holm's Horse cou'd not be found. And at last we were forced to leave Robin Hix & William Pool behind, to search narrowly for him. The Woods were so intollerably thick for near 4 Miles, that they tore the very Skins that cover'd the Bread-Bags. This hinder'd us from overtaking the Surveyors, tho' we us'd our utmost diligence to do it. We cou'd reach but 4 Miles, & were oblig'd to encamp near a small run, where our Horses came off but indifferently. However they fared very near as well as their Masters, for our Indian met with no Game, so we had nothing to entertain ourselves with, but the Scanty Remnant of Yesterday's Plenty. Nor was there much luxury at the Surveyor's Camp, either in their Lodging or Diet. However they had the Pleasure as well as we, to see the Mountains very Plain both to the North & South of the Line. Their distance seem'd to be no more than 5 or 6 Miles. Those to the North appear'd in 3 or 4 Ledges rising one above another, but those to the South made no more than one Single Ledge, and that not entire, but were rather detach't Mountains lying near one another in a Line. One was prodigiously high, & the west end of it a perpendicular Precipice. The next to it was lower but had another rising out of the East End of it, in the form of a Stack of Chimneys. We cou'd likewise discern other Mountains in the Course of the Line, but at a much greater Distance. Til this day we never had a clear View of any of these Mountains, by reason the Air was very full of Smoak. But this Morning it clear'd up & surpriz'd us with this wild Prospect all at once. At Night the Men brought Holm's Horse.

Game the whole day, so that the men were oblig'd to make a frugal
distribution of what little they left in the Morning.

We encampt upon a small Rill, where the Horses came off as temper-
ately as their Masters. They were by this time grown so thin, by hard
Travel and Spare Feeding, that henceforth, in pure Compassion we chose
to perform the greater Part of the Journey on foot. And as our Baggage
was by this time grown much lighter, we divided it, after the best Manner,
that every Horse's Load might be proportion'd to the Strength he had
left. Tho', after all the prudent Measures we cou'd take, we perceiv'd the
Hills began to rise upon us so fast in our Front, that it wou'd be impossible for us to proceed much farther.

We saw very few Squirrels in the upper parts, because the Wild Cats
devour them unmercifully. Of these there are four kinds: The Fox
Squirrel, the Gray, the Flying, and the Ground-Squirrel.

These last resemble a Rat in every thing but the Tail, and the black
and Russet Streaks that run down the Length of their little Bodies.

26. We found our way grow still more Mountainous, after extending the Line 300 Poles farther. We came then to a Rivulet that ran
with a Swift Current towards the South. This we fancy'd to be another
Branch of the Irvin, tho' some of these men, who had been Indian Traders,
judg'd it rather to be the head of Deep River, that discharges its Stream
into that of Pee Dee; but this seem'd a wild Conjecture.

The Hills beyond that River were exceedingly lofty, and not to be attempted by our Jaded Palfreys, which could now hardly drag their Legs
after them upon level Ground. Besides, the Bread began to grow Scanty,
and the Winter Season to advance apace upon us.

We had likewise reason to apprehend the Consequences of being intercepted by deep Snows, and the Swelling of the many Waters between us
and Home. The first of these Misfortunes would starve all our Horses,
and the Other ourselves, by cutting off our Retreat, and obliging us to
Winter in those Desolate Woods. These considerations determin'd us
to Stop short here, and push our Adventures no farther. The last Tree
we markt was a Red Oak, growing on the Bank of the River;[78] and to
make the Place more remarkable, we blaz'd all the Trees around it.

We found the whole Distance from Corotuck Inlet to the Rivulet Where
we left off, to be, in a Strait Line, Two Hundred and Forty-one Miles and
Two Hundred and Thirty Poles. And from the Place where the Carolina
Commissioners deserted us, 72 Miles and 302 Poles. This last part of the
Journey was generally very hilly, or else grown up with troublesome
Thickets and underwoods, all which our Carolina Friends had the Discre-
tion to avoid.

---

[78] The survey ended at Peter's Creek, on the border of Stokes County, North
Carolina.

26. We had Ambassadors from our hungry Surveyors setting forth their wants, which we supply'd in the best manner we cou'd. We mov'd towards them about 11, & found them at the Camp where they lay, near a Rivulet, which we judg'd to be the Head of Deep River, otherwise call'd the North Branch of Cape Fear. We resolv'd to encamp here, because there was great Plenty of Canes for the poor Horses, which began to grow wond'rous thin. However the Surveyors measured 300 Poles this day, which carry'd the Line to the Banks of the Rivulet. The last Line Tree they mark't, is a red Oak with the Trees around it blazed. We determin'd to proceed no farther with the dividing Line, because the way to the West grew so Mountainous that our jaded Horses were not in Condition to climb over it. Besides we had no more Bread than would last us a Fortnight at short allowance. And the Season of the Year being far advanc'd, we had reason to fear we might be intercepted by Snow, or the swelling of the Rivers, which lay betwist us & home. These Considerations check't our Inclinations to fix the Line in the Ledge of Mountains, & determin'd us to make the best of our way back the same Track we came. We knew the worst of that, & had a strait Path to carry us the nearest Distance, while we were ignorant what difficultys might be encounter'd if we steer'd any other course.

We had intended to cross at the Foot of the Mountains over to

We encampt in a dirty Valley near the Rivulet above-mention'd, for the advantage of the Canes, and so sacrificed our own Convenience for that of our Horses.

There was a Small Mountain half a Mile to the Northward of us, which we had the Curiosity to Climb up in the Afternoon, in Order to enlarge our Prospect. From thence we were able to discover where the two Ledges of Mountains clos'd, as near as we cou'd guess, about 30 Miles to the West of us, and lamented that our present circumstances wou'd not permit us to advance the Line to that Place, which the Hand of Nature had made so very remarkable.

Not far from our Quarters one of the men pickt up a pair of Elk's Horns, not very large, and discover'd the Track of the Elk that had Shed them. It was rare to find any Tokens of those Animals so far to the South, because they keep commonly to the Northward of 37 degrees, as the Buffaloes, for the most part, confine themselves to the Southward of that Latitude.

The Elk is full as big as a Horse, and of the Deer kind. The Stags only have Horns, and those exceedingly large and Spreading. Their Colour is Something lighter than that of the Red Deer, and their Flesh tougher. Their swiftest Speed is a large trot, and in that Motion they turn their Horns back upon their Necks, and Cock their Noses aloft in the Air. Nature has taught them this Attitude to save their Antlers from being entangled in the Thickets, which they always retire to. They are very shy, and have the Sense of Smelling so exquisite that they wind a man at a great distance. For this reason they are Seldom Seen but when the Air is moist, in which Case their smell is not so Nice.

They commonly herd together, and the Indians say, if one of the Drove happen by some Wound to be disabled from making his Escape, the rest will forsake their fears to defend their Friend, which they will do with great obstinacy, till they are kill'd upon the Spot. Tho' otherwise, they are so alarm'd at the Sight of a man, that to avoid him they will Sometimes throw themselves down very high Precipices into the River.

A misadventure happen'd here, which gave us no Small perplexity. One of the Commissioners was so unlucky as to bruise his Foot against a Stump, which brought on a formal Fit of the Gout.

It must be own'd there cou'd not be a more unseasonable time, nor a more improper Situation, for any one to be attackt by that cruel Distemper. The Joint was so inflam'd that he cou'd neither draw Shoe nor Boot upon it; and to ride without either wou'd have expos'd him to so many rude knocks and Bruises, in those rough Woods, as to be intolerable even to a Stoick.

It was happy, indeed, that we were to rest here the next day, being Sunday, that there might be leisure for trying some Speedy Remedy. Accordingly he was persuaded to bathe his Foot in Cold Water, in Order

the head of James River, that we might be able to describe that
Natural Boundary.   But prudence got the better of Curiosity,
which is always the more necessary when we have other Men's
welfare to consult as well as our own.   Just by our Camp we
found a pair of Elks Horns, not very large, & saw the Track of
the Owner of them.   They commonly keep more to the Northward,
as Buffalos do more to the Southward.

In the Afternoon we walk't up a high Hill North of our Camp,
from whence we discover'd an Ampitheatre of Mountains extending from the N E round by the West to the S E.   'Twas very unlucky that the Mountains were more distant just at the head of our
Line towards the West, by 30 or 40 Miles.   Our Chaplain attempted to climb a Tree, but before he got 6 Feet from the Ground,
Fear made him cling closer to the Tree, than Love wou'd make him
cling to a Mistress.   Meanwell was more venturesome, but more
unfortunate, for he bruis'd his Foot in a tender place, by which he
got a gentle Fit of the Gout.   This was an improper Situation to
have the cruel Distemper in & put my Invention upon contriving
some way or other to carry him back.   In the mean while he bath'd
his Foot frequently in cold Water, to repell the Humour if Possible for as the Case was, he cou'd neither put on Shoe nor Boot.
Our Man kill'd 2 Bears, a Buck, & a Turkey, a very seasonable
supply, & made us reflect with gratitude on the goodness of Providence.   The whole Distance from Coratuck Inlet where we began
the Line to this Rivulet where we ended it, was 241½ Miles & 70
Poles.   In the Night the Wind blew fresh at S W with moderate
Rain.

to repel the Humour and asswage the Inflamation. This made it less pain-ful, and gave us hopes, too, of reducing the Swelling in a Short time.

Our men had the fortune to kill a Brace of Bears, a fat Buck, and a Wild Turkey, all which paid them with Interest for Yesterday's Abstinence. This constant and Seasonable Supply of all our daily Wants made us reflect thankfully on the Bounty of Providence.

And that we might not be unmindful of being all along fed by Heaven in this great and Solitary Wilderness, we agreed to Wear in our Hats the Maosti, which is, in Indian, the Beard of the Wild Turkey-Cock, and on our Breasts the Figure of that Fowl with its Wings extended, and holding in its Claws a scrowl with this Motto, "VICE COTURNICUM," meaning that we had been Supported by them in the Wilderness in the room of Quails.

27. This being Sunday we were not wanting in our Thanks to Heaven for the Constant Support and Protection we had been favour'd with. Nor did our Chaplain fail to put us in mind of Our Duty by a Sermon proper for the Occasion.

We order'd a Strict Inquiry to be made into the Quantity of Bread we had left, and found no more than wou'd Subsist us a Fortnight at Short Allowance. We made a fair Distribution of our whole Stock, and at the Same time recommended to the Men to manage this, their last Stake, to the best advantage, not knowing how long they would be oblig'd to live upon it.

We likewise directed them to keep a Watchfull eye upon their Horses, that none of them might be missing the next Morning, to hinder our Return.

There fell some Rain before Noon, which made our Camp more a Bogg than it was before. This moist Situation began to infect some of the men with Fevers, and some with Fluxes, which however we soon remov'd with Peruvian Bark and Ipocoacanah.

In the Afternoon we marcht up again to the top of the Hill to entertain our Eyes a Second time with the View of the Mountains, but a perverse Fog arose that hid them from our Sight.

In the Evening we deliberated which way it might be most proper to return. We had at first intended to cross over at the foot of the Mountains to the head of James River, that we might be able to describe that Natural Boundary so far. But, on Second Thoughts, we found many good Reasons against that laudable Design, Such as the Weakness of our Horses, the Scantiness of our Bread, and the near approach of Winter. We had Cause to believe the way might be full of Hills, and the farther we went towards the North, the more danger there wou'd be of Snow. Such considerations as these determin'd us at last to make the best of our way back upon the Line, which was the Straitest,

27. This being Sunday, we gave God thanks for protecting &
sustaining us thus far by his Divine Bounty. We had also a Sermon proper for the Occasion. It rain'd small Rain in the Morning, & look't louring all day. Meanwell had the Gout in Form,
his Foot being very much swell'd; which was not more Pain to
him, than it was disturbance to the rest. I order'd all the Men to
Visit their Horses, & to drive them up, that they might be found
more easily the next Morning. When the distribution of Bread
was made among the Men, I recommended good Husbandry to
them, not knowing how long we shou'd be oblig'd to subsist upon
it. I sat by the Riverside near a small Cascade, fed by a Stream
as clear as liquid Chrystal, & the Mumur it made compos'd my
Sences into an agreeable Tranquility. We had a Fog after Sunset
that gave an Unpleasant dampness to the Air, which we endeavour'd to correct by a rousing Fire. This with the Wetness of the
Ground where we encampt made our Situation a little unwholesome; yet thank God all our Company continu'd in a perfect
Health.

and Consequently the shortest way to the Inhabitants. We knew the worst of that Course, and were sure of a beaten Path all the way, while we were totally ignorant what Difficulties and Dangers the other Course might be attended with. So Prudence got the better for once of Curiosity, and the Itch for new Discoveries gave Place to Self-preservation.

Our Inclination was the Stronger to cross over according to the Course of the Mountains, that we might find out whether James River and Appamattock River head there, or run quite thro' them. 'Tis Certain that Potomec passes in a large Stream thro' the Main Ledge, and then divides itself into two considerable Rivers. That which Stretches away to the Northward is call'd the Cohungaroota,[79] and that which flows to the South-west, hath the Name of Sharantow.[80]

The Course of this last Stream is near parallel to the Blue Ridge of Mountains, at the distance only of about three or four Miles. Tho' how far it may continue that Course has not yet been sufficiently discover'd, but some Woodsmen pretend to say it runs as far as the source of Roanoak; Nay, they are so very particular as to tell us that Roanoak, Sharantow, and another Wide Branch of the Mississippi, all head in one of the Same Mountain.

What dependence there may be upon this Conjectural Geography, I wont pretend to say, tho' 'tis certain that Sharantow keeps close to the Mountains, as far as we are acquainted with its Tendency. We are likewise assur'd that the South Branch of James River, within less than 20 Miles East of the Main Ledge, makes an Elbow, and runs due South-west, which is parallel with the Mountains on this side. But how far it Stretches that way, before it returns, is not yet certianly known, no more than where it takes its Rise.

In the mean time it is Strange that our Woodsmen have not had Curiosity enough to inform themselves more exactly of these particulars, and it is Stranger Still that the Government has never thought it worth the Expense of making an accurate Survey of the Mountains, that we might be Masters of that Natural Fortification before the French, who in some Places have Settlements not very distant from it.

It therefore concerns his Majesty's Service very nearly, and the Safety of His Subjects in this part of the World, to take Possession of so important a Barrier in time, lest our good Friends, the French, and the Indians, thro' their Means, prove a perpetual Annoyance to these Colonies.

Another Reason to invite us to Secure this great Ledge of Mountains is, the Probability that very Valuable Mines may be discover'd there. Nor wou'd it be at all extravagant to hope for Silver Mines, among the rest, because Part of these Mountains ly exactly in the same Parallel, as well

---

[79] "Which by a late Survey has been found to extend about Two Hundred miles before it reaches its Source in a Mountain from Whence Allegani one of the Branches of Mississippi, takes its Rise and runs South West as this River dos South East. (Byrd's Note.)
[80] The Shenandoah.

[Continued on page 243]

as upon the Same Continent with New Mexico, and the Mines of St. Barb.[81]

28. We had given Orders for the Horses to be brought up early, but the likelyhood of more Rain prevented our being over-hasty in decamping. Nor were we out in our conjectures, for about ten a'clock it began to fall very plentifully.

Our Commissioner's Pain began now to abate, as the Swelling encreas'd. He made an excellent Figure for a Mountaineer, with one boot of Leather and the other of Flannel. Thus accowtur'd, he intended to mount, if the Rain had not happen'd opportunely to prevent him.

Tho', in Truth, it was hardly possible for Him to ride with so Slender a Defense, without exposing his Foot to be bruis'd and tormented by the Saplings, that stood thick on either side of the Path. It was therefore a most Seasonable Rain for Him, as it gave more time for his Distemper to abate.

Tho' it may be very difficult to find a certain Cure for the Gout, yet it is not improbable but some things may ease the Pain, and Shorten the Fits of it. And those Medicines are most likely to do this, that Supple the Parts, and clear the Passage Through the Narrow Vessels, that are the Seat of this cruel Disease. Nothing will do this more Suddenly than Rattle-snake's Oyl, which will even penetrate the Pores of Glass when warm'd in the sun.

It was unfortunate, therefore, that we had not taken out the Fat of those Snakes we had kill'd some time before, for the Benefit of so useful an Experiment, as well as for the Relief of our Fellow-Traveller.

But lately the Seneca Rattle-Snake-Root has been discover'd in this Country, which being infus'd in Wine, and drank Morning and Evening, has in Several Instances had a very happy Effect upon the Gout, and enabled Cripples to throw away their Crutches and walk several Miles, and, what is Stranger Still, it takes away the Pain in half an hour.

Nor was the Gout the only Disease among us that was hard to cure. We had a man in our Company who had too Voracious a Stomach for a Woodsman. He ate as much as any other two, but all he Swallow'd stuck by him till it was carry'd off by a Strong Purge. Without this Assistance, often repeated, his Belly and Bowels wou'd swell to so enormous a Bulk that he cou'd hardly breathe, especially when he lay down, just as if he had had an Asthma; tho', notwithstanding this oddness of constitution, he was a very Strong, lively Fellow, and us'd abundance of Violent Exercise, by which 'twas wonderfull the Peristaltick Motion was not more Vigorously promoted.

---

[81] Santa Barbara, Northern Mexico, colonized by the Spanish in 1567; long famous for its silver mines.

28.   We ordered the Horses up very early, but the likelihood of more Rain prevented our decamping.   And we judg'd right, for about 10 a Clock it began to Rain in good earnest.   Meanwell made an excellent Figure with one Boot of Leather & the other of Flannel.   So accoutred, he intended to mount, but the Rain came seasonably to hinder him from exposeing his foot to be bruis'd & tormented by the Bushes.   We kept snug in the Tent all Day spending most of our time in reading, & Dr Humdrum being disturb'd at Astrolabe's reading Hudibras aloud, gabbled an Old Almanack 3 times over, to drown one Noise with another.   This Trial of Lungs lasted a full Hour, & tired the Hearers as much as the Readers.   Powell's Ague return'd for which I gave him the Bark & Pool took some Anderson's Pills to force a Passage thro' his Body.   This man had an odd Constitution, he eat like a Horse, but all he eat stay'd with him 'till it was forc'd downwards by some purging Physick.   Without this Assistance his Belly & Bowells were so swell'd he cou'd hardly Breath.   Yet he was a Strong Fellow & used a world of Exercise.   It was therefore wonderful the Peristaltick Motion was not more vigorously promoted. Page was muffled up for the Tooth-Ach, for which Distemper I cou'd recommend no medicine but Patience, which he seem'd to possess a great Share of.   It rain'd most part of the Night.

We gave this poor Man Several Purges, which only eas'd Him for the present, and the next day he wou'd grow as burly as ever. At last we gave Him a Moderate Dose of ippocoacanah,[82] in Broth made very Salt, which turn'd all its Operations downwards. This had so happy an Effect that, from that day forward to the End of our Journey, all his Complaint ceas'd, and the passages continued unobstructed.

The Rain continued most of the Day and Some part of the Night, which incommoded us much in our Dirty Camp, and made the men think of Nothing but Eating, even at the time when nobody cou'd Stir out to make provision for it.

29. Tho' we were flattered in the morning with the usual Tokens of a fair Day, yet they all blew over, and it rain'd hard before we cou'd make ready for our Departure.

This was still in favour of our Podagrous Friend, whose Lameness was now grown better, and the Inflamation fallen. Nor did it seem to need above one day more to reduce it to its Natural Proportion, and make it fit for the Boot; And effectually The Rain procur'd this Benefit for him, and gave him particular Reason to believe his Stars propitious.

Notwithstanding the falling Weather, our Hunters sally'd out in the afternoon, and drove the Woods in a Ring, which was thus performed. From the circumference of a large Circle they all march't inwards, and drove the Game towards the center. By this means they shot a Brace of fat Bears, which came very seasonably, because we had made clean Work in the Morning and were in Danger of dining with St. Anthony, or his Grace Duke Humphry.

But in this Expedition the unhappy man who had lost himself once before, Straggled again so far in Pursuit of a Deer, that he was hurry'd a second time quite out of his knowledge. And Night coming on before he cou'd recover the Camp, he was obliged to lie down, without any of the Comforts of Fire, Food or covering; Nor would his Fears suffer him to Sleep very Sound, because, to his great disturbance, the Wolves howl'd all that Night, and the Panthers scream'd most frightfully.

In the Evening a brisk North-Wester swept all the Clouds from the Sky, and expos'd the mountains as well as the Stars to our Prospect.

That which was the most lofty to the Southward, and which we call'd the Lover's Leap, some of our Indian Traders fondly fancy'd was the Kiawan mountain,[83] which they had formerly seen from the country of the Cherokees.

They were the more positive by reason of the prodigious Precipice that remarkably distinguished the West End of it.

---

[82] See Note 35, p. 62.
[83] Kiawani, also the name of an Indian of the Northwest, but most likely the association here is with the Keyauwee, a tribe living on the Yadkin in 1701.

29. In the Morning we were flatter'd with all the Signs of a fair
Day, the Wind being come about to the N W. This made us
Order the Horses to be got up very early, but the Tent Horse cou'd
not be found, And 'tis well he stop't us, for about 10, all our
hopes of fair Weather blew over, and it rain'd very smartly for
some time. This was all in Favour of Meanwell's gouty Foot,
which was now grown better, & the Inflammation asswaged. Nor did
it need above one Day more to bring it down to its natural Proportion, and make it fit for the Boot. Being confin'd to the Tent til
Dinner, I had no Amuzement but reading. But in the Afternoon
I walk't up to a Neighbouring Hill, from whence I cou'd view the
Mountains to the Southward, the highest of which our Traders
fancy'd to be the Katawa Mountain, but it seems to be too Northerly for that. Our Men went out a driveing, & had the Luck to
kill 2 Bears, one of which was found by our Indian asleep, & never
waked. Unfortunate Hamilton straggling from the rest of the
Company, was lost a Second time. We fired at least a Dozen Guns,
to direct him by their Report to our Camp, but all in Vain, we
cou'd get no tidings of him. I was much concern'd lest a disaster
might befall him being alone all Night in that dolefull Wilderness.

We seem'd however not to be far enough South for that, tho' 'tis not improbable but a few miles farther the Course of our Line might carry us to the most Northerly Towns of the Cherokees.

What makes this the more credible, is the North West Course, that our Traders take from the Catawbas for some hundred miles together, when they carry Goods that round-about way to the Cherokees.

It was a great Pity that the want of Bread, and the Weakness of our Horses, hinder'd us from making the Discovery. Tho' the great Service of such an Excursion might have been to the Country wou'd certainly have made the attempt not only pardonable, but much to be commended.

Our Traders are now at the vast Charge and Fatigue of travelling above five hundred miles for the Benefit of that traffique which hardly quits cost. Wou'd it not then be worth the Assembly's while to be at some charge to find a Shorter cut to carry on so profitable a Trade, with more advantage, and less hazard and Trouble, than they do at present? For I am persuaded it will not then be half the Distance that our Traders make it now, nor half so far as Georgia lies from the Northern Clans of that Nation.

Such a Discovery would certainly prove an unspeakable Advantage to this Colony, by facilitating a Trade with so considerable a nation of Indians, which have 62 Towns, and more than 4000 Fighting Men. Our Traders at that rate would be able to undersell those sent from the other Colonies so much, that the Indians must have reason to deal with them preferable to all others.

Of late the new Colony of Georgia has made an act obliging us to go 400 miles to take out a License to traffick with these Cherokees, tho' many of their Towns ly out of their Bounds, and we had carry'd on this Trade 80 years before that Colony was thought of.

30.   In the Morning early the man who had gone astray the day before found his way to the Camp, by the Sound of the Bells that were upon the Horses' Necks.

At nine a'clock we began our March back toward the rising Sun; for tho' we had finisht the Line, yet we had not yet near finisht our Fatigue. We had after all 200 good miles at least to our several Habitations, and the Horses were brought so low, that we were oblig'd to travel on foot great part of the way, and that in our Boots, too, to save our Legs from being torn to pieces by the Bushes and Briars. Had we not done this, we must have left all our Horses behind, which cou'd now hardly drag their Legs after them, and with all the favour we cou'd show the poor Animals, we were forc'd to set Seven of them free, not far from the foot of the Mountains.

Four men were despatcht early to clear the Road, that our Lame Commissioner's leg might be in less danger of being bruis'd, and that the Baggage Horses might travel with less difficulty and more expedition.

30.   The Clouds were all swept away by a kind N Wester, which made it pretty cold.   We were all impatient to set our Faces towards the East, which made the men more alert than Ordinary in catching their Horses.   About 7 our Stray Man found the way to the Camp, being directed by the Horse's Bells.   Tho' he had lain on the bare Ground without either Fire or Bed Cloaths, he catch't no Cold.   I gave orders that 4 Men shou'd set off early, & clear the way that the Baggage Horses might travel with less difficulty & more Expedition.   We follow'd them about 11, And the Air being clear we had a fair Prospect of the Mountains both to the N & S.   That very high one to the South, with the Precipice at the West End, we call'd the Lovers cure, because one Leap from thence wou'd put a sudden Period both to his Passion & his Pain.

As we past along, by favour of a Serene Sky, we had still, from every Eminence, a perfect view of the Mountains, as well to the North as to the South. We could not forbear now and then facing about to survey them, as if unwilling to part with a Prospect, which at the same time, like some Rake's, was very wild and very Agreeable.

We encourag'd the Horses to exert the little Strength they had, and being light, they made a shift to jog on about Eleven Miles. We Encampt on Crooked Creek, near a Thicket of Canes. In front of our Camp rose a very beautiful Hill, that bounded our View at about a Mile's Distance, and all the Intermediate space was cover'd with green canes. Tho', to our Sorrow, Fire-wood was Scarce, which was now the harder upon us, because a north-wester blew very cold from the Mountains.

The Indian kill'd a stately, fat Buck, & we pickt his Bones as clean as a score of Turkey-Buzzards cou'd have done.

By the advantage of a clear night, we made tryal once more of the Variation, and found it much the same as formerly.

This being his Majesty's Birth-Day, we drank all the Loyal Healths in excellent Water, not for the sake of the drink, (like many of our fellow subjects,) but purely for the Sake of the Toast. And because all Public Mirth shou'd be a little noisy, we fir'd several volleys of Canes, instead of Guns, which gave a loud report.

We threw them into the Fire, where the Air enclosed betwixt the Joints of the Canes, being expanded by the violent Heat, burst its narrow Bounds with a considrable explosion!

In the Evening one of the men knockt down an Oppossum, which is a harmless little Beast, that will seldom go out of your way, and if you take hold of it, it will only grin, and hardly ever bite. The Flesh was well tasted and Tender, approaching nearest to Pig, which it also resembles in Bigness. The colour of its Fur was a Goose Gray, with a Swine's Snout, and a Tail like a Rat, but at least a foot long. By twisting this Tail about the arm of a Tree, it will hand with all its weight, and swing to any thing it wants to take hold of.

It has five Claws on the fore Feet of equal length, but the hinder feet have only Four claws, and a sort of Thumb standing off at a proper Distance.

Their Feet being thus form'd, qualify them for climbing up Trees to catch little Birds, which they are very fond of.

But the greatest Particularity of this creature, and which distinguishes it from most others that we are acquainted with, is the FALSE BELLY of the FEMALE, into which her Young retreat in time of Danger. She can draw the Slit, which is the Inlet into this Pouch, so close, that you must look narrowly to find it, especially if she happen to be a Virgin.

Within the False Belly may be seen seven or eight Teats, on which the young Ones grow from their first Formation till they are big enough to fall off, like ripe Fruit from a Tree. This is so odd a method of Genera-

On the highest Ledge that stretch't away to the N. E. rose a Mount in the Shape of a Maiden's Breast, which for that reason we call'd Innocent Name. And the main Ledge itself we call'd Mount Eagle. We march't 11 Miles from the End of the Line & encampt upon Crooked-Creek near a Thicket of Cane. In the Front of our Camp was a very beautifull Hill which bounded over Prospect at a Mile's Distance, & all the intermediate Space was cover'd with Green Canes. Firewood was scanty with Us, which was the harder, because 'twas very cold. Our Indian kill'd a Deer that was extremely fat, & we pick't his Bones as clean as a Score of Turkey Buzzards cou'd have done.

By the favour of a very clear Night we made another Essary[62] of the Variation, & found it much the same as formerly 2° 30′ This being his Majesty's Birth Day we drank his Health in a Dram of excellent Cherry Brandy, but cou'd not afford one Drop for the Queen & the Roial Issue. We therefore remember'd them in Water as clear as our Wishes. And because all loyal rejoicings shou'd be a little Noisy, we fired Canes instead of Guns, which made a Report as loud as a Pistol, the heat expanding the Air shut up with the joints of this Vegetable, & making an Explosion.

The Woods being clear'd before us by the Pioneers, & the way pretty Levil we travell'd with Pleasure, encreast by the hopes of making haste home.

31.   We dispatch't away our Pioneers early to clear away the Bushes, but did not follow them till 11 a Clock. We crost Crooked Creek several times, the Banks of which being very steep, jaded our poor Horses very much. Meanwell's Baggage Horse gave out the first, & next to him one of the Bread Horses, so that we were oblig'd to drop them both by the way. The second time we crost Crooked Creek, by endeavoring to step off my Horse's Back upon the Shoar, I fell all along in the Water. I wet myself all over & bruis'd the back part of my Head; yet made no Complaint, but was the merriest of the Company at my own disaster. Our Dreamer Orion had a Revelation about it the Night before, & foretold it fairly to some of the Company.

---

[62] A corruption of essart, the art of grubbing land to make it arable.

tion, that I should not have believed it without the Testimony of mine own Eyes. Besides a knowing and credible Person has assur'd me he has more than once observ'd the Embryo Possums growing to the Teat before they were compleatly Shaped, and afterwards wacht their daily growth til they were big enough for Birth. And all this he could the more easily pry into, because the Damm was so perfectly gentle and harmless, that he could handle her just as he pleas'd.

I cou'd hardly persuade myself to publish a thing so contrary to the Course that Nature takes in the Production of other Animals, unless it were a Matter Commonly believ'd in all Countries where that Creature is produc'd, and has been often observed by Persons of undoubted credit and understanding.

They say that the Leather-winged Bats produce their Young in the same uncommon Manner. And that young Sharks at Sea, and the Young Vipers ashoar, run down the Throats of their Damms when they are closely pursued.

The frequent crossing of Crooked Creek, and mounting the Steep Banks of it, gave the finishing stroke to the foundering of our Horses: and no less than two of them made a full stop here, and would not advance a foot farther, either by fair means or foul.

We had a Dreamer of Dreams amongst us, who warned me in the Morning to take care of myself, or I shou'd infallibly fall into the Creek; I thank'd him kindly, and used what Caution I cou'd, but was not able it seems to avoid my Destiny, for my Horse made a false step and laid me down at my full Length in the water.

This was enough to bring dreaming into credit, and I think it much for the Honour of our expedition, that it was grac'd not only with PRIEST but also with a PROPHET.

We were so perplext with this Serpentine Creek, as well as in Passing the Branches of the Irvin, (which were swell'd since we saw them before,) that we could reach but 5 miles this whole day. In the Evening We pitched our Tent near Miry creek, (tho' an uncomfortable place to lodge in) purely for the advantage of the Canes.

Our Hunters killed a large Doe and two Bears, which made all other misfortunes easy. Certainly no Tartar over lov'd Horse-flesh, or Hottentot Guts and Garbage, better than Woodsmen do Bear. The truth of it is, it may be proper food perhaps for such as Work or Ride it off, but, with our Chaplain's Leave, who lov'd it much, I think it not a very proper dyet for saints, because 'tis apt to make them a little too rampant.

And now, for the good of mankind, and for the better Peopling an Infant colony, which has no want but that of Inhabitants, I will venture to publish a Secret of Importance, which our Indian disclos'd to me. I askt him the reason why few or none of his Countrywomen were barren? To which curious Question he answered, with a Broad grin upon his Face, they had an infallible SECRET for that. Upon my being importunate to

The Ground was so Mountainous, & our Horses so weak, that with all our diligence we cou'd not exceed 4 Miles. Indeed we spent some time in crossing the Dan & the Mayo, the Fords being something deeper than when we came up. We took up our Camp at Miry Creek, & regal'd ourselves with one Buck & 2 Bears, which our Men kill'd in their March. Here we promoted our Chaplain from the Deanry of Pip, to the Bishoprick of Beardom. For as these Countrys where Christians inhabit are call'd Christendome, so those where Bears take up their Residence may not improperly go by the Name of Beardom. And I wish other Bishops loved their Flock as intirely as our Doctor loves his.

know what the secret might be, he informed me that, if any Indian woman did not prove with child at a decent time after Marriage, the Husband, to save his Reputation with the women, forthwith entered into a Bear-dyet for Six Weeks, which in that time makes him so vigorous that he grows exceedingly impertinent to his poor wife and 'tis great odds but he makes her a Mother in Nine Months.

And thus I am able to say, besides, for the Reputation of the Bear Dyet, that all the Marryed men of our Company were joyful Fathers within forty weeks after they got Home, and most of the Single men had children sworn to them within the same time, our chaplain always excepted, who, with much ado, made a shift to cast out that importunate kind of Devil, by Dint of Fasting and Prayer.

Nov. 1. By the negligence of one of the Men in not hobbling his Horse, he straggled so far that he could not be found. This stopt us all the Morning long; Yet, because our Time should not be entirely lost, we endeavoured to observe the Latitude at twelve a clock. Though our observation was not perfect, by reason the Wind blew a little too fresh, however, by Such a One as we cou'd make, we found ourselves in 36° 20' only.

Notwithstanding our being thus delay'd, and the unevenness of the Ground, over which we were oblig'd to walk, (for most of us serv'd now in the Infantry,) we travell'd no less than 6 miles, Tho' as merciful as we were to our poor Beasts, another of 'em tired by the way, & was left behind for the Wolves & Panthers to feast upon.

As we marcht along, we had the fortune to kill a Brace of Bucks, as many Bears, and one wild Turkey. But this was carrying Sport to wantonness, because we butchered more than we were able to transport. We ordered the Deer to be quarter'd and divided amongst the Horses for the lighter Carriage, and recommended the Bears to our dayly attendants, the Turkey-Buzzards.

We always chose to carry Venison along with us rather than Bear, not only because it was less cumbersome, but likewise because the People cou'd eat it without Bread, which was now almost spent. Whereas the other, being richer food, lay too heavy upon the stomach, unless it were lightened by something farinaceous. This is what I thought proper to remarque, for the service of all those whose Business or Diversion shall oblige them to live any time in the Woods.

And because I am persuaded that very usefull Matters may be found out by Searching this great Wilderness, especially the upper parts of it about the Mountains, I conceive it will help to engage able men in that good work, if I recommend a wholesome kind of Food, of very small Weight and very great Nourishment, that will secure them from Starving, in case they shou'd be so unlucky as to meet with no Game. The Chief

November

1. The Pioneers were sent away about 9 a Clock, but we were detain'd til near 2, by reason John Evan's his Horse cou'd not be found, & at last we were oblig'd to leave 4 Men behind to look for him. However we made a Shift to go 6 Miles, & by the way had the Fortune to kill a Brace of Does, 2 Bears, & one Turkey. Meanwell's Riding Horse tir'd too by the way, so we were oblig'd to drop him about a Mile short of the Camp. Many more of our Horses were so weak they staggar'd under their Riders, so that in Compassion to the poor Animals we walk't great part of the way notwithstanding the Path was very rough, & in many places uneven. For the same good natur'd Reason we left our Bears behind, choosing rather to carry the Venison, for which our Bishop had like to have mutiny'd. We endeavour'd about Noon to observe the Latitude, but our Observation was something imperfect, the wind blowing too fresh. By such a one as we cou'd make we found the Latitude no more than 36° 20'. In this Camp our Horses had short Commons, and had they been able to speak like Balaam's Ass wou'd have bemoan'd themselves very much.

discouragement at present from penetrating far into the Woods in the trouble of carrying a Load of Provisions. I must own Famine is a frightful Monster, and for that reason to be guarded against as well as we can. But the common precautions against it, are so burthensome, that People can't tarry long out, and go far enough from home, to make any effectual Discovery.

The Portable Provisions I would furnish our Foresters withal are Glue-Broth and rockahomini: one contains the Essence of Bread, the other of Meat.

The best way of making Glue-Broth is after the following method: Take a Leg of Beef, Veal, Venison, or any other Young Meat, because Old Meat will not so easily Jelly. Pare off all the fat, in which there is no Nutriment, and of the Lean make a very strong Broth, after the usual Manner, by boiling the meat to Rags till all the Goodness be out. After Skimming off what fat remains, pour the Broth into a wide Stew-Pan, well tinn'd, & let it simmer over a gentle, even Fire, till it come to a thick Jelly. Then take it off and set it over Boiling Water, which is an Evener Heat, and not so apt to burn the Broth to the Vessel. Over that let it evaporate, stirring it very often till it be reduc'd, when cold, into a Solid Substance like Glue. Then cut it into small Pieces, laying them Single in the Cold, that they may dry the Sooner. When the Pieces are perfectly dry, put them into a Cannister, and they will be good, if kept Dry, a whole East India Voyage.

This Glue is so Strong, that two or three Drams, dissolv'd in boiling Water with a little Salt, will make half a pint of good Broth, & if you shou'd be faint with fasting or Fatigue, let a small piece of this Glue melt in your Mouth, and you will find yourself surprisingly refreshed.

One Pound of this cookery wou'd keep a man in good heart above a Month, and is not only Nourishing, but likewise very wholesome. Particularly it is good against Fluxes, which Woodsmen are very liable to, by lying too near the moist ground, and guzzling too much cold Water. But as it will be only us'd now and then, in times of Scarcity, when Game is wanting, two Pounds of it will be enough for a Journey of Six Months.

But this Broth will be still more heartening if you thicken every mess with half a Spoonful of Rockahominy, which is nothing but Indian Corn parched without burning, and reduced to Powder. The Fire drives out all the Watery Parts of the Corn, leaving the Strength of it behind, and this being very dry, becomes much lighter for carriage and less liable to be Spoilt by the Moist Air.

Thus half a Dozen Pounds of this Sprightful Bread will sustain a Man for as many Months, provided he husband it well, and always Spare it when he meets with Venison, which, as I said before, may be very Safely eaten without any Bread at all.

[Continued on page 257]

By what I have said, a Man needs not encumber himself with more than 8 or 10 Pounds of Provisions, tho' he continue half a year in the Woods.

These and his Gun will support him very well during that time, without the least danger of keeping one Single Fast. And tho' some of his days may be what the French call *Jours maigres*, yet there will happen no more of those than will be necessaryfor his health, and to carry off the Excesses of the Days of Plenty, when our Travellers will be apt to indulge their Lawless Appetites too much.

2. The Heavens frowned this Morning, and threaten'd abundance of Rain, but our Zeal for returning made us defy the weather, and decamp a little before Noon. Yet we had not advanct two Miles, before a Soaking Shower made us glad to pitch our Tent as fast as we could. We chose for that purpose a rising Ground, half a mile to the East of MATRIMONY CREEK. This was the first and only time we were caught in the Rain, during the whole Expedition. It us'd before to be so civil as to fall in the night, after we were safe in our Quarters, and had trencht ourselves in; or else it came upon us on Sundays, when it was no Interruption to our Progress, nor any Inconvenience to our Persons.

We had, however, been so lucky in this Particular before, that we had abundant Reason to take our present soaking patiently, and the Misfortune was the less, because we had taken the Precaution to keep all our Baggage and Bedding perfectly dry.

This Rain was enliven'd with very loud Thunder, which was echo'd back by the Hills in the Neighbourhood in a frightful Manner. There is something in the Woods that makes the Sound of this Meteor more awful, and the Violence of the Lightening more Visible. The Trees are frequently Shiver'd quite down to the Root, and sometimes perfectly twisted. But of all the Effects of Lightening that ever I heard of, the most amazing happen'd in this country, in the Year 1736.

In the Summer of that year a Surgeon of a Ship, whose Name was Davis, came ashoar at York to visit a Patient. He was no sooner got into the House, but it began to rain with many terrible Claps of Thunder. When it was almost dark there came a dreadful Flash of Lightning, which Struck the Surgeon dead as he was walking about the Room, but hurt no other Person, tho' several were near him. At the same time it made a large Hole in the Trunk of a Pine Tree, which grew about Ten Feet from the Window. But what was most surprising in this Disaster was, that on the Breast of the unfortunate man that was kill'd was the Figure of a Pine Tree, as exactly delineated as any Limner in the World could draw it, nay, the Resemblance went so far as to represent the colour of the Pine, as well as the Figure. The Lightning must probably have passed thro' the Tree first before it struck the Man, and by that means have printed the Icon of it on his breast.

2.   We lost all the Morning in hunting for Powell's Mare, so that it was 2 a Clock before we decampt. Our Zeal to make the best of our way made us set out when it was very like to rain, & it rained in good earnest before we had march't a Mile. We bore it patiently while it was moderate, & repast Matrimony Creek about 1½ Miles from our Camp. But soon after the Rain fell more violently, & oblig'd us to take up our Quarters upon an Iminence, that we might not be drown'd. This was the only time we were catch't in the Rain upon the Road during the whole Journey. It us'd to be so civil as to fall in the Night, as it did while Herod was building the Temple or on a Sunday, or else to give us warning enough to encamp before it fell. But now it took us upon the way, & made our Lodgeing uncomfortable because we were oblig'd to pitch the Tent upon wet Ground. The worst Circumstance of all was, that there was hardly any picking for the Horses, which were now grown so lean & so weak, that the Turkey-Buzzards began to follow them. It continu'd raining 'til 3 a Clock in the Morning, when to our great Joy it clear'd up with a N. Wester.

But whatever may have been the cause, the Effect was certain, and can be attested by a Cloud of Witnesses who had the curiosity to go and see this Wonderful Phenomenon.

The worst of it was, we were forced to Encamp in a barren place, where there was hardly a blade of Grass to be seen, Even the wild Rosemary failed us here, which gave us but too just apprehensions that we should not only be oblig'd to trudge all the way home on foot, but also to lug our Baggage at our Backs into the Bargain.

Thus we learnt by our own Experience, that Horses are very improper animals to use in a long Ramble into the Woods, and the better they have been used to be fed, they are still the worse. Such will fall away a great deal faster, and fail much sooner, than those which are wont to be at their own keeping. Besides, Horses that have been accustom'd to a Plane and Champaign Country will founder presently, when they come to clamber up Hills, and batter their Hoofs against continal Rocks.

We need Welsh Runts, and Highland Galloways to climb our Mountains withal; they are us'd to Precipices, and will bite as close as Banstead Down Sheep. But I should much rather recommend Mules, if we had them, for these long and painful Expeditions; tho' till they can be bred, certainly Asses are the fittest Beasts of Burthen for the Mountains. They are sure-footed, patient under the heaviest Fatigue, and will subsist upon Moss, or Browsing on Shrubs all the Winter. One of them will carry the Necessary Luggage of four Men, without any Difficulty, and upon a Pinch will take a Quarter of Bear or Venison upon their Backs into the Bargain.

Thus, when the Men are light and disengaged from everything but their Guns, they may go the whole Journey on foot with pleasure. And tho' my Dear Countrymen have so great a Passion for riding, that they will often walk two miles to catch a Horse, in Order to ride One, yet, if they'll please to take my Word for 't, when they go into the Woods upon Discovery, I would advise them by all Means to march a-foot, for they will then be deliver'd from the great Care and Concern for their Horses, which takes up too large a portion of their time.

Over Night we are now at the trouble of hobbling them out, and often of leading them a mile or two to a convenient place for Forrage, and then in the morning we are some Hours in finding them again, because they are apt to stray a great way from the place where they were turn'd out. Now and then, too, they are lost for a whole day together, and are frequently so weak and jaded, that the Company must ly still Several days, near some Meadow, or High-land Pond, to recruit them. All these delays retard their Progress intolerably; whereas, if they had only a few Asses, they wou'd abide close to the Camp, and find Sufficient food everywhere, and in all Seasons of the Year. Men wou'd then be able to travel Safely over Hills and Dales, nor wou'd the Steepest Mountains obstruct their Progress.

They might also search more narrowly for Mines and other Production

[Continued on page 261]

of Nature, without being confin'd to level grounds, in Compliment to the jades they ride on. And one may foretell, without the Spirit of Divination, that so long as Woodsmen continue to range on Horse-back, we shall be Strangers to our own Country, and a few or no valuable Discoveries will ever be made.

The FRENCH COURIERS *de Bois*, who have run from one End of the Continent to the other, have performed it all on foot, or else in all probability must have continued as ignorant as we are.

Our Country has now been inhabited more than 130 years by the English, and still we hardly know any thing of the Appallachian Mountains, that are no where above 250 miles from the sea. Whereas the French, who are later comers, have rang'd from Quebec Southward as far as the Mouth of Mississippi, in the bay of Mexico, and to the West almost as far as California, which is either way above 2000 miles.

3. A North-west Wind having clear'd the Sky, we were now tempted to travel on a Sunday, for the first time, for want of more plentiful Forage, though some of the more Scrupulous amongst us we(re) unwilling to do Evil, that good might come of it, and make our Cattle work a Good part of the Day in order to fill their Bellies at Night. However, the Chaplain put on his casuistical Face, and offer'd to take the sin upon Himself. We therefore consented to move a Sabbath Day's Journey of 3 or 4 Miles, it appearing to be a Matter of some necessity.

On the way our unmerciful Indian kill'd no less than two Brace of Deer and a large Bear. We only prim'd the Deer, being unwilling to be encumbered with their whole Carcasses. The rest we consign'd to the Wolves, which in Return seranaded us great part of the Night. They are very clamerous in their Banquets, which we know is the way some other Brutes have, in the extravagance of their Jollity and Sprightliness, of expressing their thanks to Providence.

We came to our Old camp, in Sight of the River Irvin, whose Stream was Swell'd now near four feet with the Rain that fell the Day before. This made it impracticable for us to ford it, nor could we guess when the water wou'd fall enough to let us go over.

This put our Mathematical Professor, who shou'd have set a better Example, into the Vapours, fearing he shou'd be oblig'd to take up his Winter Quarters in that doleful Wilderness. But the rest were not affected with his want of Faith, but preserv'd a Firmness of Mind Superior to such little Adverse Accidents. They trusted that the same good Providence which had most remarkably prosper'd them hitherto, would continue his goodness and conduct them safe to the End of their Journey.

However, we found plainly that travelling on the Sunday, contrary to our constant Rule, had not thriven with us in the least. We were not gainers of any distance by it, because the River made us pay two days for Violating one.

3. It was my Opinion to rest in our Camp, bad as it was, because it was Sunday: but every body was against me. They urg'd the Danger of Starving the Horses, & the Short March we made Yesterday, which might Justify making a Sabbath Day's Journey to day. I held out against all these Arguments on Account of resting the Horses, which they greatly needed, as well as because of the Duty of the Day; 'til at last the Chaplain came with a Casuistical Face, & told me it was a Case of necessity that oblig'd us to remove from a place that wou'd famish all our Horses. That Charity to those poor Animals wou'd excuse a small Violation of of the 4th Commandment. I answer'd that the Horse wou'd lose as much by the Fatigue of travelling, as they wou'd gain by the bettering their Food; that the Water was rais'd in the River Irvin, & we shou'd be forc't to stay 'til it was fallen again, & so shou'd gain no distance by travelling on the Sunday. However on condition the D^r wou'd take the Sin upon himself, I agreed to move 3 or 4 Miles, which carry'd us to the Banks of the Irvine. By the way our Indian kill'd 4 Deer & a Bear. When we came to the River, we found the Water 3 or 4 Foot higher than when we came up, so that there was no liklihood of getting over under 2 Days. This made good my Argument, & put our hasty Gentlemen into the Vapour, especially Orion, who was more impatient than any Body. I cou'd find no other Reason for it, but because he had dream't that Col° Beverley was dead, and imagined his Absence might hinder him from making Interest for his Place of Surveyor

Nevertheless, by making this Reflection, I would not be thought so rigid an observer of the Sabbath as to allow of no Work at all to be done, or Journeys to be taken upon it. I should not care to ly still and be knockt on the head, as the Jews were heretofore by Antiochus, because I believ'd it unlawful to stand upon my Defense on this good day. Nor would I care, like a certain New England Magistrate, to order a Man to the Whipping Post, for daring to ride for a Midwife on the Lord's Day.

On the contrary, I am for doing all acts of Necessity, Charity, and Self-Preservation, upon a Sunday as well as other days of the Week. But, as I think our present March cou'd not Strictly be justify'd by any of these Rules, it was but just we should suffer a little for it.

I never could learn that the Indians set apart any day of the Week or the Year for the Service of God. They pray, as Philosophers eat, only when they have a stomach, without having any set time for it. Indeed these Idle People have very little occasion for a sabbath to refresh themselves after hard Labour, because very few of them ever Labour at all. Like the wild Irish, they would rather want than Work, and are all men of Pleasure to whom every day is a day of rest.

Indeed, in their Hunting, they will take a little Pains, but this being only a Diversion, their spirits are rather rais'd than depress'd by it, and therefore need at most but a Night's Sleep to recruit them.

4. By some Stakes we had driven into the River yesterday, we perceiv'd the Water began to fall, but fell so Slowly that we found we must have patience a day or two longer. And because we were unwilling to ly altogether Idle, we sent back some of the men to bring up the two Horses that tir'd the Saturday before. They were found near the place where we had left them, but seemed too sensible of their Liberty to come to us. They were found Standing indeed, but as Motionless as the Equestrian statue at CHARING-CROSS.

We had great reason to apprehend more Rain by the clouds that drove over our Heads. The boldest amongst us were not without some Pangs of uneasiness at so very Sullen a Prospect. However, God be prais'd! it all blew over in a few Hours.

If much Rain had fallen, we resolv'd to make a Raft and bind it together with Grape Vines, to Ferry ourselves and Baggage over the River. Tho', in that Case, we expected the Swiftness of the Stream wou'd have carry'd down our Raft a long way before we cou'd have tugg'd it to the opposite shoar.

One of the Young Fellows we had sent to bring up the tired Horses entertained us in the Evening with a remarkable adventure he had met with that day.

He had straggled, it seems, from his Company in a mist, and made a cub of a year old betake itself to a Tree. While he was new-priming

Gen^{ll}. In the Evening we perceiv'd the Water began to fall in the River, which gave some of the Company the Vain hopes of getting over the next day.

4. In the Morning we measured the Marks we had set up at the River, & found the Water had not fallen above a foot, by this we were convinced, that we shou'd be obliged to halt there a day longer. We sent some Men to endeavour to bring up 2 Horses, which tired on Saturday, but the Horses were too well pleas'd with their Liberty, to come along with them. One of these Manumitted Horses belong'd to Abraham Jones, and being prick't in the Mouth he bled himself quite off his Leggs.

There being great Plenty in our Camp the Men kept eating all day to keep them out of Idleness. In the Evening it look't very dark, & menaced us with more Rain to our great Mortification, but after a few Drops, I thank God it blew over. Orion sigh'd heavily while it lasted, apprehending we shou'd take up our Winter Quarters in the Woods. John Ellis who was one of the Men we had sent to bring up the tired Horses told us a Romantick Adventure which he had with a Bear on Saturday last. He had straggled from his Company, & tree'd a Young Cubb. While he was new priming his Gun to shoot at it, the Old Gentlewoman appear'd, who seeing her Heir Apparent in Distress, came up to his Relief.

his piece, with intent to fetch it down, the Old Gentlewoman appeared, and perceiving her Heir apparent in Distress, advanc'd open-mouth'd to his relief.

The man was so intent upon his Game, that she had approacht very near him before he perceived her. But finding his Danger, he faced about upon the Enemy, which immediately rear'd upon her posteriors, & put herself in Battle Array.

The Man, admiring at the Bear's assurance, endeavour'd to fire upon Her, but by the Dampness of the Priming, his Gun did not go off. He cockt it a second time, and had the same misfortune. After missing Fire twice, he had the folly to punch the Beast with the muzzle of his Piece; but mother Bruin, being upon her Guard, seized the Weapon with her Paws, and by main strength wrenched it out of the Fellow's Hands.

The Man being thus fairly disarm'd, thought himself no longer a Match for the Enemy, and therefore retreated as fast as his Legs could carry him.

The brute naturally grew bolder upon the flight of her Adversary, and pursued him with all her heavy speed. For some time it was doubtful whether fear made one run faster, or Fury the other. But after an even course of about 50 yards, the Man had the Mishap to Stumble over a Stump, and fell down his full Length. He now wou'd have sold his Life a Penny-worth; but the Bear apprehending there might be some Trick in the Fall, instantly halted, and lookt with much attention on her Prostrate Foe.

In the mean while, the Man had with great presence of Mind resolved to make the Bear believe he was dead, by lying Breathless on the Ground, in Hopes that the Beast would be too generous to kill him over again. To carry on the Farce, he acted the Corpse for some time without dareing to raise his head, to see how near the Monster was to him. But in about two Minutes, to his unspeakable Comfort, he was rais'd from the Dead by the Barking of a Dog, belonging to one of his companions, who came Seasonably to his Rescue, and drove the Bear from pursuing the Man to take care of her Cub, which she fear'd might now fall into a second Distress.

5. We Judg'd the Waters were assuag'd this morning to make the River fordable. Therefore about Ten we try'd the Experiment, and every Body got over Safe, except one man, whose Horse Slipt from a Rock as he forded over, and threw him into the River. But being able to swim, he was not Carry'd down the Stream very far before he recover'd the North Shore.

At the Distance of about 6 miles we passt CASCADE CREEK, and 3 Miles farther we came upon the Banks of the Dan, which we crost with much Difficulty, by reason the Water was risen much higher than when we forded it before.

The Bear advanced very near to her Enemy, rear'd up on her Posteriours, & put herself in Guard. The Man presented his Piece at her, but unfortunately it only snapp't, the Powder being moist. Missing his Fire in this Manner he offer'd to punch her with the Muzzle of his Gun, which Mother Bruin being aware of, seized the Weapon with her Paws, & by main strength wrench't it out of his Hand. Being thus fairly disarm'd, & not knowing in the fright, but the Bear might turn his own Cannon upon him, he thought it prudent to retire as fast as his Legs cou'd carry him. The Brute being grown more bold by the Flight of her Adversary, immediately pursued, and for some time it was doubtfull, whether Fear made one Run faster, or Fury the other. But after a fair Course of 40 Yards, the poor man had the Mishap to stumble over a Stump, and fell down at his full length. He now wou'd have sold his Life a Penny-worth: But the Bear apprehending there might be some Trick in this Fall, instantly halted, and look't very earnestly to observe what the Man cou'd mean. In the Meantime he had with much Presence of Mind, resolved to make the Bear believe he was dead, by lying breathless on the Ground, Upon the hopes that the Bear wou'd be too generous to kill him over again. He acted a Corps in this Manner for some time, till he was rais'd from the Dead by the Barking of a Dog, belonging to one of his Companions. Cur came up seasonably to his Rescue and drove the Bear from her Pursuit of the Man, to go and take care of her innocent Cubb, which she now apprehended might fall into a Second Distress.

5. We found this Morning that the River had fallen no more than 4 Inches the whole Night, but a North Wester had swept away all the Clouds. About 10 we resolv'd to pass the River, which we did very safely, thank God, only Tom Short's Horse fell with him, & sopp't him all over. In the Distance of 6 Miles we crost Cascade Creek, & from thence proceeded in near 3 Miles to the Dan, which we forded with some difficulty, because the Water was deeper than when we came over it before. Unfortu-

Here the same unlucky Person happen'd to be duckt a Second time, and was a Second time Sav'd by Swimming. My own Horse too plunged in such a Manner that his Head was more than once under Water, but with much more ado recover'd his Feet, tho' he made so low an obeisance, that the water ran fairly over my Saddle.

We continued our march as far as LOWLAND CREEK, where we took up our Lodging, for the benefit of the Canes and Winter Grass that grew upon the rich Grounds thereabouts. On our way thither we had the Misfortune to drop another Horse, though he carry'd nothing the whole day but his Saddle. We showed the same favour to most of our Horses, for fear, if we did not do it, we should in a little time be turned into Beasts of Burthen ourselves.

Custom had now made travelling on foot so familiar, that we were able to walk ten Miles with Pleasure. This we cou'd do in our Boots, notwithstanding our way lay over rough Woods and uneven Grounds.

Our learning to walk in heavy Boots was the same advantage to us that learning to Dance High Dances in Wooden Shoes is to the French, it made us most exceedingly Nimble without them.

The Indians, who have no way of travelling but on the Hoof, make nothing of going 25 miles a day, and carrying their little Necessaries at their backs, and Sometimes a Stout Pack of Skins into the Bargain. And very often they laugh at the English, who can't Stir to Next Neighbour without a Horse, and say that 2 Legs are too much for such lazy people, who cannot visit their next neighbour without six.

For their Parts, they were utter Strangers to all our Beasts of Burthen or Carriage, before the Slothful Europeans came amongst them. They had on no part of the American Continent, or in any of the Islands, either Horses or Asses, Camels, Dromedaries or Elephants, to ease the Legs of the Original Inhabitants, or to lighten their Labour.

Indeed, in South America, and particularly in Chili, they have a useful animal call'd "paco." This creature resembles a Sheep pretty much; only in the Length of the Neck, and figure of the Head, it is more like a Camel. It is very near as high as the ass, and the Indians there make use of it for carrying moderate Burthens.

The Fleece that grows upon it is very Valuable for the fineness, length and Glossiness of the Wool. It has one remarkable Singularity, that the Hoofs of its fore-feet have three Clefts, and those behind no more than one. The Flesh of this Animal is something drier than our Mutton, but altogether as well tasted.

When it is Angry, it has no way of resenting its wrongs, but by spitting in the Face of those that provoke it: and if the Spawl happen to light on the bare Skin of any Person, it first creates an Itching, and afterwards a Scab, if no Remedy be applied. The way to manage these pacos, and make them tractable, is, to bore a hole in their ears, through which they put a Rope, and then guide them just as they please.

nate Mr Short was duck't in a Second Time by the Fall of his horse but receiv'd no hurt. My Horse made a false Step, so that his Head was all underwater, but recover'd himself with much adoe.

Having day enough left we proceeded as far as Low-land Creek, where we took up our Quarters, and had great Plenty both of Canes & Winter Grass for the Horses, but Whitlock's Horse tired 2 Miles off, and so did one of Astrolabe's. The Truth of it is, we made a long Journey, not less than 14 Miles in the round about Distance we came, tho' it did not exceed 10 upon the Line. I favour'd my Steed by walking great part of the way on foot; it being Level & well clear'd made the Fatigue more tolerable. The Indian kill'd a Young Buck, the Bones of which we pick't very clean, but want of Bear made Dr Humdrum less gay, than he used to be where that delicious Food was Plenty.

In Chili, they wear a beautiful kind of Stuff, with thread made of this Creature's Wool, which has a Gloss Superior to any Camlet, and is sold very dear in that country.

6. The Difficulty of finding the Horses among the tall Canes made it late before we decampt. We traversed very hilly Grounds, but to make amends it was pretty clear of Underwood.

We avoided crossing the Dan twice by taking a Compass round the bent of it. There was no passing by the angle of the River without halting a moment to entertain our Eyes again with that Charming Prospect. When that pleasure was over we proceeded to Sable Creek, and encampted a little to the East of it.

The River thereabouts had a charming effect, its Banks being adorn'd with green canes, sixteen feet high, which make a Spring all the year, as well as plenty of Forage all the Winter.

One of the Men wounded an Old Buck, that was gray with years, and seem'd by the Reverend Marks he bore upon him, to confirm the current Opinion of that animal's Longevity. The Smart of his Wounds made him not only turn upon the Dogs, but likewise pursue them to some Distance with great Fury.

However he got away at last, though by the blood that issued from his Wound he could not run far before he fell, and without doubt made a comfortable repast for the wolves. However the Indian had better Fortune, and supply'd us with a fat Doe, and a young Bear two years old. At that Age they are in their Prime, and, if they be fat withal, they are a Morsel for a Cardinal.

All the Land we Travell'd over this day, and the day before, that is to say from the river Irvin to Sable Creek, is exceedingly rich, both on the Virginia Side of the Line, and that of Carolina.[84] Besides whole Forests of Canes, that adorn the Banks of the River and Creeks thereabouts, the fertility of the Soil throws out such a Quantity of Winter Grass, that Horses and Cattle might keep themselves in Heart all the cold Season without the help of any Fodder. Nor have the low Grounds only this advantage, but likewise the Higher Land, and particularly that which we call the Highland Pond, which is two miles broad, and of a length unknown.

I question not but there are 30,000 Acres of least, lying Altogether, as fertile as the Lands were said to be about Babylon, which yielded, if

---

[84] Byrd is here describing the lands which he purchased from the North Carolina commissioners, who had secured them in payment for their services. Byrd called the region the Land of Eden. He inserted in the manuscript of *The Journey to the Land of Eden* a map of his purchases, which was published in Wynne's version, and is reproduced on page 271.

6. We sat not out til near 12, & past over very uneven Ground, tho' our Comfort was that it was open and clear of Bushes. We avoided crossing the Dan twice, by going round the Bent of it. About 3 we past by Mount Pleasant, and proceeded along the River Side to Sable Creek, which we crost, and encampt a little beyond it near the Banks of the Dan. The Horses fared Sumptuously here upon Canes & Grass. Hamilton wounded a Buck, which made him turn upon the Dogs, & even pursue them 40 Yards with great Fury. But he got away from us, chusing rather to give the Wolves a Supper, than to more cruel Man. However our other Gunners had better Fortune, in killing a Doe & 2 year-old Cubb. Thus Providence supply'd us every day with Food sufficient for us, making the Barren Wilderness a Theater of Plenty. The Wind blew very cold, and produced a hard Frost. Our Journey this day did not exceed 5 Miles, great part of which in Complement to my Horse, I perform'd on Foot, notwithstanding the way was Mountainous, and the Leaves that cover'd the Hills as slippery as Ice.

[Continued on page 273]

Herodotus tells us right, an Increase of no less that 2 or 300 for one. But this hath the Advantage of being a higher and consequently a much healthier, Situation than that. So that a Colony of 1000 families might, with the help of Moderate Industry, pass their time very happily there.

Besides grazing and Tillage, which would abundantly compensate their Labour, they might plant Vineyards upon the Hills, in which Situation the richest Wines are always produc'd.

They might also propagate white Mulberry Trees, which thrive exceedingly in this climate, in order to the feeding of silk-worms, and making of Raw Silk.

They might too produce Hemp, Flax and Cotton, in what quantity they pleas'd, not only for their own use, but likewise for Sale. Then they might raise very plentiful Orchards, of both Peaches and Apples, which contribute as much as any Fruit to the Luxury of Life. There is no Soil or Climate will yield better Rice than this, which is a Grain of prodigious Increase, and of very wholesome Nourishment. In short every thing will grow plentifully here to supply either the Wants of Wantonness of Man.

Nor can I so much as wish that the more tender Vegetables might grow here, such as Orange, Lemon, and Olive Trees, because then we shou'd lose the much greater benefit of the brisk North-West Winds, which purge the Air, and sweep away all the Malignant Fevers, which hover over countries that are always warm.

The Soil wou'd also want the advantages of Frost, and Snow, which by their Nitrous Particles contribute not a little to its Fertility. Besides the Inhabitants wou'd be depriv'd of the Variety and Sweet Vicissitude of the Season, which is much more delightful than one dull and Constant Succession of Warm Weather, diversify'd only by Rain and Sun Shine.

There is also another convenience, that happens to this country by cold weather—it destroys a great Number of Snakes, and other Venomous Reptiles, and troublesome Insects, or at least lays them to Sleep for Several Months, which otherwise would annoy us the whole year round, & multiply beyond all Enduring.

Though Oranges and Lemons are desirable Fruits, and Useful enough in many Cases, yet, when the Want of them is Supply'd by others more useful, we have no cause to complain.

There is no climate that produces every thing, since the Deluge Wrencht the Poles of the World out of their Place, nor is it fit it shou'd be so, because it is the Mutual Supply one country receives from another, which creates a mutual Traffic and Intercourse amongst men. And in Truth, were it not for the correspondence, in order to make up for each other's Wants, the Wars betwixt Bordering Nations, like those of the Indians and other barbarous People, wou'd be perpetual and irreconcileable.

As to Olive Trees, I know by Experience they will never stand the Sharpness of our Winters, but their Place may be Supply'd by the Plant

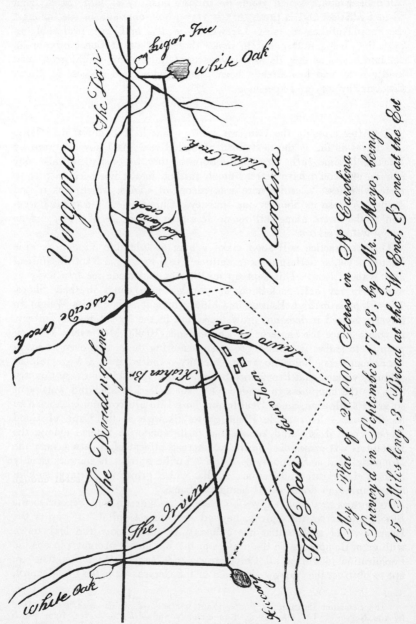

My Plat of 20,000 Acres in N° Carolina. Surveyd in September 1733, by Mr. Mayo, being 15 Miles long, 3 Broad at the W. End, & one at the Est

BYRD'S LANDS ON THE CAROLINA FRONTIER

call'd Sessamun,[85] which yields an infinite quantity of large Seed, from whence a Sweet Oyl is prest, that is very wholesome and in use amongst the People of Lesser Asia. Likewise it is us'd in Egypt, preferably to oyl olive, being not so apt to make those that eat it Constantly break out into Scabs, as they do in many parts of Italy. This would grow very kindly here, and has already been planted with good Success in North Carolina, by way of Experiment.

7. After crossing the Dan, we made a march of 8 miles, over Hills and Dales as far as the next Ford of that River. And now we were by Practice become such very able Footmen, that we easily outwalkt our Horses, and cou'd have marcht much farther, had it not been in pity to their Weakness. Besides here was plenty of Canes, which was reason enough to make us Shorten our Journey. Our Gunners did great Execution as they went along, killing no less than two Brace of Deer, and as many Wild Turkeys.

Though Practice will soon make a man of tolerable Vigour an able Footman, yet, as a Help to bear Fatigue I us'd to chew a Root of Ginseng as I Walk't along. This kept up my Spirits, and made me trip away as nimbly in my half Jack-Boots as younger men cou'd in their Shoes. This Plant is in high Esteem in China, where it sells for its Weight in Silver. Indeed it does not grow there, but in the Mountains of Tartary, to which Place the emperor of China Sends 10,000 Men every Year on purpose to gather it. But it grows so scattering there, that even so many hands can bring home no great Quantity. Indeed it is a Vegetable of so many vertues, that Providence has planted it very thin in every Country that has the happiness to produce it. Nor indeed is Mankind worthy of so great a Blessing, since Health and long Life are commonly Abus'd to ill Purposes. This noble Plant grows likewise at the Cape of Good Hope, where it is Call'd kanna, and is in wonderful Esteem among the Hottentots. It grows also on the northern continent of America, near the Mountains, but as Sparingly as Truth & Public Spirit. It answers exactly both to the Figure and vertues of that which grows in Tartary, so that there can be no doubt of its being the Same.

Its vertues are, that it gives an uncommon Warmth and Vigour to the Blood, and frisks the Spirits, beyond any other Cordial. It chears the Heart even of a Man that has a bad Wife, and makes him look down with great Composure on the crosses of the World. It promotes insensible Perspiration, dissolves all Phlegmatick and Viscous Humours, that are apt to obstruct the Narrow channels of the Nerves. It helps the Memory,

---

[85] The Sesamum Indicum, or Benne Plant, the seed of which were used as food by the Negroes. The oil was used medicinally and also the leaves, from which a gummy muscilage was derived. See Porcher, F. A. *Resources of Southern Fields and Forests*, p. 450.

7.   After dispatching away our Pioneers at 8 a Clock, we follow'd them at 10.   The Ground was very hilly, and full of Underwood, but our Pioneers had help't that Inconvenience.   Our Journey was 8 Miles by the Lines, but near 10 by our Path, which was not quite so strait.   The Hunters were more fortunate than Ordinary, killing no less than 4 Deer, and as many Turkeys.   This made them impatient to encamp early, that they might enjoy the Fruits of their good Luck.   We arriv'd at 2 a Clock on the Banks of the Dan, where we mark't out our Quarters, where the Horses had as great Plenty as ourselves.   However they were now grown so weak, that they stagger'd when we dismounted, and those which had been used to the Stable & dry Food throve least upon Grass & Canes, & were much sooner jaded than the rest.

and would quicken even Helvetian dullness. 'Tis friendly to the Lungs, much more than Scolding itself. It comforts the Stomach, and Strengthens the Bowels, preventing all Colicks and Fluxes. In one Word, it will make a Man live a great while, and very well while he does live. And what is more, it will even make Old Age amiable, by rendering it lively, chearful, and good-humour'd. However 'tis of little use in the Feats of Love, as a great prince once found, who hearing of its invigorating Quality, sent as far as China for some of it, though his ladys could not boast of any Advantage thereby.[86]

We gave the Indian the Skins of all the Deer that he Shot himself, and the Men the Skins of what they Kill'd. And every Evening after the Fires were made, they stretcht them very tight upon Sticks, and dry'd them. This, by a Nocturnal Fire, appear'd at first a very odd Spectacle, every thing being dark and gloomy round about. After they are Dry'd in this manner they may be folded up without Damage, till they come to be dress'd according to Art.

The Indians dress them with Deer's Brains, and so do the English here by their example. For Expedition's Sake they often Stretch their Skins over Smoak in order to dry them, which makes them smell so disagreeably that a Rat must have a good Stomach to gnaw them in that condition; nay, 'tis said, while that Perfume continues in a Pair of Leather Breeches, the Person who wears them will be in no Danger of that Vallainous little insect the French call Morpion. And now I am upon the subject of Insects, it may not be improper to mention some few Remedies against those that are most Vexatious in this Climate. There are two Sorts without Doors, that are great Nuisances, the Tikes, and the Horse Flies. The Tikes are either Deer-tikes, or those that annoy the Cattle. The first kind are long, and take a very Strong Gripe, being most in remote Woods, above the Inhabitants.

The other are round, and more generally insinuate themselves into the Flesh, being in all places where Cattle are frequent. Both these Sorts are apt to be troublesome during the Warm Season, but have such an aversion to Penny Royal, that they will attack no Part that is rubb'd with the Juice of that fragrant Vegetable. And a Strong Decoction of this is likewise the most effectual Remedy against Seed-tikes, which bury themselves in your Legs, when they are so small you can hardly discern them without a MICROSCOPE.

The Horse Flies are not only a great Grievance to Horses, but likewise to those that ride them. These little Vixons confine themselves chiefly to the Woods, and are most in moist Places. Tho' this Insect be no bigger than an Ordinary Fly, it bites very Smartly, darting its little Proboscis into the Skin the instant it lights upon it. These are offensive only in the hot

---

[86] Ginseng has in reality no medicinal properties and Byrd's information represents popular opinion only.

[Continued on page 277]

months, and in the Day time, when they are a great Nuisance to Travellers; insomuch that it is no Wonder they were formerly employed for one of the Plagues of Egypt. But Dittany,[87] which is to be had in the Woods all the while those Insects remain in Vigor, is a Sure Defense against them. For this purpose, if you stick a Bunch of it on the Head-Stall of your Bridle, they will be sure to keep a respectful Distance.

Thus, in what part of the Woods soever any thing mischievous or troublesome is found, kind Providence is sure to provide a Remedy. And 'tis probably one great Reason why God was pleas'd to create these, and many other Vexatious Animals, that Men sho'd exercise their Wits and Industry, to guard themselves against them.

Bears' Oyl is used by the Indians as a General Defence, against every Species of Vermin. Among the rest, they say it keeps both Bugs and Musquetas from assaulting their Persons, which wou'd otherwise devour Such uncleanly People. Yet Bears' Grease has no strong Smell, as that Plant had which the Egyptians formerly us'd against musquetas, resembling our palma Christi, the Juice of which smelled so disagreeably, that the Remedy was worse than the Disease.

Against musquetas, in Egypt, the Richer Sort us'd to build lofty Towers, with Bed-chambers in the Tops of them, that they might rest undisturbed. 'Tis certain that these Insects are no High Fliers, because their Wings are weak and their Bodies so light, that if they mount never so little, the wind blows them quite away from their Course, and they become an easy prey to the Martins, East India Bats, and other Birds that fly about in continual Quest of them.

8. As we had twice more to cross the Dan over two fords, that lay no more than 7 miles from each other, we judg'd the Distance wou'd not be much greater to go round the Bent of it. Accordingly we sent the Indian and two white Men that way, who came up with us in the Evening, after fetching a compass of about 12 Miles.

They told us that, about a mile from our last Camp, they passed a creek fortify'd with Steep Cliffs, which therefore gain'd the name of Cliff Creek. Near 3 miles beyond that they forded a Second Creek, on the Margin of which grew abundance of Tall canes and this was call'd Hix's creek, from one of the Discoverers. Between these two creeks lies a level of exceeding rich Land, full of large Trees, and cover'd with black Mould, as fruitful, if we believe them, as that which is yearly overflow'd by the Nile.

We who marched the nearest way upon the Line found the Ground rising and falling between the two Fords of the Dan, which almost broke

---

[87] Common name for labiate plants, as the *Dectanus Albus* of England and the *Cunila Mariana* of America.

8.   The Pioneers took their Departure about 9, and we sat out
upon their Track at 10, & found the Ground rising & falling all the
way between the 2 Fords of the River.   The first of these we past
at first setting out, But Robin Hix & the Indian undertook to go
round the Bent of the River, without crossing it all.   This they
perform'd, making the Distance no more than 12 Miles.   About a
Mile from our Camp, they met with a Creek whose Banks were
fortify'd with high Cliffs, which gain'd it the Name of Cliff-
Creek.   Near 3 Miles beyond that they forded over another Creek,
on whose margin grew plenty of Canes.   And this was call'd Hixe's
Creek from the Name of the Discoverer.   Between these 2 Creeks
lies a Levil of exceeding good Land, full of large Trees, and a
black Mold.   We that march't upon the Line past over Cane-
Creek something more than 4 Miles from the Camp, & 3 Miles
beyond that we forded the Dan for the last time, passing thro'

our own Wind, and the Hearts of our Jaded Palfreys. When we had passed
the last Ford, it was a Sensible Joy to find ourselves Safe over all the
Waters that might cut off our Retreat. And we had the greater Reason
to be Thankfull, because so late in the Year it was very unusual to find
the rivers so fordable.

We catcht a large Tarapin in the River, which is one kind of Turtle.
The flesh of it is wholesome, and good for Consumptive People. It lays a
great Number of Eggs, not larger but rounder than those of Pigeons.
These are Soft, but withal so tough that 'tis difficult to break them, yet
are very Sweet and invigorating, so that some Wives recommend them
earnestly to their Husbands.

One of the Men, by an Overstrain, had unhappily got a Running of the
Reins, for which I gave him every Morning a little Sweet Gumm dissolv'd
in Water, with good success. This gumm distils from a large Tree, call'd
the Sweet-Gum Tree, very Common in Virginia, and is as healing in its
Virtue as Balm of Gilead, or the Balsams of Tolu and of Peru. It is
likewise a most Agreeable parfume, very little inferior to Ambergris.

And now I have mention'd Ambergris, I hope it will not be thought an
unprofitable digression, to give a faithful Account how it is produced, in
Order to reconcile the various Opinions concerning it. It is now certainly
found to be the Dung of the Sper Maceti Whale, which is at first very
black and unsavoury. But after having been washt for some Months in the
Sea, and blanch'd in the Sun, it comes at length to be of a Gray colour,
and from a most offensive Smell, contracts the finest fragrancy in the
World.

Besides the Fragrancy of this Animal Substance, 'tis a very rich and innocent Cordial, which raises the spirits without Stupifying them afterwards,
like Opium, or intoxicating them like Wine. The Animal Spirits are
amazingly refreshed by this Cordial, without the Danger of any ill consequence, and if Husbands were now and then to dissolve a little of it in their
Broth, their Consorts might be the better for it, as well as themselves.
In the Bahama Islands (where a great Quantity is found, by reason the
Sperma Ceti Whales resort thither continually,) it is us'd as an Antidote
against the Venomous Fish which abound thereabouts, wherewith the
People are apt to Poison themselves.

We are not only oblig'd to that Whale for this rich parfume, but also
for the Sper Maceti itself, which is the Fat of that Fish's Head boil'd
and purg'd from all its impuritys. What remains is of a balsamick and
detersive Quality, very friendly to the Lungs, and usefull in many other
Cases.

The Indian had kill'd a fat Doe in the compass he took round the Elbow
of the River, but was content to Prime it only, by reason it was too far
off to lug the whole Carcass upon his Back. This, and a Brace of Wild
Turkeys which our Men had Shot, made up all our Bill of Fare this

a Forrest of Canes before we got at it. It was no small Joy to us to find ourselves safe over all the Waters that might retard our Journey home. Our Distance upon the Line was 7 Miles, & where we encampt afforded good Forrage for the Horses, which we had favour'd by walking the greater part of the way. The Indian brought us the primeings of a Fat Doe, which he had kill'd too far off for him to carry the whole. This & 2 Turkeys that our Men shot, made up our Bill of Fare this Evening.

Evening, but could only afford a Philosophical Meal to so many craving Stomachs.

The Horses were now so lean that any thing would gall those that carry'd the least Burthen; no Wonder then if Several of them had sore Backs, especially now the Pads of the Saddles and Packs were press'd flat with long and constant Use. This would have been another Misfortune, had we not been provided with an easy Remedy for it.

One of the Commissioners, believing that Such Accidents might happen in a far Journey, had furnisht himself with Plasters of Strong Glue spread pretty thick. We laid on these, after making them running hot, which, Sticking fast, never fell off till the Sore was perfectly heal'd. In the mean time it defended the part so well, that the Saddle might bear upon it without Danger of further Injury.

9. We reckon'd ourselves now pretty well out of the Latitude of Bears, to the great Grief of most of the company. There was Still Mast enough left in the Woods to keep the Bears from drawing so near to the Inhabitants. They like not the neighbourhood of Merciless Man, till Famine compels them to it. They are all Black in this part of the World, and so is their Dung, but it will make Linnen white, being tolerably good Soap, without any Preparation but only drying.

These Bears are of a Moderate Size, whereas within the Polar Circles they are white, and much larger. Those of the Southern Parts of Muscovy are of a Russet Colour, but among the SAMOEIDS, as well as in GREENLAND and NOVA ZEMBLA, they are as white as the snow they converse with, and by some Accounts are as large as a Moderate Ox.

The Excessive Cold of that Climate sets their Appetites so Sharp, that they will Attack a Man without Ceremony, and even climb up a Ship's Side to come at him. They range about and are very Mischievous all the time the Sun is above the Horizon, which is something more than Five Months; but after the Sun is Set for the rest of the Year, they retire into Holes, or bury themselves under the Snow, and Sleep away the Dark Season without any Sustenance at all. 'Tis pitty our Beggars and Pickpockets Cou'd not do the Same.

Our Journey this day was above 12 Miles, and more than half the way terribly hamper'd with Bushes. We tir'd another Horse, which we were oblig'd to leave two miles short of where we Encampt, and indeed Several others were upon the Careen almost every Step. Now we wanted one of those celebrated Musicians of Antiquity, who, they tell us, among many other Wonders of their Art, cou'd play an air which, by its Animateing Briskness wou'd make a Jaded Horse caper and curvet much better than any Whip, Spur, or even than Swearing. Tho' I fear our poor Beasts were so harast that it wou'd have been beyond the Skill of Orpheus himself so much as to make them prick up their ears.

9.   Dᵣ Humdrum got up so early, that it made him quite peevish, especially now we were out of the Latitude of Fat Bear, with which he us'd to keep up his good Humour.   It was necessary to hurry out the Pioneers by 8 a Clock because great part of the Journey was overgrown with Bushes.   However about 5 Miles of this Day's work were very open and tollerably Level.   The Distance in all was 12 Miles by the Line, tho' we made 15 of it by picking our way.   Of this I footed it at least 8 Miles, notwithstanding my Servant had scorch't my Boots by holding them too near the Fire.   The Length of our march harrass'd the Horses much, so that Page was oblig'd to leave his, 2 Miles short of our Journey's End, and several others had much adoe to drag one Leg after another.   In less than half a Mile from the Dan we crost Cocquade Creek, so call'd from our beginning there to wear the Turkey Beard in our Hats by way of Cocquade.   This we made one of the Badges of a new Order, call'd the Order of Ma-ooty, signifying in the Sapponi-Language, a Turkey's Beard.   The other Badge is a Wild Turkey in Gold, with the Wings expanded, & a Collar round its Neck, with this Motto engraven upon it, Vice Cotumicum.   As most Orders have been religious in their Original, so this was devis'd in grateful remembrance of our having been supported in the Barren-Wilderness so many weeks, with wild Turkeys instead of Quails.   From thence we continu'd our march to Buffalo-Creek, on which we encampt.   Here our Horses made better Chear than we, for the Indian kill'd nothing but one Turkey.

For Proof of the Marvellous Power of Music among the Ancients, some
Historians say, that one of those Skilful Masters took upon him to make
the great Alexander start up from his Seat, and handle his Javelin, whether
he would or not, by the force of a sprightly Tune, which he knew how
to play to Him. The King ordered the man to bring his Instrument, and
then fixing himself firmly in his chair, and determining not to Stir, he
bade him to Strike up as soon as he pleas'd. The Musician obey'd, and
presently rous'd the Hero's Spirits with such Warlike Notes, that he was
constrain'd, in Spite of all his Resolutions, to spring up and fly to his
Javelin with great martial Fury.

We can the easier credit these Prophane Stories by what we find
recorded in the Oracles of Truth, where we are told the Wonders David
performed by Sweetly touching his Harp. He made nothing of driving
the Evil Spirit out of Saul, tho' a certain rabbi assures us he could not do
so much by his Wife, MICHAL, when she happen'd to be in her Ayrs.

The greatest Instance we have of the Power of Modern Music is that
which cures those who in Italy are bitten by the little Spider called the
Tarantula. The whole method of which is perform'd in the following
manner.

In Apulia it is a common Misfortune for People to be bitten by the
Tarantula, and most about Taranto and Gallipoli. This is a gray spider,
not very large, with a narrow Streak of white along the Back. It is no
wonder there are many of these Villanous Insects, because, by a Ridiculous
Superstition 'tis accounted great Inhumanity to kill them. They believe,
it seems, that if the Spider come to a Violent Death, all those who had
been bitten by it will certainly have a Return of their Frenzy every Year
as long as they live. But if it dye a Natural Death, the Patient will have
a chance to recover in two or three Years.

The Bite of the tarantula gives no more pain than the Bite of a musqueta,
and makes little or no inflamation on the Part, especially when the Disaster happens in April or May; but, its Venom encreasing with the Heat
of the Season, has more fatal Consequences in July and August. The
Persons who are so unhappy as to be bitten in those Warm Months, fall
down on the Place in a few Minutes, and lye senseless for a considerable
time, and when they come to themselves feel horrible Pains, are very
Sick at their Stomachs, and in a Short time break out into foul Sores;
but those who are bitten in the Milder Months have much gentler Symptoms. They are longer before the Distemper Shows itself, and then they
have a small Disorder in their Senses, are a little sick, and perhaps have
some Moderate Breaking-out.

However, in both cases, the Patient keeps upon the Bed, not caring
to stir, till he is rous'd by a Tune, proper for his particular case. Therefore, as soon as the Symptoms discover themselves, a Tarantula Doctor is
sent for, who, after viewing carefully the condition of the Person, first
tries one Tune and then another, until he is so fortunate as to hit the

However with what remain'd of our former good Fortune, this was sufficient to keep Famine out of the Camp.

Phrenetic turn of the Patient. No sooner does this happen but he begins
to Wag a finger, then a Hand, and afterwards a Foot, till at last he springs
up and dances Round the Room, with a Surprising Agility, rolling his
Eyes and looking wild the whole time. This dancing-Fit lasts commonly
about 25 minutes, by which time he will be all in a Lather. Then he sits
down, falls a laughing, and returns to his Senses. So Plentiful a
Perspiration discharges to much of the Venon as will keep off the Return
of the Distemper for a whole Year. Then it will Visit Him again, and
must be remov'd in the Same Merry Manner. But three dancing Bouts
will do the Business, unless, peradventure, the Spider, according to the
Vulgar Notion, has been put to a Violent Death.[88]

The Tunes Play'd to expel this Whimsical Disorder, are of the Jigg-kind,
and exceeded not 15 in number. The Apulians are frequently dancing
off the Effects of this Poison, and no Remedy is more commonly apply'd
to any other Distemper elsewhere, than those Sprightly Tunes are to the
Bite of the Tarantula in that part of Italy.

It is remarkable that these Spiders have a greater Spight to the Natives
of the Place than they have to Strangers, and Women are oftener bitten
than Men. Tho' there may be a Reason for the last, because Women are
more confin'd to the House, where these Spyders keep, and their coats make
them liable to Attacks unseen, whereas the Men can more easily discover,
and brush them off their Legs. Nevertheless, both Sexes are cur'd the
Same way, and thereby Show the Wonderful Effects of Music.

Considering how far we had walkt, and consequently how hungry we
were, we found but Short commons when we came to our Quarters. One
Brace of Turkeys was all the Game we cou'd meet with, which almost
needed a Miracle to enable them to Suffice so many Voracious Appetites.
However, they just made a Shift to keep Famine, and consequently Mutiny,
out of the Camp. At Night we lodg'd upon the Banks of Buffalo Creek,
where none of us cou'd complain of loss of Rest, for having eaten too
heavy and Luxurious a Supper.

10. In a Dearth of Provisions our Chaplain pronounc'd it lawful to
make bold with the Sabbath, and send a Party out a-Hunting. They fired
the Dry Leaves in a Ring of five Miles' circumference, which, burning
inwards, drove all the Game to the Centre, where they were easily killed.

It is really a pitiful Sight to see the extreme Distress the poor deer are
in, when they find themselves Surrounded with this Circle of Fire; they
weep and Groan like a Human Creature, yet can't move and compassion of
those hard-hearted People, who are about to murder them. This un-

---

[88] Byrd is here describing Tarantism, a mania supposedly caused by the bite of
the tarantula, which originated in Italy during the Middle Ages and spread to other
countries of Southern Europe. A survival in modern times is the tarantilla, either
a popular dance or the music for the dance.

10.   This being Sunday we observ'd the 4th Commandment only our Hunters went out to provide a Dinner for the rest which was matter of necessity.   They fired the woods in a Ring, which burning Inwards drove the Deer to the Center, where they were easily kill'd.   This Sport is call'd Fir-hunting, & is much practiced by the Indians, & some English as barbarous as Indians.   Three Deer were Slaughter'd after this manner, of which they brought one to the Camp, and we content only to prime the other Two.   Besides these Tho Short brought in a Doe which made us live in Luxury.   William Pool complain'd that tho' his Stomach was good,

merciful Sport is called Fire Hunting, and is much practic'd by the
Indians and Frontier Inhabitants, who sometimes, in the Eagerness of their
Diversion, are Punish't for their cruelty, and are hurt by one another when
they Shoot across at the Deer which are in the Middle.

What the Indians do now by a Circle of Fire, the ancient Persians
performed formerly by a circle of Men: and the same is practis'd at
this day in Germany upon extraordinary Occasions, when any of the
Princes of the Empire have a Mind to make a General Hunt, as they call
it. At such times they order a vast Number of People to Surround a
whole Territory. Then Marching inwards in close Order, they at last
force all the Wild Beasts into a Narrow Compass, that the Prince and his
Company may have the Diversion of Slaughtering as many as they please
with their own hands.

Our Hunters massacred two Brace of Deer after this unfair way, of
which they brought us one Brace whole, and only the Primings of the rest.
So many were absent on this Occasion, that we who remained excus'd the
Chaplain from the Trouble of spending his Spirits by Preaching to so
thin a Congregation. One of the men, who had been an old Indian Trader,
brought me a Stem of Silk Grass, which was about as big as my little
Finger. But, being so late in the Year that the Leaf was fallen off, I
am not able to describe the Plant.

The Indians use it in all their little Manufactures, twisting a Thread of
it that is prodigiously Strong. Of this they make their Baskets and the
Aprons which their Women wear about their Middles, for Decency's
Sake. These are long enough to wrap quite round them and reach down
to their Knees, with a Fringe on the under part by way of Ornament.

They put on this modest covering with so much art, that the most impertinent curiosity can't in the Negligentest of their Motions or Postures
make the least discovery. As this species of Silk Grass is much Stronger
than Hemp, I make no doubt but Sail Cloth and Cordage might be made
of it with considerable Improvement.

11. We had all been so refresht by our day of rest, that we decamp'd
earlier than Ordinary, and passed the Several Fords of Hico River. The
Woods were thick great Part of this Day's Journey, so that we were forced
to scuffle hard to advance 7 miles, being equal in fatigue to double that
distance of Clear and Open Grounds.

We took up our Quarters upon Sugar-tree Creek, in the same camp we
had lain in when we came up, and happen'd to be entertained at Supper
with a Rarity we had never had the fortune to meet with before, during
the whole Expedition.

A little wide of this creek, one of the men had the Luck to meet with
a Young Buffalo of two Years Old. It was a Bull, which, notwithstanding
he was no older, was as big as an ordinary Ox. His Legs are very thick

and he eat a great deal, yet he hardly ever went to Stool without
the help of Physick. This made him very full and uneasy, giving him pains both in his Stomach and Bowels. First I gave
him a Dose of Anderson's Pills, which afforded him very little
ease. Then I prescribed a´ small Dose of Ipocoaccanna to be taken
in hot Broth well season'd with Salt, which took off the Emetick
Quality & turn'd it downwards. This not only employ'd him, and
gave him ease, but brought him to be very regular in his Evacua-
tions, by being now and then repeated. Page went out in quest
of his Horse and brought him to the Camp pretty well recruited.
The absence of most of the Men diminish't our Congregation so
much, that we who remain'd behind were contented with Prayers.
I read a great deal, and then wrote a letter with design to send
an Express with it so soon as we got amongst the Inhabitants.

11. By the favour of good Weather, and the impatience of being
at home, we decampt early. But there was none of the Company
so very hasty as Orion. He cou'd not have been more uneasy even
tho' he had a Mistress at Williamsburgh. He found much Fault
with my scrupulous observing the Sabbath. I reprov'd him for
his uneasiness, letting him understand, that I had both as much
Business, and as much Inclination to be at home as he had, but
for all that was determin'd to make no more hast than good Speed.

We crost Hico-ottomoni Creek twice in this March, and travers't
very thick and very uneven woods as far as Sugar-Tree Creek.

and very Short, and his Hoofs exceeding broad. His Back rose into
a kind of Bunch a little above the Shoulders, which I believe contributes
not a little to that creature's enormous Strength. His Body is vastly deep
from the shoulders to the Brisket, sometimes 6 feet in those that are full
grown. The portly figure of this Animal is disgrac'd by a Shabby little
Tail, not above 12 Inches long. This he cocks up on end whenever he's
in a Passion, and, instead of lowing or bellowing, grunts with no better
grace than a Hog.

The Hair growing on his Head and Neck is long and Shagged, and so
Soft that it will Spin into Thread not unlike Mohair, which might be
wove into a Sort of Camlet. Some People have Stockings knit of it,
that would have serv'd an Israelite during his forty Years' march thro'
the Wilderness.

Its horns are short and Strong, of which the Indians make large Spoons,
which they say will Split and fall to Pieces whenever Poison is put into
them. Its Colour is a dirty Brown, and its hide so thick that it is Scarce
penetrable. However, it makes very Spongy Sole Leather by the ordinary
method of Tanning, tho' this fault might by good Contrivance be mended.

As thick as this poor Beast's Hide was, a Bullet made Shift to enter it
and fetch him down. It was found all alone, tho' Buffaloes Seldom are.
They usually range about in Herds, like other cattle, and tho' they differ
something in figure, are certainly of the Same Species. There are two
Reasons for this Opinion: the Flesh of both has exactly the same taste,
and the mixed Breed betwixt both, they say, will generate. All the Difference I could perceive between the Flesh of Buffalo and Common Beef
was, that the Flesh of the first was much Yellower than that of the other,
and the Lean something tougher.

The Men were so delighted with this new dyet, that the Gridiron and
Frying-Pan had no more rest all night, than a poor Husband Subject to
Curtain Lectures. Buffaloes may be easily tamed when they are taken
Young. The best way to catch them is to carry a Milch Mare into the
Woods, and when you find a Cow and a Calf, to kill the Cow, and then
having catch'd the Calf to Suckle it upon the Mare. After once or twice
Sucking Her, it will follow her Home, and become as gentle as another
calf.

If we cou'd get into a breed of them, they might be made very usefull,
not only for the Dairy, by giving an Ocean of Milk, but also for drawing
vast and cumbersome Weights by their prodigious Strength. These, with
the other Advantages I mention'd before, wou'd make this sort of Cattle
more profitable to the owner, than any other we are acquainted with,
though they would need a world of Provender.

12. Before we marcht this Morning, every man took care to pack up
some Buffalo Steaks in his Wallet, beside what he crammed into his Belly.

This was no more than 7 Miles, but equal in fatigue to double that distance on good Ground. Near this Creek our Men kill'd a Young Buffalo of 2 Years Old, that was as big as a large Ox. He had short Legs, and a deep Body with Shagged Hair on his Head and Shoulders. His Horns were short, and very Strong. The Hair on the Shoulders is soft resembling wool, and may be spun into Thread. The Flesh is arrant Beef, all the difference is that the Fat of it enclines more to be Yellow. The Species seems to be the same, because a Calf produced betwixt Tame Cattle and these will propagate. Our People were so well pleas'd with Buffalo-Beef, that the Grid-Iron was upon the Fire all Night. In this Day's March I lost one of the Gold Buttons out of my Sleeve, which I bore more patiently because that, and the burning of my Boots were all the Damage I had suffered.

12.   We cou'd not decamp before 11, the People being so much engaged with their Beef; I found it always a Rule that the greater

When Provisions were Plenty, we always found it Difficult to get out early, being too much Embarrast with a long-winded Breakfast.

However, by the Strength of our Beef, we made a shift to walk about 12 Miles, crossing Blewing and Tewaw-hommini Creeks. And because this last Stream receiv'd its Appelation from the Disaster of a Tuscarora Indian, it will not be Straggling much out of the way to say something of that Particular Nation.[89]

These Indians were heretofore very numerous and powerful, making, within time of Memory, at least a Thousand Fighting Men. Their Habitation, before the War with Carolina, was on the North Branch of Neuse River, commonly call'd Connecta Creek, in a pleasant and fruitful Country. But now the few that are left of that Nation live on the North Side of MORATUCK, which is all that Part of Roanok below the great Falls, towards ALBEMARLE Sound.

Formerly there were Seven Towns of these Savages, lying not far from each other, but now their Number is greatly reduc'd.

The Trade they have had the Misfortune to drive with the English has furnisht them constantly with Rum, which they have used so immoderately, that, what with the Distempers, and what with the Quarrels it begat amongst them, it has proved a double Destruction.

But the greatest Consumption of these savages happen'd by the war about Twenty-Five years ago, on Account of some Injustice the Inhabitants of that Province had done them about their Lands.

It was on that Provocation they resented their wrongs a little too severely upon Mr. Lawson, who, under Colour of being Surveyor gen'l, had encroacht too much upon their Territories, at which they were so enrag'd, that they waylaid him, and cut his Throat from Ear to Ear, but at the same time releas'd the Baron de Graffenried, whom they had Seized for Company, because it appear'd plainly he had done them no Wrong.

This Blow was followed by some other Bloody Actions on the Part of the Indians, which brought on the War, wherein many of them were but (sic) off, and many were oblig'd to flee for Refuge to the Senecas, so that now there remain so few, that they are in danger of being (sic) quite exterminated by the Catawbas, their mortal Enemies.

These Indians have a very odd Tradition amongst them, that many years ago, their Nation was grown so dishonest, that no man cou'd keep any Goods, or so much as his loving Wife to himself. That, however, their God, being unwilling to root them out for their crimes, did them the honour to send a Messenger from Heaven to instruct them, and set Them a perfect Example of Integrity and kind Behavior towards one another.

But this holy Person, with all his Eloquence and Sanctity of Life, was

---

[89] These Indians belonged to the Iroquoian family, not to the Siouan. After the Tuscarora War of 1711 most of them removed North and joined the Five Nations. In the early part of the Nineteenth Century the remainder of the tribe also removed to New York.

our Plenty, the later we were in fixing out. We avoided two Miles of very uneven Ground, by leaving the Line on our Left, and keeping upon the Ridge. Something less than 3 Miles Distance from the Camp we past our Blewing Creek, and 5 Miles beyond this, over that of Tewakominy. Thence we traversed a very large Level of rich high Land near 2 Miles in breadth, and encampt on a Branch 3½ Miles beyond the last named Creek, so that our whole distance this day was more than 11 Miles. Here was very Scanty Fare for the Horses, who cou'd pick only here and there a sprig of wild Rosemary, which they are fond of, the Misfortune was, there was not enough of it. John Ellis kill'd a Bear in Revenge for the Fight one of that Species had lately put him into. Nor was this Revenge sweeter to him than a Griskin of it was to the Doctor, who of all worldly Food conceives this to be the best. Tho' in Truth 'tis too rich for a Single Man, and enclines the Eater of it strongly to the Flesh. Inasmuch that whoever makes a Supper of it, will certainly Dream of a Woman, or the Devil, or both.

able to make very little Reformation amongst them. Some few Old Men
did listen a little to his Wholesome Advice, but all the Young fellows were
quite incorrigible. They not only Neglected his Precepts, but derided
and Evil Entreated his Person. At last, taking upon Him to reprove some
Young Rakes of the Conechta Clan very sharply for their impiety, they
were so provok'd at the Freedom of his Rebukes, that they tied him to a
Tree, and shot him with Arrows through the Heart. But their God took
instant Vengeance on all who had a hand in that Monstrous Act, by
Lightning from Heaven, & has ever since visited their Nation with a continued Train of Calamities, nor will he ever leave off punishing, and
wasting their People, till he shall have blotted every living Soul of them
out of the World.

Our Hunters shot nothing this whole day but a straggling Bear, which
happen'd to fall by the Hand of the very Person who had been lately
disarm'd and put to flight, for which he declar'd War against the whole
Species.

13.   We pursued our Journey with all Diligence, and forded Ohimpamony Creek about Noon, and from thence proceeded to Yatapsco, which
we cou'd not cross without difficulty. The Beavers had dammed up the
Water much higher than we found it at our going up, so that we were
oblig'd to lay a Bridge over a part that was shallower than the rest, to
facilitate our passage.

Beavers have more of Instinct, that Half-Brother of Reason, than any
other Animal, especially in matters of Self-Preservation. In their Houses
they always contrive a Sally-Port, both towards the Land and towards the
Water, that so they may escape by One, if their Retreat shou'd happen
to be cut off at the other.

They perform all their Works in the Dead of Night, to avoid Discovery,
and are kept diligently to it by the Master Beaver, which by his age or
strength has gain'd to himself an Authority over the rest. If any of the
Gang happen to be lazy, or will not exert himself to the utmost in felling
of Trees, or dragging them (to) the place where they are made use of,
this Superintendent will not fail to chastise him with the Flat of the
Tail, wherewith he is able to give unmerciful strokes.

They lie Snug in their Houses all day, unless some unneighbourly Miller
chance to disturb their repose, by demolishing their Dams for supplying
his Mill with Water.

It is rare to see one of them, and the Indians for that Reason have hardly
any way to take them, but by laying Snares near the place where they dam
up the Water. But the English Hunters have found out a more effectual
Method, by using the following receipt. Take the large Pride of the
Beaver, Squeeze all the Juice out of it, then take the small Pride, and

13. This Morning I wrote a Letter to the Governor intending to dispatch it away by an Express from the outermost Inhabitants. We mounted about 10, and after proceeding 3 Miles crost a large Branch, and 2 Miles farther reach't Uhimpamory Creek. Beyond that $3\frac{1}{4}$ Miles, we came to Yapatsco, or Bever Creek. Here those Industrious Animals had damm'd up the Water in such a Manner, that we cou'd with difficulty Ford over it. However we all got happily over, and continued our March 3 Miles farther to Massamony Creek, so that the Day's Journey was in all $11\frac{1}{4}$ Miles. But to make the Horses Some amends, we encamp in the midst of good Forage. Both Meanwell's Horses cou'd hardly carry their Saddles, nor more being required of them, nor was it much better with many others in the Company. On our way we had the Fortune to kill a Deer, and a Turkey, sufficient for our Day's Subsistance, nor need any one Despair of his Daily Bread, whose Faith is but half so big as his Stomach.

Squeeze out about 5 or 6 Drops. Take the inside of Sassafras Bark, Powder it, and mix it with the Liquor, and place this Bait conveniently for your Steel Trap.

The Story of their biting off their Testicles to compound for their Lives, when they are pursued, is a story taken upon trust by Pliny, like many others.[90]   Nor is it the Beaver's Testicles that carry the Perfume, but they have a Pair of Glands just within the Fundament, as Sweet as Musk, that perfume their Dung, and communicate a strong scent to their Testicles, by being plac'd near them.

It is true Several creatures have Strange instincts for their Preservation, as the Egyptian Frog, we are told by Elian, will carry a whole Joint of a Reed across its Mouth, that it may not be swallow'd by the ibis.[91]

And this Long-neckt fowl will give itself a clyster with its Beak, whenever it finds itself too costive or feverish. The Dogs of that Country lap the Water of the Nile in a full Trot, that they may not be Snapped by the Crocodiles. Both Beavers and Wolves, we know, when one of their Legs is caught in a Steel Trap, will bite it off, and they may escape with the rest. The Flesh of the Beavers is tough and dry, all but the Tail, which like the Parrot's Tongue, was one of the farfetched Rarities with which Heliogabalus used to furnish his Luxurious Table.

The Fur of these creatures is very valuable, especially in the more Northern Countries, where it is longer and finer. This the Dutch have lately contriv'd to mix with their Wool, and Weave into a Sort of Drugget, that is not only warm, but wonderfully light and Soft. They also make Gloves and Stockings of it, that keep out the Cold almost as well as the Fur itself, and do not look quite so Savage.

There is a deal of Rich low Ground on Yapatsco Creek, but I believe liable to be overflow'd in a fresh. However, it might be proper enough for Rice, which receives but little Injury from Water.

We encampt on the Banks of Massamony Creek, after a Journey of more than 11 Miles. By the way we shot a fat Doe and a wild Turkey, which fed us all plentifully. And we have reason to say, by our own happy Experience, that no man need to despair of his daily Bread in the Woods, whose faith is but half so large as his Stomach.

14. Being at length happily arriv'd within 20 Miles of the uppermost Inhabitants, we despacht two Men who had the ablest Horses, to go before, and get a Beef kill'd and some Bread bak'd to refresh their Fellow Travellers, upon their arrival. They had likewise Orders to hire an

---

[90] *The Natural History*, Book XXII, Ch. 13.
[91] Apparently a reference to Claudius Albanus, *Varia Historia*, I, 3, in which the story is told of the water snake of the Nile, not the Ibis. This work was translated from Greek into Latin in the sixteenth century, and into English in 1576 and 1665.

14.   About 8 in the Morning I dispatch't 2 Men to Miles Rileys, and by the way to hire John Davis to carry my Letters to Maj^r. Mumfords with all Expedition.   I also gave them Orders to get a Beef kill'd, and likewise some Meal Ground, to refresh the Men on their Arrival amongst the Inhabitants.   We decampt after them at 11 a Clock, and at the End of 7¼ Miles crost Nutbush Creek. From thence we proceeded about 4 Miles farther to a beautiful

express to carry a Letter to the Governor, giving an Account that we were all returned in Safety. This was the more necessary, because we had been so long absent that many now began to fear we were, by this time, Scalpt and barbecu'd by the Indians.

We decampt with the rest of the People about ten a clock, and marched near 12 Miles. In our way we Crost Nutbush Creek, and 4 Miles farther we came upon a beautiful Branch of Great Creek, where we took up our Quarters. The Tent was pitched upon an Eminence, which overlookt a wide Piece of low Grounds, cover'd with Reeds and watered by a Crystal Stream, gliding thro' the Middle of it. On the Other Side of this delightful Valley, which was about half a Mile wide, rose a Hill that terminated the View, and in the figure of a Semicircle closed in upon the opposite Side of the Valley. This had a most agreeable Effect upon the Eye, and wanted nothing but Cattle grazing in the Meadow, and Sheep and Goats feeding on the Hill, to make it a Compleat Rural LANDSCAPE.

The Indian kill'd a Fawn, which, being upon its growth, was not fat, but made some amends by being tender. He also Shot an Otter, but our People were now better fed than to eat such Coarse Food. The truth of it is, the Flesh of this Creature has a rank Fishy taste, and for that reason might be a proper Regale for the Samoeids, who drink the CZAR of MUSCOVY'S health and toast their Mistresses in a Bumper of Train Oil.[92]

The Carthusians, to save their Vow of eating no Flesh, pronounce this Amphibious Animal to be a Fish, and feed upon it as such without Wounding their Consciences.

The Skin of the Otter is very Soft, and the Swedes make Caps and Socks of it, not only for Warmth, but also because they fancy it Strengthens the Nerves, and is good against all Distempers of the Brain.

The otter is a great Devourer of Fish, which are its Natural Food, and whenever it betakes itself to a Vegetable Dyet, it is as some high-Spirited Wives obey their Husbands, by pure Necessity. They dive after their Prey, tho' they can't continue long under Water, but thrust their Noses up to the Surface now and then for Breath. They are great Enemies to Weirs Set up in the Rivers to catch Fish, devouring or biting to pieces all they find there. Nor is it either easy to fright them from this kind of Robbery, or to destroy them. The best way I cou'd ever find was to float an Old Wheel just by the Weir, and so soon as the Otter has taken a large Fish, he will get upon the Wheel to eat it more at his ease, which may give you an Opportunity of firing upon him from the Shoar.

One of our People Shot a large Gray Squirrel with a very Bushy Tail, a singular use of which our merry Indian discover'd to us. He said whenever this little Animal has occasion to cross a run of Water, he launches a Chip or Piece of Bark into the Water, on which he embarks, and, holding up his Tail to the wind, he Sails over very Safely. If This be true,

---

[92] The Samogedes, obscure people of the Northern Coast of Asia and Eastern Europe.

Branch of great Creek, where we arriv'd in good order about 4 a Clock in the Afternoon.   We encamp on a rising Ground that overlookt a large extent of Green Reeds, with a Crystal Stream serpenting thro' the middle of them.   The Indian kill'd a Fawn, & one of the other Men a Raccoon, the Flesh of which is like Pork, but truly we were better Fed than to eat it.   The Clouds gather'd, and threaten'd Rain, but a brisk N. Wester swept them all away before Morning.

it is probable men learnt at first the use of Sails from these ingenious little Animals, as the Hottentots learnt the Physical use of most of their Plants from the Baboons.

15.   About three Miles from our Camp we passed GREAT CREEK, and then, after traversing very barren grounds for 5 Miles together, we crost the Tradeing Path, and soon after had the pleasure of reaching the up-permost Inhabitant. This was a Plantation belonging to colonel Mumford, where our Men almost burst themselves with Potatoes and Milk. Yet as great a Curiosity as a House was to us Foresters, still we chose to lie in the Tent, as being much the cleaner and sweeter Lodging.

The Tradeing Path above-mention'd receives its Name from being the Route the Traders take with their Caravans, when they go to traffick with the Catawbas and other Southern Indians. The Catawbas live about 250 Miles beyond Roanoke River, and yet our Traders find their Account in transporting Goods from Virginia to trade with them at their own Towne.

The Common Method of carrying on this Indian Commerce is as follows: Gentlemen send for Goods proper for such a Trade from England, and then either Venture them out at their own Risk to the Indian Towns, or else credit some Traders with them of Substance and Reputation, to be paid in Skins at a certain Price agreed betwixt them.

The Goods for the Indian Trade consist chiefly in Guns, Powder, Shot, Hatchets, (which the Indians call Tomahawks,) Kettles, red & blue Planes, Duffields, Stroudwater blankets, and some Cutlary Wares, Brass Rings and other Trinkets.

These Wares are made up into Packs and Carry'd upon Horses, each Load being from 150 to 200 Pounds, with which they are able to travel about 20 Miles a day, if Forage happen to be plentiful.

Formerly a Hundred Horses have been employ'd in one of these Indian Caravans, under the Conduct of 15 or 16 Persons only, but now the Trade is much impair'd, insomuch that they seldom go with half that Number.

The Course from Roanoke to the Catawbas is laid down nearest South-west, and lies thro' a fine Country, that is Water'd by Several beautiful Rivers.

Those of the greatest Note are, first, Tar river, which is the upper Part of Pamptico, Flat river, Little river and Eno river, all three Branches of Neuse.

Between Eno and Saxapahaw rivers are the Haw old fields, which have the Reputation of containing the most fertile high land in this part of the World, lying in a Body of about 50,000 acres.

15. We were ready to march about 10 a Clock, and at the Distance 6 miles past Great Creek. Then after traversing very barren Grounds for near 5 Miles, we crost the Trading Path used by our Traders, when they carry Goods to the S. W. Indians. In less than a mile from thence we had the Pleasure to discover a House, tho' a very poor One, the Habitation of our Friend Nat on Maj^r. Mumford's Plantation. As agreeable a sight as a House was, we chose our Tent to lie in, as much the cleanlier Lodging. However we vouchsafed to eat in the House, where nothing went down so sweetly as Potatoes & Milk. In order for that a whole Oven full of Potatoes were provided which the Men devour'd unmercifully. Here all the Company but myself were told that my little Son was dead. This Melancholly News they carefully conceal'd from me for fear of giving me uneasiness. Nothing cou'd be more good natur'd, and is a Proof that more than 30 People may keep a Secret. And what makes the wonder the greater is that 3 Women were privy to this my supposed Misfortune.

I drew out the Men after Dinner, and harrangued them on the Subject of our safe return in the Following Terms.

"Friends and Fellow-Travellors, It is with abundance of Pleas-
"ure, that I now have it in my Power to congratulate your happy
"arrival among the Inhabitants. You will give me leave to put you
"in mind, how manifestly Heaven has engaged in our Preserva-
"tion. No distress, no Disaster, no Sickness of any consequence,
"has befallen any One of us in so long and so dangerous a Jour-
"ney. We have subsisted plentifully on the bounty of Providence,
"and been day by day supply'd in the barren Wilderness with
"Food convenient for us. This surely is an Instance of Divine
"Goodness never to be forgotten, and that it may stil be more com-
"pleat, I heartily wish, that the same Protection may have been
"extended to our Families, during our Absence. But lest amidst
"so many Blessings, there may be some here who may esteem them-
"selves a little unfortunate in the loss of their Horses, I promise

This Saxapahaw is the upper Part of Cape Fair River, the falls of which lye many Miles below the Trading Path.

Some Mountains overlook this Rich Spot of Land, from whence all the soil washes down into the Plane, and is the cause of its exceeding Fertility. Not far from thence the Path crosses ARAMANCHY River, a branch of Saxapahaw, and about 40 Miles beyond that, Deep River, which is the N Branch of Pedee. Then 40 miles beyond that, the Path intersects the Yadkin, which is there half a Mile over, and is supposed to be the South Branch of the same Pedee.

The Soil is exceedingly rich on both sides the Yadkin, abounding in rank Grass nad prodigiously large Trees; and for plenty of Fish, Fowel and Venison, is inferior to No Part of the Northern Continent. There the Traders commonly lie Still for some days, to recruit their Horses' Flesh as well as to recover their own Spirits. Six Miles further is Crane Creek, so nam'd from its being the Rendezvous of great Armies of Cranes, which wage a more cruel War at this day, with the Frogs and the Fish, than they us'd to do with the Pigmies in the Days of Homer.

About three-score Miles more bring you to the first Town of the Catawbas, call'd Nauvasa, situated on the banks of Santee river. Besides this Town there are five Others belonging to the same Nation, lying all on the same Stream, within the Distance of 20 Miles.

These Indians were all call'd formerly by the general Name of the Usherees,[93] and were a very Numerous and Powerful People. But the frequent Slaughters made upon them by the Northern Indians, and, what has been still more destructive by far, the Intemperance and Foul Distempers introduc'd amongst them by the Carolina Traders, have now reduc'd their Numbers to little More than 400 Fighting Men, besides Women & Children. It is a charming Place where they live, the Air very Wholesome, the Soil fertile, and the Winters ever mild and Serene.

In Santee river, as in Several others of Carolina, a Small kind of allegator is frequently seen, which perfumes the water with a Musky Smell. They Seldom exceed Eight Feet in Length in these parts, whereas, near the Equinoctial, they come up to twelve or Fourteen. And the heat of the Climate don't only make them bigger, but more Fierce and Voracious. They watch the Cattle there when they come to drink and Cool themselves in the River; and because they are not able to drag them into the Deep Water, they make up by Strategem what they want in Force. They Swallow great Stones, the Weight of which being added to their Strength, enables them to tug a Moderate Cow under Water, and as soon as they have drown'd her, they discharge the Stones out of their Maw and then feast upon the Carcass. However, as Fierce and Strong as these Monsters are, the Indians will surprise them Napping as they float upon the Surface, get astride upon their Necks, then whip a short piece of wood like a Trunch-

---

[93] John Lederer, in 1670, calls them Ushery. (*Discoveries*, Second Expedition.) Europe. Train oil is whale oil.

"faithfully, I will do my Endeavour to procure satisfaction for
"them. And as a Proof that I am perfectly satisfy'd with your
"Service, I will receive your pay, and cause a full distribution
"to be made of it, as soon as possible. Lastly as well to gratify
"your Impatience to see your several Families as to cease the
"Expence of the Government, I will agree to your discharge, so
"fast as we shall approach the nearest distance to your respective
"Habitations."

eon into their Jaws, & holding the Ends with their two hands, hinder them from diving by keeping their mouths open, and when they are almost Spent, they will make to the shoar, where their Riders knock them on the Head and Eat them.   This Amphibious Animal is a Smaller kind of Crocodile, having the Same Shape exactly, only the Crocodile of the Nile is twice as long, being when full grown from 20 to Thirty Feet.   This Enormous Length is the more to be wonder'd at, because the Crocodile is hatcht from an Egg very little larger than that of a Goose.   It has a long Head, which it can open very wide, with very Sharp & Strong teeth. Their Eyes are Small, their Legs Short, with Claws upon their Feet.   Their Tail makes half the Length of their Body, and the whole is guarded with hard impenetrable Scales, except the Belly, which is much Softer and Smoother.   They keep much upon the Land in the day time, but towards the Evening retire into the Water to avoid the Cold Dews of the Night. They run pretty fast right forward, but are very awkward and Slow in turning by reason of their unwieldy Length.   It is an Error that they have no Tongue, without which they cou'd hardly Swallow their Food; but in eating they move the upper Jaw only, Contrary to all other Animals. The way of catching them in Egypt is, with a Strong Hook fixt to the End of a chain, and baited with a joynt of Pork, which they are very fond of.   But a live Hog is generally tyed near, the Cry of which allures them to the Hook.   This Account of the Crocodile will agree in most particulars with the Alligator, only the Bigness of the last cannot entitle it to the Name of "Leviathan," which Job gave formerly to the crocodile, and not to the Whale, as some Interpreters wou'd make us believe.

So Soon as the Catawba Indians are inform'd of the Approach of the Virginia Caravans, they send a Detachment of their Warriors to bid them Welcome, and escort them Safe to their Town, where they are receiv'd with great Marks of Distinction.   And their Courtesys to the VIRGINIA Traders, I dare say, are very Sincere, because they sell them better Goods and better Pennyworths than the Traders of Carolina.   They commonly reside among the Indians till they have barter'd their Goods away for Skins, with which they load their Horses and come back by the Same Path they went.

There are generally some Carolina Traders that constantly live among the Catawbas, and pretend to Exercise a dictatorial Authority over them. These petty Rulers don't only teach the honester Savages all sorts of Debauchery, but are unfair in their dealings, and use them with all kinds of Oppression.   Nor has their Behaviour been at all better to the rest of the Indian Nations, among whom they reside, by abusing their Women and Evil-entreating their Men; and, by the way, this was the true Reason of the fatal War which the Nations roundabout made upon Carolina in the year 1713.[94]

[94] Reference is to the Tuscarora War of 1711-13 in North Carolina, and the Yamassee of 1715, in South Carolina. In the former the Catawbas allied themselves with, and in the latter against, the English.

[Continued on page 305]

Then it was all that the Neighbouring Indians, grown weary of the Tyranny and Injustice with which they had been abus'd for many Years, resolv'd to endure their bondage no longer, but enter'd into General Confederacy against their Oppressors of Carolina.

The Indians open'd the War by knocking most of those little Tyrants on the Head that dwelt amongst them, under pretence of regulating their Commerce, and from thence Carry'd their Resentment so far as to endanger both NORTH and SOUTH CAROLINA.

16.   We gave Orders that the Horses shou'd pass Roanoak River at Monisep Ford, while most of the Baggage was transported in a Canoe.

We landed at the Plantation of Cornelius Keith, where I beheld the wretchedest Scene of Poverty I had ever met with in this happy Part of the World.   The Man, his Wife and Six Small Children, liv'd in a Penn, like so many Cattle, without any Roof over their Heads but that of Heaven. And this was their airy Residence in the Day time, but then there was a Fodder Stack not far from this Inclosure, in which the whole Family shelter'd themselves a night's and in bad weather.

However, 'twas almost worth while to be as poor as this Man was, to be as perfectly contented.   All his Wants proceeded from Indolence, and not from Misfortune.   He had good Land, as well as good Health and good Limbs to work it, and, besides, had a Trade very useful to all the Inhabitants round about.   He cou'd make and set up Quern Stones[95] very well, and had proper Materials for that purpose just at Hand, if he cou'd have taken the pains to fetch them.

There is no other kind of Mills in those remote parts, and, therefore, if the Man wou'd have Workt at his Trade, he might have liv'd very comfortably.   The poor woman had a little more Industry, and Spun Cotton enough to make a thin covering for her own and her children's Nakedness.

I am sorry to say it, but Idleness is the general character of the men in the Southern Parts of this Colony as well as in North Carolina.   The Air is so mild, and the Soil so fruitful, that very little Labour is requir'd to fill their Bellies, especially where the Woods afford such Plenty of Game.   These Advantages discharge the Men from the Necessity of killing themselves with Work, and then for the other Article of Raiment, a very little of that will suffice in so temperate a Climate.   But so much as is absolutely Necessary falls to the good women's Share to provide.   They all Spin, weave and knit, whereby they make a good Shift to cloath the whole Family; and to their credit be it recorded, many of them do it very completely, and thereby reproach their Husbands' Laziness in the most

---

[95] Stones for querns, or hand mills.

16. It was noon before we cou'd disengage ourselves from the
Charms of Madam Nat, and her Entertainments. I tipp't her
a Pistole for her Civilitys; and order'd the Horses' to the Ford,
while we and the Baggage were paddled over in the Canoe. While
the Horses were marching round. Meanwell and I made a Visit
to Cornelius Keath, who liv'd rather in a Penn than a House, with
his Wife and 6 Children. I never beheld such a Scene of Poverty in this happy part of the World. The Hovel they lay in had
no Roof to cover those wretches from the Injurys of the Weather:
but when it rain'd, or was colder than Ordinary, the whole Family
took refuge in a Fodder Stack. The poor man had rais'd a kind
of a House but for want of Nails it remain'd uncover'd. I gave
him a Note on Maj^r. Mumford for Nails for that purpose and so
made a whole Family happy at a very small Expence. The man
can read & write very well, and by way of a Trade can make &
set up Quernstones & yet is poorer than any Highland-Scot, or
Bog-trotting Irishman. When the Horses came up we moved forward to Miles Rileys another of Maj^r. Mumford's Quarters. Here
was a Young Steer kill'd for us, and meal ground, and every thing
also provided that the Place afforded. There was a huge consumption of Potatoes, milk, & Butter, which we found in great Plenty.

This day I discharg'd Robin Hix, Tho' Wilson, and Charles
Kimball, allowing them 2 Days to reach their Homes. I also dismist our honest Indian Bearskin, after presenting him with a note

inoffensive way, that is to say, by discovering a better Spirit of Industry in themselves.

From thence we mov'd forward to Colo Mumford's other Plantation, under the Care of Miles Riley, where, by that Gentleman's Directions, we were again Supply'd with many good things. Here it was we discharg'd our Worthy Friend and Fellow Travellaur, Mr. Bearskin, who had so plentifully Supplyed us with Provisions during our long Expedition. We rewarded Him to his Heart's content, so that he return'd to his Town loaden, both with Riches and the Reputation of haveing been a great Discoverer.

17. This being Sunday, we were Seasonably put in mind how much we were oblig'd to be thankful for our happy return to the Inhabitants. Indeed we had great reason to reflect with Gratitude on the Signal Mercies we had receiv'd. First, that we had, day by day, been fed by the Bountifull hand of Providence in the desolate Wilderness, Insomuch that if any of our People wanted one Single Meal during the whole Expedition, it was intirely owing to their own imprudent Management.

Secondly, that not one Man of our whole Company, had any Violent Distemper or bad Accident Befall him, from One End of the Line to the other. The very worst that happen'd was, that One of them gave himself a Smart cut on the Pan of his knee with a Tomahawk, which we had the good Fortune to cure in a Short time, without the help of a Surgeon.

As for the Misadventures of Sticking in the Mire and falling into Rivers and Creeks, they were rather Subjects of Mirth than complaint, and serv'd only to diversify our Travels with a little farcicall Variety. And, lastly, that many uncommon Incidents have concurr'd to prosper our Undertaking. We had not only a dry Spring before we went out, but preceding Winter, and even a Year or two before, had been much dryer than Ordinary. This made not only the Dismal, but likewise most of the Sunken Grounds near the Sea-Side, just hard enough to bear us, which otherwise had been quite unpassible.

And the whole time we were upon the Business, which was in all about Sixteen Weeks, we were never catch't in the Rain except once, Nor was our Progress Interrupted by bad Weather above 3 or 4 days at most. Besides all this, we were Surpriz'd by no Indian Enemy, but all of us brought our Scalps back Safe upon our Heads.

of £3 on Maj^r. Mumford, a Pound of Powder with Shot in proportion. He had besides the Skins of all the Deer he had kill'd
in the whole Journey, and had them carry'd for him into the Bargain. Nothing cou'd be happier than this honest Fellow was with
all these Riches, besides the great Knowledge he had gain'd of
the Country. He kill'd a Fat Buck, great part of which he left us by
way of Legacy, the rest he cut into pieces, toasted them before the
Fire, & then strung them upon his Girdle to serve him for his
Provisions on his way to Christanna-Fort, where his Nation liv'd.
We lay in the Tent, notwithstanding there was a clean Landlady,
and good Beds, which gave the Men an Opportunity of getting a
House over their Heads, after having for 2 Months had no covering but the Firmaments.

17.   Being Sunday besides performing the Dutys of the day, we
christen'd Tho. Page one of our Men, who had been bred a Quaker,
and Meanwell & I were his Gossips. Several of the Neighbours
came, partly out of curiosity, and partly out of Devotion.
Amongst the rest came a young Woman which lives in comfortable
Fornication with Cornelius Cargil, and has several Children by
him. Meanwell bought a Horse of this man, in which he was
Jockyed. Our Eyes as well as our Taste were blest with a Surloin
of Roast Beef, and we drank pleasure to our Wives in a Glass of
Shrub. Not content with this Moderate Refreshment, my Friends
carry'd on the Joke with Bambo made of execrable Brandy, the
manufacture of the place. I preach't against it, tho' they minded
me as little at Night, as they had Humdrum in the Morning, but
most of them paid for it by being extremely Sick. This day I discharg'd John Holms and Tho. Page, with a reasonable allowance
of Days for their return home.

This cruel Method of Scalping of Enemies is practis'd by all the Savages in America, and perhaps is not the least proof of their Original from the Northern Inhabitants of Asia. Among the Ancient Scythians it was constantly us'd, who carry'd about these hairy Scalps as Trophies of Victory. They serv'd them too as Towels at home, and Trappings for their Horses abroad. But these were not content with the Skin of their Enemies' Heads, but also made use of their Sculls for cups to drink out of upon high Festival days, & made greater Ostentation of them than if they had been made of Gold or the purest crystal.

Besides the Duties of the Day, we christen'd one of our Men who had been bred a Quaker. The Man desir'd this of his own mere Motion, without being tamper'd with by the Parson, who was willing every one shou'd go to Heaven his own way. But whether he did it by the Conviction of his Own Reason, or to get rid of some Troublesome Forms and Restraints, to which the Saints of that Perswasion are Subject, I can't Positively say.

18.   We proceeded over a Levil Road 12 Miles, as far as George Hixe's Plantation, on the South Side Meherrin River, Our Course being for the most part North-East. By the way we hired a Cart to transport our Baggage, that we might the better befriend our Jaded Horses.

Within 2 Miles of our Journey's End this day, we met the Express We had sent the Saturday before to give Notice of our Arrival. He had been almost as Expeditious as a carrier Pigeon, rideing in 2 Days no less than 200 Miles.

All the Grandees of the Sappony Nation did us the Honour to repair hither to meet us, and our worthy Friend and Fellow Traveller, Bearskin, appear'd among the gravest of them in his Robes of ceremony. Four Young Ladies of the first Quality came with them, who had more the Air of cleanliness than any copper-Colour'd Beauties I had ever seen; Yet we resisted all their Charms, notwithstanding the long Fast we had kept from the Sex, and the Bear Dyet was had been so long engag'd in. Nor can I say the Price they sat upon their Charms was at all Exorbitant. A Princess for a Pair of Red Stockings can't, surely, be thought buying Repentance much too dear.

The Men had something great and Venerable in their countenances, beyond the common Mien of Savages; and indeed they ever had the Reputation of being the Honestest, as well as the bravest Indians we have ever been acquainted with.

This People is now made up of the Remnant of Several other Nations, of which the most considerable are the Sapponys, the Occaneches, and

18.   This day we endeavour'd to set out early but were hinder'd by Powel's not finding some of his Horses.   This Man had almost been negligent in that particular, but amongst the Inhabitants was more careless than ordinary.   It was therefore thought high time to discharge him, and carry our Baggage as well as we cou'd to Cornelius Cargill's, who liv'd about 7 Miles off, and there hire his Cart to transport it as far as Maj^r. Mumfords.   We made the best Shift we cou'd, and having crost Mr Riley's hand with a Pistole, we mov'd toward Cargils, where we arriv'd about 2 a Clock.   Here we put the heavy Baggage into the Cart, tho' I order'd mine to continue on my own Horse, lest some disaster might happen to this frail Vehicle.   Then appointing a Guard to attend the Baggage, we proceeded 5 Miles farther to George Hixes Plantation, where preparation was made to entertain us.

By the way we met John Davis that brought me Letters from home, & from Maj^r. Mumford, in answer to those I had sent to them by this Express.   He had indeed been almost as Epeditious as a Carrier-Pigeon, for he went from Miles Richleys on Saturday, and he met us this day, being Monday, early in the Afternoon 3 miles before we got to George Hixes.   By the Letters he brought I had the pleasure to hear that all my Family was well.

Steukenhocks,[96] who not finding themselves Separately Numerous, enough for their Defence, have agreed to unite into one Body, and all of them now go under the Name of the Sapponys.

Each of these was formerly a distinct Nation, or rather a Several clan or Canton of the Same Nation, Speaking the Same Language, and using the same Customs. But their perpetual Wars against all other Indians, in time, reduc'd them so lo as to make it Necessary to join their Forces together.

They dwelt formerly not far below the Mountains, upon Yadkin River, about 200 Miles West and by South from the Falls of Roanoak. But about 25 Years ago they took Refuge in Virginia, being no longer in condition to make Head not only against the Northern Indians, who are their Implacable enemies, but also against most of those to the South. All the Nations round about, bearing in mind the Havock these Indians us'd formerly to make among their Ancestors in the Insolence of their Power, did at length avenge it Home upon them, and made them glad to apply to this Government for protection.

Colo Spotswood, our then lieut. governor, having a good Opinion of their Fidelity & Courage, Settled them at Christanna, ten Miles north of Roanoak, upon the belief that they wou'd be a good Barrier on that Side of the Country, against the Incursion of all Foreign Indians. And in Earnest they wou'd have Serv'd well enough for that Purpose, if the White People in the Neighbourhood had not debauch't their Morals, and ruin'd their Health with Rum, which was the Cause of many disorders, and ended at last in a barbarous Murder committeed by one of these Indians when he was drunk, for which the poor Wretch was executed when he was sober.

It was a matter of great Concern to them, however, that one of their Grandees should be put to so ignominious a Death. All Indians have as great an Aversion to hanging as the Muscovites, tho' perhaps not for the same cleanly reason: These last believing that the Soul of one that dies in this manner, being forc'd to Sally out of the Body at the Postern, must needs be defiled. The Sapponys took this Execution so much to Heart, that they soon after quitted their Settlement and remov'd in a Body to the Cataubas.

The Daughter of the TETERO KING went away with the Sapponys, but being the last of her Nation, and fearing she Shou'd not be treated according to her Rank, poison'd herself, like an Old Roman, with the Root

---

[96] Probably the Conestoga, who for a short time in the early eighteeenth century lived on the Roanoke River. Earlier, in 1608, they live on the Rappahannock River and were called Mannahoac. Spotswood speaks of the Stenkennocks as one of the tribes whose interests he represented at the Albany Conference in 1722. (*N. Y. Doc. Col. Hist. V*, 673). The Occoneechi in 1670 lived on an island in the Roanoke River near Clarksville, Virginia, but by 1701 they had moved westward to the region of Hillsboro, North Carolina, and in 1722 were at Christanna. Later they moved North with the Saponi and Tutelo. (See Note 62.)

That my Heir Apparent had been extremely ill, but was recover'd, nevertheless the Danger he had been in gave Birth to the Report that he was dead. All my Company expected that now the bad News wou'd be confirmed. This made Meanwell take a convenient Station to observe with how much Temper I shou'd receive such Melancholly Tydings. But not finding any change in my countenance, he ventur'd to ask me how it fared with my Family. And I must greatfully own, that both he and the whole Company discover'd a great deal of Satisfaction that the Report prov'd false. They then told me with how much care they had conceal'd from me the Fame of his being dead, being unwilling to make me uneasy upon so much incertainty.

We got to Geo. Hixes before 4 a Clock, and both he and his lively little Wife receiv'd us courteously. His House Stands on an Emminence, from whence is a good Prospect. Every thing lookt clean and wholesome, which made us resolve to quit the Tent, and betake ourselves to the House.

All the Grandees of the Sapponi Nation waited here to see us, and our Fellow-Traveller Bearskin was amongst the gravest of them. Four Ladys of Quality graced their visit, who were less besmear'd with Grease and Dirt, than any Copper-colour'd Beauty's I had ever seen. The Men too had an air of decency very uncommon and what was a greater curiosity, Most of the Company came on Horseback. The Men rode more awkwardly than Sailors, and the Women who sat astride, were so basfull they wou'd not mount their Ponys til they were quite out of Sight.

Christanna Fort where these Indians live, lies 3 Miles from George Hixes Plantation. He has considerable dealings with them, and supplys them too plentifully with Rum, which kills more of them than the Northern Indians do, and causes much disorder amongst them. Maj. Mumford was so good as to send me a Horse, believing that mine was sufficiently jaded, and Col° Bolling sent me another.[65] With the last I complemented Orion, who had march't on Foot good part of the way from the Mountains.

---

[65] Colonel John Bolling (1700-1757), son of Major John Bolling (1676-1729) and grandson of Robert Bolling (1646-1709) who came to Virginia in 1660 and married Jane Rolfe, grand-daughter of John Rolfe and Pocahontas. The residence referred to was "Cobbe" in Chesterfield, now Henrico County. See "The Ancestors and Descendants of John Rolfe," (*Virginia Mag. Hist. and Biog.*, Vol. XXII, p. 103.)

of the Trumpet-Plant. Her Father dy'd 2 Years before, who was the most
intrepid Indian we have been acquainted with. He had made himself
terrible to all other Indians by His Exploits, and had escaped so many
Dangers that he was esteem'd invulnerable. But at last he dy'd of a
Pleurisy, the last Man of his Race and Nation, leaving only that unhappy Daughter behind him, who would not long survive Him.

The most uncommon Circumstance in this Indian visit Was, that they all
came on Horse-back, which was certainly intended for a Piece of State,
because the Distance was but 3 Miles, and 'tis likely they had walk't a
foot twice as far to catch their Horses. The Men rode more awkwardly
than any Dutch Sailor, and the Ladies bestrode their Palfreys a la mode
de France, but were so bashful about it, that there was no persuading
them to Mount till they were quite out of our Sight.

The French Women use to ride a-straddle, not so much to make them
sit firmer in the Saddle, as from the hopes the same thing might peradventure befall them that once happen'd to the Nun of ORLEANS, who
escaping of a Nunnery, took Post en CAVALIER, and in ten Miles' hard
riding had the good Fortune to have all the Tokens of a Man break out
upon her.

This Piece of History ought to be the more credible, because it leans
upon much the same Degree of Proof as the Tale of Bishop Burnet's Two
Italian NUNS, who, according to his Lordship's Account, underwent the
Same happy Metamorphosis, probably by some other Violent Exercise.[97]

19. From hence we despatch't the Cart with our Baggage under a
Guard, and crosst MEHERRIN River, which was not 30 Yards wide in that
Place. By the help of Fresh Horses that had been sent us we now began
to mend our Pace, which was also quicken'd by the Strong Inclinations
we had to get home.

In the Distance of 5 Miles we forded MEHERRIN creek, which was very
near as broad as the River. About 8 Miles farther we came to STURGEON-
Creek, so call'd from the Dexterity an OCCAANECHY Indian shewed there
in Catching one of those Royal Fish, which was perform'd after the following Manner.

In the Summer time 'tis no unusual thing for Sturgeons to Sleep on
the Surface of the Water and one of them having wander'd up into this
Creek in the Spring, was floating in that drowsy condition.

The Indian, above mention'd, ran up to the Neck into the Creek a little
below the Place where he discover'd the Fish, expecting the Stream wou'd

---

[97] Burnett, *Some letters containing An Account of what seemed most remarkable in
Switzerland, Italy, etc., written by G. Burnet, D.D. to T. H. B. B.* (Rotterdam,
1686) pp. 246-247.

When we saluted Mrs Hix, she bobb'd up her mouth with more than Ordinary Elasticity, and gave Us a good Opinion of her other Motions.   Captain Embry who lives on Notoway River met us here, and gave us an invitation to make our next Stage at his House.   Here I discharged John Evans, Stephen Evans, William Pool, George Tilman, George Hamilton, and James Patillo, allowing them for their Distance Home.   Our course from Miles Rileys inwards held generally about N E. and the Road Levil.

19.   We dispach't away the Cart under a Guard by 9 a Clock, and after Complementing our Landlord with a Pistole for Feeding us and our Horses, we follow'd about 11.   About a Mile from the House, we crost Meherrin River, which being very low was not more than 20 Yards wide.   About 5 miles farther we past Meherrin Creek almost as wide as the River.   From thence 8 Miles we went over Sturgeon Run, and 6 Miles beyond that we came upon Wick-quoy Creek where the Stream is swift, and tumbles over the Rocks very solemnly, this makes broad low Grounds in many places, and abundance of rich Land.   About 2 Miles more brought us to our worthy Friends Capt. Embry's Habitation, where we found the House keeping much better than the House.   In that the Noble Capt. is not very curious, His Castle consisting of one Dirty Room, with a dragging Door to it that will neither Open nor Shut.   However my Landlady made us

soon bring his Game down to Him. He judg'd the Matter right, and as Soon as it came within his Reach, he whip't a running Noose over his Jole. This waked the Sturgeon, which being Strong in its own Element darted immediately under Water and dragg'd the Indian after Him. The Man made it a Point of Honour to keep his Hold, which he did to the Apparent Danger of being drown'd. Sometimes both the Indian and the Fish disappear'd for a Quarter of a Minute, & then rose at some Distance from where they dived. At this rate they continued flouncing about, Sometimes above, and sometimes under Water, for a considerable time, till at last the Hero Suffocated his Adversary, and haled his Body ashoar in Triumph.

About Six Miles beyond that, we passed over Wicco-quoi creek, Named so from the Multitude of Rocks over which the water tumbles in a Fresh, with a bellowing Noise. Not far from where we went over, is a Rock much higher than the rest, that Strikes the Eye with agreeable Horror, and near it a very Talkative Eccho, that, like a fluent Helpmeet, will return her good Man Seven Words for one, & after all, be Sure to have the Last. It speaks not only the Language of Men, but also of Birds & Beasts, and often a Single Wild Goose is cheated into the Belief that Some of his Company are not far off, by hearing his own cry multiply'd; & 'tis pleasant to see in what a flutter the Poor Bird is, when he finds himself disappointed.

On the Banks of this creek are very broad low-Grounds in many Places, and abundance of good high-Land, tho' a little Subject to Floods.

We had but two Miles more to Capt. EMBRY'S, where we found the Housekeeping much better than the House. Our Bountifull Landlady had set her Oven and all her Spits, Pots, Gridirons and Saucepans to work, to diversify our Entertainment, tho' after all it prov'd but a Mahommetan Feast, there being Nothing to drink but Water. The worst of it was, we had unluckily outrid the Baggage, and for that Reason were oblig'd to Lodge very Sociably in the Same Apartment with the Family, where, reckoning Women and Children, we muster'd in all no less than Nine Persons, who all pigg'd loveingly together.

20. In the Morning colo Bolling,[98] who had been Surveying in the Neighbourhood, and Mr. Walker, who dwelt not far off, came to visit us; And the last of these Worthy Gentlemen, fearing that our drinking so much Water might incline us to Pleurisys, brought us a kind Supply both of Wine and cyder.

It was Noon before we cou'd disengage Ourselves from the Courtesies of this Place, and then the two Gentlemen above-mention'd were so good as

---

[98] See Notes 63, Secret History; and Virginia Mag. Hist. and Biog. XXII, p. 103.

amends by providing a Supper Sufficient for a Battalion. I was a little Shocked at our first alighting with a Sight I did not expect. Most of the Men I discharg'd yesterday were got here before us, and within a few good downs of being drunk. I shew'd so much concern at this, that they had the Modesty to retire. Mr Walker met us here, and kindly invited us to his House, being about 5 Miles wide of this place. I shou'd have been glad to accept of his Civility but cou'd not with decency put a Slur upon our good Friend the Captain, who had made abundant Provision for us. For this reason we chose to drink Water, and stow thick in a dirty Room, rather than give our black-Ey'd Landlady the Trouble of making a Feast to no purpose. She had set all her Spits, Pots, Frying pans, Grid Irons and Ovens at work to pamper us up after fasting so long, in the Wilderness. The worst point of her Civility was that she made us eat of everything, which oblig'd 2 of the 9 that lay in the Room to rise at a very unseasonable time of Night.

20. Mr Walker came to us again in the morning and was so kind as to bring us some Wine and Cyder along with him. He also lent Meanwell [a] Horse for himself, and me another for one of my men. We had likewise a visit from Col^o Bolling, who had been surveying in the neighbourhood. Our Landlord, who is a dealer in Rum, let me have some for the men, & had the humility, tho' a Captain, to accept of a Pistole for our Entertainment. I discharg'd John Ellis & James Whitlock, at this Place. It was 12 a clock before we cou'd get loose from hence, and then we past Nottoway River just below Capt. Embrys house, where it was about 15 yards over. This River divides Prince George County from Brunswick. We had the Company of Col^o Bolling & Mr Walker along with us, who cou'd not heartily approve of our Lithuanian Custome of walking part of the way. At the distance of 11 miles we crost stony ·creek, and 5 miles farther we went over Gravelly Run, which is wide enough to merit the name of a creek. We past by Saponi Chappel and after 30 good miles arriv'd safe at Col^o Bollings, where we were entertained with much Plenty & civility. Among abundance of other good things he regaled us with excel-

to accompany us that day's Journey, tho' they cou'd by no means approve
of our LITHUANIAN Fashion of Dismounting now and then, in order to
walk part of the way on foot.

We cros't Nottoway River not far from our Landlord's House, where it
seem'd to be about 25 Yards over. This River divides the County of
Prince George from that of BRUNSWICK. We had not gone 8 Miles
father before our Eyes were bless'd with the Sight of Sapponi chappel,
which was the first House of Prayer we had seen for more than two
calendar Months.

About 3 Miles beyond that, we passed over Stony Creek, where One
of those that Guarded the Baggage kill'd a Polcat, upon which he made
a comfortable Repast. Those of his company were so SQUEAMISH
they cou'd not be persuaded at first to tast, as they said, of so unsavoury
an Animal; but seeing the Man Smack his Lips with more pleasure than
usual, they ventur'd at last to be of his Mess, and instead of finding the
Flesh rank and high-tasted, they owned it to be the Sweetest Morsel they
had ever eat in their Lives.

The ill Savour of this little Beast lys altogether in its Urin, Which
Nature has made so detestably ill-scented on purpose to furnish a helpless
Creature with Something to defend itself. For as some Brutes have Horns
and Hoofs, and others are arm'd with Claws, Teeth and Tushes for their
Defence; and as Some Spit a Sort of Poison at their Adversaries, like the
Paco; and others dart Quills at their Pursuers, like the Porcupine; and as
some have no Weapons to help themselves but their Tongue, and others
none but their Tails; so the poor Polcat's safety lies altogether in the
irresistible Stench of its Water; insomuch that when it finds itself in
Danger from an Enemy, it Moistens its bushy Tail plentifully with this
Liquid Amunition, and, then with great fury, Sprinkles it like a Shower
of Rain full into the Eyes of its Assailant, by which it gains time to make
its Escape.

Nor is the Polcat the only Animal that defends itself by a Stink. At
the CAPE OF GOOD HOPE is a little Beast, call'd a Stinker, as big as a
Fox, and Shap't like a Ferret, which being pursued has no way to save
himself but by farting and Squittering. And then such a Stench ensues
that None of its Pursuers can Possibly stand it.

At the End of 30 good Miles, we arriv'd in the Evening at colo Bolling's,
where first, from a Primitive Course of Life, we began to relapse into
Luxury. This Gentleman lives within Hearing of the Falls of Appamatuck
River, which are very Noisy whenever a Flood happens to roll a greater
stream than ordinary over the Rocks.

The River is Navigable for Small Craft as high as the Falls, and at
Some distance from thence fetches a compass, and runs nearly parallel
with James River almost as high as the Mountains.

While the Commissioners fared Sumptuously here, the poor Chaplain
and two Surveyors, stoppt Ten Miles Short at a poor Planter's House, in

lent Cyder. While Meanwell and I fared deliciously here, our 2 Surveyors & the Rev. Doctor in complement to their horses stuck close to the Baggage. They reach't no farther than 18 miles, & took up their Quarters at James Hudsons, where the Horses were better provided for than their Masters. There was no more than one bed to pig into, with one Cotten Sheet and the other of Brown Ozzenbrugs made brouner by a months Persperation. This mortify'd Orion to the Soul, so that the other 2 were happy enough in laughing at him. Tho I think they ought all to have been perfectly satisfy'd with the mans hospitality who was content to lye out of his own Bed to make room for them.

21. These Gentlemen quitted their sweet Lodging so early, that they reacht Col° Bollings time enough for Breakfast. M˚ Mumfords pretty Wife was very ill here, which had altered her pretty face beyond all knowledge. I took upon me to prescribe to her and my advice succeeded well as I understood afterwards. About 11 a clock we took leave and proceeded to Maj˚ Mumfords, when I discharged the Cart, and the few men that remained with me, assureing them that their Behaviour had engaged me to do them any service that lay in my power. I had no sooner settled these affairs but my Wife & Eldest Daughter arriv'd in the Chair to meet me. Besides the pleasure of embraceing them, they made me happy by letting me understand the rest of the Family were extreamly well. Our treatment was as civil as possible in this good Family. I wrote a Letter to send by Orion to the Governour, and the Evening we spent giving an account of our Travels and drinking the best cyder I ever tasted.

22. I sent away Meanwells Baggage and my own about ten a clock, he intending to take Westover in his way home. When we had fortify'd our selves with a meat Breakfast, we took leave about 12. My Wife and I rode in the Chair, and my Daughter on an easy pad she had borrow'd. Mrs Mumford was so kind as to undertake to spin my Buffalo's Hair, in order to knit me a Pair of Stockins. Orion took the nearest way to Williamsburgh, Astro-

Pity to their Horses, made a Saint ANTHONY'S Meal, that is, they Supp't upon the Pickings of what Stuck in their Teeth ever since Breakfast. But to make them amends, the good Man laid them in his own Bed, where they all three nestled together in one cotton Sheet and one of Brown Oznabrugs, made Still Something Browner by two Months' Copious Perspiration.

21.   But those worthy Gentlemen were so alert in the Morning after their light Supper, that they came up with us before Breakfast, & honestly paid their Stomachs all they ow'd them.

We made no more than a Sabbath day's Journey from this to the next Hospitable House, namely, that of our great Benefactor, Colo Mumford. We had already been much befiended by this Gentlemen, who, besides sending Orders to his Overseers at ROANOAK to let us want for nothing, had, in the Beginning of our Business, been so kind as to recommend most of the Men to us who were the faithful Partners of our Fatigue.

Altho, in most other ATCHIEVEMENTS those who command are apt to take all the HONOUR to themselves of what perhaps was more owing to the Vigour of those who were under them, Yet I must be more just, and allow these brave Fellows their full Share of credit for the Service we perform'd, & must declare, that it was in a great Measure owing to their Spirit and indefatigable Industry that we overcame many Obstacles in the Course of our Line, which till then had been esteem'd unsurmountable.

Nor must I at the Same time omit to do Justice to the Surveyors, and particularly to Mr. Mayo, who besides an eminent degree of Skill, encounter'd the same Hardships and underwent the Same Fatigue that the forwardest of the Men did, and that with as much Chearfulness as if Pain had been his Pleasure, and Difficulty his real Diversion.

Here we discharg'd the few Men we had left, who were all as Ragged as the GIBEONITE AMBASSADORS, tho', at the Same time, their Rags were very honourable, by the Service they had so Vigorously performed in making them so.

22.   A little before Noon we all took leave and dispers't to our Several Habitations, where we were so happy to find all our Familys well. This crown'd all our other Blessings, and made our Journey as prosperous as it had been painfull.

Thus ended our Second Expedition, in which we extented the Line within the Shadow of the Chariky Mountains, where we were oblig'd to Set up our Pillars, like Hercules, and return Home.

labe to Goochland, and Humdrum to Mount Misery. We call'd on Mr FitzGerald, to advise him what method to take with his sick child: but nature had done the business, before we came. We arriv'd at coggins Point about 4, where my servants attended with both Boats, in order to transport us to Westover. I had the happiness to find all the Family well. This crown'd all my other Blessings, and made the Journey truly prosperous, of which I hope I shall ever retain a gratefull remembrance. Nor was it all, that my People were in good health, but my Business was likewise in good order. Everyone seem'd to have done their duty, by the joy they express't at my Return. My Neighbours had been kind to my Wife, when she was threaten'd with the loss of her Son & Heir. Their assistance was kind as well as seasonable, when her child was threaten'd with fatal Symptomes, and her Husband upon a long Journey expos'd to great variety of Perils. Thus surrounded with the most fearfull apprehensions, Heaven was pleas'd to support her spirits, and bring back her child from the Grave, and her Husband from the mountains, for which Blessings may we be all sincerly thankfull.

THE NAMES of the Commissioners to direct the running of the Line between Virginia and North Carolina.

Commissioners for Virginia
        Steaddy   Meanwell
        Firebrand

Commissioners for North Carolina
        Judge Jumble   Plausible
        Shoebrush   Puzzlecause

Surveyors for Virginia
        Orion   Astrolabe

Surveyors for N. Carolina
        Bo-otes   Plausible

The Revd Dr Humdrum.   Chaplain

[Continued on page 320]

NAMES of the Men employ'd on the part of Virginia to run
the Line between that Colony and N. Carolina

On the first Expedition

1. Peter Jones	11. George Hamilton.
2. Thomas Short.	12. Robert Allen.
3. Thomas Jones.	13. Thomas Jones Junr.
4. Robert Hix.	14. John Ellis Junr.
5. John Evans.	15. James Pettillo.
6. Stephen Evans.	16. Richard Smith.
7. John Ellis.	17. John Rice.
8. Thomas Wilson.	18. William Calvert
9. George Tilman.	19. James Whitlock
10. Charles Kimball.	20. Thomas Page

On the 2^d Expedition

Peter Jones.	Charles Kimball.
Thomas Short.	George Hamilton.
Thomas Jones.	Edward Powell.
Robert Hix.	Thomas Jones Junr.
John Evans.	William Pool.
Stephen Evans.	James Pettillo.
John Ellis.	Richard Smith.
Thomas Wilson.	Abraham Jones.
George Tilman.	

ACCOUNT of the Expence of running the Line between Virginia
and N. Carolina.

To the Men's wages in Current Money	£277"10"0
To Sundry Disbursements for Provisions, &c	174"01"6
To paid the Men for 7 Horses lost	44"00"0
The Sum of £495"11"6 Current Money	£495"11"6
reduc't at 15 Per Cent to Sterling amounts to	£430"08"10

We had now, upon the whole, been out Sixteen Weeks, including going and returning and had travell'd at least Six Hundred Miles, and no Small part of that Distance on foot. Below, towards the Sea Side, our Course lay through MARSHES, SWAMPS, and great Waters; and above, over Steep HILLS, Craggy ROCKS, and Thickets, hardly penetrable. Notwithstanding this variety of Hardships, we may say, without Vanity, that we faithfully obey'd the King's Orders, and perform'd the Business effectually, in which we had the Honour to be employ'd.

Nor can we by any Means reproach Ourselves of having put the Crown to any exorbitant Expense in this difficult affair, the whole Charge, from Beginning to End, amounting to no more than One Thousand Pounds. But let no one concern'd in this painful Expedition complain of the Scantiness of his Pay, so long as His Majesty has been Graciously pleas'd to add ao our Reward the HONOUR of his ROYAL approbation, and to declare, notwithstanding the Desertion of the CAROLINA COMMISSIONERS, that the Line by us run shall hereafter Stand as the true Boundary betwixt the GOVERNMENTS OF VIRGINIA AND NORTH CAROLINA.

to paid Steddy	142″05″7
To Paid Meanwell	142″05″07
To paid Firebrand	94:00:00
To paid the Chaplain, Humdrum	20:00:00
To paid Orion	75:00:00
To paid Astrolabe	75:00:00
To paid for a Tent and Marquis	20:00:00
	£1000:00:00

This Sum was discharg'd by a Warrant of his Majesty'd Quit-rents from the Lands in

VIRGINIA.

THE DISTANCES OF PLACES

mention'd in the foregoing History
of the Dividing Line between Virginia
and North Carolina.

	M.Q.D.
From Coratuck Inlet to the Dismal	21:2:16
The Course thro' the Dismal	15:0:00
To the East Side of Blackwater River	20:1:43
We came down Blackwater to the Mouth of	
Nottoway 176 Poles, from whence to Meherrin	13:2:46
To Meherrin River again	0:1:67
To Meherrin River again	2:0:40
To the Ferry Road	1:2:60
To Meherrin again	0:0:22
To Meherrin the 5th and last Time	2:3:66
To the Middle of Jack's Swamp	11:0:25
To a Road	1:2:52
To Beaver pond Creek the first time	3:3:08

APPENDIX

To the Foregoing Journal, containing the second Charter to the Proprietors of CAROLINA, confirming and enlarging the first, and also several other acts to which it refers. These are plac'd by themselves at the End of the Book, that they may not interrupt the Thread of the Story, and the Reader will be more at liberty whether he will please to read them or not, being something dry and unpleasant.

The Second Charter granted by KING CHARLES 2D to the Proprietors of CAROLINA[1]

CHARLES, by the GRACE OF GOD, &c.: WHEREAS, by our LETTERS PATENT, bearing date the four and twentieth day of march, in the fifteenth year of our Reign, we were graciously pleas'd to grant unto our right trusty and right well beloved cousin and councellor, Edward, Earl of Clarendon, our high Chancellor of England, Our right trusty and right entirely beloved Cousin and Counsellor, George, Duke of Albemarle, Master of our Horse, our right trusty and well beloved William, now Earl of Craven, our Right trusty and well beloved Counsellor, Anthony, Lord Ashley, Chancellor of our Exchequer, our right trusty and well beloved Counsellor, Sir George Carterett, Knight and Baronet, vice Chamberlain of our household, our right trusty and well beloved, Sir John Colleton, Knight and Baronet, and Sir William Berkley,[2] Knight, all that Province Territory, or Tract of Ground, called Carolina, situate, lying and being within our Dominions of America, extending from the North End of the Island called Duke Island, which lys in the Southern Virginia Seas, and within Six and thirty Degrees of the Northern Latitude; and to the West as far as the South Seas; & so respectively as far as the River of Nathias, which bordereth upon the Coast of Florida, & within one and thirty Degrees of the Northern Latitude, and so west in a direct line as far as the South Seas aforesaid. Now know ye, that, at the humblest request of the said Grantees in the aforesaid Letters Patent named, and as a further mark of our especial favour towards them, we are graciously pleas'd to enlarge our said Grant unto them according to the Bounds & Limits hereafter Specify'd & in favour to the pious and noble purpose of the said Edward, Earl of Clarendon, George, Duke of Albemarle, William, Earl of Craven, John, Lord Berkley, Anthony, Lord Ashley, Sir George Carterett, Sir John Colleton, and Sir William Berkley, we do give and grant to them, their Heirs and Assigns, all that Province, Territory, or tract of Ground,

---

[1] Here follows the text of the Charter. Only the beginning, the part which concerns boundaries, is here given. The complete document is easily accessible to the general reader. It may be found in the *Colonial Records of North Carolina*, Vol. I, p. 102.

[2] The name of Lord John Berkeley is omitted.

To a Road from Bedding-field Southward	11:0:37
To Poa-hill Creek	3:1:33
To a Road	2:0:30
To Lizzard Creek	0:3:38
To Pigeon-roost Creek	3:1:72
To Cockes Creek	2:3:24
To Roanoke River	0:2:48
To the West Side of D°	0:0:49
To the Indian Trading Path	3:0:20
To Great Creek	4:3:28
To Nut-bush Creek	7:0:6
To Massamony Creek	7:1:4
To Yapatsco Creek	3:0:30
To Ohimpamony Creek	3:1:38
To Tewa-ho-mony Creek	8:2:54
To Blewing Creek	4:3:10
To Sugar Tree Creek	2:3:10
To Hico-ottomony Creek	3:1:76
To the same	18
To the same	2:64
To the same	2:66
To the same again	0:0:42
To Buffalo Creek	1:2:40
To Cocquade Creek	11:3:6
To the South Branch of Roanoke call'd the Dan	1:26
To the West Side including the Island	:34
To Cane Creek	2:2:42
To Dan River the 2ᵈ time	4:1:38
To the West Side of D°	24
To Dan River the 3ᵈ time	8:0:68
To the N W Side a Slant	53
To the Dan River the 4ᵗʰ time	1:0:7
To the West Side	21
To Low Land Creek	3:2:56
To Dan River the 5ᵗʰ Time	1:0:18
To the N W Side aslant	66
To Cascade Creek	2:3:10

Situate, lying and being within our Dominions of America aforesaid, extending North and Eastward as far as the North end of Carahtuke River or Inlet, upon a Streight westerly line to Wyonoake Creek, which lys within or about the Degrees of thirty-six and thirty Minutes Northern Latitude, and so West in a Direct line as far as the South Seas; & south and westward as far as the Degrees of twenty-nine inclusive Northern Latitude, & so west in a direct line as far as the South seas; together with all and Singular ports, harbours, Bays, rivers, & inlets belonging unto the Province or Territory aforesaid, etc.

At the Court of St. James's the 1st day of March, 1710.—
Present, The Queen's most Excellent Majesty in Council.

Upon reading this day at the Board a Representation from the Rt Honble the Lords Commissioners for trade & Plantations, in the Words following: In pursuance of your Majesty's Pleasure, Commissioners have been appointed on the Part of your Majesty's Colony of Virginia, as likewise on the Part of the Province of Carolina, for the settling the Bounds between those Governments; And they have met several times for that purpose, but have not agreed upon any one Point thereof, by reason of the trifleing delays of the Carolina Commissioners, & of the many difficulties by them rais'd in relation to the proper Observations & survey they were to make. However, the Commissioners for Virginia have deliver'd to your Majesty's Lieut Governor of that Colony an Account of their proceedings, which Account has been under the Consideration of your Majesty's Council of Virginia, &c they have made a Report thereon to the said Lieut Governor, who haveing lately transmitted unto us a Copy of that Report, we take leave humbly to lay the Substance thereof before your Majesty, which is as follows:

That the Commissioners of Carolina are both of them Persons engag'd in Interest to obstruct the Settling the Boundarys between that Province and the Colony of Virginia; for one of them has for several Years been Suveyor General of Carolina, has acquired to himself great Profit by surveying Lands within the controverted Bounds, & has taken up several Tracts of Land in his own Name, & sold the same to others, for which he stands still oblig'd obtain Patents from the Government of Carolina. The other of them is at this time Surveyor General, & hath the same Prospect of advantage by making future surveys within the said Bounds. That the Behavior of the Carolina Commissioners has tended visibly to no other End than to protect and defeat the Settling this Affair; and particularly Mr. Moseley has us'd so many Shifts & Excuses to disappoint all Conferences with the Commissioners of Virginia, as plainly shew his Aversion to proceed in a Business that tends so manifestly to his disadvantage. His prevaricating on this occasion has been so undiscreet and so unguarded, as to be discover'd in the presence of the Lieut Governor of Virginia. He started so many objections to the Powers granted to the Commission-

To Irvin River a Branch of the Dan	6:0:30
To Matrimony Creek	4:0:31
To Miry Creek	7:1:68
To Mayo-River another Branch of the Dan	0:1:36
To Dan River the 6th and last time	0:1:2
To Crooked Creek the first time	2:1:77
To Ne plus ultra Camp	13:0:35
To a Red Oak mark'd on 3 Sides with 4 Notches, & the Trees blaz'd about it, on the East Bank of a Rivulet, suppos'd to be either a Branch of Roanoke, or Deep River	3:60

The whole Distance   241:2:70

(Here ends the Secret History.—Editor.)

ers of that Colony, with design to render their conferences ineffectual, that his Joint Commissioner cou'd hardly find an excuse for him. And when the Lieut Governor has with much adoe prevail'd with the said Mr. Moseley to appoint a time for meeting the Commissioners of Virginia, & for bringing the necessary Instruments to take the Latitude of the Bounds in dispute, which Instruments he owned were ready in Carolina, he not only fail'd to comply with his own appointment, but after the Commissioners of Virginia had made a Journey to his House, and had attended him to the Places proper for observing the Latitude, he wou'd not take the trouble of carrying his own Instrument, but contented himself to find fault with the Quadrant produc'd by the Virginia Commissioners, tho that Instrument had been approv'd by the best Mathematicians, and is of universal Use. From all which it is evident how little hopes there are of Settling the Boundaries abovementioned, in concert with the present Commissioners for Carolina. That tho the Bounds of the Carolina Charter are in express words limited to Weyanock Creek, lying in or about 36° 30' of Northern Latitude, yet the Commissioners for Carolina have not by any of their Evidences pretended to prove any such Place as Wayanoak Creek, the amount of their Evidence reaching no further than to prove which is Weyanoak River, & even that is contradicted by affidavit taken on the part of Virginia; by which affidavits it appears that, before the Date of the Carolina Charter to this day, the place they pretend to be Weyanoak River was, & is still, called Nottaway River. But supposing the same had been called Weyanoak River, it can be nothing to their purpose, there being a great difference between a River & a Creek. Besides, in that Country there are divers Rivers & Creeks of the same Name, as Potomeck River & Potomeck Creek, Rappahannock River, & Rappahannock Creek, & Several others, tho there are many Miles' distance between the mouths of these Rivers and the mouths of these Creeks. It is also observable, that the Witnesses on the Part of Carolina are all very Ignorant persons, & most of them of ill fame & Reputation, on which Account they had been forced to remove from Virginia to Carolina. Further, there appeared to be many contradictions in their Testimonys, whereas, on the other hand, the witnesses to prove that the Right to those Lands is in the Government of Virginia are Persons of food Credit, their knowledge of the Lands in question is more ancient than any of the witnesses for Carolina, & their Evidence fully corroborated by the concurrent Testimony of the Tributary Indians. And that right is farther confirm'd by the Observations lately taken of the Latitude in those parts, by which tis plain, that the Creek proved to be Weyanock Creek by the Virginia Evidences, & sometimes call'd Wicocon, answers best to the Latitude described in the Carolina charter, for it lys in 36° 40', which is ten Minutes to the Northward of the Limits described in the Carolina grant, Whereas Nottoway River, lys exactly in the Latitude of 37°,[1] and can by no construction be sup-

---

[1] The commissioners in 1728 found that it was really in 36° 30½'.

pos'd to be the Boundary described in their Charter; So that upon the whole Matter, if the Commissioners of Carolina had no other view than to clear the just right of the Proprietors, such undeniable Demonstrations wou'd be Sufficient to convince them; but the said Commissioners gave too much Cause to suspect that they mix their own private Interest with the Claim of the Proprietors, & for that reason endeavor to gain time in order to obtain Grants for the Land already taken up, and also to secure the rest on this occasion, we take notice, that they proceed to survey the Land in dispute, notwithstanding the assurance given by the Government of Carolina to the Contrary by their letter of the 17th of June, 1707, to the Government of Virginia, by which letter they promised that no lands shou'd be taken up within the controverted bounds till the same were settled.

Whereupon we humbly propose, that the Lords Proprietors be acquainted with the foregoing Complaint of the trifleing delays of their Commissioners, which delays tis reasonable to believe have proceeded from the self-Interest of those Commissioners, and that therefore your Majesty's pleasure be signify'd to the said Lords Proprietors, that by the first Opportunity they send Orders to their Governour or Commander in Chief of Carolina for the time being, to issue forth a new Commission, to the purport of that lately issued, thereby constituting two other Persons, not having any personal Interest in, or claim to, any of the Land lying within the Boundary's in the room of Edward Moseley & John Lawson. The Carolina Commissioners to be appointed being strictly required to finish their Survey, & to make a return thereof in conjunction with the Virginia Commissioners, within six months, to be computed from the time, that due notice shall be given by your Majesty's Lieut Governor of Virginia to the Governor or Commander in Chief of Carolina, of the time & place, which your Majesty's said Lieut Governor shall appoint for the first meeting of the Commissioners on one part & the other. In order whereunto we humbly offer, that directions be sent to the said Lieut Governor, to give such Notice accordingly; & if after Notice so given, the Carolina Commissioners shall refuse or neglect to Join with those on the part of Virginia, in making such survey, as likewise a Return thereof within the time before mention'd; that then and in such Case, the Commissioners on the part of Virginia be directed to draw up an Account of the proper observations and Survey which they shall have made for ascertaining the Bounds between Virginia & Carolina, and to deliver the same in Writing under their Hands and Seals to the Lieut Governor and Council of Virginia, to the end the same may be laid before your Majesty, for your Majesty's final Determination therein, within, with regard to the Settling of those Boundarys; the Lords Proprietors haveing, by an Instrument under their Hands, submitted the same to Your Majesty's royal determination, which instrument, dated in March, 1708, is lying in this office.

And lastly, we humbly propose, that your Majesty's further pleasure be signifyd to the said Lords Proprietors, and in like manner to the Lieut Governor of Virginia, that no Grants be pass'd by either of those Governments of any of the Lands lying within the controverted Bounds, until such Bounds shall be ascertain'd and settled as aforesaid, whereby it may appear whether those Lands do of Right belong to your Majesty, or to the Lords Proprietors of Carolina.

Her Majesty in Council, approving of the said Representation, is pleas'd to order, as it is hereby ordered, that the Rt Honble the Lords Commissioners for Trade & Plantations Do signifye her Majesty's pleasure herein to her Majesty's Lieut Governor or Commander in Chief of Virginia for the time being, and to all Persons to whom it may belong, as is propos'd by their Lordships in the said Representation, and the Rt Honble the Lords Proprietors of Carolina are to do what on their part does appertain.

EDW SOUTHWELL.

PROPOSALS *for determining the Controversy relating to the Bounds between the Governments of Virginia and North Carolina, most humbly offered for his Majesty's Royal Approbation, and for the Consent of the Rt Honble the Lords Proprietors of Carolina.*

Forasmuch as the dispute between the said two Governments about their true Limits continues still, notwithstanding the several meetings of the Commissioners, and all the proceedings of many Years past, in order to adjust that affair, & seeing no speedy Determination is likely to ensue, unless some Medium be found out, in which both Partys may incline to acquiesce, wherefore, both the underwritten Governors having met, and consider'd the prejudice both to the King & the Lords Proprietors' Interests, by the continuance of this contest, and truly endeavoring a Decision, which they Judge comes nearest the Intention of Royal Charter granted to the Lords Proprietors, do, with the advice & consent of their respective Councils, propose as follows:

That from the mouth of Corotuck River or Inlet, & setting the Compass on the North Shoar, thereof a due West Line be run & fairly mark'd, & if it happen to cut Chowan River, between the mouths of Nottoway River and Wicocon Creek, then shall the same direct Course be continued towards the Mountains, and be ever deem'd the Sole dividing line between Virginia & Carolina.

That if the said West Line cuts Chowan River to the Southward of Wicocon Creek, then from point of Intersection the Bounds shall be allow'd to continue up the middle of the said Chowan River to the middle of the Entrance into the said Wicocon Creek, and from thence a due West Line shall divide the said two Governments.

That if a due West Line shall be found to pass through Islands or to cut out small Slips of Land, which might much more conveniently be included in one Province or the other by Natural Water Bounds, In such Cases the Persons appointed for runing the Line shall have power to settle Natural Bounds, provided the Commissioners of both Sides agree thereto, and that all such Variations from the West Line, be particularly Noted in the Maps or Plats, which they shall return, to be put upon the Records of both Governments, all which is Humbly submitted by

CHARLES EDEN.

A. SPOTSWOOD.

Order of the King and Council upon the foregoing Proposals, At the Court of St. James's the 28th day of March, 1729.[1] Present, the King's most Excellent Majesty in Council.

WHEREAS it has been represented to his Majesty at the Board, that for adjusting the disputes, which have Subsisted for many Years past, between the Colonys of Virginia and North Carolina, concerning their true Boundarys, the late Governors of the said colonys did some time since agree upon certain Proposals for regulating the said Boundarys for the future, to which Proposals the Lords Proprietors of Carolina have given their assent; And whereas the said Proposals were this day presented to his Majesty as proper for his Royal Approbation.

His Majesty is thereupon pleas'd, with the Advice of his Privy Council, to approve of the said Proposals, a copy whereof is hereunto annex't, and to order, as it is hereby order'd, that the Governor or Commander in Chief of the Colony of Virginia, do settle the said Bondarys, in conjunction with the Governor of North Carolina, agreeable to the said Proposals.

EDWARD SOUTHWELL.

The Lieut Governor of Virginia's Commission in obedience to His Majesty's Order.

George the second, by the Grace of God, of great Britain, France and Ireland King, Defender of the Faith, to our trusty and well beloved William Byrd, Richard Fitz-William, and William Dandridge, Esqrs., members of our council of the Colony and Dominion of Virginia, Greeting: Where as our late Royal Father of Blessed memory was graciously pleas'd, by Order of his Privy Council, bearing date the 28 day of March 1727, to approve of certain Proposals agreed upon by Alexander Spotswood, Esqr. late Lieut Governor of Virginia, on the one part, and Charles Eden, Espr. late Governor of the Province of North Carolina, for determining the Controversy relating to the Bounds between the said two Governments, and was farther pleased to direct and Order, that the said Boundarys shoud be laid out & settled agreeable to the said Proposals. Know

---

[1] It should be 1727.

ye, therefore, that reposing special trust and confidence in your Ability & Provident circumspection, have assign'd, constituted & appointed, & by these presents do assign, constitute & appoint you & every of you jointly & severally, our Commissioners for & on behalf of our Colony & Dominion of Virginia, to meet the Commissioners appointed or to be appointed on the part of the Province of North Carolina, and in conjunction with them to cause a Line or Lines of Division to be run and markt, to divide the said two Governments according to the proposals above-mention'd, & the order of our late Royal Father, Copies of both which you will herewith receive, and we do further give and grant unto you, and in case of the Death or absence of any of you, such of you as shall be present, full power and authority to treat & agree with the said Commissioners of the Province of North Carolina on such rules and Methods as you shall Judge most expedient for the adjusting and finally determining all disputes or controversies which may arise, touching any Islands or other small Slips of Land which may happen to be intersected or cut off by the dividing Line aforesaid, and which may with come conveniency be included in the One Province or the other by natural water bounds, agreeable to the proposals aforemention'd, and generally to do and perform all matters and things requisite for the final determination and Settlement of the said Boundarys, according to the said Proposals. And to the end our Service herein may not be disappointed through the refusal or delay of the Commissioners for the Province of North Carolina, to act in Conjunction with you in settling the Boundarys aforesaid, we do hereby give & grant unto you, or such of you as shall be present at the time and place appointed for running the dividing Line aforesaid, full power and Authority to cause the said Line to be run and mark'd out, conformable to the said proposals, having due regard to the doing equal Justice to Us, and to the Lords Proprietors of Carolina, any refusal, disagreement, or opposition of the said Commissioners of North Carolina notwithstanding. And in that case we hereby require you to make a true report of your proceedings to our Lieut Governor, or Commander in Chief of Virginia, in order to be laid before us for our approbation, and final determination herein. And in case any Person or Persons whatsoever shall presume to disturb, Molest or resist you, or any of the Officers or Persons by your direction, in running the said Line, and executing the Powers herein given you, wo do by these presents Give and Grant unto you, or such of you as shall be attending the service aforesaid, full power & authority by Warrant under your or any of your hands Seals, to order and command all and every the Militia Officers in our counties of Princess Anne, Norfolk, Nansemond, & Isle of Wight, or other the adjacent Counties, together with the Sheriff of each of the said Counties, or either of them, to raise the Militia & posse of the said Several Counties, for the removing all force and opposition, which shall or may be made to you in the due Execution of this our Commission, & we do hereby will and require, as well the Officers of the said militia. as all other our Officers & loving Subjects within the said Counties, & all others whom it may concern, to be obedient, aiding & assisting unto you in all & Singular the Premises. And we do in like manner command & require you, to cause fair Maps & descriptions of the said Dividing Line, and the remarkable places through which it shall pass, to be made and return'd to our Lieut Governor or Commander in Chief of our said Colony for the time being, in order to be entered on Record in the proper Offices within our said Colony. Provided that you do not, by colour of this our Commission, take upon you or determine any Private man's property, in or to the Lands which shall by the said dividing Line be included within the Limits of Virginia, nor of any other matter or thing that doth not relate immediately to the adjusting, settling & final Determination of the Boundary aforesaid, conformable to the Proposals hereinbefore mention'd, and not otherwise. In Witness whereof we have caused these presents to be made. Witness our trusty and well beloved William Gooch, Esqr. our Lieut Governor & Commander in Chief of our Colony & Dominion of Virginia, under the seal of our said Colony, at Williamsburg the 14th day of December, 1727, in the first Year of our Reign.

WILLIAM GOOCH.

The Governor of N. Carolina's Commission in Obedience to His Majesty's Order.

Sir Richard Everard, Baronet, Governor, Captain General, Admiral, and Commander in Chief of the said Province: To Christopher Gale, Esq. Chief Justice, John Lovick, Esqr., Secretary, Edward Moseley, Esqr., Surveyor General & William Little, Esqr., Attorney General, Greeting: Whereas many disputes & differences have formerly been between the Inhabitants of this province and those of his Majesty's Colony of Virginia, concerning the Boundarys and Limits between the said two Governments, which having been duly considered by Charles Eden, Esqr., late Governor of this Province, and Alexander Spotswood, Esqr., late Governor of Virginia, they agreed to certain proposals for determing the said controversy, & humbly offer'd the same for his Majesty's Royal Approbation, and the consent of the true & absolute Lords Proprietors of Carolina. and his Majesty having been pleas'd to signify his Royal approbation of those proposals (consent'd unto by the true and absolute Lords Proprietors of Carolina) and given directions for adjusting & settling the Boundarys as near as may be to the said Proposals:

I, therefore, reposing especial trust and confidence in you the said Christopher Gale, John Lovick, Edward Moseley and William Little, to be Commissioners, on the part of the true and absolute Lords Proprietors, and that you in conjunction with such Commissioners as shall be nominated for Virginia, use your utmost Endeavors, and take all necessary care in adjusting and settling the said boundarys, by drawing such a distinct

Line or Lines of Division between the said two Provinces, as near as reasonable you can to the Proposals made by the two former Governors, and the Instructions herewith given you. Given at the Council Chamber in Edenton, under my hand, and the Seal of the Colony, the 21st day of February, *anno Dom* 1727,[1] and in the first year of the Reign of our sovereign Lord, King George the Second.

RICHARD EVERARD.

The Protest of the Carolina Commissioners, against our Proceeding on the Line without them.

We the underwritten Commissioners for the Government of N. Carolina, in conjunction with the Commissioners on the part of Virginia, having run the Line for the division of the two Colonys from Corotuck Inlet, to the South Branch of Roanoak River; being in the whole about 170 Miles, and near 50 Miles without the Inhabitants, being of Opinion we had run Line as far as would be requisite for a long time, Judged the carrying it farther would be a needless charge and trouble. And the Grand Debate which had so long Subsisted between the two Governments, about Wyanoke River or Creek, being settled at our former meeting in the Spring, when we were ready on our parts to have gone with the Line to the utmost Inhabitants, which if it had been done, the Line at any time after might have been continued at an easy expense by a Surveyor on each side; and if at any time hereafter there shou'd be occasion to carry the Line on further than we have now run it, which we think will not be in an Age or two, it may be done in the same easy manner, without the great Expense that now attends it. And on the Conference of all the Commissioners, we have communicated our sentiments thereon, and declar'd our Opinion, that we had gone as far as the Service required, and thought proper to proceed no further; to which it was answered by the Commissioners for Virginia, that they Should not regard what we did, but if we desisted, they wou'd proceed without us. But we, conceiving by his Majesty's Order in Council they were directed to Act in conjunction with the Commissioners appointed for Carolina, & having accordingly run the Line jointly so far, and Exchanged Plans, thought they cou'd not carry on the Bounds singly; but that their proceedings without us wou'd be irregular & invalid, and that it wou'd be no Boundary, and thought proper to enter our Dissent thereto. Wherefore, for the reasons aforesaid, in the name of his Excellency the Lord Palatine, and the rest of the true and absolute Lords proprietors of Carolina, we do hereby dissent and Disallow of any further proceedings with the Bounds without our Concurrence, and pursuant to our Instructions do give this our DISSENT in Writing.

EDWARD MOSELEY.   C. GALE.
WILL LITTLE.   J. LOVICK.

October 7th, 1728.

---
[1] February 21, 1728, by New Style.

The Answer of the Virginia Commissioners to the foregoing protest.

WHEREAS, on the 7th of October last, a paper was deliver'd to us by the Commissioners of N. Carolina, in the Stile of a Protest, against our carrying any farther, without them, the dividing Line between the 2 Governments, we, the underwritten Commissioners on the part of Virginia, having maturely considered the reasons offer'd in the said PROTEST, why those Gentlemen retir'd so soon from that Service, beg leave to return the following answer:

They are pleas'd in the first place to allege, by way of Reason, that having run the Line near 50 Miles beyond the Inhabitants, it was Sufficient for a long time, in their Opinion for an Age or two. To this we answer that, by breaking off so soon, they did but imperfectly obey his Majesty's Order, assented to by the Lords Proprietors. The plain meaning of that Order was, to ascertain the Bounds betwixt the two Governments as far towards the Mountains as we cou'd, that neither the King's Grants may hereafter encroach on the Lords Proprietors', nor theirs on the Right of his Majesty. And tho the distance towards the great Mountains be not precisely determined, yet surely the West line shou'd be carry'd as near them as may be, that both the King's Lands and those of their Lordships, may be taken up the faster, and that his Majesty's Subjects may as soon as possible extend themselves to that Natural Barrier. This they will certainly do in a few Years, when they know distinctly in which Government they may enter for the Land, as they have already done in the more northern parts of Virginia. So that 'tis Strange the Carolina Commissioners should affirm, that the distance only of 50 Miles above the Inhabitants wou'd be sufficient to carry the Line for an Age or two, especially considering that, two or three days before the date of their Protest, Mr. Mayo had enter'd with them for 2000 Acres of Land, within 5 Miles of the Place where they left off. Besides, if we reflect on the richness of the soil in those parts, & the convenience for Stock, we may foretell, without the Spirit of Divination, that there will be many Settlements higher than those Gentlemen went, in less than ten Years, and Perhaps in half that time.

Another reason mention'd in the Protest for their retiring so soon from the Service is, that their going farther wou'd be a needless charge and Trouble. And they alledge that the rest may be done by one Surveyor on a side, in an easy manner, whenever it shall be thought necessary.

To this we answer, that Frugality for the Public is a rare virtue, but when the public Service must suffer by it, it degenerates into a Vice. And this will ever be the Case when Gentlemen Execute the orders of their Superiors by halves, but had the Carolina Commissioners been sincerely frugal for their Government, why did they carry our Provisions Sufficient to support them and their Men for ten Weeks, when they intended not to tarry half that time? This they must own to be true, since they brought 1000 lbs. of Provisions along with them. Now, after so great an Expence in their preparations, it had been no mighty addition to their Charge, had they endured the Fatigue 5 or 6 Weeks longer. It wou'd at most have been no more than they must be at, whenever they finish their Work, even tho they shou'd fancy it proper to trust a matter of that consequence to the Management of one Surveyor. Such a one must have a Number of Men along with him, both for his assistance and Defense, and those Men must have Provisions to Support them.

These are all the reasons these Gentlemen think fit to mention in their protest, tho they had in truth a more Powerful argument for retiring so abruptly, which, because they forgot, it will be neighbourly to help them out. The provisions they intended to bring along with them, for want of Horses to carry them, were partly droppt by the way, & what they cou'd bring was husbanded so ill, that after 18 days, (which was the whole time we had then in our Company,) they had no more left, by their own confession, than two Pounds of Biscuit for each Man, to carry them home. However, tho this was an unanswerable Reason for Gentlemen for leaving the Business unfinisht, it was none at all for us, who had at that time Bread Sufficient for 7 Weeks longer. Therefore, lest their want of Management might put a stop to his Majesty's Service, & frustrate his Royal intentions, we judg'd it our Duty to proceed without them, and have extended the Dividing Line so far West as to leave the great Mountains on each hand to the Eastward of us. And this we have done with the same fidelity & exactness as if the Gentlemen had continued with us. Our surveyors (whose Integrity I am perswaded they will not call in Question) continued to Act under the same Oath, which they had done from the beginning. Yet, notwithstanding all this, if the Government of N. Carolina shou'd not hold itself bound by that part of the Line which we made without the assistance of the Commissioners, yet we shall have this benefit in it at least, that his Majesty will know how far his Lands reach towards the South, & consequently where his Subjects may take it up, & how far they may be granted without Injustice to the Lords Proprietors. To this we may also add, that having the Authority of our Commission to act without the Commissioners of Carolina, in Case of their disagreement or refusal, we thought ourselves bound upon their Retreat to finish the Line without them, lest his Majesty's Service might Suffer by any honour or neglect on their part.

WILLIAM DANDRIDGE.   W. BYRD.

The Names of the Commissioners to direct the running of the Line between Virginia and North Carolina.

WILLIAM BYRD,   WILLIAM DANDRIDGE,
RICH'D FITZ-WILLIAM,

Esqrs.
Commissioners for Virginia.

CHRISTOPHER GALE, EDWARD MOSELEY,
JOHN LOVEWICK, W'M LITTLE,

Esqrs.

Commissioners for Carolina.

ALEX'R IRVIN, WILLIAM MAYO,
Surveyors for Virginia.

EDW'D MOSELEY, SAM'LL SWAN,
Surveyors for N. Carolina.

THE REV'D PETER FOUNTAIN, Chaplain.

*Names of the Men employ'd on the part of Virginia to run the Line
between that Colony and N. Carolina.*

On the first expedition.	On the 2nd expedition.
1. Peter Jones,	Peter Jones,
2. Thomas Jones,	Thomas Jones,
3. Thomas Short,	Thomas Short,
4. Robert Hix,	Robert Hix,
5. John Evans,	John Evans,
6. Stevens Evans,	Stephen Evans,
7. John Ellis,	John Ellis,
8. John Ellis, Jr.	John Ellis, Jr.,
9. Thomas Wilson.	Thomas Wilson,
10. George Tilman,	George Tilman,
11. Charles Kimbal,	Charles Kimbal,
12. George Hamilton,	George Hamilton,
13. Robert Allen,	Thomas Jones, Junr.
14. Thomas Jones, Junr.	James Petillo,
15. James Petillo,	Rich'd Smith,
16. Richard Smith,	Abraham Jones,
17. John Rice,	Edward Powell,
	William Pool,
	William Calvert,
	James Whitlock,
	Thomas Page.

*Account of the Expence of running the Line between
Virginia and N. Carolina.*

To the Men's Wages in Current Money_____ 227 10 0[1]
To Sundry Disbursements for Provisions, &c._____ 174 01 6
To Paid the Men for 7 Horses lost_____ 44 0 0

---

[1] There is an error in the sum of these figures.

The Sum of £495 11 6 Current Money_____£495 11 6

---

reduc't at 15 Per Cent to Sterling amounts to_____	£430	08	10
To Paid to colo Byrd _____	142	5	7
To paid to colo Dandridge _____	142	5	7
T paid to Mr. Fitz-William_____	94	0	0
To paid to the Chapdain, Mr. Fountain_____	20	0	0
To paid to Mr. William Mayo_____	75	0	0
To paid to Mr. Alex Irvin _____	75	0	0
To paid for a Tent and Marquis _____	20	0	0

£1000 0 0

This Summ was discharg'd by a Warrant out of His Majesty's Quitrents from the Lands in Virginia.

INDEX

A CATALOG OF SELECTED

DOVER BOOKS

IN ALL FIELDS OF INTEREST

A CATALOG OF SELECTED DOVER BOOKS IN ALL FIELDS OF INTEREST

CONCERNING THE SPIRITUAL IN ART, Wassily Kandinsky. Pioneering work by father of abstract art. Thoughts on color theory, nature of art. Analysis of earlier masters. 12 illustrations. 80pp. of text. 5⅜ × 8½. 23411-8 Pa. $2.95

LEONARDO ON THE HUMAN BODY, Leonardo da Vinci. More than 1200 of Leonardo's anatomical drawings on 215 plates. Leonardo's text, which accompanies the drawings, has been translated into English. 506pp. 8⅜ × 11¾. 24483-0 Pa. $11.95

GOBLIN MARKET, Christina Rossetti. Best-known work by poet comparable to Emily Dickinson, Alfred Tennyson. With 46 delightfully grotesque illustrations by Laurence Housman. 64pp. 4 × 6¾. 24516-0 Pa. $2.50

THE HEART OF THOREAU'S JOURNALS, edited by Odell Shepard. Selections from *Journal*, ranging over full gamut of interests. 228pp. 5⅜ × 8½. 20741-2 Pa. $4.50

MR. LINCOLN'S CAMERA MAN: MATHEW B. BRADY, Roy Meredith. Over 300 Brady photos reproduced directly from original negatives, photos. Lively commentary. 368pp. 8⅜ × 11¼. 23021-X Pa. $14.95

PHOTOGRAPHIC VIEWS OF SHERMAN'S CAMPAIGN, George N. Barnard. Reprint of landmark 1866 volume with 61 plates: battlefield of New Hope Church, the Etawah Bridge, the capture of Atlanta, etc. 80pp. 9 × 12. 23445-2 Pa. $6.00

A SHORT HISTORY OF ANATOMY AND PHYSIOLOGY FROM THE GREEKS TO HARVEY, Dr. Charles Singer. Thoroughly engrossing non-technical survey. 270 illustrations. 211pp. 5⅜ × 8½. 20389-1 Pa. $4.95

REDOUTE ROSES IRON-ON TRANSFER PATTERNS, Barbara Christopher. Redouté was botanical painter to the Empress Josephine; transfer his famous roses onto fabric with these 24 transfer patterns. 80pp. 8¼ × 10⅞. 24292-7 Pa. $3.50

THE FIVE BOOKS OF ARCHITECTURE, Sebastiano Serlio. Architectural milestone, first (1611) English translation of Renaissance classic. Unabridged reproduction of original edition includes over 300 woodcut illustrations. 416pp. 9⅜ × 12¼. 24349-4 Pa. $14.95

CARLSON'S GUIDE TO LANDSCAPE PAINTING, John F. Carlson. Authoritative, comprehensive guide covers, every aspect of landscape painting. 34 reproductions of paintings by author; 58 explanatory diagrams. 144pp. 8⅜ × 11. 22927-0 Pa. $5.95

101 PUZZLES IN THOUGHT AND LOGIC, C.R. Wylie, Jr. Solve murders, robberies, see which fishermen are liars—purely by reasoning! 107pp. 5⅜ × 8½. 20367-0 Pa. $2.00

TEST YOUR LOGIC, George J. Summers. 50 more truly new puzzles with new turns of thought, new subtleties of inference. 100pp. 5⅜ × 8½. 22877-0 Pa. $2.50

THE MURDER BOOK OF J.G. REEDER, Edgar Wallace. Eight suspenseful stories by bestselling mystery writer of 20s and 30s. Features the donnish Mr. J.G. Reeder of Public Prosecutor's Office. 128pp. 5⅜ × 8½.

24374-5 Pa. $3.95

ANNE ORR'S CHARTED DESIGNS, Anne Orr. Best designs by premier needlework designer, all on charts: flowers, borders, birds, children, alphabets, etc. Over 100 charts, 10 in color. Total of 40pp. 8¼ × 11.

23704-4 Pa. $2.50

BASIC CONSTRUCTION TECHNIQUES FOR HOUSES AND SMALL BUILDINGS SIMPLY EXPLAINED, U.S. Bureau of Naval Personnel. Grading, masonry, woodworking, floor and wall framing, roof framing, plastering, tile setting, much more. Over 675 illustrations. 568pp. 6½ × 9¼.

20242-9 Pa. $9.95

MATISSE LINE DRAWINGS AND PRINTS, Henri Matisse. Representative collection of female nudes, faces, still lifes, experimental works, etc., from 1898 to 1948. 50 illustrations. 48pp. 8⅜ × 11¼.

23877-6 Pa. $3.50

HOW TO PLAY THE CHESS OPENINGS, Eugene Znosko-Borovsky. Clear, profound examinations of just what each opening is intended to do and how opponent can counter. Many sample games. 147pp. 5⅜ × 8½.

22795-2 Pa. $3.50

DUPLICATE BRIDGE, Alfred Sheinwold. Clear, thorough, easily followed account: rules, etiquette, scoring, strategy, bidding; Goren's point-count system, Blackwood and Gerber conventions, etc. 158pp. 5⅜ × 8½.

22741-3 Pa. $3.50

SARGENT PORTRAIT DRAWINGS, J.S. Sargent. Collection of 42 portraits reveals technical skill and intuitive eye of noted American portrait painter, John Singer Sargent. 48pp. 8¼ × 11⅛.

24524-1 Pa. $3.50

ENTERTAINING SCIENCE EXPERIMENTS WITH EVERYDAY OBJECTS, Martin Gardner. Over 100 experiments for youngsters. Will amuse, astonish, teach, and entertain. Over 100 illustrations. 127pp. 5⅜ × 8½.

24201-3 Pa. $2.50

TEDDY BEAR PAPER DOLLS IN FULL COLOR: A Family of Four Bears and Their Costumes, Crystal Collins. A family of four Teddy Bear paper dolls and nearly 60 cut-out costumes. Full color, printed one side only. 32pp. 9¼ × 12¼.

24550-0 Pa. $3.50

NEW CALLIGRAPHIC ORNAMENTS AND FLOURISHES, Arthur Baker. Unusual, multi-useable material: arrows, pointing hands, brackets and frames, ovals, swirls, birds, etc. Nearly 700 illustrations. 80pp. 8⅜ × 11¼.

24095-9 Pa. $3.75

DINOSAUR DIORAMAS TO CUT & ASSEMBLE, M. Kalmenoff. Two complete three-dimensional scenes in full color, with 31 cut-out animals and plants. Excellent educational toy for youngsters. Instructions; 2 assembly diagrams. 32pp. 9¼ × 12¼.

24541-1 Pa. $4.50

SILHOUETTES: A PICTORIAL ARCHIVE OF VARIED ILLUSTRATIONS, edited by Carol Belanger Grafton. Over 600 silhouettes from the 18th to 20th centuries. Profiles and full figures of men, women, children, birds, animals, groups and scenes, nature, ships, an alphabet. 144pp. 8⅜ × 11¼.

23781-8 Pa. $5.95

25 KITES THAT FLY, Leslie Hunt. Full, easy-to-follow instructions for kites made from inexpensive materials. Many novelties. 70 illustrations. 110pp. 5⅜ × 8½.
22550-X Pa. $2.50

PIANO TUNING, J. Cree Fischer. Clearest, best book for beginner, amateur. Simple repairs, raising dropped notes, tuning by easy method of flattened fifths. No previous skills needed. 4 illustrations. 201pp. 5⅜ × 8½.   23267-0 Pa. $3.50

EARLY AMERICAN IRON-ON TRANSFER PATTERNS, edited by Rita Weiss. 75 designs, borders, alphabets, from traditional American sources. 48pp. 8¼ × 11.
23162-3 Pa. $1.95

CROCHETING EDGINGS, edited by Rita Weiss. Over 100 of the best designs for these lovely trims for a host of household items. Complete instructions, illustrations. 48pp. 8¼ × 11.   24031-2 Pa. $2.95

FINGER PLAYS FOR NURSERY AND KINDERGARTEN, Emilie Poulsson. 18 finger plays with music (voice and piano); entertaining, instructive. Counting, nature lore, etc. Victorian classic. 53 illustrations. 80pp. 6½ × 9¼. 22588-7 Pa. $2.25

BOSTON THEN AND NOW, Peter Vanderwarker. Here in 59 side-by-side views are photographic documentations of the city's past and present. 119 photographs. Full captions. 122pp. 8¼ × 11.   24312-5 Pa. $7.95

CROCHETING BEDSPREADS, edited by Rita Weiss. 22 patterns, originally published in three instruction books 1939-41. 39 photos, 8 charts. Instructions. 48pp. 8¼ × 11.   23610-2 Pa. $2.00

HAWTHORNE ON PAINTING, Charles W. Hawthorne. Collected from notes taken by students at famous Cape Cod School; hundreds of direct, personal *apercus*, ideas, suggestions. 91pp. 5⅜ × 8½.   20653-X Pa. $2.95

THERMODYNAMICS, Enrico Fermi. A classic of modern science. Clear, organized treatment of systems, first and second laws, entropy, thermodynamic potentials, etc. Calculus required. 160pp. 5⅜ × 8½.   60361-X Pa. $4.50

TEN BOOKS ON ARCHITECTURE, Vitruvius. The most important book ever written on architecture. Early Roman aesthetics, technology, classical orders, site selection, all other aspects. Morgan translation. 331pp. 5⅜ × 8½. 20645-9 Pa. $6.95

THE CORNELL BREAD BOOK, Clive M. McCay and Jeanette B. McCay. Famed high-protein recipe incorporated into breads, rolls, buns, coffee cakes, pizza, pie crusts, more. Nearly 50 illustrations. 48pp. 8¼ × 11.   23995-0 Pa. $2.00

THE CRAFTSMAN'S HANDBOOK, Cennino Cennini. 15th-century handbook, school of Giotto, explains applying gold, silver leaf; gesso; fresco painting, grinding pigments, etc. 142pp. 6⅛ × 9¼.   20054-X Pa. $3.95

FRANK LLOYD WRIGHT'S FALLINGWATER, Donald Hoffmann. Full story of Wright's masterwork at Bear Run, Pa. 100 photographs of site, construction, and details of completed structure. 112pp. 9¼ × 10.   23671-4 Pa. $7.95

OVAL STAINED GLASS PATTERN BOOK, C. Eaton. 60 new designs framed in shape of an oval. Greater complexity, challenge with sinuous cats, birds, mandalas framed in antique shape. 64pp. 8¼ × 11.   24519-5 Pa. $3.95

THE BOOK OF WOOD CARVING, Charles Marshall Sayers. Still finest book for beginning student. Fundamentals, technique; gives 34 designs, over 34 projects for panels, bookends, mirrors, etc. 33 photos. 118pp. 7¾ × 10⅝.   23654-4 Pa. $3.95

CARVING COUNTRY CHARACTERS, Bill Higginbotham. Expert advice for beginning, advanced carvers on materials, techniques for creating 18 projects— mirthful panorama of American characters. 105 illustrations. 80pp. 8⅜ × 11.
24135-1 Pa. $2.95

300 ART NOUVEAU DESIGNS AND MOTIFS IN FULL COLOR, C.B. Grafton. 44 full-page plates display swirling lines and muted colors typical of Art Nouveau. Borders, frames, panels, cartouches, dingbats, etc. 48pp. 9⅜ × 12¼.
24354-0 Pa. $6.95

SELF-WORKING CARD TRICKS, Karl Fulves. Editor of *Pallbearer* offers 72 tricks that work automatically through nature of card deck. No sleight of hand needed. Often spectacular. 42 illustrations. 113pp. 5⅜ × 8½.   23334-0 Pa. $3.50

CUT AND ASSEMBLE A WESTERN FRONTIER TOWN, Edmund V. Gillon, Jr. Ten authentic full-color buildings on heavy cardboard stock in H-O scale. Sheriff's Office and Jail, Saloon, Wells Fargo, Opera House, others. 48pp. 9¼ × 12¼.
23736-2 Pa. $4.95

CUT AND ASSEMBLE AN EARLY NEW ENGLAND VILLAGE, Edmund V. Gillon, Jr. Printed in full color on heavy cardboard stock. 12 authentic buildings in H-O scale: Adams home in Quincy, Mass., Oliver Wight house in Sturbridge, smithy, store, church, others. 48pp. 9¼ × 12¼.   23536-X Pa. $4.95

THE TALE OF TWO BAD MICE, Beatrix Potter. Tom Thumb and Hunca Munca squeeze out of their hole and go exploring. 27 full-color Potter illustrations. 59pp. 4¼ × 5½. (Available in U.S. only)   23065-1 Pa. $1.75

CARVING FIGURE CARICATURES IN THE OZARK STYLE, Harold L. Enlow. Instructions and illustrations for ten delightful projects, plus general carving instructions. 22 drawings and 47 photographs altogether. 39pp. 8⅜ × 11.
23151-8 Pa. $2.95

A TREASURY OF FLOWER DESIGNS FOR ARTISTS, EMBROIDERERS AND CRAFTSMEN, Susan Gaber. 100 garden favorites lushly rendered by artist for artists, craftsmen, needleworkers. Many form frames, borders. 80pp. 8¼ × 11.
24096-7 Pa. $3.95

CUT & ASSEMBLE A TOY THEATER/THE NUTCRACKER BALLET, Tom Tierney. Model of a complete, full-color production of Tchaikovsky's classic. 6 backdrops, dozens of characters, familiar dance sequences. 32pp. 9⅜ × 12¼.
24194-7 Pa. $4.50

ANIMALS: 1,419 COPYRIGHT-FREE ILLUSTRATIONS OF MAMMALS, BIRDS, FISH, INSECTS, ETC., edited by Jim Harter. Clear wood engravings present, in extremely lifelike poses, over 1,000 species of animals. 284pp. 9 × 12.
23766-4 Pa. $9.95

MORE HAND SHADOWS, Henry Bursill. For those at their 'finger ends," 16 more effects—Shakespeare, a hare, a squirrel, Mr. Punch, and twelve more—each explained by a full-page illustration. Considerable period charm. 30pp. 6½ × 9¼.
21384-6 Pa. $1.95

SURREAL STICKERS AND UNREAL STAMPS, William Rowe. 224 haunting, hilarious stamps on gummed, perforated stock, with images of elephants, geisha girls, George Washington, etc. 16pp. one side. 8¼ × 11.   24371-0 Pa. $3.50

GOURMET KITCHEN LABELS, Ed Sibbett, Jr. 112 full-color labels (4 copies each of 28 designs). Fruit, bread, other culinary motifs. Gummed and perforated. 16pp. 8¼ × 11.   24087-8 Pa. $2.95

PATTERNS AND INSTRUCTIONS FOR CARVING AUTHENTIC BIRDS, H.D. Green. Detailed instructions, 27 diagrams, 85 photographs for carving 15 species of birds so life-like, they'll seem ready to fly! 8¼ × 11.   24222-6 Pa. $3.00

FLATLAND, E.A. Abbott. Science-fiction classic explores life of 2-D being in 3-D world. 16 illustrations. 103pp. 5⅜ × 8.   20001-9 Pa. $2.00

DRIED FLOWERS, Sarah Whitlock and Martha Rankin. Concise, clear, practical guide to dehydration, glycerinizing, pressing plant material, and more. Covers use of silica gel. 12 drawings. 32pp. 5⅜ × 8½.   21802-3 Pa. $1.00

EASY-TO-MAKE CANDLES, Gary V. Guy. Learn how easy it is to make all kinds of decorative candles. Step-by-step instructions. 82 illustrations. 48pp. 8¼ × 11.
     23881-4 Pa. $2.95

SUPER STICKERS FOR KIDS, Carolyn Bracken. 128 gummed and perforated full-color stickers: GIRL WANTED, KEEP OUT, BORED OF EDUCATION, X-RATED, COMBAT ZONE, many others. 16pp. 8¼ × 11.   24092-4 Pa. $3.50

CUT AND COLOR PAPER MASKS, Michael Grater. Clowns, animals, funny faces...simply color them in, cut them out, and put them together, and you have 9 paper masks to play with and enjoy. 32pp. 8¼ × 11.   23171-2 Pa. $2.95

A CHRISTMAS CAROL: THE ORIGINAL MANUSCRIPT, Charles Dickens. Clear facsimile of Dickens manuscript, on facing pages with final printed text. 8 illustrations by John Leech, 4 in color on covers. 144pp. 8⅜ × 11¼.
     20980-6 Pa. $5.95

CARVING SHOREBIRDS, Harry V. Shourds & Anthony Hillman. 16 full-size patterns (all double-page spreads) for 19 North American shorebirds with step-by-step instructions. 72pp. 9¼ × 12¼.   24287-0 Pa. $5.95

THE GENTLE ART OF MATHEMATICS, Dan Pedoe. Mathematical games, probability, the question of infinity, topology, how the laws of algebra work, problems of irrational numbers, and more. 42 figures. 143pp. 5⅜ × 8½.
     22949-1 Pa. $3.50

READY-TO-USE DOLLHOUSE WALLPAPER, Katzenbach & Warren, Inc. Stripe, 2 floral stripes, 2 allover florals, polka dot; all in full color. 4 sheets (350 sq. in.) of each, enough for average room. 48pp. 8¼ × 11.   23495-9 Pa. $2.95

MINIATURE IRON-ON TRANSFER PATTERNS FOR DOLLHOUSES, DOLLS, AND SMALL PROJECTS, Rita Weiss and Frank Fontana. Over 100 miniature patterns: rugs, bedspreads, quilts, chair seats, etc. In standard dollhouse size. 48pp. 8¼ × 11.   23741-9 Pa. $1.95

THE DINOSAUR COLORING BOOK, Anthony Rao. 45 renderings of dinosaurs, fossil birds, turtles, other creatures of Mesozoic Era. Scientifically accurate. Captions. 48pp. 8¼ × 11.   24022-3 Pa. $2.50

JAPANESE DESIGN MOTIFS, Matsuya Co. Mon, or heraldic designs. Over 4000 typical, beautiful designs: birds, animals, flowers, swords, fans, geometrics; all beautifully stylized. 213pp. 11⅜ × 8¼. 22874-6 Pa. $7.95

THE TALE OF BENJAMIN BUNNY, Beatrix Potter. Peter Rabbit's cousin coaxes him back into Mr. McGregor's garden for a whole new set of adventures. All 27 full-color illustrations. 59pp. 4¼ × 5½. (Available in U.S. only) 21102-9 Pa. $1.75

THE TALE OF PETER RABBIT AND OTHER FAVORITE STORIES BOXED SET, Beatrix Potter. Seven of Beatrix Potter's best-loved tales including Peter Rabbit in a specially designed, durable boxed set. 4¼ × 5½. Total of 447pp. 158 color illustrations. (Available in U.S. only) 23903-9 Pa. $12.25

PRACTICAL MENTAL MAGIC, Theodore Annemann. Nearly 200 astonishing feats of mental magic revealed in step-by-step detail. Complete advice on staging, patter, etc. Illustrated. 320pp. 5⅜ × 8½. 24426-1 Pa. $5.95

CELEBRATED CASES OF JUDGE DEE (DEE GOONG AN), translated by Robert Van Gulik. Authentic 18th-century Chinese detective novel; Dee and associates solve three interlocked cases. Led to van Gulik's own stories with same characters. Extensive introduction. 9 illustrations. 237pp. 5⅜ × 8½. 23337-5 Pa. $4.95

CUT & FOLD EXTRATERRESTRIAL INVADERS THAT FLY, M. Grater. Stage your own lilliputian space battles. By following the step-by-step instructions and explanatory diagrams you can launch 22 full-color fliers into space. 36pp. 8¼ × 11. 24478-4 Pa. $2.95

CUT & ASSEMBLE VICTORIAN HOUSES, Edmund V. Gillon, Jr. Printed in full color on heavy cardboard stock, 4 authentic Victorian houses in H-O scale: Italian-style Villa, Octagon, Second Empire, Stick Style. 48pp. 9¼ × 12¼. 23849-0 Pa. $4.95

BEST SCIENCE FICTION STORIES OF H.G. WELLS, H.G. Wells. Full novel *The Invisible Man,* plus 17 short stories: "The Crystal Egg," "Aepyornis Island," "The Strange Orchid," etc. 303pp. 5⅜ × 8½. (Available in U.S. only) 21531-8 Pa. $4.95

TRADEMARK DESIGNS OF THE WORLD, Yusaku Kamekura. A lavish collection of nearly 700 trademarks, the work of Wright, Loewy, Klee, Binder, hundreds of others. 160pp. 8¾ × 8. (EJ) 24191-2 Pa. $5.95

THE ARTIST'S AND CRAFTSMAN'S GUIDE TO REDUCING, ENLARGING AND TRANSFERRING DESIGNS, Rita Weiss. Discover, reduce, enlarge, transfer designs from any objects to any craft project. 12pp. plus 16 sheets special graph paper. 8¼ × 11. 24142-4 Pa. $3.95

TREASURY OF JAPANESE DESIGNS AND MOTIFS FOR ARTISTS AND CRAFTSMEN, edited by Carol Belanger Grafton. Indispensable collection of 360 traditional Japanese designs and motifs redrawn in clean, crisp black-and-white, copyright-free illustrations. 96pp. 8¼ × 11. 24435-0 Pa. $4.50

CHANCERY CURSIVE STROKE BY STROKE, Arthur Baker. Instructions and illustrations for each stroke of each letter (upper and lower case) and numerals. 54 full-page plates. 64pp. 8¼ × 11. 24278-1 Pa. $2.50

THE ENJOYMENT AND USE OF COLOR, Walter Sargent. Color relationships, values, intensities; complementary colors, illumination, similar topics. Color in nature and art. 7 color plates, 29 illustrations. 274pp. 5⅜ × 8½. 20944-X Pa. $4.95

SCULPTURE PRINCIPLES AND PRACTICE, Louis Slobodkin. Step-by-step approach to clay, plaster, metals, stone; classical and modern. 253 drawings, photos. 255pp. 8⅛ × 11. 22960-2 Pa. $7.50

VICTORIAN FASHION PAPER DOLLS FROM HARPER'S BAZAR, 1867-1898, Theodore Menten. Four female dolls with 28 elegant high fashion costumes, printed in full color. 32pp. 9¼ × 12¼. 23453-3 Pa. $3.95

FLOPSY, MOPSY AND COTTONTAIL: A Little Book of Paper Dolls in Full Color, Susan LaBelle. Three dolls and 21 costumes (7 for each doll) show Peter Rabbit's siblings dressed for holidays, gardening, hiking, etc. Charming borders, captions. 48pp. 4¼ × 5½. (USCO) 24376-1 Pa. $2.50

NATIONAL LEAGUE BASEBALL CARD CLASSICS, Bert Randolph Sugar. 83 big-leaguers from 1909-69 on facsimile cards. Hubbell, Dean, Spahn, Brock plus advertising, info, no duplications. Perforated, detachable. 16pp. 8¼ × 11.
24308-7 Pa. $3.50

THE LOGICAL APPROACH TO CHESS, Dr. Max Euwe, et al. First-rate text of comprehensive strategy, tactics, theory for the amateur. No gambits to memorize, just a clear, logical approach. 224pp. 5⅜ × 8½. 24353-2 Pa. $4.50

MAGICK IN THEORY AND PRACTICE, Aleister Crowley. The summation of the thought and practice of the century's most famous necromancer, long hard to find. Crowley's best book. 436pp. 5⅜ × 8½. (Available in U.S. only)
23295-6 Pa. $6.95

THE HAUNTED HOTEL, Wilkie Collins. Collins' last great tale; doom and destiny in a Venetian palace. Praised by T.S. Eliot. 127pp. 5⅜ × 8½.
24333-8 Pa. $3.00

ART DECO DISPLAY ALPHABETS, Dan X. Solo. Wide variety of bold yet elegant lettering in handsome Art Deco styles. 100 complete fonts, with numerals, punctuation, more. 104pp. 8⅛ × 11. 24372-9 Pa. $4.50

CALLIGRAPHIC ALPHABETS, Arthur Baker. Nearly 150 complete alphabets by outstanding contemporary. Stimulating ideas; useful source for unique effects. 154 plates. 157pp. 8⅜ × 11¼. 21045-6 Pa. $5.95

ARTHUR BAKER'S HISTORIC CALLIGRAPHIC ALPHABETS, Arthur Baker. From monumental capitals of first-century Rome to humanistic cursive of 16th century, 33 alphabets in fresh interpretations. 88 plates. 96pp. 9 × 12.
24054-1 Pa. $4.50

LETTIE LANE PAPER DOLLS, Sheila Young. Genteel turn-of-the-century family very popular then and now. 24 paper dolls. 16 plates in full color. 32pp. 9¼ × 12¼. 24089-4 Pa. $3.95

KEYBOARD WORKS FOR SOLO INSTRUMENTS, G.F. Handel. 35 neglected works from Handel's vast oeuvre, originally jotted down as improvisations. Includes Eight Great Suites, others. New sequence. 174pp. 9⅜ × 12¼.
24338-9 Pa. $7.50

AMERICAN LEAGUE BASEBALL CARD CLASSICS, Bert Randolph Sugar. 82 stars from 1900s to 60s on facsimile cards. Ruth, Cobb, Mantle, Williams, plus advertising, info, no duplications. Perforated, detachable. 16pp. 8¼ × 11.
24286-2 Pa. $3.50

A TREASURY OF CHARTED DESIGNS FOR NEEDLEWORKERS, Georgia Gorham and Jeanne Warth. 141 charted designs: owl, cat with yarn, tulips, piano, spinning wheel, covered bridge, Victorian house and many others. 48pp. 8¼ × 11.
23558-0 Pa. $1.95

DANISH FLORAL CHARTED DESIGNS, Gerda Bengtsson. Exquisite collection of over 40 different florals: anemone, Iceland poppy, wild fruit, pansies, many others. 45 illustrations. 48pp. 8¼ × 11.
23957-8 Pa. $2.50

OLD PHILADELPHIA IN EARLY PHOTOGRAPHS 1839-1914, Robert F. Looney. 215 photographs: panoramas, street scenes, landmarks, President-elect Lincoln's visit, 1876 Centennial Exposition, much more. 230pp. 8⅜ × 11¾.
23345-6 Pa. $9.95

PRELUDE TO MATHEMATICS, W.W. Sawyer. Noted mathematician's lively, stimulating account of non-Euclidean geometry, matrices, determinants, group theory, other topics. Emphasis on novel, striking aspects. 224pp. 5⅜ × 8½.
24401-6 Pa. $4.50

ADVENTURES WITH A MICROSCOPE, Richard Headstrom. 59 adventures with clothing fibers, protozoa, ferns and lichens, roots and leaves, much more. 142 illustrations. 232pp. 5⅜ × 8½.
23471-1 Pa. $3.95

IDENTIFYING ANIMAL TRACKS: MAMMALS, BIRDS, AND OTHER ANIMALS OF THE EASTERN UNITED STATES, Richard Headstrom. For hunters, naturalists, scouts, nature-lovers. Diagrams of tracks, tips on identification. 128pp. 5⅜ × 8.
24442-3 Pa. $3.50

VICTORIAN FASHIONS AND COSTUMES FROM HARPER'S BAZAR, 1867-1898, edited by Stella Blum. Day costumes, evening wear, sports clothes, shoes, hats, other accessories in over 1,000 detailed engravings. 320pp. 9⅜ × 12¼.
22990-4 Pa. $10.95

EVERYDAY FASHIONS OF THE TWENTIES AS PICTURED IN SEARS AND OTHER CATALOGS, edited by Stella Blum. Actual dress of the Roaring Twenties, with text by Stella Blum. Over 750 illustrations, captions. 156pp. 9 × 12.
24134-3 Pa. $8.95

HALL OF FAME BASEBALL CARDS, edited by Bert Randolph Sugar. Cy Young, Ted Williams, Lou Gehrig, and many other Hall of Fame greats on 92 full-color, detachable reprints of early baseball cards. No duplication of cards with *Classic Baseball Cards.* 16pp. 8¼ × 11.
23624-2 Pa. $3.50

THE ART OF HAND LETTERING, Helm Wotzkow. Course in hand lettering, Roman, Gothic, Italic, Block, Script. Tools, proportions, optical aspects, individual variation. Very quality conscious. Hundreds of specimens. 320pp. 5⅜ × 8½.
21797-3 Pa. $5.95

HOW THE OTHER HALF LIVES, Jacob A. Riis. Journalistic record of filth, degradation, upward drive in New York immigrant slums, shops, around 1900. New edition includes 100 original Riis photos, monuments of early photography. 233pp. 10 × 7⅞. 22012-5 Pa. $9.95

CHINA AND ITS PEOPLE IN EARLY PHOTOGRAPHS, John Thomson. In 200 black-and-white photographs of exceptional quality photographic pioneer Thomson captures the mountains, dwellings, monuments and people of 19th-century China. 272pp. 9⅜ × 12¼. 24393-1 Pa. $13.95

GODEY COSTUME PLATES IN COLOR FOR DECOUPAGE AND FRAMING, edited by Eleanor Hasbrouk Rawlings. 24 full-color engravings depicting 19th-century Parisian haute couture. Printed on one side only. 56pp. 8¼ × 11. 23879-2 Pa. $3.95

ART NOUVEAU STAINED GLASS PATTERN BOOK, Ed Sibbett, Jr. 104 projects using well-known themes of Art Nouveau: swirling forms, florals, peacocks, and sensuous women. 60pp. 8¼ × 11. 23577-7 Pa. $3.95

QUICK AND EASY PATCHWORK ON THE SEWING MACHINE: Susan Aylsworth Murwin and Suzzy Payne. Instructions, diagrams show exactly how to machine sew 12 quilts. 48pp. of templates. 50 figures. 80pp. 8¼ × 11. 23770-2 Pa. $3.95

THE STANDARD BOOK OF QUILT MAKING AND COLLECTING, Marguerite Ickis. Full information, full-sized patterns for making 46 traditional quilts, also 150 other patterns. 483 illustrations. 273pp. 6⅞ × 9⅝. 20582-7 Pa. $5.95

LETTERING AND ALPHABETS, J. Albert Cavanagh. 85 complete alphabets lettered in various styles; instructions for spacing, roughs, brushwork. 121pp. 8¾ × 8. 20053-1 Pa. $3.95

LETTER FORMS: 110 COMPLETE ALPHABETS, Frederick Lambert. 110 sets of capital letters; 16 lower case alphabets; 70 sets of numbers and other symbols. 110pp. 8⅛ × 11. 22872-X Pa. $4.50

ORCHIDS AS HOUSE PLANTS, Rebecca Tyson Northen. Grow cattleyas and many other kinds of orchids—in a window, in a case, or under artificial light. 63 illustrations. 148pp. 5⅜ × 8½. 23261-1 Pa. $2.95

THE MUSHROOM HANDBOOK, Louis C.C. Krieger. Still the best popular handbook. Full descriptions of 259 species, extremely thorough text, poisons, folklore, etc. 32 color plates; 126 other illustrations. 560pp. 5⅜ × 8½. 21861-9 Pa. $8.50

THE DORÉ BIBLE ILLUSTRATIONS, Gustave Doré. All wonderful, detailed plates: Adam and Eve, Flood, Babylon, life of Jesus, etc. Brief King James text with each plate. 241 plates. 241pp. 9 × 12. 23004-X Pa. $8.95

THE BOOK OF KELLS: Selected Plates in Full Color, edited by Blanche Cirker. 32 full-page plates from greatest manuscript-icon of early Middle Ages. Fantastic, mysterious. Publisher's Note. Captions. 32pp. 9¾ × 12¼. 24345-1 Pa. $4.50

THE PERFECT WAGNERITE, George Bernard Shaw. Brilliant criticism of the Ring Cycle, with provocative interpretation of politics, economic theories behind the Ring. 136pp. 5⅜ × 8½. (EUK) 21707-8 Pa. $3.95

THE RIME OF THE ANCIENT MARINER, Gustave Doré, S.T. Coleridge. Doré's finest work, 34 plates capture moods, subtleties of poem. Full text. 77pp. 9¼ × 12.
22305-1 Pa. $4.95

SONGS OF INNOCENCE, William Blake. The first and most popular of Blake's famous "Illuminated Books," in a facsimile edition reproducing all 31 brightly colored plates. Additional printed text of each poem. 64pp. 5¼ × 7.
22764-2 Pa. $3.50

AN INTRODUCTION TO INFORMATION THEORY, J.R. Pierce. Second (1980) edition of most impressive non-technical account available. Encoding, entropy, noisy channel, related areas, etc. 320pp. 5⅜ × 8½.
24061-4 Pa. $5.95

THE DIVINE PROPORTION: A STUDY IN MATHEMATICAL BEAUTY, H.E. Huntley. "Divine proportion" or "golden ratio" in poetry, Pascal's triangle, philosophy, psychology, music, mathematical figures, etc. Excellent bridge between science and art. 58 figures. 185pp. 5⅜ × 8½.
22254-3 Pa. $4.50

THE DOVER NEW YORK WALKING GUIDE: From the Battery to Wall Street, Mary J. Shapiro. Superb inexpensive guide to historic buildings and locales in lower Manhattan: Trinity Church, Bowling Green, more. Complete Text; maps. 36 illustrations. 48pp. 3⅞ × 9¼.
24225-0 Pa. $2.50

NEW YORK THEN AND NOW, Edward B. Watson, Edmund V. Gillon, Jr. 83 important Manhattan sites: on facing pages early photographs (1875-1925) and 1976 photos by Gillon. 172 illustrations. 171pp. 9¼ × 10.
23361-8 Pa. $9.95

HISTORIC COSTUME IN PICTURES, Braun & Schneider. Over 1450 costumed figures from dawn of civilization to end of 19th century. English captions. 125 plates. 256pp. 8⅜ × 11¼.
23150-X Pa. $7.95

VICTORIAN AND EDWARDIAN FASHION: A Photographic Survey, Alison Gernsheim. First fashion history completely illustrated by contemporary photographs. Full text plus 235 photos, 1840-1914, in which many celebrities appear. 240pp. 6½ × 9¼.
24205-6 Pa. $6.00

CHARTED CHRISTMAS DESIGNS FOR COUNTED CROSS-STITCH AND OTHER NEEDLECRAFTS, Lindberg Press. Charted designs for 45 beautiful needlecraft projects with many yuletide and wintertime motifs. 48pp. 8¼ × 11. (EDNS)
24356-7 Pa. $2.50

101 FOLK DESIGNS FOR COUNTED CROSS-STITCH AND OTHER NEEDLE-CRAFTS, Carter Houck. 101 authentic charted folk designs in a wide array of lovely representations with many suggestions for effective use. 48pp. 8¼ × 11.
24369-9 Pa. $2.25

FIVE ACRES AND INDEPENDENCE, Maurice G. Kains. Great back-to-the-land classic explains basics of self-sufficient farming. The one book to get. 95 illustrations. 397pp. 5⅜ × 8½.
20974-1 Pa. $6.50

A MODERN HERBAL, Margaret Grieve. Much the fullest, most exact, most useful compilation of herbal material. Gigantic alphabetical encyclopedia, from aconite to zedoary, gives botanical information, medical properties, folklore, economic uses, and much else. Indispensable to serious reader. 161 illustrations. 888pp. 6½ × 9¼. (Available in U.S. only)
22798-7, 22799-5 Pa., Two-vol. set $17.00

DECORATIVE NAPKIN FOLDING FOR BEGINNERS, Lillian Oppenheimer and Natalie Epstein. 22 different napkin folds in the shape of a heart, clown's hat, love knot, etc. 63 drawings. 48pp. 8¼ × 11.   23797-4 Pa. $2.25

DECORATIVE LABELS FOR HOME CANNING, PRESERVING, AND OTHER HOUSEHOLD AND GIFT USES, Theodore Menten. 128 gummed, perforated labels, beautifully printed in 2 colors. 12 versions. Adhere to metal, glass, wood, ceramics. 24pp. 8¼ × 11.   23219-0 Pa. $3.50

EARLY AMERICAN STENCILS ON WALLS AND FURNITURE, Janet Waring. Thorough coverage of 19th-century folk art: techniques, artifacts, surviving specimens. 166 illustrations, 7 in color. 147pp. of text. 7⅞ × 10¾. 21906-2 Pa. $9.95

AMERICAN ANTIQUE WEATHERVANES, A.B. & W.T. Westervelt. Extensively illustrated 1883 catalog exhibiting over 550 copper weathervanes and finials. Excellent primary source by one of the principal manufacturers. 104pp. 6⅛ × 9¼.
24396-6 Pa. $3.95

ART STUDENTS' ANATOMY, Edmond J. Farris. Long favorite in art schools. Basic elements, common positions, actions. Full text, 158 illustrations. 159pp. 5⅜ × 8½.   20744-7 Pa. $3.95

BRIDGMAN'S LIFE DRAWING, George B. Bridgman. More than 500 drawings and text teach you to abstract the body into its major masses. Also specific areas of anatomy. 192pp. 6½ × 9¼.   22710-3 Pa. $4.50

COMPLETE PRELUDES AND ETUDES FOR SOLO PIANO, Frederic Chopin. All 26 Preludes, all 27 Etudes by greatest composer of piano music. Authoritative Paderewski edition. 224pp. 9 × 12. (Available in U.S. only)   24052-5 Pa. $7.50

PIANO MUSIC 1888-1905, Claude Debussy. Deux Arabesques, Suite Bergamesque, Masques, 1st series of Images, etc. 9 others, in corrected editions. 175pp. 9⅜ × 12¼.
22771-5 Pa. $6.95

TEDDY BEAR IRON-ON TRANSFER PATTERNS, Ted Menten. 80 iron-on transfer patterns of male and female Teddys in a wide variety of activities, poses, sizes. 48pp. 8¼ × 11.   24596-9 Pa. $2.25

A PICTURE HISTORY OF THE BROOKLYN BRIDGE, M.J. Shapiro. Profusely illustrated account of greatest engineering achievement of 19th century. 167 rare photos & engravings recall construction, human drama. Extensive, detailed text. 122pp. 8¼ × 11.   24403-2 Pa. $7.95

NEW YORK IN THE THIRTIES, Berenice Abbott. Noted photographer's fascinating study shows new buildings that have become famous and old sights that have disappeared forever. 97 photographs. 97pp. 11⅜ × 10.   22967-X Pa. $7.50

MATHEMATICAL TABLES AND FORMULAS, Robert D. Carmichael and Edwin R. Smith. Logarithms, sines, tangents, trig functions, powers, roots, reciprocals, exponential and hyperbolic functions, formulas and theorems. 269pp. 5⅜ × 8½.   60111-0 Pa. $4.95

HANDBOOK OF MATHEMATICAL FUNCTIONS WITH FORMULAS, GRAPHS, AND MATHEMATICAL TABLES, edited by Milton Abramowitz and Irene A. Stegun. Vast compendium: 29 sets of tables, some to as high as 20 places. 1,046pp. 8 × 10½.   61272-4 Pa. $21.95

REASON IN ART, George Santayana. Renowned philosopher's provocative, seminal treatment of basis of art in instinct and experience. Volume Four of *The Life of Reason*. 230pp. 5⅜ × 8.   24358-3 Pa. $4.50

LANGUAGE, TRUTH AND LOGIC, Alfred J. Ayer. Famous, clear introduction to Vienna, Cambridge schools of Logical Positivism. Role of philosophy, elimination of metaphysics, nature of analysis, etc. 160pp. 5⅜ × 8½. (USCO)
                                                                    20010-8 Pa. $2.95

BASIC ELECTRONICS, U.S. Bureau of Naval Personnel. Electron tubes, circuits, antennas, AM, FM, and CW transmission and receiving, etc. 560 illustrations. 567pp. 6½ × 9¼.   21076-6 Pa. $9.95

THE ART DECO STYLE, edited by Theodore Menten. Furniture, jewelry, metalwork, ceramics, fabrics, lighting fixtures, interior decors, exteriors, graphics from pure French sources. Over 400 photographs. 183pp. 8⅜ × 11¼.
                                                                    22824-X Pa. $7.95

THE FOUR BOOKS OF ARCHITECTURE, Andrea Palladio. 16th-century classic covers classical architectural remains, Renaissance revivals, classical orders, etc. 1738 Ware English edition. 216 plates. 110pp. of text. 9½ × 12¾.
                                                                    21308-0 Pa. $11.95

THE WIT AND HUMOR OF OSCAR WILDE, edited by Alvin Redman. More than 1000 ripostes, paradoxes, wisecracks: Work is the curse of the drinking classes, I can resist everything except temptations, etc. 258pp. 5⅜ × 8½.
                                                                    20602-5 Pa. $4.50

THE DEVIL'S DICTIONARY, Ambrose Bierce. Barbed, bitter, brilliant witticisms in the form of a dictionary. Best, most ferocious satire America has produced. 145pp. 5⅜ × 8½.   20487-1 Pa. $2.95

ERTÉ'S FASHION DESIGNS, Erté. 210 black-and-white inventions from *Harper's Bazar*, 1918-32, plus 8pp. full-color covers. Captions. 88pp. 9 × 12.
                                                                    24203-X Pa. $7.95

ERTÉ GRAPHICS, Erté. Collection of striking color graphics: *Seasons, Alphabet, Numerals, Aces* and *Precious Stones*. 50 plates, including 4 on covers. 48pp. 9⅜ × 12¼.   23580-7 Pa. $6.95

PAPER FOLDING FOR BEGINNERS, William D. Murray and Francis J. Rigney. Clearest book for making origami sail boats, roosters, frogs that move legs, etc. 40 projects. More than 275 illustrations. 94pp. 5⅜ × 8½.   20713-7 Pa. $2.50

ORIGAMI FOR THE ENTHUSIAST, John Montroll. Fish, ostrich, peacock, squirrel, rhinoceros, Pegasus, 19 other intricate subjects. Instructions. Diagrams. 128pp. 9 × 12.   23799-0 Pa. $5.95

CROCHETING NOVELTY POT HOLDERS, edited by Linda Macho. 64 useful, whimsical pot holders feature kitchen themes, animals, flowers, other novelties. Surprisingly easy to crochet. Complete instructions. 48pp. 8¼ × 11.
                                                                    24296-X Pa. $1.95

CROCHETING DOILIES, edited by Rita Weiss. Irish Crochet, Jewel, Star Wheel, Vanity Fair and more. Also luncheon and console sets, runners and centerpieces. 51 illustrations. 48pp. 8¼ × 11.   23424-X Pa. $2.75

YUCATAN BEFORE AND AFTER THE CONQUEST, Diego de Landa. Only significant account of Yucatan written in the early post-Conquest era. Translated by William Gates. Over 120 illustrations. 162pp. 5⅜ × 8½. 23622-6 Pa. $3.95

ORNATE PICTORIAL CALLIGRAPHY, E.A. Lupfer. Complete instructions, over 150 examples help you create magnificent "flourishes" from which beautiful animals and objects gracefully emerge. 8⅛ × 11. 21957-7 Pa. $3.50

DOLLY DINGLE PAPER DOLLS, Grace Drayton. Cute chubby children by same artist who did Campbell Kids. Rare plates from 1910s. 30 paper dolls and over 100 outfits reproduced in full color. 32pp. 9¼ × 12¼. 23711-7 Pa. $3.50

CURIOUS GEORGE PAPER DOLLS IN FULL COLOR, H. A. Rey, Kathy Allert. Naughty little monkey-hero of children's books in two doll figures, plus 48 full-color costumes: pirate, Indian chief, fireman, more. 32pp. 9¼ × 12¼. 24386-9 Pa. $3.50

GERMAN: HOW TO SPEAK AND WRITE IT, Joseph Rosenberg. Like *French, How to Speak and Write It.* Very rich modern course, with a wealth of pictorial material. 330 illustrations. 384pp. 5⅜ × 8½. 20271-2 Pa. $4.95

CATS AND KITTENS: 24 Ready-to-Mail Color Photo Postcards, D. Holby. Handsome collection; feline in a variety of adorable poses. Identifications. 12pp. on postcard stock. 8¼ × 11. 24469-5 Pa. $2.95

MARILYN MONROE PAPER DOLLS, Tom Tierney. 31 full-color designs on heavy stock, from *The Asphalt Jungle, Gentlemen Prefer Blondes,* 22 others. 1 doll. 16 plates. 32pp. 9⅜ × 12¼. 23769-9 Pa. $3.95

FUNDAMENTALS OF LAYOUT, F.H. Wills. All phases of layout design discussed and illustrated in 121 illustrations. Indispensable as student's text or handbook for professional. 124pp. 8⅛ × 11. 21279-3 Pa. $4.50

FANTASTIC SUPER STICKERS, Ed Sibbett, Jr. 75 colorful pressure-sensitive stickers. Peel off and place for a touch of pizzazz: clowns, penguins, teddy bears, etc. Full color. 16pp. 8¼ × 11. 24471-7 Pa. $3.50

LABELS FOR ALL OCCASIONS, Ed Sibbett, Jr. 6 labels each of 16 different designs—baroque, art nouveau, art deco, Pennsylvania Dutch, etc.—in full color. 24pp. 8¼ × 11. 23688-9 Pa. $3.95

HOW TO CALCULATE QUICKLY: RAPID METHODS IN BASIC MATHEMATICS, Henry Sticker. Addition, subtraction, multiplication, division, checks, etc. More than 8000 problems, solutions. 185pp. 5 × 7¼. 20295-X Pa. $2.95

THE CAT COLORING BOOK, Karen Baldauski. Handsome, realistic renderings of 40 splendid felines, from American shorthair to exotic types. 44 plates. Captions. 48pp. 8¼ × 11. 24011-8 Pa. $2.50

THE TALE OF PETER RABBIT, Beatrix Potter. The inimitable Peter's terrifying adventure in Mr. McGregor's garden, with all 27 wonderful, full-color Potter illustrations. 55pp. 4¼ × 5½. (Available in U.S. only) 22827-4 Pa. $1.75

BASIC ELECTRICITY, U.S. Bureau of Naval Personnel. Batteries, circuits, conductors, AC and DC, inductance and capacitance, generators, motors, transformers, amplifiers, etc. 349 illustrations. 448pp. 6½ × 9¼. 20973-3 Pa. $7.95

CATALOG OF DOVER BOOKS

SOURCE BOOK OF MEDICAL HISTORY, edited by Logan Clendening, M.D. Original accounts ranging from Ancient Egypt and Greece to discovery of X-rays: Galen, Pasteur, Lavoisier, Harvey, Parkinson, others. 685pp. 5⅜ × 8½.
20621-1 Pa. $11.95

THE ROSE AND THE KEY, J.S. Lefanu. Superb mystery novel from Irish master. Dark doings among an ancient and aristocratic English family. Well-drawn characters; capital suspense. Introduction by N. Donaldson. 448pp. 5⅜ × 8½.
24377-X Pa. $6.95

SOUTH WIND, Norman Douglas. Witty, elegant novel of ideas set on languorous Meditterranean island of Nepenthe. Elegant prose, glittering epigrams, mordant satire. 1917 masterpiece. 416pp. 5⅜ × 8½. (Available in U.S. only)
24361-3 Pa. $5.95

RUSSELL'S CIVIL WAR PHOTOGRAPHS, Capt. A.J. Russell. 116 rare Civil War Photos: Bull Run, Virginia campaigns, bridges, railroads, Richmond, Lincoln's funeral car. Many never seen before. Captions. 128pp. 9⅜ × 12¼.
24283-8 Pa. $7.95

PHOTOGRAPHS BY MAN RAY: 105 Works, 1920-1934. Nudes, still lifes, landscapes, women's faces, celebrity portraits (Dali, Matisse, Picasso, others), rayographs. Reprinted from rare gravure edition. 128pp. 9⅜ × 12¼.
23842-3 Pa. $8.95

STAR NAMES: THEIR LORE AND MEANING, Richard H. Allen. Star names, the zodiac, constellations: folklore and literature associated with heavens. The basic book of its field, fascinating reading. 563pp. 5⅜ × 8½.   21079-0 Pa. $7.95

BURNHAM'S CELESTIAL HANDBOOK, Robert Burnham, Jr. Thorough guide to the stars beyond our solar system. Exhaustive treatment. Alphabetical by constellation: Andromeda to Cetus in Vol. 1; Chamaeleon to Orion in Vol. 2; and Pavo to Vulpecula in Vol. 3. Hundreds of illustrations. Index in Vol. 3. 2000pp. 6⅛ × 9¼.   23567-X, 23568-8, 23673-0 Pa. Three-vol. set $37.85

THE ART NOUVEAU STYLE BOOK OF ALPHONSE MUCHA, Alphonse Mucha. All 72 plates from *Documents Decoratifs* in original color. Stunning, essential work of Art Nouveau. 80pp. 9⅜ × 12¼.   24044-4 Pa. $8.95

DESIGNS BY ERTE; FASHION DRAWINGS AND ILLUSTRATIONS FROM "HARPER'S BAZAR," Erte. 310 fabulous line drawings and 14 *Harper's Bazar* covers, 8 in full color. Erte's exotic temptresses with tassels, fur muffs, long trains, coifs, more. 129pp. 9⅜ × 12¼.   23397-9 Pa. $8.95

HISTORY OF STRENGTH OF MATERIALS, Stephen P. Timoshenko. Excellent historical survey of the strength of materials with many references to the theories of elasticity and structure. 245 figures. 452pp. 5⅜ × 8½. 61187-6 Pa. $9.95

Prices subject to change without notice.

Available at your book dealer or write for free catalog to Dept. GI, Dover Publications, Inc., 31 East 2nd St. Mineola, N.Y. 11501. Dover publishes more than 175 books each year on science, elementary and advanced mathematics, biology, music, art, literary history, social sciences and other areas.